Introduction to Social Policy

Elizabeth Dickerson Huttman, Ph.D.

Professor of Sociology and Social Service
California State University, Hayward

McGraw-Hill Book Company
New York   St. Louis   San Francisco   Auckland   Bogotá   Hamburg
Johannesburg   London   Madrid   Mexico   Montreal   New Delhi
Panama   Paris   São Paulo   Singapore   Sydney   Tokyo   Toronto

Cover and chapter-opening photographs by Dorothea Lange, Lange Collection, Oakland, California, Museum, with the cooperation of Therese Heyman, curator.

This book was set in Times Roman by Black Dot, Inc. (ECU).
The editors were Nelson W. Black and David Dunham;
the production supervisor was Donna Piligra.
The cover was designed by Jane Moorman.
R. R. Donnelley & Sons Company was printer and binder.

INTRODUCTION TO SOCIAL POLICY

1 2 3 4 5 6 7 8 9 0 DODO 8 9 8 7 6 5 4 3 2 1 0

Library of Congress Cataloging in Publication Data

Huttman, Elizabeth D   date
   Introduction to social policy.

   Bibliography: p.
   Includes index.
   1. Social policy. 2. United States—Social policy.
I. Title.
HN13.H87   361.6'1   80-15147
ISBN 0-07-031548-5

To
Irene Case Dickerson, for her long-time cheerful friendship,
and
Alma Dickerson Winberg, who has been an inspiration for her
courageous spirit in the face of physical handicaps
and
Lottie Dickerson Smith, who presents an inspiring model,
with her joyful outlook on life and deep faith
and also
to
the memory of Dorothea Lange and to
her husband and my great professor, Paul Taylor

Contents

1

NEED FOR SOCIAL POLICY

2

SOCIAL POLICY STRATEGIES

3

SOCIAL POLICY IN SPECIFIC SOCIAL SERVICE FIELDS

Preface

This book is a simplified introduction to social policy issues. Its purpose is not only to explain and illustrate the many aspects of policy strategies in easy terms but also to apply these strategies to a number of social service areas, such as child welfare, income maintenance, services to the elderly, juvenile justice, housing, and the environment. This book gives the beginning student historical background on the development of social services and the values embodied in providing them. It also covers changes in American life that will affect social policy.

Many people have been helpful in the preparation of this book. Dr. Terry Jones, of California State University, Hayward, wrote the chapter on juvenile justice. Arnold Katz of the University of Illinois has provided lengthy, helpful suggestions. Norman Goroff, of the University of Connecticut, and Dorothy Gibson, of San Francisco State University, have also read the manuscript and made useful comments, as has Larry Northwood, of the University of Washington. I would like to thank Paul Taylor and Therese Heyman for their assistance in bringing together Dorothea Lange's photographs.

I am appreciative of the efforts made in typing the manuscript by Sandra and Dorothy Schwab and Polly Schmid. Anna Dickerson has provided continuing support in a number of ways. As ususal my friends in Zermatt, including Sonja Truffer, Stephan and Brigitte Grutter, Ruth Grob, Edith Imark, the Aufdenblattens, Irene Graven, and the late Ruth Rinderknecht Perren have over the years of writing the book provided the quiet friendly atmosphere in which to work.

I would also like to express my appreciation to my editors, Nelson Black and Rhona Robbin, and to the development editor, David Dunham, as well as the editorial assistant Debbie Ritorze. I also appreciate the help of Eric Munson, sociology editor.

And last of all, I would like to recognize the patience and helpfulness of my husband, John Huttman.

Elizabeth Dickerson Huttman

Introduction to Social Policy

Chapter 1

Introduction

FOCUS OF THIS BOOK

This book introduces the student to the major components of social policy development and, in Part Two, to specific social policy issues in the social services fields of child welfare, income maintenance or welfare assistance, juvenile justice, services to the elderly, race relations, and housing assistance. The book also covers the historical perspective on policy, in both Europe and America.

AIMS OF SOCIAL POLICY

Every industrial society makes organized efforts to meet personal and group needs that individuals find difficult to take care of on their own. The aims of social policy measures are to assist people in need of help, to alleviate social problems, to improve the individual's and the group's social and economic situation, and to provide an environment conducive to growth and satisfaction. An underlying goal of many social policies is to promote greater social equality. Social policies, as plans of action and strategies for providing services, also have the goal of improving intrasocial human relations by eliminating the dysfunctioning of individuals and groups caused by external forces and personal problems. In sum, the policymaker's overall goal is to improve the quality of life and circumstances of living of individuals and groups.

Many students enter social work with these kinds of goals in mind. They want to help people who have problems. The questions dealt with in this book are *how* to help them and what strategies and what types of programs to initiate. Social policy's function is to formulate courses of action, choices, and priorities—usually on the macro level, as through national legislation—that result in effective programs to meet these aims. Each student in his or her future work in social work programs or governmental bodies will have to work under a set of regulations, principles, rules of action, or even detailed guidelines for the program that have been laid down by legislation or policy documents. These legislated policies often dictate that one must provide help to those in need in a certain, structured way. The policies may mean the program gives considerable assistance to some types of individuals in need and little to other types simply because that is the way policymakers have set up the program. For example, in the United States, government financial help is given *only* to poor children, through Aid to Families with Dependent Children (AFDC), while in Canada and most European countries it is given to *all* children, through children's allowances or small payments per child.

In the agency work world, social workers often have to follow guidelines they do not agree with. In the AFDC program, for example, they have to ask the divorced or deserted mother for information about the father's whereabouts. The practitioners, whether they are eligibility workers, caseworkers (in a variety of agencies), community organizers (in settlement houses, neighborhood programs, or whatever), or administrators of any of many local programs, are affected by social policy decisions made by others for programs and activities in their fields.

Some would say they are the victims of such policies; increasingly, however, their role is one of taking some minor part in deciding on policies in their field. If nothing else, social workers may modify and reshape national or state policies in their own agency work or, if administrators for a whole agency, give testimony on how the policy changes will work out in their agency. As members of a professional group, whether the National Association of Social Workers (NASW), the Child Welfare League, or the National Association for Mental Health, or the many other organizations representing social service interests, they may be asked to pressure legislators, state or national, on certain provisions of a particular piece of social welfare legislation. As professionals in direct services whom the community and even legislators consider knowledgeable on social service issues, they may be asked to give expert advice on courses of action to be taken in a certain social service field. All these are compelling reasons why those who plan to go into social work should understand the methods of analysis, the strategies, and the stages of formulation in the broad field of social policy.

COURSE EMPHASIS

In social policy decision making, one needs not only to have an intimate knowledge of a social service field but also to be able to analyze the choices and priorities involved, as well as to know what policies, in a real-world setting, will work or pass a legislative body. Thus an introductory course in social policy differs from one in social services; the latter is mainly of a descriptive nature, providing the history of social work and then describing various fields of social work—such as child welfare—and types of social work—such as casework, group work, and community organization. A course in social policy also differs from a social problems course because the latter is mainly concerned with the extent of the social problem and causes of the problem, while a social policy course is concerned with what to do about the problem.

This book emphasizes strategies and methods of providing a service. For example, one goes beyond looking at the cause of poverty in such a course to considering the policies that could decrease it. Using as an example the Community Action Program (CAP) of the "War on Poverty" or the OEO (the Office of Economic Opportunity, which implemented the Economic Opportunity Act) program introduced by the federal government in the 1960s, one can say that assessing the degree of poverty was only the first step in policy. Other policy decisions in the CAP program of the War on Poverty legislation included, first, who should be eligible for benefits. In many CAP programs the allocation of benefits was to all those in the target poverty area rather than to individuals who took a poverty or means test to prove eligibility. Second, decisions were made on what type of programs to offer; instead of cash benefits, such services as personnel training, educational tutoring, and health services were offered by CAP programs in various target areas. In addition, emphasis was put on giving the poor power as well as services by making them participants on local CAP boards or paraprofessional workers in CAP programs in target areas. Another area of policy decisions was how to deliver the services. In many areas the CAP did not use existing voluntary agencies or public agencies but used new CAP councils. The CAP had little coordination with existing, traditional social welfare agencies in many cities. As far as staffing decisions were concerned, these CAP programs in some areas employed a large number of paraprofessionals.

These are all policy strategies. Each plan of action was chosen from a number of alternative strategy choices that could have been utilized.

These CAP decisions were influenced by values in a number of cases. Value judgments arose, first, from the democratic idea that the poor should be able to make decisions for themselves and shape their own programs and, second, from the belief that past elitist decision making had not served the needs of the poor. The value orientation was that power itself was an important commodity and giving power should be emphasized as much as providing money or skills. At the same time, many CAP programs were based on the idea of opening up opportunities for the poor, by giving them educational and technical skills, rather than the idea of redistribution of resources, including income, to the poor.

Historical precedent also influences policy decisions. In the CAP programs historical precedent was often not followed; in some areas the CAP acted outside the traditional social welfare agencies and had ties mainly to the federal bureaucracy of OEO and to the local OEO-CAP council rather than to the local city hall. Second, the CAP program broke tradition in including the poor in their decision-making councils and as staff in their programs.

The power struggles between various interest groups are important in determining policy direction. In the CAP program's decision making, many fights occurred between city hall and the various local minority organizations. These were of continuing significance in shaping CAP policy. Volumes of literature have been written on the struggles that went on in the OEO's CAP programs in different cities.

All these aspects of the CAP story—the jobs of assessing need, setting goals, and deciding who is eligible for benefits, what type of benefits to provide, and what organizational structure and staff to use to deliver them—are policy analysis issues. Policy analysis also includes taking into account value premises and power relationships. In this book chapters are devoted to each of these.

The first policy activity discussed is methods and sources for assessing needs or social problems, at both the local and the national level (Chapter 2). This includes discussing the theories on change and their consequences in terms of need. Chapter 3 describes the major changes in American society in the postwar period, including changes in the family, in urban life, in demographic composition, in economic conditions, in the position of women, and in the status of minorities. Chapters 5 to 7, which make up Part Two, are devoted to alternative policy strategies for meeting needs. Chapter 5 is on whom to assist, that is, how to allocate benefits; and Chapter 6 is on the type of benefits to give, such as cash, material assistance, or services. Chapter 7 deals with alternatives for the delivery of services. These are the kinds of technical issues the social policy expert deals with.

In the real world of politics and public opinion, the value orientations and ideological positions of both concerned interest groups and the mass public play a dominant role in policy decisions. Chapter 4 describes value orientations concerning those in need over the centuries and historical precedents, from the British poor law days of the 1600s onward through America's frontier days and the post–World War II period. Power relationships are mentioned here, as well as in the chapters in Part Three that outline specific policy developments and issues in such fields as welfare assistance (Chapter 8), services to the elderly (Chapter 10), child welfare (Chapter 9), housing assistance (Chapter 12), juvenile justice (Chapter 11), and race relations (Chapter 13). The influence of interest groups and political parties on policy formulation can never be ignored, for in determining the final shape of policy actions it often greatly outweighs the importance of the rational plans the expert policymaker systematically works out.

ELABORATION OF THE DEFINITION OF SOCIAL POLICY

The foregoing section gives a broad idea of the ingredients of social policy analysis. Before proceeding to the chapters on these aspects we should elaborate on the definition of social policy and on what social services it encompasses. Social policy can be considered strategies for action on problems or needs of a social nature. Kahn (1973) talks of social policy as "a strategy, direction and posture, the wedding of reality assessment and choice, of empiricism and preference." Kahn further says that policy is "an explicit and implicit core of principles or the continuing line of decisions and constraints, behind specific programs, legislation, administrative practices, or priorities."

Some writers see policy as the *process,* or stages, of developing a plan of action, of assessing need, examining alternatives, and selecting strategies; and others see policy as the *product,* or final result, of such work, such as a report along the order of the British government white papers on policy in particular areas. Others see policy as rules, regulations, and principles. This book deemphasizes the stages approach; that is, the study of the political struggles and strategy debates over a particular policy, as found in Daniel Moynihan's 1973 book on the welfare reform debates during the Nixon administration, or in Meyerson and Banfield's description of the political struggles in Chicago over the siting of public housing in *Politics, Planning, and the Public Interest* (1955), or in Edward Hayes's *Who Rules Oakland?* (1972). This book instead concentrates on the substantive strategy choices and the final product.

As for what the word "social" in "social policy" means, some writers consider "social" to mean welfare benefits. For example, T. H. Marshall, the dean of British social policy writers, defines social policy as "policy of governments with regard to action having a direct impact on the welfare of citizens, by providing them with services or income. The central core consists, therefore, of social insurance, public (or national) assistance, the health and welfare services, and housing policy" (Marshall, 1965, p. 7).

Some stress that "social" policy concerns the quality of life. Freeman and Sherwood (1970) say social policy "consists of the conclusions reached by persons concerned with the betterment of community conditions and social life, and with the amelioration of deviance and social disorganization" (p. 13).

The National Association of Social Workers (NASW) touches more on the mutual support–interpersonal relations aspect, saying, "Public social policy . . . consists of those laws, policies and practices of government that affect the social relationships of individuals and their relationship to the society of which they are a part" (Gil, 1973, p. 22).

These definitions do not focus on a major goal of social policy, namely, its social equality and income redistribution effects, which are so important to such leading policy experts as Martin Rein, S. M. Miller, and David Gil. Rein (1970) defines social policy as planning for social externalities, redistribution, and the equitable distribution of social benefits, especially social services.

Many definitions mention that policies often take the form of laws. One should also mention they can be judicial decisions. Some courses are primarily concerned with legislation and court decisions. There is no question but that one must cover laws when discussing income maintenance policies as well as many other areas of policy. Second, one must be aware of major court decisions, such as the 1954 *Brown* desegregation case in the Supreme Court, when discussing race relations. Many court decisions, such as this one, have started a whole set of administrative actions.

Social policy can also include actions of nongovernmental bodies, such as unions and voluntary organizations, as Gil (1973) points out.

In whatever loci it occurs, policy is above all strategies, actions, or plans for alleviating a social problem or meeting a social need after analyzing alternative choices.

RANGE OF SOCIAL SERVICES COVERED BY THE TERM "SOCIAL POLICY"

Social policy is more actively debated in many industrialized societies of Europe, where the social welfare system is considered an important, ongoing institution and covers a broad range of government-sponsored services. In these countries, which include Holland, Denmark, West Germany, France, Sweden, and Britain, the services are often considered part of what is called the "welfare state" system, which is to take care of basic social and medical needs "from cradle to grave," as the British policymaker Lord Beveridge phrased it. These services go to many members of the community, rich and poor, as we shall see under "The Welfare State Philosophy" in Chapter 4. In our country, where social welfare is less likely to be seen as an ongoing *institution* than as a stopgap or temporary assistance to a few who cannot meet their needs themselves in the marketplace, usually because of income deficiencies—in other words, where social welfare has a *residual* function—fewer services and benefits are of interest to social policy experts. Second, even when American policy experts try to outline strategy courses in some areas, such as housing and health, their work is less likely to be enacted into law or administrative policy, because to a large degree the service is handled by the private market.

The basic services included within every definition of social policy are income maintenance programs, which include social insurance such as old-age, survivors, and disability insurance (OASDHI); unemployment insurance and workers' compensation; and other programs of cash assistance to the poor, such as Aid to Families with Dependent Children (AFDC), Supplemental Security Income (SSI), and General Assistance (GA). Another would be the food-stamp voucher program. Social policy also includes cash benefits from the Veterans Administration and other bodies. In other countries it would include family or child allowances and housing allowances.

Most policy experts would also include traditional casework and group work services performed by trained social workers, such as family counseling, child welfare services, and mental health counseling, as well as community organization services with neighborhood groups and other entities. The various services to specific groups, such as the elderly, the handicapped, new immigrants, rural farm migrants, and minority groups, are also included. Probation and parole services, delinquency prevention programs, and assistance to ex-convicts are others usually included. Family planning activities and homemaker services also are a focus of social policymakers. Certain recreational-social integration programs, such as the Big Brothers and the Girl Scouts, are also included.

Most social policy experts would include housing assistance programs for low- and moderate-income persons, such as public housing, and also neighborhood improvement activities, such as the Model Cities program and urban renewal. They also would assume that certain aspects of medical services related to income maintenance, such as Medicaid and Medicare, and certain social services in the medical setting, would be within the boundaries of social policy interests.

Some experts would expand the list to include educational programs, but education policy is such a large field in itself that it often involves a separate group of policymakers. However, some programs for disadvantaged children, such as Head Start, or for special groups, such as the mentally retarded, may be of interest to social policy experts. The experts also may be concerned with race relations in the schools or with the role of the school social worker.

Occupation- and employment-oriented services are also included by some social policy scholars. These include manpower training programs, special vocational training for the handicapped, youth opportunity center programs, the Job Corps, retirement counseling, and unemployment insurance.

Kahn (1973) classifies these various social services as those for socialization and development; those for therapy, help, rehabilitation, and social protection; and those for information on access to the other services, which make potential clients aware of their rights to use the program.

ACTORS INVOLVED IN DIFFERENT STAGES OF SOCIAL POLICYMAKING

Another major aspect of social policy discussion the student should be introduced to in the beginning chapter is the stages of development of social policy and the different actors taking part at different stages or playing different roles in the overall formulation of policy. As already mentioned, this is a *process* type of study of policy, with power struggles and strategies of different interest groups taken into account. The whole process is one of moving from simple concern to organizational action, to research and publicity, to specific formulation of programs, and finally to enactment of laws or administrative actions. While for some policies one stage may be more prominent than others and some stages skipped, in general there are chronological steps in the development of policy. In the early stages, concerned lay persons decide something must be done about an unmet need. They may be the individuals affected, such as families of handicapped children or alcoholics, or mothers concerned with the need for day care. They form a group of concerned persons, who may then be joined by concerned practitioners and academics. For example, a student working on a volunteer basis developed an alternative facility for young offenders who would otherwise be sent to a correctional facility; she was helped in her efforts to establish a small halfway house by two probation officers in the county who were dissatisfied with the existing places of treatment for youthful offenders. They all worked to get funding and to staff this halfway house and organize a program.

The initial concern of lay citizens, students, individual practitioners, and the like can lead to the involvement of *professional organizations,* which focus on the problem at meetings. Federal and state agencies operating in the area may develop an interest. Research funding organizations may investigate the problem or fund academic scholars to do so. Such organizations as social planning councils may collect statistics. Findings and reports are then often published and circulated to concerned groups and even the general public. At this point the researchers' reports are on the *extent and characteristics of the problem,* rather than on the social policy strategies to meet the need. The personnel involved in such research include social welfare administrators, special research staff, and academics.

The next stage is the development of general policy solutions and goals that are workable, acceptable to allies, and cost-efficient. Both academic scholars and organizational leaders may be involved in these. In addition, at this stage there are often task forces of civil servants in government agencies or of members of Congress established to explore potential solutions. The academic researchers are trained in a variety of disciplines. Some are in schools of social work, as are Alfred Kahn, Alvin Schorr, Wilbur Cohen, David Gil, Richard Cloward, and Neil Gilbert. Others, such as S. M. Miller, Frank Reissman, and T. H. Marshall, are sociologists. Others are in planning departments, as are Martin Rein and Leonard Duhl. In Britain a number have been on social administration faculties, as have David Donnison, Della Nevitt, and the late Richard Titmuss.

A number of economists, such as Kenneth Boulding and Sar Levitan, have also contributed to social policy decisions. Economists' roles were especially important in income maintenance research—the large New Jersey negative-income experiment—as well as the housing allowance experiments and the personnel training demonstrations.

These various actors may also take part in the later step of formulating operational policy and guidelines, in the form of actual legislation to bring before Congress or a state body. However, the politicians become the principal actors at this stage, and the representatives of various interest groups, such as NASW, the AFL-CIO, and various religious bodies, take on a lobbying role. Politicians act in a complex world where many external factors are weighed for or against a provision in the legislation; they often make trade-offs on other legislation they need to pass. They give consideration to the values of their constituents, campaign backers, and political party. They take into consideration their own priority system of different kinds of legislative measures; some give social policy measures low priority. They are influenced by pressure groups and lobbies. They take into account the costs of any legislation in relation to those of other legislation they are already committed to, perhaps defense measures, or they measure those costs in accordance with their overall fiscal out-look. They interact with other actors, such as the president's executive staff, Cabinet members, and leaders of organizations sponsoring the legis-lation.

Another group of actors, involved in policy decisions from another government base of action, is judges in federal and state courts. The Supreme Court in the postwar years has been a source of far-reaching policy decisions in race relations, such as the 1954 *Brown* decision on desegregation of schools. The courts have also made rulings on welfare regulations, such as the legality of state residency requirements for receiving welfare assistance; the Court's negative vote on this has increased the welfare rolls in a number of states. In the correctional field, the *Gault* decision, which gives youths before a juvenile court the right to counsel, has had a major effect on the whole structure of the juvenile court system.

As indicated, these different actors are involved in various stages of policy development. Let us now outline these stages.

Stages of Policymaking

I   Concern over an unmet need or social problem or gap in services
   A   Symptoms of unmet needs—Individual cases of stress, indica-tions of tensions and strains between institutions, and evidence that traditional institutions are not covering need in this area
      1   Evidence of income need, deviant acts, or hostile out-breaks
   B   Development of informal concerned groups, outcries from moral innovators, and upsurge of instigators of action and advocates of new programs, among them practitioners
   C   Media spotlight on this unmet need or social problem and professional and academic group interest in problem
      1   Conferences on subject, academic papers, special articles or television shows on the topic
II Development of formal, structured groups, both lay and government-sponsored
III Structured information gathering on the scope and characteristics of users
   A   Collection of data through systematic research and gathering together of statistics, by academic sources and social welfare coordinating groups, such as social planning councils, as well as by the organization newly established to deal with the problem
      1   Investigation by national professional standard-setting agency, such as the Child Welfare League of America
      2   Fact-finding hearings in Congress or in the state legislature

    B Development of exploratory theories and theoretical orientations regarding the problem

    C Communication of findings to various publics, such as academics, professionals, and lay publics, including concerned organizations

IV Development of general policy solutions and goals

    A Exploration of possible policy alternatives

    B Attention to workable possibilities within the social reality and the value context of that society

    C Taking into account objectives of a variety of allies that would offer support or resistance to the program

    D Envisioning both the manifest and expected functions of this general policy and the latent functions or unintended consequences

    E Estimating the numerical size and characteristics of the population on which this policy will be concentrated

    F Assessing the cost of alternative solutions and of coverage of different groups in the need category

V Lobbying for change by formal concerned organizations

    A Gaining support from politicians and civil servants

    B Seeking out possible allies and gaining the help of general institutional groups such as churches; developing coalitions and compromising to meet their demands

VI Formulation of an operational policy and laws

    A Setting up task forces to put policy into operation and to write provisions of the law, possibly in research organizations or the research arm of an agency, or in a social planning council or planning division of a professional group

    B Narrowing strategies to a particular workable group, keeping in mind alternative methods of provision and the cost of the program

    C Shaping policy into operational guidelines, including the type of provision, the method of provision and degree of provision, organizational structure, financing, and allocation of responsibility among different administrative levels, such as federal, state, and local

    D Adding or compromising on or deleting provisions, due to action of Congressional or state legislature committees or reactions of overall board of national professional organizations or other enacting groups, such as local community chest or local council

VII Actual enactment of law, agency program

    A Statement of agreed-upon final provisions or program structure

    B Setup of agency or other structure to run the program

VIII Implementation of the program

    A Translating laws, executive orders, or operational guidelines into provision of the services or benefits at the local level

    B   Setting up an organizational structure and staffing its components

    C   Structuring a delivery system at the agency-client level

    D   Facilitating access to the service through information, advocacy, and acessibility mechanisms such as neighborhood offices, use of simpler forms, shorter waiting lists

IX   Evaluation and assessment of program

    A   Research to judge whether the program meets the needs of intended target groups and reaches stated objectives and decreases the problem

    B   Assessment of latent functions or impacts

    C   Detection of bottlenecks in delivery

    D   Integration of policy program into overall social, political, and economic institutions in the society

    E   Examination of alternative policies

Birth of Budget Item

Last April [1977], Secretary of Health, Education and Welfare Joseph A. Califano, Jr., saw some statistics on teenage pregnancies—one million youngsters, one of every ten, get pregnant every year.

"When Joe saw those numbers, they just dazzled him," recalled Laura Miller, one of his assistants.

That moment was one small link in a chain of events that ended yesterday, when President Carter sent his [1978] budget to Congress. Included was $142 million for programs that would help prevent teenage pregnancies or aid young women if they became mothers.

In a budget of $500 billion, the teenage pregnancy program represents an infinitesimal fraction of the total. But a case study of how and why that money wound up in the budget provides some insights into the decision-making process.

Teenage pregnancy and motherhood was gaining public attention long before Carter took office. Outside government, the Alan Guttmacher Institute had published a powerful booklet called "Eleven Million Teenagers," a reference to the number of youngsters who are "sexually active."

This booklet, which has had wide circulation among professionals and public officials, contains the startling statistic that impressed Califano. Moreover, it adds, 600,000 young women between ages 15 and 19 carry their babies to term. Pregnancy is the most common reason for young women dropping out of school. Teenage mothers face far greater risks of unemployment, welfare and divorce. The younger a woman is when she gives birth, the poorer her family is likely to be.

Within the government, HEW had a variety of programs that touched on the issue, from family planning to child health to Medicaid. In June, 1976, the department evaluated those programs and found them ineffective.

When the Carter administration took office, the problem received immediate attention for at least two reasons. Because Carter and Califano both opposed the use of public funds to finance abortions, they were under strong political pressure to produce alternatives to deal with unwanted pregnancies.

The second major factor was the attitude Califano brought to his Cabinet post. "I think the secretary has a real burden for young people," noted Miller, his assistant. "Maybe it's because he has three children of his own." Moreover, noted another aide, when Califano ranked all department programs in order of importance, he placed top priority on preventive efforts, not cures. Curbing teenage pregnancies fit two of his major concerns.

As he started educating himself, Califano sprayed his staff with questions. Of those one million pregnancies, he asked Miller during the spring, how many involved girls under age 15? The answer: 30,000—a significant number.

By all accounts, the Secretary was also influenced by his close friends Sargent and Eunice Shriver, who have been deeply involved in the issue through their work with the Kennedy Foundation. The foundation finances a project in Baltimore that focuses on the needs of teenage parents for post-natal care, job counseling, and help to continue their education.

From the beginning, then, there were two motives behind administration thinking—political and practical, and the practical divided into two issues: preventing pregnancy and helping youngsters who, for whatever reason, get pregnant and have their babies.

Califano ordered an intensive study of the issue and of current programs to deal with it.

Public hearings were held in July, and Peter H. Schuck, deputy assistant secretary of HEW, recalls that he was particularly struck by a delegation representing The Door, a community center for teenagers in Manhattan.

"They had created a real community in which hard-core inner-city kids seemed to come alive and prosper," Schuck said. "Family planning was not really the focus. It was really a teen center, but pulled in kids who wouldn't be caught dead in a family planning clinic."

The Door, Schuck added, helped "plant the seeds" for the concept that was now emerging—a comprehensive program that would cut across the various problems plaguing teenagers.

A study group put together an ambitious program to provide preventive and post-natal care for young mothers, which was approved by Califano after intensive discussion within the department.

Then the program went to the Budget office, and on the first go-round the new program was virtually knocked out. An appeal was filed with James T. McIntyre, Jr., the acting budget chief, but when his mediation could not resolve the impasse, Califano took up the issue with Carter in December.

Finally, a compromise was reached. The new program would be approved, but it would get only $60 million—a good deal less than requested. A second new piece of legislation would expand Medicaid to cover the teenagers while they were pregnant, and after they gave birth, at a cost of $18 million.

The final $64 million would go to existing programs—family planning, community health centers, research and training—on the understanding that the additional funds would be aimed toward teenagers.

It now faces an uncertain future on Capitol Hill.

Source: *New York Times,* January 24, 1978.

Note: This case is an example of the stages of policy development and the political considerations brought to bear on policy formulation. In this case one early source of concern over an unmet need (item I in the outline) was the Guttmacher Institute, which expressed that concern in a publication. This group had done some structured information gathering (III). From other information we know there were also pressure groups (I.*B*) demanding that any alternative to the policy of letting Medicaid pay for abortions be effective. Another influence was the experience of the Kennedy Foundation with a demonstration program and a communication of its findings (III.*C*) on this.

Activity moved on to the next, more formal stage, development of general policy solutions (IV), where policy alternatives (IV.*A*) were explored, including present programs, through hearings, where allies for the program (IV.*C*) appeared.

General policy decisions were set up, such as using a *preventive* approach in a nonthreatening setting where other youth activities occurred. This was followed by a study of the estimated numerical size and characteristics of the group (IV.*E*). After that, Califano's group lobbied to get the funding for the program in the budget (V.*A*) and, one would assume, sought out possible allies (V.*B*). Finally, the types of aid were changed and narrowed (VI). This is a good example of a few of the many factors that go into the formulation of policy.

FRAMEWORK FOR POLICY ANALYSIS

An outline of the stages of development of policy and a description of the actors involved gives the student some idea of the dynamic chronological development of policy, or what is called the "process" of policymaking. Such an approach does not give the student the *substance* of policy strategies, that is, a detailed knowledge of such alternative methods as means testing or universal provision. In this book the main focus is on substance.

Ours is a broad approach. In many such *product* books, as Gilbert and Specht (1974) point out, the "analyses of choice usually focuses upon one or another issue of choice that is germane to a specific policy, but there is no systematic framework for placing the generic issues of policy design in a broad context." In this book an attempt is made to describe a number of substantive policy alternatives and to develop a framework of basic policy choice questions to be answered in making policy decisions. Separate chapters of the book cover such essential policy questions as what is the need (Chapter 2); and the goals or objectives of the policy; what is the strategy in meeting the need in terms of what persons are helped (Chapter 5), how they are helped (Chapter 6), and what organizational and staff structure is used (Chapter 7); and what are the values, ideologies, and historical precedents involved in the policy choice (Chapters 3 and 4). Each of these is a substantive issue that requires detailed coverage of the dimensions of the different choices, such as the different types of provision (cash, material help, or services; see Chapter 6).

Within this framework of essential questions, we ask about political influence. We discuss it in brief in the chapters in Part Three on development of policy in specific fields, such as income maintenance (Chapter 8), just as we also answer all the other framework questions in terms of the specific policy issue we are concerned with in each of these later chapters. When assessing political influences, one looks at the relative power, the size, and the degree of interest particular power bases, such as the business community or unions, have in the policy issue under study. One can ask whether there is an elitist power model, with one group, such as the business community, influencing the policy decisions, or a pluralistic model, with a number of groups concerned with the policy issue and forcing compromises on final action.

The major questions included in this broad framework for analysis of policy are given in the following outline, under the appropriate headings.

Framework for Policy Analysis

I   Assessing unmet needs
    A   What particular needs or social problems will this policy address?
    B   What are the dimensions of this problem, including the size and characteristics of the group affected?
    C   What changes in American society and what gaps in institutional performance of basic societal functions will this policy cover?

II   Identification of goals and outcomes of this policy
    A   What will be the goals or outcomes in terms of—
        1   Greater social equality, that is, income or resource redistribution
        2   Greater opportunities for disadvantaged groups
        3   Changing the power position of the poor in comparison to other groups
    B   To what degree will this policy improve the quality of life of those affected and the community in general?
    C   To what degree will this policy improve societal functioning?
    D   To what extent will this policy improve intrasocial relations and decrease individual and group tensions and conflicts?
    E   What will be the indirect or side effects of this policy, and will it generate other social problems?

III   Policy implementation strategies in terms of eligibility requirements, type of assistance given, and type of organization and staff utilized
    A   What part of the target group will be eligible for benefits, as determined by such policy decisions as means testing? In other words, to whom will these benefits be allocated?
    B   What type of benefits are provided—cash, material goods, or services?
    C   What type of organization and staff is used in providing services, and to what degree does the organizational arrangement fulfill the need of consumer accessibility and coordination of services?
    D   Will the rules and regulations of this policy be workable at the user level?

IV   Scientific basis for policy
    A   Is this policy in accord with research findings?
    B   Does this policy follow social work principles and practice?

V   Values embodied in this policy
    A   What types of basic value premises are embodied in this policy?
    B   Will influential groups with different values provide opposition to implementation of this policy?
    C   Are there value compromises in the policy?
    D   To what extent is the policy influenced by historical precedent and present and past institutional arrangements?

VI Power bases for support for this policy
    A What interest groups and power bases will support or oppose this policy, and what is their respective strength and size?
    B How much interest do these respective groups have in the policy?
    C Is political decision making on this policy likely to be of the elitist or of the pluralistic type?
    D In general, will the policy be politically acceptable?

VII Resource scarcity and policy
    A What is the resource situation of the funding body (usually, a national government), and what proportion can be used for this policy, under strictly traditional budgetary allocations or under special conditions caused by the economic and political climate?
    B What demand will this policy put on changing the priorities in resource allocation, say between defense and social welfare spending?
    C Is the policy economically feasible?

VIII Costs and benefits related to this policy
    A What is the cost-effectiveness of this program versus the present program or other alternatives in terms of the degree to which it will reduce the problem, help a large number of people, or give high levels of help?
    B What are the funding mechanisms, and are these cost-effective?

CONCLUSION

In this chapter the explanation of what social policy is concerned with has been detailed. A list of the social services covered has been given. An outline has been presented of stages of policy development, or the chronological process of making policy. Last, a substantive framework for the analysis of policy alternatives and outcomes has been given. The last forms the basis for the chapters of this book.

Need for Social Policy

Part One introduces the ideas of unmet needs and need assessment. Gaps in meeting need exist in all societies, especially a fast-changing one like our own. The social services are called on to help fill this gap or vacuum. In this section are discussed the theories of change and of functional analysis that are helpful in identifying unmet needs. Then we move to the practical level and discuss how local communities discover unmet needs through need-assessment studies and how identification of need at the national level is made with the aid of social indicators.

In Chapter 3 we discuss the changes in American society that cause these unmet needs or gaps in institutional functioning. These include changes in the family, in the role of women, in the employment situation, in the size of the population and its concentration in cities, in income distribution, and in the status of minorities. All these changes affect social policy.

The last chapter of this part, Chapter 4, provides a historical picture of how values affect the provision of social services. It gives the major values from early Christian days onward, especially seventeenth- and eighteenth-century American values, and it shows how they affected the delivery of help to those in need. It then discusses the twentieth-century idea of the welfare state and gives factual information on how it works.

Chapter 2

Assessing Unmet Needs

DEFINITION OF NEEDS

In any society there are a number of needs that must be met. Social service agencies are seen as need-meeting agencies. Social workers make the assumption that certain universal or primary physical, mental, economic, and social needs must be met for people of every age and condition of life (Meyer, 1972).

Social needs can be defined as those requirements of society's members necessary for survival, growth, and fulfillment. Implicit in the definition of social needs is the idea that there is a standard or quality of life to be maintained and that when this is not being met a social need becomes a social problem. As Wolins (1967) says, "Need may be thought of as a tension state in the human organism which demands reduction."

Basic survival needs are shelter, food, and clothing, but beyond this there are needs for socialization, education, health care, and recreation. And Meyer adds the need for love, intimacy, and human relationships. A need for a decrease in inequality in income is a primary thrust in Wilcox (1969), while meeting a need for opportunity or access to education for minorities is a focus of many social workers and sociologists. The need for reduction of income insecurity through social insurance programs is a related concern.

The need for participation and some degree of power has been stressed by many recipients and such social policy scholars as Piven and Cloward (1971). A need for neighborhood and general urban improvement is stressed by Kahn (1973).

Towle, in her classic book, *Common Human Needs* (1965), gives as major need categories physical welfare and personality development. She points out that inadequate provision for physical needs may affect personality development. Towle further adds that one should comprehend "the interrelatedness of man's needs and the fact that frequently basic dependency needs must be met first in order that man may utilize opportunities for independence." And Wolins (1967) points out that "not all needs have the same order of priority. The organic usually prevail over the social. Hunger and thirst, when sufficiently severe, can displace all other tensions to the point of eradication, but when these are satisfied, other tension states (needs)—sex, alienation, for example—become expressed with a substantial urgency" (pp. 110–111).

Another group of needs Towle lists are emotional growth and the development of intellectual capacity, adding that "in America this need [intellectual capacity] has been considered more sympathetically than many other common needs. While the establishment of public school systems at first evoked some of the protests that public assistance programs have encountered," now, she says, "the taxpayer takes it for granted that the opportunity for an education is every man's inalienable right."

Towle lists social relations as a major need, stating, "It is generally agreed that the human personality grows, develops, and matures through relationships with others."

Needs or goals are given in a different way in the 1974 Title XX amendment on social service funding to the Social Security Act, as described in Mott (1976). The five goals given by Mott include maintaining economic self-support and self-sufficiency to avoid dependency; preventing neglect, abuse, or exploitation of children and adults unable to protect their own interests; preserving families; preventing inappropriate institutional care by providing community-based or home-based care; and securing institutional care when appropriate or providing services to individuals in institutions.

Some, such as Austin et al. (1977), put emphasis on the unmet needs of communities rather than individuals and suggest that one assess how many persons are in need—not just what needs individuals have—to determine whether there is an indication of a real unmet community need.

Others, closer to the casework approach, focus on individual needs. Thus, Pincus and Minahan (1973) discuss assessment of the problems of the individual, but unlike a number of other writers oriented toward casework diagnosis of needs, they also direct readers to look at the "public issues" side. They say that a problem (or need), while it may be a "private trouble," may also be linked to the lack of sufficient community resources, a public issue. They add, "While [the worker] has a primary responsibility for dealing with private troubles of his client, when he is aware of the related public issue he has also a professional obligation to address himself to it" (Pincus and Minahan, 1973, p. 107). Besides looking at individuals' deficiencies for coping, or their own individual behavior problems, they say one should identify and study the social systems in which these problems are rooted and try to find the reasons why informal, formal, and societal resource systems may be failing to provide needed resources.

NORMAL NEED-MEETING INSTITUTIONS

Certain parts of the social system are considered normal need-meeting social institutions, with some cultural variations. The family is a traditional institution taking care of many needs, such as affection, child care, and sexual needs. Other institutions include the economy, the educational system, the political system, the religious system, and the health system.

Yet the traditional institutions for meeting needs are often not able to perform their job in our industrialized and urbanized society. Meyer, speaking of the social work profession, says:

> The thrust of professional attention has been in those structures where people end up because these normal institutions of life somehow failed to meet their needs. Thus, institutions for the sick, the mentally ill, the penal offender, the neglected child, the neglected aged person appear to have overtaken those that are appropriate to the mainstream of life.

Meyer adds, "The family no longer is the locus of production, socialization, religious training, education, or authority," and it remains "structurally dependent on external systems, making it impossible for the family to exist as an entirely self-sufficient unit" (Meyer, 1972, p. 91). Meyer relates this to factors of urban living, while Wilensky and Lebeaux in their classic work *Industrial Society and Social Welfare* (1965) relate it to industrialization.

A BROAD THEORETICAL GUIDE TO NEED ASSESSMENT

The question always is, To what degree are the above needs left unmet and do gaps in provision occur? A broad framework or theoretical orientation for answering this question, that is, how to detect unmet needs, is given here, followed by a discussion of practical approaches to gathering data on unmet needs, including the local needs-assessment approach and the national compilation of social indicators of need.

The theoretical orientations give us ways of thinking useful to assessing human needs. The theories start with a picture of the way society is organized and how changes occur. They explain how changes have caused tensions and caused gaps in society's ability to meet certain needs. In Chapter 3 changes in American society are described. In the present chapter there is more of a focus on what change in general means, according to several theories.

Change in society can be seen as a normal state of affairs, as such social change theorists as Ogburn (1922) and Bennis (1961) point out. Even in the most traditional and static societies some changes in values and in institutions or social structures emerge. Often change comes not from conscious or deliberate effort but from certain normal developments, such as population growth or decline, improvement of the standard of living, or increased urbanization.

In industrializing societies, changes have resulted from the emphasis on technological developments and scientific advancement in the material side of culture. Such changes as automation seriously affect the nonmaterial side of culture. This nonmaterial side, Ogburn pointed out, changes more slowly, because it is laden with tradition and sentiment, values, and institutions. *Cultural lag* develops where the nonmaterial culture still holds on to the ways of the past instead of adjusting to the technological changes.

Change causes strains and tensions because adjustment is hard to make. Some institutions, such as the family, find it hard to react or adjust to changes in other institutions, such as the economy. They may even find it impossible to do so. These strains due to changes take many forms, whether conflict over proper role performance or loss of functions of institutions.

Pressures occur in the working of accepted institutions because of some changes in other parts of the social structure. These strains or disorganizations due to changes may cause large groups in society to find their conventional routine disrupted, their values threatened, and their social position challenged. Sometimes these pressures can be reduced or drained off; sometimes they start a chain effect of many changes in different parts of the social system; sometimes they cause the development of a counterforce to resist the change, itself an adjustment to the situation.

Anyone involved in social welfare need assessment and planning in this world of rapid change must give adequate attention to the strains constantly taking place and the shifts in the way society's needs are being

met, the ways social structures are functioning, and the ways values are being modified or replaced.

The function of the social reformer, according to Romanyshyn (1973), includes "enabling society to recognize the existence of a new social reality that permits it to aspire to change conditions once seen as unalterable" (p. 112).

In trying to identify this new social reality in its broadest sense we need to look at the functioning of the whole society and its institutions or subsystems. If the new reality is that a certain institution is no longer filling a function, such as child care, because of change, we must look at the whole system to see the cause. This change may be due to changes in another institution, such as the economy, in this example increased jobs for women. Then we look at the result of this change—Who takes care of the children? Is there an unmet need due to this change, this failure of the traditional need-filling institution to cover the need? In such an investigation of coverage of need one notes the interdependence of the institutions or subsystems in a society.

One broad theoretical approach helpful in orienting one toward an investigation of needs is called "functional" or "functional-structural analysis" by sociologists, or "general systems theory," although the words "systems theory," while used by such social work scholars as Compton and Galaway (1979), Kahn (1973), Fodor (1979), Romanyshyn (1971), Rivlin (1971), and Wolins (1967), have been interpreted differently by certain social work writers. Starting with the idea already covered that there are basic needs or jobs to be done in any society (here called functional prerequisites), such as child care, this functional or systems theory adds that there are in each culture social structures or institutions to carry out these functions. Some of the units or institutions or subsystems one thinks of are the family, the economy, the political system, the religious institution, the educational system, and even the welfare system. Each of the subsystems performs certain functions, stemming from basic needs. For example, we think of the family as taking care of childrearing, procreation, the emotional function, and in most societies many more needs. The political system takes care of the function of maintaining social order. The functions of the religious institution may include providing an explanation of the unknown and contributing to social stability. All these units work together to fill the functions as a more or less integrated whole, and the whole (society) is greater than the sum of the parts. Each part contributes to the survival or effective functioning of the society.

While in our analysis the parts or subsystems are institutions or social structures, they can be other kinds of social units. For example, Compton and Galaway give the example of the social units for a mentally ill girl: the primary systems, which include intimate social groups, such as her immediate family, her grandparents, and another group; and the community social system, which includes the school system, the mental health center, and the social agency.

Whatever the method of classification used, the important idea that the functional or general systems analysis contributes to a study of need is that there is an interdependence among institutions. As Buckley (1971) says, each component of the system is related to others in a causal network. And, as Kahn (1973) points out, "The performance of one component is affected by the performance of another component" (p. 142).

This particular point from the functional or systems theory is what makes the theory so useful to the social scientist. According to the prominent sociologist Alvin Gouldner, this way of thinking "forewarns the applied social scientist of the possibility that a change in one part of the system may yield unforeseen and undesirable consequences in another part of the system, due to the interdependence of its elements" (Gouldner, 1970, p. 648). This shifts the attention from a discrete unit in society and isolated changes in it to the *interaction* between units (or institutions) and their interdependence on each other (Compton and Galaway, 1979). It makes one look at the larger picture and take account of the range of major interacting variables (Kahn, 1973). If a change occurs in the economy and causes unemployment and then the proportion of household heads in the work force decreases, there is likely to be a change in the family system, and this causes a need for income maintenance.

One of the most obvious ways of using systems theory in social work "is to draw attention to the multiplicity of systems of different levels of complexity that *influence* any particular situation" (Fodor, 1979, p. 102). This in turn makes possible a review of a wider range of possible targets for intervention—referred to as "target systems." As Fodor adds, systems theory provides "the framework for a wider view of personal and social problems than has commonly been employed by social workers in their practice."

Two other ideas from systems or functional theory that help us assess needs and ways to meet them are the idea of *gaps* or *vacuums* in meeting need and the idea of *functional alternatives*. One starts out with the assumption already given that changes in the institutions mean the institutions' functions are not adequately filled. There is a disequilibrium, which means all parts of the system are not working together smoothly or are out of balance. Functionalists, who consider the whole society in a dynamic, moving state, believe that this disequilibrium is temporary; the society moves to a new equilibrium or stable state because adjustments occur to take care of tensions caused by changes. As Compton and

Galaway (1979) point out, "Although the system [or society] is viewed as a constantly changing whole that is always in the process of movement toward a selected purpose, its parts are assumed to interact within a more or less stable structure at any particular point in time" (p. 78).

Gaps in Filling Functions

While functionalists find that society easily adjusts to changes, one can cite cases where, as an institution of society changes and does not fill certain functions any longer, other institutions *do not* take on that function. For example, changes in the economy cause unemployment, and this loss of function causes tensions and strains that often go unresolved for a long period of time. There is a gap or vacuum in filling the function.

It is often the job of the social policy planner to detect the needs caused by this vacuum, try to point them out to the public, and, if no other normal need-meeting institutions respond, see that the social welfare system provides a temporary or permanent program to meet this need. For example, the planner may observe that many children whose parents both work are "key" children, who come home from school and have no one there to watch them for several hours. The social policy person may push the social welfare institution to establish such a program if other institutions won't do it. Other examples exist in relation to changes in the economy; for instance, men over 55, if laid off, often cannot find other employment and eventually must turn to home relief (meager county assistance) for funds until they reach age 62 and can qualify for social security retirement payments; there is a gap in meeting need. A functional alternative is required.

Functional Alternatives

Of course, most of the time gaps, vacuums, or unmet needs are filled by some institution, usually a traditional one; if not, the social welfare institution eventually fills the gap. Theorists call this a use of functional alternatives; that is, when changes cause the normal need-meeting institution to have difficulty in filling a function, an alternative institution takes over. Either the society has automatically adjusted to this change, or the social policy planner or other professional has stepped in and provided a program. If a parent can't meet the after-school needs of a child, a functional alternative, such as a recreational program, can step in to cover the function. It is very important to the social policy expert to realize there are functional alternatives, that is, that a function can be performed by different institutions in the society; or, conversely, that several institutions can perform the same or similar functions. The family is not the only institution that can carry on the function of care of the elderly; the social welfare institution (or, some would say, that arm of the political institution) can carry on this function, as has indeed happened. The function of childrearing can be performed in a day care center as well as in the family.

THE CHANGE AGENT

Social policy students not only must watch for changes in where these functions are being performed but in some cases also may be instigators of such functional alternatives, simply because there is a need for them. Warren (1977) speaks of purposive change, or deliberate action by social workers and others.

There is a gap in need meeting that must be taken care of. The social worker can be seen as a *change agent,* or intervenor, where there are tensions and strains and functions not taken care of. The worker uses the systems theory as an aid in examining all parts of the system to locate the primary target for remedies. According to Compton and Galaway (1979), this theory not only will influence social workers in identifying all the subsystems that make up the client system but will also help them to "determine what elements in the subsystem will be involved in the change efforts. The system analysis will help to show them where to intervene" (p. 79).

As social workers more and more take on the role of change agents, a terminology Bennis, Benne, and Chin (1961) have popularized, this way of thinking becomes helpful. Bennis et al. talk of planned change as a new discipline, a linkage between theory and action; and Bennis adds that planned change "plays this role by converting variables from the basic disciplines into strategic instrumentation and programs" (p. 65). Both Bennis and Saunders (1975) separately stress that planned change starts with the identification of strategic variables and fact finding. But Bennis's list of the problems that such change agents must take into account includes much more than needs or gaps in meeting need and the lack of functional alternatives that we are talking about here. It includes problems of identification of mission and values; of collaboration and conflict; of control and leadership; of resistance and adaptation to change; of utilization of human resources; of communications; and of management development—in other words, the many policy issues discussed in Chapter 1. In fact, both Bennis and Saunders's description of the change agent is as another term for the policy expert, though in this case one who is also action-oriented, as is the community organization worker. Warren, Bennis, and Saunders all speak of *change agents* or planners who through their community organization efforts try to change policies and bring about new programs and even new laws.

THE SOCIAL WELFARE INSTITUTION AS A
FUNCTIONAL ALTERNATIVE

Both the society and the change agent (or the entire social work profession) now assume that often the profession must intervene and give a normal need-meeting institution, such as the family, help or, in many cases, provide a functional alternative. There are now many social services in existence as functional alternatives for the family's traditional functions, such as nursing homes for the care of chronically ill elderly parents.

Wolins (1967) says that personal malfunction has to be cared for by the social welfare institution. Stating that some degree of institutional malfunctioning often exists, such as the inability of the family to offer adequate child care, he adds:

> Even when a system operates well, there will always be some members who fail to know its rules or who are unable or unwilling to fulfill its requirements. But there is no assurance that the systems (institutions) of our major concern—E(economy), F(family), and P(polity)—will recognize need in their members and stand ready to meet it. That is, they may not operate well. Failure to recognize or acknowledge need may be due to many causes, but evidence of it abounds.

Wolins sees the necessity for the social welfare institution to step in:

> Need must be met. Tension states within the organism must be reduced. Failing that, the person or institution or both are in jeopardy. . . . Social welfare is a systematic provision whose purpose has been to make it more likely that personal and institutional change will be of the former type [in the direction of conformity to the system]. [Pp. 114–115]

Kahn (1973) also assumes that because of changes in the family and the economy the social welfare institution will either have to take on the job of being a substitute for meeting a need or an institution providing support to the traditional need-meeting institutions. He predicts that social services strengthening the family will function in ongoing roles, providing new institutional outlets to replace the roles formerly discharged by the family in the areas of socialization, development, and assistance; and that new institutional forms will develop for new activities essential in a complex urban society and unknown in a simple society.

Sometimes, of course, the alternatives provided do not work. One questions the quality of the performance of such functional alternatives as the nursing home. To correct this we are providing more home care to help adults take on the job of caring for their aging parents, as they do in

Denmark and Holland. As social policy experts, we must ask, What function is the family failing to meet and what institution can best take care of this function today, and how can we enable that institution to do a high-quality job?

Latent Functions

The systems theory also warns us that these functional alternatives we social workers may instigate may have *latent* functions as well as *manifest* functions; that is, they may have consequences we did not expect. For example, some legislators fear that a latent function of a guaranteed annual income will be to decrease work incentive. A latent function or consequence of using correctional institutions for young delinquents is that placement in them gives youths a negative label or bad reputation when they get back into society. The latent function can also have a good effect; for example, providing a Head Start program means giving parents as well as children a new value system and broadening their horizons. In fact we might be more interested, in some cases, in promoting the latent or hidden function of the program than the manifest or announced one. Instead of a frontal attack on a problem we use indirect manipulation, as Gouldner (1964) says; he adds that our knowledge of subsystem interdependence directs us to multiple possibilities of intervention.

CONTRIBUTIONS FROM CONFLICT THEORY

Ideas from conflict theory can also help us in assessing need. Because functional or systems theory assumes that after change the subsystems adjust, some scholars say it is too static a theory. It does, however, contain many ideas on change and on the tensions and strains caused by problems in filling functions. As Fodor (1979) says, systems theory, which some regard as providing a consensus view of society, can include conflict ideas if one abandons the equilibrium model. The theory, he says, "leaves open the possibility of a much wider range of developments. . . . there is plenty of room within the theory for inclusion of conflict, and for conflict to be seen as having a more positive role" (p. 102).

The conflict theory puts the stress on struggle between classes or groups with different interests. Some groups are seen as powerful and some as powerless. They are in a struggle for scarce goods. These scarce goods include power itself, as well as a higher occupational position and a larger share of the income.

Here tension and strain are seen as a natural and continuous state of affairs; conflict rather than cooperation between institutions and societal groups is a normal state. Change is often due to this struggle. The powerless in the struggle demand concessions from the powerful, often using such physical actions as demonstrations or strikes to get better jobs or participation in decision-making activities. The powerless group may even replace the present power elite and possibly change the existing political structure.

In the ideas of Marx, the father of conflict theory, the workers would struggle with the bourgeoisie or capitalists. Today these conflict theories have been reshaped by a number of writers to fit the contemporary scene.

The conflict theory warns us that, in assessing need, what the community power structure perceives as needs may not be what the powerless poor identify as needs. The decision making on what needs to fill will usually come from certain influential power bases, at the national level, as Mills (1956) showed, and at the local level, as Hunter (1953) found for Atlanta and Hayes (1972) found for Oakland. Decisions on welfare and housing needs, they demonstrated, may be made by elitist business power bases without input from other groups in a pluralistic society. These findings alert the social worker to the need to obtain the opinions of the powerless, who, after all, are usually the target group and should know their own needs.

This general conflict theory also warns us that powerful groups may be mainly interested in the latent functions or consequences they see stemming from the meeting of certain social needs. For example, the powerful may support welfare payments to the unemployed in times of serious recession because it keeps these ex-workers from expressing political discontent, as Piven and Cloward (1971) point out, by actions such as riots or activities to bring in political parties of the left.

Conflict between groups in itself can warn us of unmet need. The March on Washington in the 1930s of unemployed workers was a call for action on the need for employment. Riots in the period 1964–1967 were considered a crying out of discontent by black urban masses. In reports trying to explain the riots, expert after expert was quoted as saying they were due to the lack of improvement in the condition of the black population after hopes were raised by the 1954 Supreme Court decision on school desegregation. Protests by American Indians and other groups again warn of the many needs of these groups. The long struggle of farm workers, mainly Chicano, through the United Farm Workers again has brought attention to a major area of need in our society.

Social Movements

The aforementioned movements represent an organized mechanism for bringing needs to the attention of society. As Warren (1977) points out, conflict actions of an organized type are one strategy that change agents use to change institutions.

A social movement, whether a civil rights, labor, or welfare rights movement, has certain stages of development and a certain character. Starting with a small group that stands out as radicals or deviants protesting an injustice, the group, if it centers on a real need for grievance of a large part of the population—a dissatisfaction and tension in society—will gather followers. It will likely use dramatic tactics, such as demonstrations, strikes, mass rallies, marches, fasts, and going to jail to bring the issue to the attention of the public and gain further support. A large movement is likely to have intellectual leaders who can communicate ideas to the society and a cadre of marchers or adherents willing to protest and take the abuse of the establishment. The social movement often has a charismatic leader, such as Martin Luther King, Jr., who was able to capture the loyalty of the followers and the imagination of the public and turn them toward the cause. At first a movement is often considered very radical and its members are treated as criminals, harassed by the police, jailed, or even exiled in the struggle with the power structure. As its message appeals to a wider and wider audience it is often joined by many other groups in society, some of whom are close to legitimate organizations. The group's demands are often acted on and it and its leaders often become more and more part of the establishment. For example, in the 1930s, during the United Auto Workers' strikes, police were used; Walter Reuther, the union's leader, was jailed; and the movement was called radical. By the 1960s Reuther was a close friend to President Kennedy; the union was very much an institution, with large headquarters across from the White House; and it was considered natural for the union to bargain collectively with the motor companies each year.

In recent times we have had several major social movements. Cesar Chavez's United Farm Workers at this writing is still going through the middle stages of becoming an accepted representative of farm workers. The success of the union is changing the position of workers in the fields to one similar to that of industrialized workers and has many consequences for the welfare of this class of workers. A *latent* function of the movement is to heighten respect for the Mexican-American, among the rest of society, to further bring this group's problems to the attention of the whole society, and to further encourage the growth of a political organization of Mexican-Americans. Legitimate social service agencies are being affected by this movement because they are being forced to be aware of an almost ignored clientele, the Chicanos, or Mexican-Americans, and their needs, and to add or restructure services to meet these needs. This includes adding Spanish-speaking staff and even Mexican-American representatives to agency boards. In many areas new social service agencies are springing up and receiving funding from the traditional sources for their work with the Mexican-American community. One can even go so far as to say that concern with increasing the number of college students of Mexican-American background has come partly as a result of Chavez's movement.

METHODS OF ASSESSING NEEDS

The theories on social change and functional alternatives described above, as well as social movement, give us a way of thinking that alerts us to change and unmet needs. There are also systematic methods that practitioners can use to acquire data on needs. Prigmore and Atherton (1978) point out that "one should start from a needs assessment in which as many relevant as possible participate. The needs assessment leads the social worker to set some goals" (p. 45).

Today, needs assessment has become very popular. Many local communities have done such a study. In addition studies of social indicators have been done on a national level by the U.S. Census Bureau.

Local Needs Assessment Studies

Such fact finding on the local level can be done by looking at available statistics on the degree to which a need is met and comparing it with the population at risk. One could, for example, look at the number of children in all child care facilities in a city compared to the number of young children of working mothers in the city. One could get data on the number of children of different ages of low-income families in summer camp and compare it with the actual number of such children in the community. Many studies provide just the first half of the data, not the comparison data.

One example of a highly praised model for a community needs assessment is the Hayward, California, one, done by appointed community groups, staff, and consultants. With the use of a careful design, extensive data on needs and on resources was gathered by a variety of techniques and combined to give an up-to-date and well-organized picture of the situation in the city of Hayward in eight problem areas: education, health, housing, income and employment, recreation and leisure, safety and justice, social environment, and transportation.

For each problem the data collected were organized into an outline containing a number of useful categories. For example, for the health problem, the physical illness section was organized under the heading "problem identification: social indicators of physical illness," and under this were the subheads: *(A)* infant mortality statistics for the last five years; *(B)* venereal disease statistics; *(C)* incidence of communicable diseases; *(D)* weight of children at birth; *(E)* incidence of tuberculosis; and *(F)* percentage of population with medical insurance. This report on the health situation then had a section on resource identification, including the number of hospitals and private physicians.

The "problem identification" or "social indicators" section for each of the eight problems used a variety of information sources. These included, besides standard statistical data from the census and other government reports, data from a scientifically planned needs assessment survey done by consultants. Over 500 residents were interviewed, answering a total of seventy-six questions. In addition, census tract meetings were held in nineteen neighborhoods to get opinions on needs. A community resource conference of community agency personnel and residents was held, in which 100 people in a needs assessment workshop gave opinions. In-depth interviews were conducted with ninety-eight community leaders, including business and ethnic leaders, government administrators, and social service directors. The latter were also asked about resource availability. All these data gave a many-sided and comprehensive picture of unmet needs for this city of 100,000.

Voluntary Agencies' Efforts at Need Assessment

Many voluntary associations concerned with broad social service areas also do need assessment of different problem groups. For example, some members and leaders in the Mental Health Association of San Francisco saw a need for services to the families of the irreversibly brain-damaged adults, who deteriorate slowly in health and drag their families down emotionally and financially. Research showed these cases were not coverable under private health insurance. The association set up a family survival project to look into the need; with grants from a foundation and the state public health department they did a study. They produced a report and a sociolegal handbook for the families. A group of 400 family members was organized. The association and the group pushed the state to provide funds for services. On the basis of information on need, the state passed a bill to fund counseling for brain-damaged adults and their families.

Social Indicators

Nationally, a massive effort has been made by the Census Bureau's Office of Federal Statistical Policy and Standards to gather many basic national statistics and assemble them in table form "to provide a factual basis for independent assessments of our current social conditions and the directions in which we appear to be evolving as a society." This statistics-gathering effort was made under the Advisory Committee on Social Indicators, with the aid of high-level consultants. Eleven major social areas are covered, with a number of tables for each area of concern; they include population, family, housing, education, social security and welfare, health and nutrition, public safety, work, income, and several others. This report was put out under the title *Social Indicators* in 1973 and 1976.

As *Social Indicators 1976* says, in regard to each area and its tables, "All of these concerns relate, directly or indirectly, to the quality of our lives." They add:

> In order to reveal these relationships, the concerns which have been identified in each of the broad social areas are represented by selected statistics or statistical measures—social indicators which describe the general status of the population with respect to certain aspects of each concern. . . . Where these indicators are available in the form of time series of observations, they also reflect trends in the particular characteristic or condition, so that the reader can gauge the direction of major social changes or developments over time. [Pp. xxiii–xxiv]

This report assesses needs in three ways. It gives social indicators of system performance, such as the average public expenditure per recipient for unemployment insurance; indicators of economic well-being; and the public's perception of its degree of well-being and of its needs or concerns, from national attitudinal surveys.

PROBLEMS IN ASSESSING NEEDS

Both local needs assessment studies and national ones, whether of one need or a number of needs, suffer from several problems. As Kahn (1973) points out, most needs, except major physical ones, are conditioned by societal context; expectations are developed by the culture. The form and level of need satisfaction is culturally set. The form of satisfying people's housing needs, for example, is deciding whether to build houses instead of apartments or just to provide tents. Setting the *level* of need satisfaction here is determining whether to provide one room per person or one room for a whole family. In some developing countries educational need is satisfied with elementary education; in the United States we now think of elementary school through junior college as a need.

Estimates of need and unmet need are often in terms of certain standards, such as teacher-student ratios. There is always the question of who sets the standards and what motivation is behind it. What kind of personnel is required to meet a need? One way health needs in a country or area are judged is in terms of the proportion of doctors to population. However, an increase in the number of nurse-practitioners and even licensed midwives could decrease the need for doctors. In doing this personnel substitution or in using alternative programs, one runs across the problem of discussing the "boundaries" of each need. Thus, while cataloging need seems simple, these issues of boundaries and alternatives make it more difficult.

Another problem is that the degree of scientific knowledge used to determine need standards may be low, as Kahn (1973) states. He says:

> Service standards (number of teachers per 100 pupils, number of doctors per 100,000 population, and so on) are occasionally validated empirically as assuring a defined level of service. More often they incorporate some elements of folklore and faith. They always assume a specific pattern of operations, and the pattern may not be acceptable to innovators and reformers. [P. 61]

A related problem Kahn mentions is that need satisfaction changes over time; thus a need standard may become outmoded. As our society becomes more affluent we set higher standards for meeting a need. In fact, a situation that was considered tolerable in 1948 may be considered an unmet need in 1979. Increased aspirations, improved communication, or scientific progress, as well as affluence, influence need standards, Kahn points out. He also adds that policy decisions themselves, such as equality, affect levels of expectations. One could say that since the 1954 school desegregation decision and the 1964 Civil Rights Act minorities have had greater aspirations, often unmet, and this was a partial cause of the city riots of 1964 to 1967.

Another source of difficulty in needs assessment work is the fact that different people have a different perception of what a problem or need is. Gilbert and Specht (1974) point out that:

> The basis for institutional policy change is sometimes an unrecognized or unmet need in the community. . . . The perception of the problem and the institution's responsibility are related to the political, economic, social and institutional forces that the originator perceives. . . . What people define as problems is related in part to their institutional positions. [P. 16]

Certain behavior may be considered deviant and in need of corrective action by some while it is considered acceptable and normal by others. Different groups or individuals may define the same situation in different ways, as Austin et al. (1977) point out in giving the example of the merchant whose windows are regularly broken. The merchant speaks of "young hoodlums," while the social worker, looking at groups, is concerned with "teenaged gangs" and the parents talk about their kids' "having no place to play."

Priorities

Another aspect of needs assessment is assigning priority to needs and then to programs to alleviate needs. These judgments not only relate to how far below a standard a problem falls (say a shortfall in the number of doctors per 100,000 population) but also involve value judgments on how serious the need in general is *in comparison* to other needs. If resources are plentiful, Kahn (1973) mentions, fewer priority choices have to be made, but, as he states strongly, "The reality is that resources are always scarce and never unlimited" (p. 61). Does one give high priority to education, as we do in the United States, or to health insurance, as is done in some northern European countries?

All these problems make needs assessment a difficult task. Yet it is the starting point for any policy formulation.

SOCIAL CHANGE AND NEEDS

New needs develop as society changes. Needs may be inadequately met because traditional need-meeting institutions can no longer carry on the job. We have already covered the functional analysis of how interdependence exists between institutions or subsystems of the social system and how disequilibriums and gaps in taking care of functional prerequisites come about.

A knowledge of recent social changes in American society also makes the student aware of new needs. The very quick pace in American life causes needs to come upon us very suddenly and sometimes to remain unmet for a long period. Kahn (1973) noted:

> An analysis of social change in modern society . . . suggests that social services will be essential in the predictable future and perhaps should be given a higher priority if certain amenities and protections are not to be ignored. [P. 62]

The present course of American society, as Chapter 3 details, demands that a higher priority be given to addressing unmet social needs.

Chapter 3

Changes in
American Society

INTRODUCTION

Social policies must be based on an accurate, up-to-date understanding of American society. A first step in policy formulation is assessing need. Society's institutions are continually changing, and the changes cause new needs and new gaps in meeting functions.

In this chapter some aspects of American life, such as the family, are looked at in terms of the changes that have occurred that affect policy. An awareness of current trends is very necessary for successful policy formulation. One has to know what situation exists before strategies can be developed to intervene and give assistance. For example, Lampman (1971) pointed out that in making income maintenance policy one must take into account the rate of economic growth; changes in the composition of the population, in family size, and in the level of immigration; and many other factors.

This chapter, then, will describe major changes affecting many areas of social service provision. It will not outline goals or policies in particular fields such as child welfare or juvenile justice; this is done in later chapters.

CHANGES IN FAMILY LIFE IN AMERICA

The family is a major social institution in our society that is undergoing change. As a subsystem in the social system of interrelated institutions, it has traditionally filled many functions for its members. It performs a number of jobs or functions for other subsystems, such as starting the child on the road to education or giving the young person training useful in the job world.

The changes that are going on in the American family influence social policies in a number of ways. The drastic increase in one-parent families means a number of policies must be formulated taking this phenomenon into account. Meeting the needs of this increasing group becomes a goal. The phenomena of marital dissolution and the new nonmarital social bonds require new policy orientations.

The decrease in the functions the family fills must be recognized and policies evolved to take this into account. Thus, the goal of stabilizing the family and helping it meet its normal functions may be too simplistic. There must be policy goals that find a number of innovative approaches, of a universal nature, to the complex arrangements that now replace the lifelong nuclear family (husband, wife, and children), which today represents only a small proportion of the actual families in our society. It is the purpose of this section to make the student aware of the changes in the family. Specific policies are given in the chapters in Part Three.

Response to Outside Forces

The family in the twentieth century has been forced to respond to a variety of changes occurring on the American scene, especially in the economic realm. As Romanyshyn (1971) has pointed out, the family is asked to respond to changes in other organizations and to adapt itself and its members to external factors—a depression in the economic subsystem, for example, or something like the increased need for female workers in World War II. He adds that "this little understood and unappreciated adaptive function of the family has a heavy human cost, inequitably distributed. Change imposes stress. In the absence of adequate societal supports, disorganization of family life may be the consequence" (p. 324).

Rodman (1965) gives as an example, "If the social and economic system functions to deprive lower class males of adequate jobs, this limits opportunities for stable marriages for lower class women, thus increasing the risk of illegitimacy and female-based households."

The family is not a powerful institution but one that must bend to new needs and trends in other institutions. In fact, one modern job the family has is socializing the person to the requirements of these other institutions, as through education. The family has had to deal with the consequences of the strain industrialization imposed on family life when it disrupted the pattern of farm living, in which the whole family had often worked the farm together. The family has been equally vulnerable to the related stress of urbanization, which has often separated it from supportive relatives. In our present, postindustrial era, the family has had to develop the geographic mobility needed for many corporate jobs, which again separates it from relatives. Policies must take into account this mobility and the frequent lack of relatives living close by.

As future changes come in the larger society, the family must again respond and change, because, as Keller (1971) points out, "You cannot tamper with a society without expecting the family to be affected and vice versa. . . . We are in the presence of a feedback system" (p. 45). Even scientific changes have had their effect on the family. Through science we have had the development of the pill and other contraceptives, a major force in determining family size. Through technology we have been given all sorts of labor-saving home helpers, from dishwasher, and microwave ovens to TV dinners, to facilitate the wife's entry into the job market.

Attitudes have also been changing toward birth control, abortion, adoption, and illegitimacy, and this affects the family. The attitudes of individualism, personal competition, and self-fulfillment fostered in the industrial and postindustrial eras—along with technological developments that make individual self-sufficiency possible in comparison to the mutual cooperation required between husband, wife, and children in the farm family—all work to downgrade the desire or need for a family. As Keller (1971) points out:

> As individual self-sufficiency, fed by economic affluence or economic self-constraint, increases, so does one's exemption from unwanted economic as well as kinship responsibilities. Today the important frontiers seem to lie elsewhere, in science, politics, and outerspace. This must affect the attractions of family life for both men and women. For men, because they will see less and less reason to assume full economic and social responsibilities for four to five human beings in addition to themselves as it becomes more difficult and less necessary to do so. This, together with the continued decline of patriarchal authority and male dominance—even in the illusory forms in which they have managed to hang on—will remove some of the psychic rewards which prompted many men to marry, while the disappearance of lineage as mainstays of the social and class order, will deprive paternity of its social justification. [P. 47]

Interest in Other Roles

The women's movement has made the female partner to the marriage aware of her potential for more than the childbearing and housewife roles. The attitudes of independence have been matched by increased opportunities for women in a broader range of available jobs, and more role models are successful in the career woman–housewife combination. Several studies have shown that newlywed women now have a variety of goals, as Sherlock and Moeller (1977) found of college-educated newlyweds; a third of the newlyweds in this study did not plan to have children, and another large group were deferring children until they had obtained certain material possessions, such as a house, or until the career of one spouse or both was more fully launched.

In one large sample, many female students did not consider children to be the most important reason for marriage, disapproved of large families, and thought it possible for a woman to pursue family and career simultaneously.

The Lessening of the Family's Responsibility for Certain Functions

In many cases traditional functions of the family are now shared with other institutions or taken over by them. The American family has long shared the job of socializing and educating the child, and now this often occurs as early as the child's second or third year, in day care and preschool programs. This means that a policy to meet the child's needs can no longer be assumed to be executed through the family.

The family no longer takes a great responsibility for the recreational function. Even young children spend many of their leisure hours away from the home, and policy must take this into account.

The social insurance or social welfare function is to a large degree no longer a family responsibility, partly because the modern family, small in size and constrained by the urban setting, has been unable to fulfill this social insurance need to help poor and ill relatives and partly because, as a greater need has finally been recognized, the government has stepped in. Under social security one's aged parents are given financial help; the disabled, the blind, widows, and deserted women are given cash. Care of the children in cases of family dismemberment or disruption has been taken over by the state through foster care or institutional care. The emotionally disturbed have been put in institutions or day care programs. This, of course, has not occurred in every case, and especially in regard to the elderly the social insurance responsibility is shared between adult offspring and government institutions, although in some areas, such as nursing homes, the state has been assumed somewhat responsible but in reality has left a major gap.

There is a policy dilemma here. The state stepped in, especially in the Depression of the 1930s, because the family could not adequately fill the social insurance function. Today the attitude of many is that the state and not the family should carry that function, with the result that the state is forced into greater expenditures; yet, because the public wants to keep the cost down, there are inadequate expenditures per capita, leaving those in need only partially covered. Serious gaps in state coverage exist, for example, for adequate homemaker services for the elderly, and many families are unwilling to fill that gap.

The function of reproduction has stayed in the family, but since the number of children per family has gone down and in some cases there are no children, childbearing and childrearing do not consume as long a period in a woman's life. Since some experts have considered parenthood the pivotal factor in marriage and the family, its diminished importance may be a signal of the family's deterioration.

One function that has possibly actually increased in the modern American family is the emotional-affectional function, even though the number of family members involved in this intimate interaction now is smaller. Because Americans are mobile and because they now usually live in an urban environment, the intensity of their interaction with the community has often greatly decreased. Many don't know their neighbors and town leaders; if they do, they often move and have to reestablish contacts in a new group. In their often competitive jobs they do not become overly friendly with fellow employees, and frequent job changes or promotions discourage close friendships. Thus, the family is the place of intimate relations, the place where one presents one's natural self, gives out confidences and emotional feelings, unburdens the soul in times of tragedies and failures, and shares happiness in times of special events and successes. Since there are now fewer family members to relate to, this greater closeness can put a strain on the few there are when it is failure or anger that has to be shared.

The Structure of the Family

A changed structure is one cause of the trouble the family has filling these various functions. While the structure differs from family to family, the most common type is the model nuclear family with only husband, wife, and children living in the same unit. Another type gaining in importance is the female-headed family; by 1975, 17 percent of all children under 18 were living in single-parent families. (See Table 3-1.) These are smaller units and have fewer adult members than the old-fashioned extended families found in the early 1900s even in the United States. The family of an earlier period was a three- or more-generation family in which adult offspring and their spouses and children lived with or near the parents in the farm community. It was the type of family that could handle many functions because it had many adult members.

In rural areas of the United States today and even in urban areas, some families are modified extended families, with relatives living nearby,

Table 3-1   Children Under 18 Years Old in Families, by Presence of Parents and Race of Children: 1960 and 1975

Children under 18 years	1960			1975		
	Total	White	Black	Total	White	Black
All children under 18 in families, thousands	62,873	54,492	8,381	65,711	55,252	9,365
Percent*	100.0	100.0	100.0	100.0	100.0	100.0
Living with both parents	88.9	91.9	69.2	80.8	85.8	50.0
Living with mother only	8.1	6.2	20.6	15.6	11.3	41.3
Living with father only	1.2	1.0	2.1	1.5	1.5	1.8
All other†	1.8	.8	8.2	2.1	1.3	6.8

*Detail may not add to 100.0 because of rounding.
†Children under 18 living with friends, neighbors, or relatives other than parents, or as adopted or foster children.
Source: U.S. Department of Commerce, Bureau of the Census, Current Population Reports, Series P-20, No. 291, and Series P-23, No. 50.

that still allow interaction between relatives and provide social and economic support. This structure is more often characteristic of working-class and minority families than of white-collar families, which have greater geographic mobility and more interaction with outsiders with similar interests.

The dominant nuclear family is a weak unit, since it has the burden of children and only two adults. The female-headed household, missing the male support force, is, of course, extremely overburdened in trying to carry out its functions. For this lone adult to carry out the socialization process or other functions on a round-the-clock, day-in, day-out basis is difficult. Yet, in the last few years there has been a heavy increase in the number of single-parent, usually female-headed, households. Illegitimate births have increased, especially among teenagers, thus upping the number of single-parent families; 15 percent of all births in 1974 were illegitimate, half of them to teenagers; half of black births were illegitimate.

In 1977 there were 5.3 million single-parent households with children under 18, three million with a full-time working mother. While there were still 24.9 million husband-wife families with children under 18, one no longer can say it is the norm. Nor can one think of the typical two-parent family as husband-breadwinner, wife-homemaker-mother, and two or more children. Of these 24.9 million husband-wife-children families, 11.4 million, or almost half, had *both* parents working. In addition, half of all American families now have no children under 18.

Also, a new type of family has gained some prominence: the *blended* family, where children of several marriages are living with mother and *present* husband, or, less often, with father and present wife; in some cases, children of both spouses' former marriages are living under the same roof. One estimate is that in 1977 about 18 million stepchildren from the remnants of what used to be called "broken" families were blended into the new kind of family unit. If the divorce rate goes higher, one can expect even more of this.

The Increased Divorce Rate

The divorce rate in the United States is the highest in the world, and in the period 1970–1977 alone it went up around 60 to 70 percent. (See Figure 3-1.) Social policies must deal with this situation in a variety of ways.

Number per 1000 population

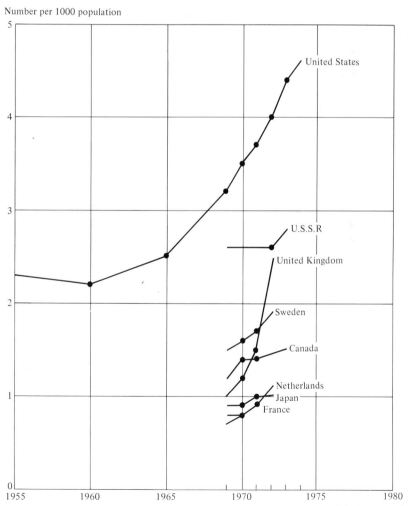

Figure 3-1 Divorce rates, selected countries: 1955–1975. (*Source:* U.S. Bureau of the Census, *Social Indicators, 1976.*)

For every three marriages in a year in the United States there is one divorce. In California 1 out of 2 marriages end in divorce; in some rich suburban counties there are three times as many divorces as marriages recorded. In America, between 1890 and 1970 the divorce rate increased by 300 percent. It is estimated there are 12 million or more children under 18 from divorced families today. Divorce rates are highest among teenagers, but often, of course, divorce occurs for those married twenty years as well as for those married one year or less. As many as 30 to 40 percent of these divorces involve children, and the proportion is increasing each year. In some cases there is a second or third divorce; for example, a study of all California divorces in 1966 showed that one-third of the divorces were among couples for whom there had been at least one previous marriage, and in some cases more. In this study, 15 percent of the marriages had lasted under one year. Twenty-four percent of these divorces were among Catholics even though the Catholic Church is adamantly against divorce.

Looking at these statistics, one can of course be too pessimistic about the instability of the American family. Nearly two-thirds of all couples do remain married until death, and even of the couples that had divorced, 75 percent of the women and 83 percent of the men remarried within three years of their divorce. In summary, 96 percent of American adults marry, a very high percentage; 38 percent of those will divorce; and of this group 79 percent will remarry. However, of those who remarry, 44 percent will again divorce. It was predicted that 4 out of 10 children born in 1970 would spend part of their childhood in a single-parent family, usually with the mother, as a result of divorce, desertion, or illegitimacy.

What are the social welfare ramifications of all this? One is the need for income maintenance. Child support is low, as Pearce (1978) has shown; in 1976, 40 percent of absent fathers contributed nothing, while the average payment provided by the other 60 percent was less than $2000; this was at a time when the median income for all families was over $13,000. That is why a number of divorced women must turn to welfare.

Not that there isn't some attempt to locate these runaway fathers. For example, in San Francisco the city has a family support division that works at this as a collection and transmittal agency. As an assistant said, "If you locate the fathers, the chances [of collecting] are pretty good. We file an action here; they put the screws on him and he pays or goes to jail." There were, in one period alone, 2400 child support cases on file. Even if the father cannot pay, this office tries to make him maintain a psychological link with the family. Many fathers have steady jobs and can pay something. Often, as one man said, "I got tired of paying. I haven't seen the kids for years. The arrearage kept getting larger." One social worker said, "Some of these men, not seeing the children, somehow forget those kids are the same ones they brought into this world" (Emch, 1973, p. 9).

Nationwide, collection of child support has not been good; it may be that the man is not locatable or that the jurisdiction he lives in does not cooperate fully.

Child support is not the only type of payment awarded in a divorce. Many men prefer paying alimony rather than child support, because this former is tax-deductible to the payer. Second, alimony is paid usually only until the wife remarries, so that the husband may be relieved of the burden when she remarries. For this reason, some women with alimony support establish a cohabitation relationship rather than a legal one in the next permanent union, rather than lose their alimony from the first husband.

In any case, the wife and children are usually worse off than before the break. As one major divorce lawyer said, "If I represent the wife, I look upon the result as good if she ends up within 10 percent to 15 percent of her husband's take-home money" (Watten, 1977, p. 10). Many get much less.

Some women get a settlement at the time of divorce. In the majority of states, they also get half the property because there is a community property law; the house may need to be sold in order to divide the property.

While no-fault divorce, in which no accusations are made, exists in almost all states, the courtroom financial battle over the support amounts, especially for middle-class families, can be painful. Children are often used as pawns in these battles. Arguments are waged over what is owned in common. No issue is too trivial for a fight here. Who gets to keep the couch? the family dog?

As one frustrated court official adds, "Judges will say, 'give me a good clean murder.'" He adds, "They don't want to get involved in family disputes. It's too messy. Somehow, in this society, what happens to the children isn't important. Then we wonder why they go wrong, why they get into trouble. I don't understand it."

The mother is also affected emotionally and financially. As Hawley says, the woman takes the brunt (Watten, 1977):

> Despite women's lib and so forth, they're at a disadvantage. After years of marriage, the husband looks around and decides he'd like a new model. It takes 6 months to obtain a final. He can be married again within a month. But not the woman. The woman has problems; a financial problem, a rejection problem. [P. 10]

Yet, for the husband as well as the wife, divorce can be painful, dealing an emotional jolt to him and calling for heavy adjustment away from the married way of life. The man must adjust to being single, to living in a small apartment, to cooking and cleaning for himself, and worst of all, being separated from his children. The wife moves to single-adult status, but now with twenty-four hours' unshared child care, except in times when the children visit the father. She moves down in income and must now master the finances. She may cling desperately to the old married identity, but in reality both she and the husband often lose the support of mutual friends. As one woman said, "The other day I was at the store and spotted the mother of one of Jimmy's classmates. She actually ducked down an aisle to avoid me. This town is like Noah's Ark; if you aren't part of a pair, they shut you out."

The wife may feel lonely and treat the children as companions and even as substitute male household heads. The wife's feeling of rejection may hurt the care of the children, as in this example:

> Dorothy, 36, divorced by her husband, has spent the past four months crying constantly. Her two children are ignored and are out of control, taking off on their own without orders on what time to return. Bills have gone unpaid and now she has been served with an eviction notice.

If the man does remarry, his financial situation suffers, since he has only half or two-thirds of his income to share with his second wife and the children of that marriage; and second, he suffers guilt pains about the limited visitation rights to the children of the first marriage. Also, if the man remarries, he may have a new problem, that of relating to his new wife's children. He may suffer from both role ambiguity and frequent guilt feelings about negative attitudes he has to the new partner's children.

Children of divorced parents, of course, suffer in a number of ways. In a Toronto study, the children of divorce were found to be unhappy because when their mother remarried they were required to respond to the mother's new mate as though he were their "real father," and this often gave rise to feelings of hostility, rebellion, or withdrawal (Schlesinger, 1970, p. 117).

Just as likely is the situation where after remarriage the mother is unhappy about having the children of her former marriage with her, reflecting the new mate's negative feelings toward the children or the financial problems of meeting the needs of these children, who are often teenagers. The unwanted children may be boarded with grandparents or other relatives.

Even before remarriage there are problems for the child whose parents divorce. Children may have a guilty feeling that they are the cause of the parental discord. After the divorce the child also has the problem of divided loyalty. The mother may demand that the child be completely loyal to her and encourage the child to look on the father as the wrongdoer, sinner, or enemy. The mother may make it difficult for the child to visit the father.

The Family Service Agency and other groups recognizing these problems faced by children of divorced parents are now providing therapy sessions for these children and even the divorced woman in some locations.

In conclusion, social policies must take into account the new structure of many families and the increased tensions caused by their breakup or loss of function.

WOMEN IN THE WORK FORCE

A major development in the last twenty years has been the great increase in the number of women in the work force. A number of these women are, of course, divorced women. Over half the adult women in the United States were in the work force or looking for work in 1978; this totaled over 38 million women over the age of 20 out of 76 million adult women in the country. Barry Chiswick, formerly of the President's Council of Economic Advisers, calls this increased female work participation "one of the most important changes in the American economy in this century" (Chiswick and O'Neill, 1977, p. 137).

In 1900 about 20 percent of all women were in the work force. From 1945 to 1965, that figure ran from about 35 to 39 percent, but by 1977 it was over 50 percent. Some of this increase can be attributed to the fact that women today marry later, hold off childbearing after they marry, and on the average have fewer children, so that the burden of child care is less. Last, they have longer life expectancies these days and so have more years to be in the work force.

Yet the significant increase in labor-force participation has been not only in the group without school-aged and preschool children but also among those with children. By March 1974, almost 27 million children in the United States, or 42 percent of those under 18, had mothers who were working or seeking work. About 1 of every 4 of these children (6.1 million) were below regular school age, requiring some kind of care in their working mother's absence. The most startling finding, however, is that more than a third of the mothers whose children were under age 6 were in the work force. (See Table 3-2.) Of mothers with toddlers under 3, 36 percent of black mothers worked at full-time jobs in 1974 and 17 percent of white mothers did. Black mothers with older children were also more likely to work than white mothers.

Female-headed households with children were, of course, highly represented in the work force. In 1974, 1 of 10 white children and 4 of 10 black children were in *working*-female–headed families. Some were

Table 3-2   Labor force status of married women, husband present, by age of children, March 1974
(Numbers in Thousands)

Presence and age of children	Population 16 years old and over	Labor force	Labor force participation rate, %
Total	47,324	20,367	43.0
No children under 18 years old	21,804	9,365	43.0
Children under 18 years old	25,520	11,002	43.1
Children 6 to 17 years only	13,268	6,792	51.2
Children 3 to 5 years old, none under 3 years	5,027	1,967	39.1
Children under 3 years old	7,225	2,243	31.0

Source: U.S. Department of Labor, *Marital and Family Characteristics of the Labor Force*, March 1974, p. 61.

illegitimate children, and many were children of divorced parents. The Department of Labor report (1974) giving the above data also states, "In fact, the absolute 1970–1974 increase in the number of children with working mothers occurred almost exclusively in the fatherless, one-parent families, with distinct differences between whites and blacks" (pp. 65–66). The report further states that among white women those who are divorced have a historical pattern of much higher labor-force participation rates than married women.

A main reason women are in the work force is an urgent economic one, especially for these female-headed households. However, some wives, because of a desire for a higher standard of living and a concern with inflation, turn to work to supply the needed income, such as money for a down payment on a house or a car. Another reason is that more women are receiving college educations and then want more participation in the labor force.

One can also say that work in the marketplace now looks more attractive than work in the home; and because machines and innovations have somewhat lightened work in the home, this substitution is possible to a greater degree than in the early 1900s. Some new job opportunities have also opened up, particularly in the service sector of the economy.

This fact of heavy service-sector employment to some degree explains women's lower earning power than men's, although the fact that women are much less likely to be continuously in the work force over many years compared to men is another factor to take into account. For example, although 59.8 percent of the women 24 to 54 years old were in the labor force at one time or another during 1971, Chiswick (1977) reports only 38.2

percent were in the labor force for 50 to 52 weeks during the year. The in-and-out work force of women with children makes them remain newcomers on the job or lower-rung workers, although prejudice against women supervisors has a similar effect.

Earnings data shows that in 1971 the annual median earnings for women 14 years old and over, if the comparison is restricted to year-round, full-time workers, were 60 percent of men's (Chiswick, 1977). Another major difference, according to Chiswick, is that "the incomes of women do not *increase with age* in anything like the same way men's do." He does state that for older women in continuous work for a number of years the situation was considerably better, as it was for those in professional jobs. Yet Hartley (1974) reports that even in the high-ranking professions women are usually found in the lower-level positions and median income is only 39 to 53 percent of that of males in professions requiring similar schooling, licensing, and commitment on the job (e.g., physician, lawyer, architect, and economist).

The problem is not only that women are likely to be in and out of the work force but that they are mainly in low-paying occupations. Pearce (1978) says, "Women are much more concentrated in relatively few occupations than are men; 60 percent of all women are in ten occupations." These occupations are low-paying ones. In fact, the higher the percentage of workers that are female in an occupation, the lower the average income. For example, 81 percent of the workers in apparel manufacture were female in January 1973, and the average weekly wage was $93, Pearce points out; in motor vehicle sales only 11 percent were female, and the average weekly earnings were $152; and for construction they were $223. Sawhill (1976) found that over half of the female-dominated occupations were ones with poverty-level wages. Pearce says that "within occupationally segregated ghettos, the demand for *cheap* labor and the demand for *female* labor became synonymous" (pp. 6–7). She also mentions that often women not only get low pay but also do not get the fringe benefits many men do, because they are either temporary or part-time workers or newcomers to the job.

The low pay of women is a reason many are on work and welfare. Another reason is that a number of women who want to work cannot find work. The Women's Bureau in 1977 reported almost twice as many women as men classified as discouraged workers (neither working nor actively looking for work). The female unemployment rate is considerably higher than the male unemployment rate, 8.6 percent as against 7 percent in 1976. Women are often not well qualified for work because of inadequate education, job skills, or past work experience. A special group is the older, "displaced homemakers," who have lost their husbands because of death, desertion, or divorce and are forced into the job market. They have never developed job skills, career confidence, or employment experience. They are considered too old for beginning-level jobs by many employers.

Role Changes Due to Employment

It is inaccurate to think of married women and divorced mothers in America mainly as housewives centering their activities in the home. A very large group are filling a dual role of employee and homemaker. As Hartley says, many are finding rewards in labor-force activity, not only monetary rewards, but also symbolic recognition and intrinsic satisfaction in work beyond the nuclear family.

Some women have taken on these dual roles in order to fill a vacuum when the children leave home, and others because a husband has divorced or deserted them, but many young married women today assume they will play the dual role of employee and homemaker. This changes the role of the man, as both husband and father. There is more sharing of household tasks and care of the children. There is more use of alternative homemaking and child care services, such as through day care centers.

In many areas of social policy one must keep in mind that the woman in the family is likely to be working outside the home. Such realization changes our perception of the degree to which one can depend on the female adult for a variety of supports, whether in the child welfare area, in the care of elderly parents, or in relation to the delinquent child.

FLUCTUATIONS IN THE ECONOMIC SYSTEM AND THEIR EFFECTS ON EMPLOYMENT

It is a commonsense conclusion that in periods of economic recession or depression there will be a greater need for government policies. As the unemployment rate goes up, people laid off turn to the government for financial assistance and jobs as well as for counseling and other services related to their problems; in other words, fluctuations in the economy have a serious effect on government policies.

The government has to respond to a downturn in the economy. Its policies can include measures to decrease the unemployment rate and stimulate jobs through economic growth incentives or monetary system adjustments. Various policies, such as tax incentives, can be used to get private industry to provide more jobs, or the government itself can take on the task of providing public service jobs. The government can also focus on measures to increase the employment of highly vulnerable groups through a variety of actions, such as encouraging industries to move into depressed rural or inner-city areas, pushing for affirmative action for minority and women workers, or upgrading the skills of teenagers.

On the other hand, the government's strategy can be instead to encourage, by use of subsidies, certain groups, such as college students and the elderly, to stay out of the labor market. Or the government can be more forceful in keeping illegal immigrants out of the country. Its policies can also include extending unemployment benefit periods.

The Depression of 1929 to 1935 provides historic evidence of how a serious downturn in the economy can mean a need for government assistance to workers. With millions of unemployed people standing in soup lines, peddling pencils on street corners, or queuing up for the few jobs available, a need for government intervention was obvious. Out of this need came a variety of programs to provide jobs, such as the Works Progress Administration (WPA) and Civilian Conservation Corps (CCC), or to provide income, such as the Social Security Act of 1935 with its Aid to Dependent Children (ADC, now AFDC), OASDHI, and other provisions, including an unemployment compensation system.

Increases in Unemployment

Today our economy still goes through downturns or recession periods, such as the 1974–1975 recession. The growth rate of the gross national product (GNP) has slowed down somewhat (to below 3 percent in 1979), and so while there are some new jobs there are not enough to fully employ the "baby boom" group now entering the job market or the older females entering the labor force.

For several years our unemployment rate has been from 6 to over 7 percent; in the 1950s and 1960s a rate about 4 percent was felt abnormal. Table 3-3 shows the increase in the unemployment rate by group between 1956 and 1977. The change for some groups has been great. The difference was lowest for white males at 1.1 percent, while the greatest increase in unemployment was among teenagers, who now account for one-fourth of

Table 3-3   Unemployment Rate by Group, 1956 and 1977, %

	1956	1977
Overall rate	4.1	7.0
White adult women	3.7	6.2
Black teenagers	18.2	39.5
Black adults	7.5	11.1
White adult males	2.6	3.7

Source: U.S. Department of Labor.

those looking for work, and other large increases occurred among blacks and, to a lesser extent, women. The unemployment rate would be even higher for these particular groups if "discouraged workers," those no longer looking for work, were included.

The reason today's high overall unemployment rate is tolerated is that the most powerful group in the labor force, the white adult male, has a fairly low unemployment rate compared to the other groups.

One of the reasons for the higher unemployment rate of teenagers and women is that they are new entrants to the labor market. This knowledge should not lessen our concern over the 1 million male teenaged (16 to 19) unemployed or the almost 4 million females unemployed in December 1976. Nor can one ignore a 39 percent unemployment rate in 1977 among black teenagers, a majority of them high school graduates. A University of Michigan survey in 1977 saw a bleak job outlook for young blacks, finding that two-thirds of the surveyed blacks between 20 and 29 were unemployed *at least once* during the period from 1967 to 1974 and that black earnings over the 8-year period grew less than half as fast as those of whites.

This black unemployment situation, especially among teenagers, is sometimes seen as a threat to the system, a potential cause of riots and crime. Conant (1961) called this teenage out-of-work, out-of-school situation one of "social dynamite," with large gatherings of youth, not inured to job routines and work habits, standing on street corners and getting into trouble with the law. Some will drift about and take drugs and some will get arrested for illegal activities and find it even harder, with an arrest record, to get a job. By the age of 25 these black teenagers are often "dead-ended." Ward (1977) warns that an entire generation of black youth have become useless, expendable, nonfunctional, nonproductive human refuse.

The government, in fear of disruptive activities, has taken on the business of creating summer jobs and year-round public works jobs. In 1979 the Comprehensive Employment and Training Act (CETA) public works program had between 0.5 and 0.75 million workers, and over a million more were in manpower training programs. President Carter credited the CETA program with playing an important role in lowering the country's overall unemployment rate.

Another reason why the high unemployment rate is tolerated is that the period of unemployment compensation benefits is sometimes extended; it was increased to a maximum of sixty-five weeks in 1975 in places with high unemployment, although it was lowered when the unemployment rate went down.

These factors have caused a tolerance that has let the Carter Administration center its economic manipulation efforts in 1978 on controlling inflation rather than providing full employment; in many northern European countries, with heavy political backing by labor parties, the economic policy has centered instead in providing full employment. With on the average over 7.5 million Americans officially unemployed in 1977, it seems that policy measures need to be considered.

Changes in the Industrial Complex and Their Effect on the Economy

Many changes have come about in our economy in the last few decades. In some areas of innovation, such as the electronics industry, other countries now produce cheaper and sometimes more innovative equipment and flood our markets, decreasing the number of American jobs in these areas. Some of our own firms, turned into multinational corporations, produce their products abroad in such places as Taiwan and Korea and other cheap-labor areas as well as, or instead of, the United States. This is again a loss of work for the American labor force.

Ironically, as this happens the United States is providing residence for a number of both legal and illegal immigrants who compete for the unskilled and semiskilled jobs we do have. Over 400,000 legal immigrants came in each year in 1975 to 1977, with an increasing number from Asia. In addition, special consideration was given to Vietnamese refugees. Added to these groups are the large number of illegal immigrants, especially from Mexico, who reside in the United States, estimated between 2 and 12 million a year.

Another long-range development in the economy is automation. The machine is now able to take on a number of manual jobs and also many white-collar tasks. The changing technology makes certain skills obsolete and demands a flexible work force willing to tool up in new specializations and to change job and geographic location and adapt to market needs.

In many industries production has gone up while the number of workers has gone down. For example, though steel capacity increased 20 percent between 1956 and 1960, the number of workers needed to operate the industry's plants, even at full capacity, dropped 17,000 (Michael, 1962). In the clerical area, the computer now does the addition, subtracts, writes bills, and types out letters. With the help of the computer, the U.S. Census Bureau was able to use fifty statisticians in 1960 to do the tabulations that required 4100 in 1950.

In the service area, food can be bought from a machine, parking fees paid to a machine, elevators operated by a button, and so on. In many cases the machine has displaced the unskilled and semiskilled worker.

What does this all mean? The young person with only a minimum of skills has little chance in today's job market. In some cases, one who is a high school dropout may never hold more than a temporary job.

Education, including some college education, becomes essential; apprenticeships, job training, and vocational education programs are important.

SOCIAL INEQUALITY: THE DISTRIBUTION OF INCOME AND WEALTH IN SOCIETY

In all societies there is some degree of unequal distribution of valued economic resources. Many researchers feel there is an excessive difference in this country between the economic resources held by the poorest one-fifth of American households and the richest one-fifth, that the range between the bottom and the top may be too great. Social policy experts want to narrow the range of incomes so that, say, the top fifth of all households earns only five times as much and not twenty times as much as the bottom fifth.

The main interest in this section is to document the degree of income disparity that exists in the United States; income equality as a value is discussed in Chapter 4. The picture we will give is one of the *relative* deprivation of the poor in the United States; it will show where they stand in resources compared to the rest of society. In Chapter 8 the actual income level of the poor over time—and of different groups of the poor—is given. These data, one should warn, are given mainly in terms of income, an inaccurate measure because there have been very few studies of how much wealth the rich have, on account of the difficulty in counting in all the assets, and these few studies were done in the 1960s. The problem is that the very rich have many assets in nonliquid form; with most of us, the major proportion of our assets is in calculable salaries and wages and possibly a house. For certain categories of the poor, it is mainly in government-provided benefits.

Income Distribution

Income measurements include only salaries and wages, interest, dividends, rent, social security, public assistance, unemployment insurance, and a few related items, rather than *total assets*. The household units in the nation are divided into fifths of the total units. The U.S. Census Bureau (1977) reports that the highest fifth had 44.5 percent of all the aggregate income in 1975. Actually, the top 5 percent of the units had 17 percent of the income. If one took the top 40 percent of all household units, it had almost double the aggregate income it would have had if all aggregate income was equally divided; that is, this 40 percent had 69.4 percent of the aggregate income. On the other end, the 20 percent of the households with the lowest proportion of the aggregate income had 3.9 percent of all such income. Even the second-lowest fifth had only 9.9 percent. Together this 40 percent of all household units had 13.8 percent of all aggregate income.

Suggestions have been made that slightly higher taxes on the rich, or the elimination of tax loopholes for the rich, although only slightly affecting their relative income position in relation to the lower quintiles of households, would allow somewhat more money for income transfers to the poor.

Wealth

Wealth is defined as the total economic assets—including equity in homes, stocks, trusts, and other assets—possessed by people. The major study of wealth in the United States was done by the Federal Reserve Board in 1962; there has been nothing as extensive since. It was found that there was an even greater disparity in wealth than in aggregate income; the 20 percent of all units that had the most wealth had 76 percent of all wealth in the United States in 1962, mostly in investments, while the lowest, or poorest, 20 percent of all consumer units had only 0.2 percent of the wealth. Even the lowest 40 percent of all consumer units had only 2.3 percent of the total wealth.

If one looks at such an asset as stocks, the richest 1 percent of persons in the nation in 1969 had 51 percent of the corporate stocks (Smith, 1974). Thus the top 1 percent really have a very high proportion of the total assets. Even the middle class is very underrepresented.

Another way of seeing the disparities is to look at family income levels. In 1975 the upper income limit of the lowest-income 20 percent was $4514; for the middle 20 percent it was $13,500. Again, this shows a considerable degree of social inequality. This inequality would be even greater if we took into account family size, since those in lower income brackets generally have larger families. In fairness to the richest 20 percent, we must also say that many of them are older and many are at the peak of their lifetime earnings.

This situation, wherein the top fifth holds the major share of total assets and income and the poor have a very small share of either, has changed little from early postwar years to now; it is hard to say that the poor are doing better today. The poorest fifth had 3.5 percent of the income in 1947 and 3.9 percent in 1975. Each year the gap between the average AFDC-household income and American median family income widens.

Tax Loopholes

The wealthy, much more than the middle and working classes, are able to keep their money away from the tax collector and thus perpetuate it year after year and pass it on to their children. Taxing is regressive, though meant to be progressive. "Progressive" describes a system in which people with more income and assets pay a larger portion of their wealth in taxes;

thus, in 1974 the tax rate was around 15 percent for a $4000 *taxable* income (income after deductions), compared to a rate over 40 percent for a $76,000 taxable income. In actuality, many rich pay much less *proportionately* than middle-class taxpayers. Some even pay no tax, because they have tax shelters.

Stern (1972) estimated that the structural tax rate for persons in the $200,000 to $500,000 category was 58 percent but that the taxes they *actually* paid were at the rate of 29.6 percent; for the average citizen the two rates were much closer. This shows that in actuality income taxes are *regressive,* with the poorer and middle-income households paying a higher *proportion* of their income in taxes than the well-off.

The reason the rich can end up paying less or, in some cases, no taxes is that they are able to claim various deductions before arriving at their taxable income that, in effect, are allowable only to the wealthy. Working-class people and even many of the middle class do not have the types of investments and expenses that would make it possible for them to take these allowable tax deductions or loopholes. For example, the expenses of owning a piece of business property and a high depreciation rate in the first years of ownership can be subtracted from rents or other profits on the property so that, even though the property's value is increasing, in one's tax calculations a loss can be written off against other income. Certain types of investments are called "tax shelters," whereby income can escape from taxation. Turner and Starnes (1976) mention cattle ranching, mining, farming, and other investments; only the rich are able to take advantage of these types of tax shelters and protect their income by a large paper loss or deduction on their tax form.

We mention in passing that another regressive tax is the state or local general sales tax. The sales tax rate on goods bought in the store is the same for everyone, so that the tax takes a larger proportion of the incomes of the working class and the poor, especially because a much larger proportion of the income of low-income people is used for purchases—they don't have much left over to invest.

The Effect of Tax Loopholes on the Poor   How do these tax loopholes affect income distribution? First, the loopholes allow the rich to stay rich and can be said to be partly responsible for the great disparity between the assets of the top 1 percentile and top fifth, on the one hand, and those of the rest of the population on the other. The federal revenue loss from these tax loopholes also means the government has less money to use for social welfare programs and other programs that might benefit low-income groups. Surrey (1973) has calculated that without the loopholes, on the average, the government would have collected $1729 more from each person in the $25,000 to $50,000 group in 1972, and $216,751 more from each individual in the income group $500,000 to $1 million. It would collect only slightly more from those in the $10,000 to $15,000 income group.

Turner and Starnes (1976) suggest that since the middle class's benefits from the loopholes are so low, it should support elimination of:

> . . . at least some wealth fare [government subsidies to the rich] abuses. The money collected in this way could be used to increase welfare benefits, to provide higher wages in existing jobs and to create public service jobs. These changes would reduce some of the privilege of the wealthy and much of the poverty of the poor. The middle groups would probably be relatively unaffected by these changes as the income and wealth levels began to regress toward the middle income and wealth fifths. [P. 156]
>
> These changes in the system of distribution, one could suggest, would lessen tension and conflict between the poor and the affluent rest of the society; would mean less crime; and would decrease the general guilt over having, in our prosperous country, the embarrassing poverty holdouts—the slums, the rural shacks, the undernourished children, the penniless elderly, the none-too-good infant mortality rate.

One estimate for 1972 was that in total the federal government would have recovered in the realm of $65 to $70 billion if it had closed the tax loopholes. This $65 to $70 billion contrasts with the same year's approximately $12 billion in transfer payments to the poor from the direct expenditure budget.

Of course, some would say redistributing income from the rich is not a good idea because those who accumulate private property are essential to economic progress, since only vast accumulations can provide sufficient capital for ventures that create as well as exploit resources. Part of this thinking is that the investments will keep vital industries going and stimulate the economy and jobs will then be provided and benefits will trickle down to the poorer members. To heavily tax the rich is to kill the incentive to work, invest, and accumulate capital, the incentive to take the business risks necessary in a free-enterprise, capitalist society. Others would argue that the wealth the top one-fifth has accumulated is excessive and that if this group had 66 percent instead of 76 percent of the wealth it would not be greatly deprived of incentive or rewards, while this slight redistribution might greatly improve the welfare of the whole society. Today benefits given to the poor must be paid out of the pockets of the middle class and the upper working class, who pay out disproportionately for benefits they themselves could use but are denied because the service is available only to those below the poverty line; medical assistance through Medicaid is an example. It is these groups that are revolting against greater welfare benefits to the poor.

This cry against greater taxation for welfare benefits has come not only in the United States, through California's Proposition 13 and the like, but in such welfare-state countries as Denmark and Sweden, where a tremendous variety of welfare services and cash assistance are provided the citizens. There, taxation is high for both the rich and the middle class.

A 1977 study by the Organization for Economic Cooperation and Development (OECD) shows that taxes and social security contributions as a proportion of total personal income are slightly over 30 percent for Holland and Sweden. In these two countries much of the national budget goes for social benefits.

In Sweden and Holland about 6 percent of GNP in 1971 was for social security insurance–type programs (not welfare); in West Germany, about 7.6 percent; but in the United States, only 3.4 percent. For public health care programs it was over 6 percent of GNP for Sweden, over 4 percent in Holland, and only around 2 percent in the United States. In these European countries taxes go to pay for many services for all citizens, not just the poor, that in the United States the private citizen would have to pay for out of pocket.

Taking major welfare services, including social security, medical assistance, and public assistance, Wilensky (1975), after a massive study involving most industrial countries, finds that the payout in these programs may be progressive, or in favor of the poor, even though financing of them is somewhat *regressive,* with the rich, as we have shown, not paying their proportionate share of financing through taxes.

Even though the poor may get more out of these programs as a *proportion* of their income, Branch (1975) shows that the middle class is likely to benefit more in actual dollars. By including such universal-type programs as social security, veteran's disability, unemployment benefits, worker's compensation, and railroad retirement benefits, as well as the means-tested welfare programs of AFDC and SSI, Branch calculated in the early 1970s that people earning below $5000 got $269 per person and those with incomes of $25,000 to $40,000 got $1146.

Public Subsidies to the Middle Class

One should realize that certain government subsidies, both indirect and direct, benefit mainly the middle and upper classes, so that while Wilensky is right that certain subsidies will disproportionately benefit the poor, *others he does not mention* are mainly directed at middle-income people. Various higher-education subsidies to those attending public colleges and even private colleges go for the most part to the children of the middle class, for they are the ones who usually attend college. Subsidization of medical students is a prime example.

The middle class receives a number of housing subsidies, such as VA-

and FHA-insured loans and rehabilitation loans; and, as homeowners, indirect subsidies, by being able to write off their mortgage interest and the property tax on their homes as deductions on their federal income tax, thus causing the federal government to lose more than an estimated $70 billion a year in revenue (Aaron, 1972).

In concluding this section, we reiterate that income distribution is very unequal in the United States and, thus, that in developing any income maintenance programs and services the redistribution effect is an important factor to take into account. One should ask, Does this program bring the poor nearer to the middle class in regard to income or income equivalents? Does it decrease relative deprivation?

POPULATION CHANGES IN THE LAST FEW DECADES

Population or demographic shifts have a variety of effects on the structure of society and its needs. The very dramatic changes in the birthrate in the last fifty years in the United States are causing a number of problems and reshaping American society. Social policies in the 1980s must take into account the decreasing youth population, and thus the fact there is a smaller proportion of the population to educate or likely to be involved in crimes of youth. At the same time, the startling growth of the elderly population, especially those over 75, means that social policies must be shaped to meet their needs. For example, with the large number of retirees and the smaller proportion of the population in the work force, the whole social security insurance system (OASDHI) may need to be revamped, since the number of recipients will be larger in relation to the number of contributors. Changes in where the population resides—inner cities, suburban areas, or rural communities—again influence general policy guidelines; if inner cities house only the poor, certain policies to attract the middle class back may be in order.

From the Depression period of the 1930s through World War II, America had a low birthrate. Then a very different stage began, a postwar *baby boom,* which lasted from 1946 to about 1961. At first this high birthrate was caused when men came back from the war and formed families; but then the high rate continued, partly because of American families' affluence and partly because of the greater desire of people to have children. These changes meant that in comparison to the birth of only 40 million children between 1931 and 1946, in 1946 to 1961, 60 million were born. Then, in the early 1960s, a "baby bust" stage was reached; *even with more women in the childbearing years* of 14 to 44, the birthrate dropped. This downward trend in births has continued until very recently, when in 1977 to 1978 a slight rise in births occurred.

Aside from birthrates, another way to compare the baby boom period with the later baby bust period is to show the change in the rate at which women on the average were bearing children. At the peak of the baby boom in 1959, the rate was 3.8 children in a woman's lifetime; in 1976 to 1977, the rate was around 1.8 births per woman, below the replacement rate. (See Figure 3-2.)

This drop in the birthrate, in turn, has changed the median age of our population, for, if there are fewer children born, the young make up a smaller proportion of the population. In 1978 one could say the American population was aging, because the median age was over 29. Also, the life expectancy is going up, so that more and more people, especially women,

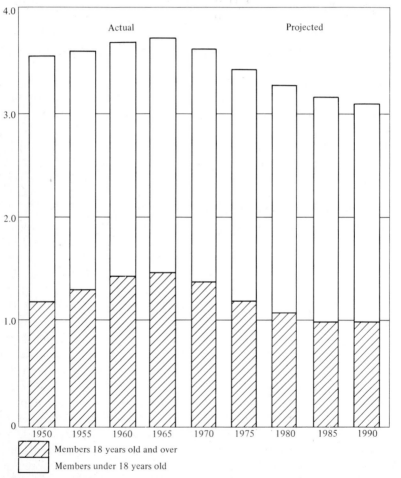

Figure 3-2 Average size of families, by age of members: 1950–1990, United States. *(Source:* U.S. Bureau of the Census, *Social Indicators, 1976.)*

are living into their eighties; the elderly population 65 and over is now over 10 percent of our total population, around 24 million in 1978.

Today in America the people going through the different life stages can be identified with the three different birth trends: the low-birthrate group of the 1930s and 1940s (and those born earlier), with their youngest member (born in 1945) 33 years old in 1978; then the baby boom group, aged 18 to 32 in 1978; and the baby bust group, 17 and younger in 1978. Because the middle group is so much bigger than the other two the population is like a snake with a bulge in its middle area but gradually moving toward one end.

The large baby boom group faces different problems at each stage of life and causes strains on the social and economic structure in various ways. First there were not enough schools for this group, then they overfilled the colleges. Now they are becoming a bulging labor-market force, with too many workers for too few jobs. The high rate of unemployment of teenagers and now of the 20- to 24-year-olds is related to the size of this group entering the work force.

One could add, it could be worse if so many weren't enrolled in college. College enrollment rose in 1976, with 25 percent of the college-age group going to college, compared to 11 percent in 1952. Yet because of their larger numbers, fewer of these college graduates find suitable jobs. Many will be forced into service-level and blue-collar jobs, which have not normally required a college degree. In 1976 some 656,000 graduates were in blue-collar jobs, compared with only 179,000 in 1970. Competition for jobs at any level has become fierce. The baby boom group will have to downgrade its ambitions, which may be hard for a group raised in an era of expansion and affluence. It can lead to a turn to individualistic solutions and a deemphasis on jobs and an increased focus on the arts and such. For example, many young people have joined a movement back to basics, sometimes practicing organic farming and simple crafts, which are less competitive and less environmentally destructive than the mainstream economy.

Implications of a Low Birthrate

When the large baby boom group enters the retirement stage, say in the early 2000s, there will be a new problem, a strain on the pension and social security system. At that time the dependency ratio will also be different. The people born later than this group, in the baby bust years, which some see continuing indefinitely, make up a much smaller group. This group will find itself supporting pensions for the much larger baby boom group. By the 2030s the dependency ratio (the ratio of wage earners to dependents) is expected to fall from its current level of 3.2 to 1 to less than 2 to 1. The smaller younger group is likely to complain it cannot support this older group and to demand changes in the social security contribution system, even the amount of the payment and the year at which one can retire. Even today the social security system is suffering from an increase in beneficiaries and an escalation in payments per beneficiary.

In this post–baby boom period we have seen many elementary and middle-level schools close. Now we see college enrollments going down. We will likely also see the crime rate go down as youth, those under 25 (who commit over 75 percent of the burglaries, robberies, and auto thefts in the United States) decrease in number.

With the extremely low birthrate from 1961 on, by the mid-1980s, when the first part of the baby bust group comes into the job market, there might be a scarcity of labor for beginning-level jobs, jobs hiring young people. If this group itself should have fewer children, then it will indeed be well off.

Studies show many enjoy the affluence possible without children. Sherlock and Moeller (1977) found a third of a sample of newlyweds seeing themselves not having children and another large group postponing having children, giving priority instead to acquiring houses and a number of material goods and settling into careers. Robert Clark (1978) says current social and economic trends suggest that fertility will tend to stay somewhat below the replacement level. These trends include falling marriage and rising divorce rates; deferred childbearing; the upswing in numbers of single parents, two–wage earner families, and individual households; and higher educational levels. Add to this the increased work experience among young women, the high cost of rearing and educating children, and the ever-increasing use of effective birth control techniques.

Birthrates actually rose slightly in 1977. The reason given is that women born in the baby boom era who held off having babies are now entering their thirties and have to make "now or never" decisions on whether to have children.

However, for reasons given above, the birthrate is unlikely to rise much. The fact that women are marrying later means they are less likely to have many children. In 1960 there were only 1.6 million never-married women aged 20 to 24, and in 1977 there were 4.4 million. And a 1977 Population Reference Bureau study found nearly 2 million people living as couples without being married.

The very high use of contraceptives by married couples indicates how much these couples control their childbearing. A 1975 national survey showed that an estimated 75 percent of all married couples of childbearing age were using the pill, the IUD (intrauterine device), or sterilization. Catholics and minorities, especially black women, have considerably increased their use of contraceptives in the last few years.

Abortion is another way of controlling births, and after the 1973 Supreme Court decision making early abortions legal, the number increased dramatically. Medicaid coverage of abortion costs for the poor up to 1977 also gave impetus for teenagers, AFDC mothers, and other poor women to seek this solution. New 1978 rulings limiting federal Medicaid coverage to abortions in only a few special categories may cut the abortion rate. Yet, in 1976 in California there were 142,593 *known* abortions, with about half paid for by Medicaid. One-third of the abortions were received by women aged 15 to 19. One-fifth of the women were terminating their fourth or later pregnancy, and the largest group their second or third. In New York City, the Health Department found that, of women who became pregnant during 1975, forty-five percent sought abortions.

The implications of a low birthrate are numerous. Effects include the closing of schools and now possibly of colleges. City life is likely to become more acceptable for the group that remains childless or has only one child. Crime is likely to go down and AFDC cases decrease. Maternity wards of hospitals will continue to close. And eventually a labor shortage may occur.

Some policymakers say measures should be taken to increase the birth rate, for example, by increasing children's allowances. East Germany, faced with a low birthrate and a large elderly population, is giving home mortgage assistance, free bassinets, and generous maternity leaves to change the trend.

In the United States, some population experts say fewer children means better-educated and healthier ones.

Immigration

One factor influencing a country's birthrate is the number of young immigrants coming in and the rate at which they have children. Since the 1965 immigration law was passed, an increasingly large group of Chinese, Filipinos, and other Asians have been arriving. They are moving to the top ranking among incoming immigrants. To them are added the many Mexican-Americans, many illegal as well as legal and most having large families. Estimates of the number of resident illegal immigrants range from 2 million upward. Over 445,000 legal immigrants came in from Mexico from 1971 to 1975, and 319,000 came in from the Philippines. A total of around 400,000 legal immigrants (plus special groups) came in during each year in this period.

Demographic Geography

Geographic demographic imbalance also affects social change and calls for special policy considerations. In the postwar period the population has been increasingly unevenly dispersed, with certain industrial states gaining greatly in population and rural areas losing population. Heavy concentrations of population exist between Boston and Washington; in the Chicago

area; in the Los Angeles area; and in a few other areas. Almost 1 out of 3
Americans live in the thirteen large metropolitan areas in the United
States. In 1975 the Census Bureau reported that the New York City region,
including nine metropolitan areas in New York, New Jersey, and Connecticut, had 17.2 million inhabitants and Los Angeles and suburbs, 10 million,
and Chicago and suburbs, 7.6 million. This meant there were many areas,
such as Montana, Wyoming, Arkansas, and Mississippi, with very low
population density. In the mid-1970s a population commission recommended that government inducements be given to move people and
industry to medium-sized towns and low-density states. Actually, the
government has given subsidies to industry to do just that. One purpose
was to decrease traffic, overbuilding, and pollution in these thirteen
metropolitan areas; many regional scientists considered city size to have
reached the point of inefficiency.

Around 1970 to 1975 a small trend of population movement away
from these metropolitan areas began to develop. While this is only a slight
change in a situation in which about three-fourths of the American
population still live in urban areas, it may be a continuing one.

The Sunbelt states continued to lead in *growth* in population, with
Arizona and Florida growing by over 29 percent between 1970 and 1977.
Old industrial areas were up only very small amounts.

Urbanization   By the 1970s urban areas had been divided into central
cities and suburbs, with population loss a trait of central cities. Two-thirds
of the American population growth found in the 1970 census was in the
suburbs. In 1975, the suburbs had 39 percent of the population and the
cities had only 29 percent. (See Table 3-4.)

This "white flight" to the suburbs has been a post–World War II
phenomenon. Some say it has divided America into two Americas, the
affluent white suburb, which now includes shopping centers and industrial
parks that fulfill many of the functions of the central city, and the other
America, the deteriorating central city, with its poor, its minorities, its
deviants, and its old.

Statistics from the Department of Labor show retail sales have been
much greater outside than inside central cities; that an increasing proportion of total employment is in these suburban areas; and that a large
proportion of new commercial and industrial buildings are being built in
suburban areas. Department stores in central cities have closed, central
business districts have lost their vitality, and after dark many downtown
areas have become deserted. These central cities are left with a decreasing
tax base, both for residential taxes from middle-class families and for
industrial and commercial property taxes. These cities often have an
obsolete physical structure and are in need of urban renewal. Above all,

Table 3-4 Metropolitan and Nonmetropolitan Residence of the Population, by Race: 1960 and 1975

Area and race	1960[1] Number, thousands	1960[1] Percent	1975[2] Number, thousands	1975[2] Percent
All classes				
Total	179,323	100.0	209,747	100.0
In metropolitan areas[3]	119,581	66.7	142,721	68.0
Central city[4]	59,947	33.4	61,158	29.2
Outside central city	59,634	33.3	81,564	38.9
Nonmetropolitan areas	59,742	33.3	67,026	32.0
White				
Total	158,832	100.0	182,581	100.0
In metropolitan areas[3]	105,817	66.6	121,914	66.8
Central city[4]	49,420	31.1	45,765	25.1
Outside central city	56,397	35.5	76,149	41.7
Nonmetropolitan areas	53,015	33.4	60,667	33.2
Black and other races				
Total	20,491	100.0	27,167	100.0
In metropolitan areas[3]	13,764	67.2	20,807	76.6
Central city[4]	10,527	51.4	15,392	56.7
Outside central city	3,237	15.8	5,415	19.9
Nonmetropolitan areas	6,728	32.8	6,359	23.4
Black and other races as a percent of total				
Total	11.4	(X)	13.0	(X)
In metropolitan areas[3]	11.5	(X)	14.6	(X)
Central city[4]	17.6	(X)	25.2	(X)
Outside central city	5.4	(X)	6.6	(X)
Nonmetropolitan areas	11.3	(X)	9.5	(X)

X Not applicable.
[1] Based on complete count.
[2] April-centered annual averages from the Current Population Survey.
[3] Population of the 243 SMSAs as defined in 1970 publications.
[4] 1975 data for the central cities refer to their January 1, 1970, boundaries and exclude areas annexed since 1970; 1970 data relate to 1970 corporate boundaries; 1960 data relate to 1960 corporate boundaries.
Source: U.S. Department of Commerce, Bureau of the Census, *1960 Census of Population*, Vol. I; *1970 Census of Population and Housing*, PHC(2)-1, *United States Summary.*

they need funds to pay for services to their increasingly poor minority and elderly population. In a number of these central cities, 1 out of 7 persons are on welfare. In some, such as Washington, Gary, Detroit, and Atlanta, blacks make up over half the population. Bankruptcy is near in several of these older core cities, with New York City being the prime example. In 1975 alone New York City felt it necessary to decrease the work force by 39,000, although this hardly solved its problems. Many cities have had to decrease services, with those affecting the poor often going first; New York City closed twenty-eight day care centers in 1975 alone. The cities' other alternative, of trying to get higher taxes out of the industries and commercial activities and even residents left behind, only hastens their exodus. Taxes on parking lots and the city sales tax all cause shoppers to turn to suburban shopping centers. Federal subsidy policies in the postwar period have had considerable impact on the growth of suburbs. Federal and state transportation policy up until the mid-1970s has been to build new highways into suburbia, making it easier for the commuter. Even mass transit systems connect the suburbs to the cities.

Federal housing policy had also mainly been directed at insuring single-family dwellings' mortgages, through FHA- and VA-insured loans in the 1950s and 1960s. This encouraged developers to build tract home developments across the countryside, and a new type of suburbia was launched, not for the rich, but for the lower middle class and even the skilled working class.

The suburbs themselves have changed as they have grown and aged in the last thirty years. While still having few minorities, they have a somewhat less homogeneous population. They are no longer just families with children; they now include singles, sometimes themselves products of suburbia, and childless couples. The single-family dwelling still dominates, but a number of apartment complexes now exist in suburbia. There is still little low-cost housing for the poor in suburbia, but some older suburbs, with notable commercial centers, have become mini–central cities, with some old, cheap units.

Suburban schools differ from city ones in that they do not face the problems of busing or desegregation, a phenomenon in the central cities that has pushed many families toward suburbia. However, integration in the suburbs, through residential location, usually does not exist, since most blacks are in segregated enclaves.

THE CHANGING STATUS OF AMERICAN MINORITIES

A long-time problem in American society has been discrimination against ethnic and racial minorities. The Kerner Commission report cited "white racism" as a main cause of the urban riots of 1965 to 1967 and referred to America as two "separate societies," white and black; and Myrdal (1944) wrote of an "American Dilemma." Many other minorities are also, to varying degrees, segregated from the mainstream of American society. Those considered today to be most likely to suffer from discriminatory practices are blacks, Asians such as Chinese-Americans, Hispanic groups, and American Indians.

The dominant American response to these racial and ethnic minorities in the last half century has been to perpetuate economic, political, and social inequality for these groups. Such a situation has been created and maintained because of official and unofficial acts at all levels of government and society. Because of past and present discrimination and its varied long-term consequences, the socioeconomic status of these groups falls far below that of most other groups in society. Yet there have been changes in the situation of these groups in some areas of living over the last twenty years.

The situation of our largest racial minority, the black population, especially those who live in the South, has changed considerably in regard to some dimensions of life since the 1950s, even though, as statistics on employment and income show in Chapter 13, it is still bleak for many.

Segregation statutes still existed in the South in the 1950s and until the mid-1960s. Such public facilities as libraries, parks, and schools were segregated. Such public accommodations as restaurants and hotels were often off limits to black citizens or were divided into whites-only and Negro sections; even restrooms were.

In a 1965 Mississippi Civil Rights Commission document a young black serviceman reported how his accidental entry into a white café brought quick reaction to his violation of these segregation customs. He and a fellow black serviceman were chased by white men and then badly beaten up.

An Example of the Struggle for Basic Civil Rights in the South

Blacks were violently stopped from voting in the South up to 1964; few did in most areas. One early member of the Mississippi voter rights struggle, Hartman Turnbow, recalled how "when I got big enough to learn about conditions the first thing I learned was white people beatin' Negroes and killin' 'em and all that kind of stuff. And my grandmomma and my grandpoppa what raised me, they would tell me all that stuff about the advantages the white people had and the Negroes didn't have no chance and no rights."

Turnbow tells how in 1963 in Mississippi the voter rights struggle encountered extreme resistance. He reports:

We had been reading 'bout the civil rights movement 'for it ever got here. . . . Finally a little fellow came in here once and asked could he have a meetin' with us. So we got together . . . [then] he came back [for the second meeting] and there was so many folk there till the church wouldn't hold 'em they was all outside. So he went through the same talk. . . . So we told him we'll accept citizenship school . . . we have never voted, and that kind of stuff . . . we'd go down every night, having some lessons . . . we went that away 'bout two weeks. . . .

Turnbow then reports:

[Finally] it was about 70 of us goin' to the court house the next day and redish to vote. Was right funny. Out of 70 only 20 showed up. We don't care what it cost. We left our cars on the outer edge of town so they can't say we parked wrong or done nothin' . . .

So we went on there walking two by two and we met Mr. Sheriff. . . . He said, "Where in the hell is you all going?" We said we come to redish to vote. We had John Ball, he was a leadin' us. Mr. Sheriff grabbed his pistol and his blackjack . . . he looked at us, all huddled there, 20 of us under that tree. He slapped one hand on his pistol, the other on his blackjack. He said, "All right, now, who'll be first?"

Turnbow goes on:

Them guys commence lookin' at one another right fast. They was fixin to run. . . . I told him, yeah, I'll be first. . . . I went in there. . . .

Turnbow goes on:

. . . The lady said [the voter registrar] is not here. . . . I stay there till 12 [then lunch]. . . . At one o'clock I came back. . . . He was in there. . . . I said I come to redish to vote. . . . He just handed me the book. I stood there and filled out them questions. . . . So all of us redished to vote and left. Didn't none of us get beat up, but hit might of been more trouble if there wasn't an FBI man there at the crowd watchin'.

Four or five nights later Turnbow and his wife and their youngest daughter returned home from a citizenship meeting at the church. Their dog was missing. They went to bed.

Round 'bout one o'clock they throwed two firebombs right through that window in here . . . and then they throwed a firebomb in the back living room. An' then commenced to shootin'. There are bullet holes right there. My wife and daughter, they run out, but I didn't run out till I got my rifle. I got my rifle and then I run out. . . . a guy started shootin' at me, and I started shootin' at him. So they run on off. . . . then we went down to some boys and told 'em to call the Justice Department in Washington, D.C.

That night the Holmes County sheriff came to Turnbow's house and arrested him. He stayed in jail two nights. Justice Department attorney John Doar intervened and the charges against Turnbow were dropped as groundless.

Source: Haynes Johnson in the *Sunday Examiner & Chronicle,* San Francisco, October 24, 1976. Permission granted from the New York Times Company.

Separation of blacks and whites in all aspects of life in the South was enforced by various types of violence. Blacks were to sit at the back of the bus and to keep in their subordinate position in a variety of black-white situations. Any violation was dealt with severely by the white power structure. Violence was also used up to the mid-1960s against blacks who tried to vote in the Deep South. Attempts of black citizens to register to vote were often followed by shootings or beatings by white men, often members of the Ku Klux Klan, as in Hartman Turnbow's experience.

De jure segregation enforced by law existed in the South, but in the North de facto (unofficial) segregation produced the same conditions, although without laws behind them. Segregated schools existed in most Northern cities. Blacks were very limited in where they could rent or buy housing in the North as well as in the South. Claude Brown (1965) describes the Negroes who migrated north in the 1940s and 1950s to reside in the "Promised Land" only to find in such ghettos as Harlem a troubled and demoralized, poor, segregated slum.

In the South up to the late 1960s most occupations were segregated. Some occupations were considered whites-only jobs while others were considered jobs for blacks.

To varying degrees other minorities suffered similar treatment. For example, Japanese-Americans could not buy land under the 1913 California Alien Land Act; Chinese suffered a similar fate and were mainly limited to the Chinatowns of large cities. Many jobs were not open to them. Japanese-Americans suffered their worst discrimination in 1942, when 110,000 of them, including 70,000 American citizens, were rounded up and placed in "relocation centers."

Mexican-Americans in many Southwestern cities in early days were limited in the use of public facilities, as have also been the American Indians. The Indian's history is one of losing land and fishing and hunting rights to later settlers and being pushed onto reservations governed by an outside force, the U.S. Bureau of Indian Affairs. Even in 1970 over half of the 790,000 American Indians lived on reservations under trusteeship of the Bureau of Indian Affairs. While they have in the last decade had a greater part in running reservation affairs, as in the case of the Navajo Council, they are still generally under the regulations of the Bureau. The

American Indian Movement, founded in 1973, has pushed for the return of Indian lands, as in Maine, or reimbursement for the loss of them. Confrontations between Indians and law enforcement agencies still go on, as at Wounded Knee.

American Indians are considered the poorest of the minority groups. Their median income is less than half that of whites. On the reservation many are unemployed and living in unsanitary housing. For example, in the Navajo Nation territory 80 percent of the houses have no running water or plumbing and 60 percent no electricity. Over half the adults in this population of 137,000 are either unemployed or working part-time. Only 1 out of 5 adults has a high school diploma. Per capita income is $1000, as of 1975.

Hispanic groups also are the victims of discrimination and racism. Here there is the additional situation of newcomers to the United States versus long-time residents. Many Mexican-Americans have had roots in the Southwest for decades, even since before it became part of the United States in 1848, while others are very recent arrivals. The same situation is true for Puerto Ricans, who since 1917 have been declared American citizens; over 1.8 million live on the American mainland, mainly in and around New York City, but a number go back and forth to Puerto Rico. These ties to other countries and such movement back and forth may be a reason protest has been slower from Hispanic groups. However, by the late 1960s the Mexican-Americans, or Chicanos, had begun to organize for group solidarity and political action.

Some early protests by blacks for change occurred in World War II (although, of course, one can also mention very early protests, such as slave revolts). The demand for nondiscriminatory recruitment of workers and an end to segregation of jobs resulted in a 1941 Presidential Executive order recommending nondiscrimination in jobs in war plants under government contract.

A major change in 1954 came from the Supreme Court, which reversed its long-standing decision made in *Plessy v. Ferguson* in 1896 that separate but equal schools were acceptable. In *Brown v. Board of Education* (1954) the Supreme Court said separate but equal was no longer acceptable, since the separation of the races suggested that the Negro group was inferior and this assumption affected the motivation of a child to learn.

The *Brown* decision gave the Southern Negro hope that black-white relations would improve. In 1954, seventeen states required segregation of races in public schools and four additional states authorized segregation at the option of local school boards. But efforts to desegregate schools were very slow, so that even ten years later, Dye (1972) reports, only about 2 percent of the Negro schoolchildren in the eleven Southern states were attending integrated schools.

Other developments to change race relations, sparked by discouragement over progress since the 1954 *Brown* decision, occurred under the name "civil rights movement" from 1955 on. In 1955 in Montgomery, Alabama, Rosa Parks refused to sit in the back of the bus, and a nonviolent bus boycott was born, led by Martin Luther King, Jr. In Greensboro, North Carolina, black students were refused service at a lunch counter, and this again sparked a protest campaign.

These developments all ignited the spirits of those unhappy about segregation and resulted in demonstrations, picket lines, sit-ins, wade-ins, and the like all over the South to change the Jim Crow laws on use of public facilities. Northern religious leaders, liberals, and students went south in the early 1960s to join the movement. Such marches as the Selma March drew 100,000 people. In the North, groups formed, such as the Congress of Racial Equality (CORE) and Student Nonviolent Coordinating Committee (SNCC), to protest the lack of hiring of minority workers, to picket, to sit in, and to hold protest marches.

Out of the civil rights movement came a number of policy changes, described in Chapter 13. Many were written into the Civil Rights Act of 1964, which forbade discrimination in many areas of life, especially public accommodations, voter registration, and jobs. This monumental act was a manifesto that was to reduce discrimination against many minorities. A feeling of change was in the air. Public facilities were opened; the black was no longer treated as a nonperson.

However, ghettos remained, and black unemployment stayed high. In Northern cities in the hot summers of 1965 and 1966, black persons, especially teenagers, rioted. In Watts, Los Angeles, alone thirty-four persons died and 600 buildings were damaged. One explanation of these outbreaks was frustrated hopes due to unfulfilled expectations aroused by the great judicial and legislative victories of the civil rights movement.

When Martin Luther King, Jr., was assassinated in April 1968 the civil rights movement had already slowed to a murmur, although the Civil Rights Bill of 1968, which included a fair housing provision, was enacted.

The problem was that such statutes did not make for instant equality of the groups. As Dye (1972) says, "The problem of racial inequality between Blacks and whites in income, health, housing, employment, education and so on, is more than a problem of *direct legal discrimination* even though the first important step toward equality was the elimination of Jim Crow" (p. 44). Blacks no longer had to eat at separate lunch counters, but for many blacks, their low income and lack of work, as well as their ghetto location, limited their ability to join the mainstream of American life.

In fact, in some ways a very large proportion of the black population was less likely to be in the mainstream in 1970 than earlier; the cities where they lived were increasingly inhabited by minority groups; whites in very large numbers had moved to the suburbs, which had few blacks. Thus America increasingly became two separate nations, making school integration difficult and access to new job opportunities, often in the suburbs, equally difficult for central-city minorities.

Black-white power arrangements in the central city became strained. Some black activists and scholars complained that a neocolonial situation existed, where a small white power group controlled a large black ghetto population. Turner (1969) compared the inner-city situation to Fanon's (1966) colonialism: "It is instructive to ask, for example, if Black people comprise 47 percent of the population of Newark—then why don't they occupy anywhere near 47 percent of the land?" The police forces of the urban black reserves (ghettos) were virtually all white and completely controlled by and responsible to the interests of the white community and he felt this was another indication of neocolonialism. Even where there was a black mayor, the police were likely to go their own way, as Jones (1977) points out, and clashes sparked riots.

On a more optimistic note, by 1976 blacks, even in Newark, did have more political power. By 1976, there were over 4000 black elected officials, including mayors, of such cities as Los Angeles, Atlanta, and Detroit.

Another optimistic sign was that under affirmative action measures professional and managerial jobs were opening up to blacks in the late 1960s and early 1970s, especially the young, better-educated black males, as we shall see in Chapter 13.

Yet by the mid-1970s the recession canceled out some gains, causing high unemployment. Those without skills or work experience, especially black teenagers, found it even more difficult to enter the labor market.

What did increase was the number of female-headed households, to around 4 out of each 10 black families, with the economic handicaps that situation has always brought.

The educational attainments of the black population had improved by 1970. Years of school attendance had considerably increased, and an increasingly large number in the youth group were going on to college. This was partly due to affirmative action and desegregation policies and financial assistance. Desegregation of schools, however, was slow.

The 1964 Civil Rights Act and the United States Office of Education threatened a cutoff of funds to schools that did not desegregate. In 1969 in the *Mississippi* case the Supreme Court demanded that states move ahead to desegregate with "all deliberate speed."

Although many tense situations existed in connection with desegregation in various Southern cities, often leading to temporary conflict, by 1972 many black children in the South were attending schools with whites. In the North whites were fleeing to the suburbs, leaving the central-city school population largely minority children. In 1979 Supreme Court orders still had to be used to get such cities as Dayton and Columbus, Ohio, to carry out desegregation plans. The Court in 1979 let stand a ruling that the school board in Austin, Texas, intentionally discriminated against Mexican-Americans.

The point here is that changes in the educational system have been very slow and twenty-five years after the 1954 *Brown* decision most black children go to segregated or only tokenly integrated schools. Residential segregation has made it difficult to integrate, and desegregation through busing across city lines, between suburbs and cities, has hardly existed.

In sum, by the late 1970s many changes had come through laws and court actions to provide minorities with equal treatment. In public accommodations, the barriers had come down. In jobs, minorities were represented in many occupational fields that had formerly been closed to them (although they were represented primarily at the entry level). An increasing number were also attending colleges and universities. However, many were still in poverty, lived in ghettos, and did not yet enjoy the American dream. Recessions and the growth of the whites-only suburbs in fact had the effect of worsening their position over the decade.

At the same time, white America had cooled its interest in doing more for these groups, many feeling that blacks and other minorities had pushed too fast or got too much special treatment. As the number of available jobs dropped, competition for positions caused whites to take a less benevolent attitude to their minority brothers. The phrase "reverse discrimination" became popular; that is, minorities were thought to be given special treatment and to be put into programs in preference to whites. The racial goals were contested. In the *Bakke* medical school case, the Supreme Court ruled out the use of specific quotas, although it allowed race as a factor to be taken into account in admissions. In *Weber* (1979) the Court said private employers could legally give special preference to black workers for training programs to correct past discrimination and eliminate "manifest racial imbalance" in traditionally whites-only jobs.

The rumblings about reverse discrimination, an indicator of white backlash, continue. While the government pushes for greater enforcement of affirmative action programs, many firms are slow to respond.

The ironic thing is that polls show a greater willingness of whites in the 1970s to have integrated schools than in earlier decades. In the South the change was dramatic; on a Gallup poll in 1963, 78 percent of Southern white parents objected to sending their children to school where half of the children were black and 61 percent to a school where a few were black; by 1975, it was 35 percent where half were black and 15 percent where a few were black. In the North in 1963 it was 35 percent where half were black and 10 percent where a few were black; by 1975, it was down to 24 percent and 3 percent.

The slowdown of interest in carrying out affirmative action plans or school desegregation at present is also ironical in that it comes at a time when many Negro families are worse off in relation to white families than they have been in the past. This situation causes black discontent, especially among the teenagers and the sizable group of female-headed low-income households. Jordan (1977) said, regarding the 1977 New York City looting incident, "All our cities contain large numbers of people who have no stake in this society, who are without jobs or hope, whose despair and anger simmers continually, until it boils over, past the limits of accepted behavior" (p. 4).

For Mexican-American youth and many Chinese-American youth the situation is somewhat the same, and the "boiling over" may again occur. Dramatic policy measures are necessary. The present policies are discussed in Chapter 13.

SUMMARY

In this chapter a number of major changes in American society have been covered. The great change for minorities has been the end of blatant discrimination, such as that in public places and certain occupations. However, change has left them in midstream, halfway between the old castelike customs and full racial and ethnic equality.

Changes in urban life keep occurring, the most prominent development of the last few decades being the move of the white population to the suburbs, which has left the central cities to minorities. Other major population changes affecting policy are the baby boom and baby bust phenomena; these are related to changes in the family.

Loss of function is the most marked change in the family; many other institutions have had to take over the family's functions. This is partly due to the increased instability of the family, with its high divorce rate and many female-headed households. The great increase in the proportion of married women in the labor force is another change in the family.

A related continuing change affecting a variety of policies is fluctuations in the economy and the decreasing need for unskilled labor.

In the chapters in Part Three, when we discuss policy in specific areas, such as income maintenance and child welfare, these changes must be kept in mind.

American Values and Changes in American Society

American Values and Changes in American Society

Values, that is, the beliefs and attitudes people hold, are a major factor in determining the types of social policies existing in a society and, in fact, the priority given to social service needs. The policies on income assistance, such as Aid to Families with Dependent Children, have been largely determined by our historical values and present attitudes. The form of such social services as casework is likewise influenced by the society's values.

EARLY HISTORICAL ROOTS OF VALUES

Values regarding the poor and those in trouble have historical roots. Although they have changed over time, the often conflicting values existing today are a carryover of different historical outlooks. Very early expressions of attitudes toward the poor and the unfortunate are found in Hebrew or Judaic social thought centuries before the birth of Christ. The value of social justice was often expressed, as well as that of compassion for human suffering.

Christianity also stressed compassion for the poor and a life of service, as well as forgiveness of sins. One was to love one's neighbor. In the medieval period, when the church was dominated by the ideas of St. Augustine, doing good works for one's own salvation and reward in the next world, rather than because of an interest in one's fellow human beings, was stressed. Second, one gave alms to the institutionalized source of assistance to the poor, the church, and let it do with it as it saw fit. Monasteries became guardians and regulators of the poor and the troubled.

The church was gradually replaced by the local community as the provider of assistance, although the community gave assistance grudgingly and with many restrictions, and with punishment for begging and vagrancy. Community relief began as early as the mid-1500s in some German, Swiss, and Austrian towns at the instigation of Martin Luther and others. By the mid-1700s several cities, such as Hamburg and Elberfeld, financed their relief by taxation as well as individual collections and gifts.

In England, especially after Henry VIII's destruction of the church system in the mid-1500s, relief came from local authorities. The breakdown of the feudal system and its welfare supports and the loss of common lands for the peasants after the Enclosure Acts, as well as wars, had caused an increase in the mobile poor population begging throughout the country. Towns established laws against begging and vagrancy. One could say the towns, while taking on a communal responsibility, a value expressed in early Judaic and Christian writings, limited their help to local residents, forcing nonresident beggars to leave their area by threats of severe punishment. Second, they separated out the able-bodied poor and made them accept any employment.

The British Poor Law of 1601 and subsequent poor laws were a codification of these trends in relief for the poor, and they made even clearer the distinctions between residents and nonresidents and among the classes of poor: the able-bodied poor and the beggars who were considered able to work; second, the deserving or impotent poor, who included the sick, aged, blind, or otherwise physically handicapped, and mothers with young children; and the third group, dependent children, such as orphans or those deserted by their parents. These laws established the very negative orientation to able-bodied poor that has lasted even beyond the 300 years of poor laws. These laws also continued the disdain and repression of the poor who applied for aid and the stigmatization of them. The system was deliberately intended to operate as an assault on personal dignity and self-respect, as Titmuss (1969) points out in regard to the New Poor Laws of 1834. Eligibility for aid was determined by stringent income tests. The infamous workhouse for the poor existed in part of this period. For a century reformers were crying out against the philosophy of the poor laws; in fact, up to World War II and the period of the welfare state reforms this value orientation dominated the British welfare system, and it still dominates American welfare thinking.

PHILOSOPHIES SUPPORTING THE POOR LAW ORIENTATION

Some of the schools of thought that negatively influenced the treatment of the poor are what may be called "Social Darwinism," the Protestant ethic, laissez faire economic theories and the related idea of individualism, and the application of Freudian theory to social work.

The Protestant Ethic

As part of the rise of a mercantile class and the breakaway from feudalism and the control of the aristocracy, the Protestant Reformation, teaching a different philosophy from Catholicism, developed. Its first spokesman was Martin Luther, who openly challenged the Roman Catholic Church in 1517 in Wittenberg. Luther emphasized work, something the new middle class very much practiced, as a salvation in heaven and as a service to God. Any type of work, in whatever vocation one was in, was considered admirable and a good deed in the eyes of God. Those who did not work to their fullest ability, were, of course, considered contemptible. Thus this Protestant ethic, especially as later expressed by John Calvin in Switzerland, endowed work with a religious significance. The subsequent rise of Puritanism out of the Reformation movement branded illness as bad. The use of the workhouse for the poor was a natural outgrowth.

Diligence and work were now the supreme virtues in the eyes of the church. As the Industrial Revolution developed in England and other places, this theme of hard work was especially useful in mobilizing a population to labor in the factories. In early America, with its new frontiers to conquer and land and other resources to develop, hard work was indeed considered a proper theme. It was assumed anyone who worked hard could get ahead, with the abundance of resources available to tame. Those who did not succeed must be lazy or nonworkers.

Values of Success and Achievement The values of success and achievement were a natural outgrowth of this hard work orientation. In America, achievement and mobility had become almost a sacred value. In colonial America, failure was to be despised.

Tropman (1976) says, regarding this success–social mobility orientation today, "This dominant value touches almost every part of the lives of most Americans and becomes the operational vehicle through which many of the other values are expressed. Along with some corollary values, it provides a basis for judging men and women" (p. 75). The problem, as Romanyshyn (1971) says, is that if Americans organize society as a game called "occupational achievement" someone has to be the "loser." Merton (1957) saw this when he made this "success" value, and the repetitive preaching to all Americans that they should and could be successful, the center of his theory of "anomie and social structure." Those who had barriers to achieving these success goals, such as the poor and minorities, he hypothesized, used illegal means to reach these goals, such as crime, or they gave up on the goals, as in the case of such retreatists as drug addicts.

Success goals are something apart from the hard work value; some, such as Max Lerner (1957), feel that in the twentieth century success and money have replaced work, thrift, and achievement as the major values. In an impersonal, urban society, in contrast to a rural or small-town environment, one has little knowledge about how hard others have worked; being rich in itself means success.

Social Darwinism

The idea that a person was a failure because he or she was unsuccessful on account of deficiencies, such as a lack of hard work and an inability to utilize the opportunities available, was reinforced as early as 1852 by the idea of unfitness expressed in Social Darwinism. Based on the evolutionary idea of the development of new species, this theory saw an evolution among human beings caused by the survival of the fittest and a natural extermination of the unfit. One of the main proponents, Herbert Spencer, speaking of the fate of the unfit in 1852, said, "Nature is a little cruel that it can be very kind." The theme here was that it was useless to help the poor (the unfit) because one just prolonged an unhappy and indeed unnatural situation by keeping the poor at a near starvation level when actual starvation was better. It fit in with Malthus' ideas (1798) that human fecundity would outstrip food supply and any social doctoring to mediate suffering would be self-defeating since it would put more pressure on the food supply and mean real starvation. Such philosophies, of course, considered relief to the poor as a misplaced use of resources and condemned agencies that engaged in such relief.

A leading American Social Darwinist, William Graham Sumner, in 1879 gave the essence of this value orientation when he said:

> Here "the strong" and "the weak" are terms which admit to no definition unless they are made equivalent to the industrious and the idle, the frugal and the extravagant. . . . the socialist desideratum—a plan for nourishing the unfittest and yet advancing in civilization—no man will ever find. [Reprint ed., 1934, p. 56]

Most Americans would not fully subscribe to this harsh treatment of the poor. In a 1964 Harris survey, 74 percent of the public felt government should be used to protect the weak. Yet a 1965 Gallup poll showed a carryover of Social Darwinism; one-third of the Americans polled nation-wide felt that lack of effort on one's own part was more often to blame if one was poor than circumstances beyond one's control.

Individual Pathology

As Macarov (1978) states, the theme of Social Darwinism strengthened the belief that the cause of social problems lay in the *individuals* afflicted with them rather than in the rest of society. Macarov points out that "mostly as a result of the influence of Spencer and Sumner, the American Charity Organization Society movement [of the nineteenth century] accepted Social Darwinism as a theoretical base for its activities" (p. 196). This voluntary charity movement was the main source of help to American poor in this period, since the federal government gave little help until 1935 and public efforts in general were minor. This social work orientation emphasizes the individual pathology approach. As Henry Miller (1968) says in an article on social work values explaining the themes of this approach:

> The social work profession presumes to confront a large number of people with the judgment that they are unhappy, confused, deviant, ill, maladapted—this list could be extended indefinitely. . . . This judgment is based on either the conclusions of society . . . or the diagnostic acumen of our own expert knowledge. In the latter instance we look upon an individual and say that he suffers from an ailment, and we can say this because we are experts; he may not realize that he is afflicted—he may not even care that he is afflicted—but we know he is and it is our responsibility to minister to him. In the former instance we concur in the judgment of society that he is ailing and we accept the charge of that society to effect a remedy. [P. 27]

This diagnosis of the client as ill or deviant or out of step with society is a common one among social workers. It does not focus on the fact that the institutions in the society rather than the person may need changing. The focus is on counseling (nonvoluntary) and on rehabilitating the individuals and fitting them into society.

As Romanyshyn (1971) states, critics have blamed social work for having a fixation on individual casework to the neglect of social reform. Macarov (1978) feels that the theories of Sigmund Freud, with emphasis on the inner self rather than outer reality, helped turn social workers to individual adjustment as a goal. He says, "Social work, partly due to Freud's theories, became deeply engaged with the one-to-one relationship and casework assumed a predominance in social-work activities" (p. 239). Freud's medical model, whereby the patient is brought to the therapist and assumed ill, became accepted. Because in Freudian theory the presented problem is thought not to be the real problem, correcting the former is thought not to solve anything. This inhibits social reform attempts.

Such a therapeutic approach even ignores the fact that the poor need money, as Schorr (1966) points out; it instead concentrates on their discovering their psychological problems by talking out their situation, something many poor have trouble doing.

The most recent major analysis of this individual pathology outlook is Ryan (1971), in which it is termed "blaming the victim." Ryan states that "the multi-problem poor, it is claimed, suffer the psychological effects of impoverishment, the culture of poverty and the deviant value system of the lower classes; consequently, though unwittingly, they cause their own troubles." Ryan also gives examples of other problems where the victim is blamed; for example "The miserable health care of the poor is explained away on the grounds that the victim has poor motivation and lacks health information" (p. 173).

The plight of various minority groups is also explained in Social Darwinism terms, with the group itself blamed if it does not make progress up the success ladder. Immigrant groups were seen over time or in stages moving up the success ladder and becoming assimilated into American society. If they didn't make it, it was due to the character and values of the group (they were not hardworking) or the unwillingness of the group to assimilate (to learn a new language or make use of educational opportunities).

Laissez Faire Attitudes and Individualism

The interests of the eighteenth-century mercantile class and industrialists were served by the economist Adam Smith of England who in his famous *Wealth of Nations* (1776) put forth the theory of individualism and the laissez faire orientation of business. Smith felt that persons who were under a minimum of government restraints could produce the best social good through individual action. Adam Smith felt that individuals should work to maximize their own economic condition and, although this might seem selfish, in the end society would profit. The orientation was toward individual competition, with the most efficient winning out. The government should not interfere with the free functioning of the market and with this individual competition. It was also felt that the state should not interfere to relieve social misery or else the beneficial results of self-seeking would be upset. As Titmuss (1969) points out, the nineteenth century chose the laissez faire solution, that is, to allow the social costs of the system to lie where they fell rather than provide social services.

Economic growth in the private sector became the god of progress.

There was a feeling, in fact, that such economic growth in itself would solve social problems; affluence would put an end to poverty. All activities were to be done through the private sector. People, if at all possible, should buy needed services through the private sector. If provided in the private sector the service might be considered in economic terms, in profit terms, as today nursing homes and many day care center chains are, with listings on the stock market. There would be agency competition for customers.

This feeling that all objectives should be met through the marketplace Kahn (1975) considered a major American ideological block to provision of services. The private sector was seen by laissez faire theory as economically efficient, and efficiency was valued over humanitarianism. The public sector, in contrast, was seen as wasteful. As Abel-Smith (1966) says, public spending was considered an extravagance while private spending was acceptable. Galbraith expressed the same idea in *The Affluent Society* (1958), pointing out how this philosophy promoted production of useless goods that people must be persuaded by advertising to buy, while production in the public sector of such services as hospital care was seen in a negative light. For example, the health service and public retirement pensions have been seen as an economic burden in balance of payments crises in Britain in the 1960s.

The Land of Opportunities—The Optimism Theme

The themes of individualism, laissez faire economics, and private market activities fit in with the situation in the United States in the eighteenth and nineteenth centuries. Americans were optimistic about the opportunities to develop the vast resources of this country. The plains, the forests, the mines were all there to develop, in contrast to the European areas many of the early pioneers had come from, as Henry Steele Commager points out. The opportunities to develop these resources seemed real if one worked hard. Example after example of moving from rags to riches during one's life was there; Horatio Alger stories were common. As Commager says, Americans were visionary, seeing their greatest dreams realized. They had an optimism, he says, that nothing was beyond their power. There was an atmosphere of independence and encouragement of enterprise; the vast spaces were an invitation to mobility. This supported a tradition of individualism, of cutting out one's empire and conquering new frontiers.

This economic reality of the frontier reinforced the other value themes, as Heilbroner concludes when he says, "The rampage of Social Darwinism in late nineteenth-century America, with its long-abiding legacy of antiwelfare attitudes in the twentieth, cannot be divorced from the myth (and the reality) of the frontier or the facts of economic life itself" (1976, p. 62).

Equal Opportunity A value in such an environment was equal opportunity. The rigid class structure of many European countries did not exist in America. The European peasant could move to the top of the system in America.

Equal opportunity means an equal chance to obtain a share of a scarce good. It means the legal right to compete for a resource, or equal treatment in taking part in the competition, whether for a top-level job, education, desirable housing, or income. It does not ensure equal *results,* that everyone will have equal income, equal-level jobs, or education. Equal opportunity, many would say, is the type of equality Americans have supported, especially through civil rights bills in the 1960s.

Equal opportunity means that the system offers equal chances to be unequal. Some, if they have a fair start, will be more likely to obtain a major share due to such virtues as hard work. As Miller (1974) says, "Provision of equal opportunity is a change in sorting and selection, not a change in the structure of the social stratification system; the equality of opportunity approach does not attempt to change the rewards to positions but to give everyone a similar chance of getting to desirable positions."

The problem with this approach, as Miller sees it, is that "in practice it is not possible to provide an equal footing, an equal start for those who have come from many different places [such as different classes or ethnic and racial groups] in society. It is exceedingly difficult to achieve equal opportunities without prior equal conditions" (1974, p. 4).

For ethnic-racial or religious minorities and women, legal attempts have been made to open up equal opportunities. Miller calls this "representative equality," to increase the representation of underrepresented groups in occupations and higher-education admissions, as in medical schools. Targets, quotas, and preferences have been used; terms like "affirmative action," "compensatory opportunity," "positive discrimination" have been created. The target of such measures is only some slight definite movement in the direction of some greater proportionality and not exactly proportional representation.

Equality of *outcome* or *result* or an equal share is a very different thing from equal opportunity. It is redistribution of resources, including income and assets, so that the lower income group is closer to the middle group and the higher group. Many social policymakers consider resource redistribution the major concern today rather than opportunity of access to an equal share. They want the poor to have a greater proportion of the total resources or income of society and the money differentials between the rich and other groups to be lessened.

VALUES OPPOSED TO THE POOR LAW ORIENTATION

Income Redistribution

In all societies there are rich families and poor families. In many developing countries there is a small elite and a very large poor population. On the other hand, there could be a country where the income distribution is such that all samplings of the households have an equal share of the economic resources, a situation we do not have even in so-called classless societies of the communist world.

The value one is talking of here is decreasing this inequality of income, working toward some degree of redistribution or a system of transfers of money and nonmonetary benefits so that members of a given group, such as the poor, end up with a balance different from that created by market transactions. One might simply be trying for a certain level of distribution justice; some talk of guaranteeing a socially defined minimum standard of living to everyone, but as Rainwater (1967) and Miller (1974) both point out, this must not be a static income floor but a dynamic amount *relative* to the median income. As Miller says, "The issue is no longer bringing people up to some poverty line, even if adjusted for changes in the average standard of living; the issue is rather that of comparative or relative position of degrees of inequalities rather than sheer insufficiency as implied in the poverty line approach" (1974, p. 11).

These goals of redistribution are very important ones to social policy scholars, as Gil (1973) stresses, saying, "The distribution of rights in a society, and the criteria underlying this distribution are, no doubt, most significant issues of social policy development. For no other factor seems to have a stronger, direct impact on the circumstances of living of individuals and groups than the nature and scope of their rights with respect to control over material and symbolic resources, goods and services" (p. 22). Rein (1970) defines social policy as "planning for social externalities, redistribution and the equitable distribution of social benefits, especially social services" (p. xiii).

The late Richard Titmuss, the top British scholar on social policy, very much related the goal of income redistribution to social welfare policies when he said:

> All three categories of social policy [direct public provision of services in kind, direct payment of benefits, *and* fiscal welfare *and* occupational welfare] have a great deal in common in terms of redistribution. They are all concerned with changing the individual and family pattern of current and future claims on resources set by the market . . . and set by the allocations made by governments to provide for national defense and other non-market sectors. Social welfare changes the pattern of claims by, for instance, directly providing

in-kind education or mental hospital care either free or at less than the market cost. . . . [1965, pp. 17–18]

Besides welfare benefit transfers to the poorer groups, increased taxes on the richer groups are seen as the main means of lessening income differences.

One must point out, however, that a part of the academic community does not support the value of greater equality of incomes. These academics back the Davis and Moore theory (1945) of functional bases of a stratification or unequal reward system. This theory says some must get greater rewards in terms of income, privileges, and power because they are filling the most needed functions, where greater rewards are necessary in order to obtain the best talent and most extensive training needed, for example, for medical doctors. Many argue with this Davis-Moore theory, saying that people will take on these important jobs anyway without these rewards because they are interested in the work and, second, that important positions are often in reality not filled by the best talent but by those from a privileged background.

Democracy as a Value

A value closely related to equal opportunity, and sometimes the umbrella under which such equality occurs, is the democratic creed, that is, the belief that all the people should participate in the decision-making process. Such a creed espouses universal suffrage and is considered opposed to totalitarian rule by a narrow elite. True democracy could be said to require the participation of all races, ethnic groups, and religious minorities. Today an extension of this principle is citizen participation in social service programs, as covered in Chapter 7.

Collective or Societal Responsibility

Collective responsibility is a value stressed in the welfare state philosophy described later in this chapter. It represents a twentieth-century value orientation that has penetrated Western Europe and to some degree the United States. Under this philosophy the state guarantees to cover a minimum standard of living and to meet the basic necessities for all its citizens through health insurance, disability payments, pensions, and the like rather than leave these to citizens' individual efforts. A further step in collective responsibility is the socialist value of state ownership of the means of production. While, in general, individual enterprise has dominated in the United States, as Galbraith (1967) points out, government has played a major role in recent years in a number of industrial activities, such as the defense industries, utilities, and energy resource enterprises. While seldom the outright owner of the firms, the state is the major subsidizer and regulator. American public opinion has backed this heavy state support of certain firms.

CHANGES IN THE AMERICAN VALUES SYSTEM
RELATED TO CHANGES IN AMERICAN SOCIETY

The situation that supported the old value orientations started to change in the late nineteenth century in America. Economic activities began to be run on a large scale so that there were railroad barons, great mining speculators, and steel trusts. Cities grew with industrialization and the heavy influx of immigrant workers. Economic instability occurred with a great strike in 1886 and a bank panic in 1893. By 1912 Woodrow Wilson was proclaiming, "The man with little capital is finding it harder and harder to get into the field and more and more impossible to compete with the big fellow," and saying that antitrust laws were needed. Franklin Roosevelt, in one of his early policy statements in 1924, summarized the situation then:

> [In Jeffersonian times] . . . individualism was made the great watchword of American life. The happiest of economic conditions made the day long and splendid on the Western frontier; land was substantially free. No one who did not shirk the task of earning a living was entirely without the opportunity to do so. . . .
>
> It was in the middle of the nineteenth century that a new force was released and a new dream created. The force was what is called the industrial revolution, the advance of steam and machinery and the rise of the forerunner of the modern industrial plant. . . . Our industrial plant is built. Our last frontier has long since been reached and there is practically no more free land. More than half of our people do not live on the farms or on lands and cannot derive a living by cultivating their own property.
>
> There is no safety valve in the form of a Western prairie to which those thrown out of work by the Eastern economic machines can go for a new start. . . . [Rattner, 1964, pp. 134–135]

Handlin (1963) said that the nineteenth-century situation brought a radical change in attitudes, with a growing conviction that the state needed reconstruction to advance the welfare of the people and that the republic bore the responsibility for helping people master forces set loose by industrialization. When Teddy Roosevelt came in, he was elected on the ideas of strong government to control the economy, including regulating (rather than busting) trusts. Various types of legislation came in at the federal level. Some were in the area of social welfare, a field that in the nineteenth century had been left mostly to voluntary agencies, with some help from local relief boards, which subsidized these private groups or directly gave outdoor relief. (The local agencies also put the poor—

especially in the 1800s—in local workhouses or almshouses or boarded them out to the lowest-bidding family.)

By the mid-1800s orphanages had been established for young children in many areas and mental hospitals were built to house the insane. The federal government very slowly and reluctantly got involved, for the most part in the period after 1912, and services to veterans and to immigrants also began early (a U.S. Marine hospital existed as early as 1798).

The Depression, from 1929 to 1935, was the period when new attitudes to social welfare and to government provision came in. The complete breakdown of the economic system, beginning on the stock market's Black Thursday, October 24, 1929, called forth changes. By 1932 over 12 million were out of work. Then President Hoover took those steps that followed from his values, namely, an appeal to big business and a call for a reliance on the spirit of charity and mutual self-help through voluntary giving; he also stressed the responsibility of local government, as distinguished from appropriations from the federal treasury.

In 1933 President Franklin Roosevelt, unlike Hoover, proposed many federal programs, such as the Federal Emergency Relief Administration (FERA), providing relief to as many as 18 million people. In introducing such assistance, Roosevelt pointed out that the individual had little control over conditions due to the economic crisis; it was not individual social pathology that caused need but the economic situation.

FERA was replaced by other programs, the best-known being the WPA, or Works Progress Administration, which supplied jobs itself through its many projects. It engaged in construction of roads, dams, playgrounds, and public buildings, such as hospitals and libraries, and also employed artists to do murals. It furnished jobs to almost 8 million individuals.

Another job corps, CCC, or Civilian Conservation Corps, was established for unemployed youth. There were forest camps, over 1500 in number, from which the boys went out to build forest breaks and dams, plant trees, clear hiking paths, clear marshland, and do related activities.

Much of the relief was in keeping with the hard work ethos, that is, providing jobs, and was considered temporary.

The provisions of the Social Security Act of 1935 were of a more revolutionary and more permanent nature. Some provisions were of a type new to the United States, of a universal type of contributory insurance, that is, retirement and survivors' pensions as well as help to the disabled (OASDHI), and an unemployment insurance scheme. These programs were for all citizens in those categories, rich and poor, without an income (means) test.

Some other programs under the Social Security Act were means-tested programs for certain categories of those in need, such as dependent children (through AFDC) and the needy old and disabled (now through SSI). This act also provided for maternal and child health services.

Such pension insurance schemes for workers already existed in some northern European countries. Bismarck of Germany, as a politically expedient measure to avoid industrial conflict, had introduced compulsory insurance and sickness schemes for industrial workers by the mid 1880s. There was an acceptance in such insurance programs that industrialization was partly the cause of the problems. Fabian leaders stressed, speaking of the English pension plan brought in in 1908, that such measures were needed "to lift the burden of hopelessness and insecurity from the lives of the aged" (Webb and Webb, 1909).

Thus, while the Social Security Act of 1935 was a revolutionary one in America, its most startling proposal, a universal contributory insurance program for the retired, their spouses, and then their survivors, rich and poor alike, had long existed in Europe.

THE WELFARE STATE PHILOSOPHY

From the late 1800s onward, social reformers in Britain, opposed to the poor law welfare system, were fighting for social service assistance as a right. The Fabian Society, with such leaders as Beatrice and Sidney Webb, rejected the poor law idea of the means test and of the use of the workhouse.

Other British insurance programs came in. The philosophy toward welfare was changing. Hall (1955) sums up the shifting attitudes, saying, "The nineteenth century witnessed changes in political philosophy and economic doctrine from the laissez-faire individualism of the early part of the century to the Fabian socialism of its closing years."

The full flowering of this welfare state philosophy came in with the British Beveridge Report in 1942, the historic document in which Lord Beveridge and his colleagues outlined the shape of the postwar social service program. In the United States, the OASDHI part of the Social Security Act is still the legislation closest to this philosophic orientation.

Philosophies embodied in the Beveridge Report were formulated in a period of war, when the British were facing extreme deprivations and making great sacrifices, sharing the battles and the burdens as a cohesive group rather than as separate class groups. This situation encouraged attitudes of collectivism of concern for all citizens and promises to the less fortunate ones that conditions, the quality of life, in Britain would be better for them after the war. As Beveridge said, it was:

. . . the assumption by the community, acting through the state, of the responsibilities for providing the means whereby all its members can reach minimum standards of health, economic security, and civilized living, and can share according to their capacity in its social and cultural heritage. [1942, p. 12]

Birch (1974) says that national collectivist policies under the welfare state also had the goal of maintaining a high level of employment and providing decent housing, a favorable environment, and a system of education in which no talent is wasted.

This system was to be one of pooling of risks, a radically widened form of social insurance, in which one single contribution was to open the door to a number of assorted benefits, Beveridge pointed out. This pooling of risks meant risks were to be borne collectively by society; for example, the perennially healthy would bear the burden of the chronic sick. The state or community as a whole was to reduce insecurity for all citizens by meeting "social contingencies," such as illness or unemployment or financial bankruptcy in old age, by giving protection from the cradle to the grave. The welfare state was to guarantee a minimum income level to the citizen.

A reason for this collective responsibility is the acceptance that it was the state's role to compensate the citizens for any disservice the progress of the society, the industrialization and urbanization, had caused them. This philosophy accepted that needy individuals were the victims of societal forces beyond their control rather than problems they themselves had caused. As Titmuss (1969) explained:

[Social benefits] represent partial compensations for disservices, for social costs and social insecurities which are the product of a rapidly changing industrial-urban society. They are part of the price we pay to some people for bearing part of the cost of other people's progress: the obsolescence of skills, redundance, premature retirements, accidents, many categories of disease and handicaps, urban blight and slum clearance, smoke pollution and a hundred-and-one other socially generated disservices. They are the socially-caused diswelfares; the losses involved in aggregate welfare gains. [P. 133]

In other words, according to this philosophy, for society to progress to a higher standard of living, there are some casualties—some unemployed or otherwise affected—and social benefits must be given to them as compensation.

A brief description of the changed programs that came in under this welfare state policy might illuminate how the philosophy applied. Titmuss (1969) reported that:

Gradually in Britain . . . we began to discard the use of discriminatory and overtly redistributive services for second-class citizens. The social services or minimum standards for all citizens crept apologetically into existence. In common with other countries, we invented contributory national insurance or social security and provided benefits as of right. The actuary was called in to replace the functions of the public assistance relieving officer. Free secondary education for all children, irrespective of the means of their parents, was enacted in 1944 as part of a comprehensive educational system. Public housing authorities were called upon in 1945 to build houses for people and not just for working-class people. A limited and second-class health insurance scheme for working men was transformed in 1948, into a comprehensive and free-on-demand health service for the whole population. [Pp. 190–191]

A major principle of this welfare state philosophy was that welfare assistance, mainly insurance programs, was a *right* the citizen was entitled to from the state. Freedom of want was no longer to be something citizens had to beg for but a right they could demand from the state, as Beveridge stated.

Franklin Roosevelt, in pushing his New Deal legislation, with its universal social insurance system, was also talking of a government that would guarantee the citizen as a *right* certain basic assistance. Roosevelt said in 1934, "Government has the definite duty to use all its powers and resources to meet social problems with new social controls—to ensure to the average person the right to his own economic and political life, liberty, and the pursuit of happiness" (Birch, 1961, p. 5). However, in America welfare as a right was not to be the dominant philosophy it was in Britain and the Scandinavian countries.

In the British welfare state orientation, as Beveridge (1942) outlined, charity should be reduced to a minimum by the creation of social rights, that is, giving universal, nondiscriminatory service to rich and poor alike. This would cut down on the abortive use of the stigmatic poor law means test these British social reformers disliked so much.

The universal social insurance system of the welfare state would allow assistance to be given with dignity and to be nonjudgmental of each person's individual case in financial and moral terms. The fact that it was nondiscriminatory and without class distinctions instead of being available only to those of the poor who stood up to beg was seen as a positive change, although by the late 1960s Titmuss (1969) was somewhat bothered by the outcome of this universal policy, saying, "We have learnt from fifteen years' experience of the Health Service that the higher income groups know how to make better use of the service." Yet in an evaluation of the welfare state's National Health System in 1967, he says:

The major positive achievement which has resulted from the creation of direct, universalist social services in kind has been the erosion of formal discriminatory barriers. One publicly approved standard of service, irrespective of income, class or race, replaced the double standard which invariably meant second-class services for second-class citizens [the poor]. [P. 195]

This ending of second-class service for the poor was a major theme of the welfare state philosophers.

The increased role of government versus private services meant that the state's provision of social services could no longer be looked on as a *residual* activity, a temporary filling of need, with the family and the market the natural, desirable sources of help. Instead, the social services became ongoing societal institutions in their own right, such as the National Health Service. They were part of the structure of society. Marshall (1965) pointed this out:

> The social services were not to be regarded as regrettable necessities to be retained only until the capitalist system had been reformed or socialized; they were a permanent and even a glorious part of the social system itself. [P. 77]

There was great growth of social service institutions in most northern European countries after World War II. Titmuss (1950) said, "It was increasingly regarded as a proper function of government to ward off stress and strain not only among the poor but among almost all classes of society" (p. 8). This was different from the prewar philosophy, a philosophy still held in many circles in the United States, that no one should get a social service from the state who either can pay for it in the private market or doesn't need it.

In the welfare state philosophy, provision through a public source was accepted on the basis of the idea that some elements of civilized life ranked above the market economy and must be achieved by superseding the market, as Marshall (1965) reported. There was a suspension of the free play of economic forces in one area, the social services. The market system was seen to have the objectives of profit and efficiency, objectives that might be at odds with the provision of social services. To extract profit from a nursing home or from a day care center might mean lowering the quality of care needed by the recipient. Or one could take the example of private insurance and public insurance and say again that each sector has different ends to meet, as Titmuss (1969) concluded. The private economic sector may find it expedient to discriminate against the elderly and other groups, while the public sector, with other aims and objectives, would be less likely to do so.

The fact was that the welfare state's objectives were not economic profit or market expansion as an end in itself but instead the improvement of the quality of life. As Abel-Smith (1966) said, "Why do we want economic growth if not to promote social and not economic ends, that is, higher levels of living?" He adds, "Do we want increased private material consumption, such as of cars, as we have in this decade of the 1960–70's, and public service starvation?" (p. 10).

Another important provision of the welfare state was that it was to be redistributive. Even the *Times* of London during the war called for more equitable distribution of income and wealth as part of the future welfare state. Titmuss (1969) said, "Built into the public model of social policy in Britain since 1948 there are two major roles or objectives: the redistributive objective and the non-discriminatory objective" (p. 191).

Redistribution was seen as the main aim of governmental social policies by such welfare state scholars as Donnison (1975), with government deliberately influencing the distribution of resources, status, opportunities, and life chances among social groups and categories within the country. Welfare state insurance measures would give the poor a greater proportion of the income and the resources of the society.

The Success of the Welfare State

Britain, with all its fine philosophizing about the welfare state, put down in document after document, did not do so well under the welfare state measures as other northern European countries, such as Sweden, Norway, Denmark, West Germany, and Holland. But then Britain started the welfare state in a period marked by wartime devastation, an impossible situation of housing shortages and deterioration, an old and outworn industrial base, a large group in poverty, and a rigid class situation characterized by broad income differentials. Second, its welfare spending as a percent of GNP was considered below that of most welfare state leaders.

In another statistic, the proportion below the poverty level in per capita income, the other welfare states did better; Sweden in 1979 had 3 percent below the poverty level and West Germany, 2.5 percent. West Germany was judged to have a rather equal distribution of earnings among manual workers, better than Britain's, but wide gaps between manual and nonmanual and among nonmanual workers. Sweden also had a fairly equal distribution of earnings, and both West Germany and Sweden were much better than the United States; Britain was also judged better than the United States, a 1979 *Economist* article reports, in distribution of income, although salaries were lower than those in the United States.

In Sweden the welfare state was highly redistributive in supplying a variety of services free to all or, in some cases, free or with employer contributions to those below professional salary levels. These services included pensions, day care, housing allowances, and a health service, including a variety of maternity and child care services. Because of the type of taxation needed to raise money for health services, the tax contribution for the service was slightly "regressive"; that is, it required of the low-income family a proportionately higher tax contribution for the services. But, as Sidel and Sidel (1979) point out from their extensive study:

> It must be remembered that taxation for health services is only a small part of total taxation in Sweden, and that the bulk of the tax pattern and the service pattern outside medicine, is heavily redistributive. Furthermore, since there are relatively few barriers, geographic or financial, to the use of health services in Sweden, utilization seems relatively equitably distributed among all groups in society in relation to their needs. [P. 8]

Swedes have certainly had tangible results in the improvement of their health, with (1) one of the best (lowest) infant mortality rates in the world, (2) a low age-specific mortality rate, and (3) a long life-expectancy rate. Sweden has considerably surpassed the United States in the first and third factors and done somewhat better in the second.

Wilensky (1975), after extensive analysis of different leading welfare-state countries, gives an optimistic answer to the question whether the welfare state is redistributive. He says:

> Sweden, like some of the other countries at the top of our list of welfare leaders [of 22 countries studied], not only distributes medical care more aggressively and fairly but also invests heavily in health-relevant programs of housing, nutrition, health education and child care, and draws the income floor for everyone higher and more uniformly; in short it assures the least privileged of its population a higher standard of living. It is likely that the entire package—the interaction of all of these programs—is a major source of Sweden's superior health performance. [P. 102]

Wilensky also answers the question, Does the welfare state work, by saying of the redistribution of resources:

> If the focus is on its effects on the equality of income distribution in some recent year, there are more than hints in English and German data that as a whole the impact is substantially equalitarian. . . . If the focus is not on economic equality but on psychological and economic security, the case for the welfare state seems plain. Does anyone believe that the family or any overloaded institution could soften the risks of modern life as effectively as the seven or eight major social security programs do?

From these data Wilensky concludes that for welfare leader countries, the payout in provision of social services is progressive; that is, the poor get far more payout than they put in compared to better-off groups, and thus the welfare state could be said to foster "short run equality." He adds:

> Much of social insurance goes to them [the poor]. The aged and the poor are more often sick; they receive a disproportionate share of public expenditures on health. Large families and women heading broken homes are over-represented among the poor; family allowances and public assistance go disproportionately to them. For the time of their travail, the unemployed and job-injured are concentrated among low-income families; again the payout is progressive. [P. 90]

The Future Shape of the Welfare State

Rainwater and Rein (1978) discuss the future in terms of stages. Stage two is the post–World War II phase of consolidation of the (stage one) early programs. The emphasis in stage two is on collective universal protection against the economic forces that depleted individuals of their own resources. Derthick (1979) says that in the United States (from 1939 to 1972) for social security legislation, stage two was an expansion phase in which social security was depoliticized. With the present slowing down of economic growth in both Europe and the United States, some see the third or present stage as one where expansion of growth in coverage and costs are accompanied by an increase in taxation to pay the bill. In this stage, people feel the burden of social provision but not its benefits.

In the revolt against taxes by voters in California under Proposition 13 and in Denmark, one could agree there are signs that the third stage has been reached. As Rainwater and Rein quote Heclo (1978), in this stage cost controls (like Proposition 13) will be more prominent when there is no economic surplus to distribute on account of slow economic growth, and attention will be given to *maximum* standards as well as minimum standards. The fiscal manager will become prominent. Or, as Derthick adds for the United States:

> In this period [1972 on] of maturity, tough political issues must be faced because the system [OASDHI] is almost universal, the ratio of taxpayers to beneficiaries is unfavorable, benefit flexibility tied to indexing decreases flexibility, social security taxation becomes more visible, and the aggregate size of the program in the economy becomes more evident. [In Rainwater and Rein, 1978, p. 6]

Certainly we have seen this happen in the United States, where more and more groups, such as divorced wives, have been included under social security, as benefit amounts have increased with the cost-of-living index, and as the total number of recipients has increased in relation to the working population. Angry workers are calling for a cutback in contributions and in the number of groups covered.

This may be a period of integrating state social service provisions and the private provision of benefits given as entitlement with steady jobs. In some countries, such as Japan and the United States, private provision plays a dominant role. But in northern Europe, where state social welfare expenditures have been much higher as a percentage of GNP than in Japan, a "social wage" system is emerging, in which unions and employers and the government all negotiate or plan together a wide range of social and economic policies. Some benefits are given by the state, such as government pensions, housing subsidies, and health coverage. Others, such as the degree of wage increases the government allows different unions, are negotiated between the state and employees, as in Britain. Kuhnle (1978), speaking of Scandinavian social policy in 1978, also saw this type of government-unions-employer policymaking happening. He said:

> The growth of social policy legislation has—together with legislation on labour market, and economic and industrial policies—made the market mechanism less and less important as a mechanism for deciding the distribution of rewards in society. A most discernible trend, at least in Norway, is one of making the setting of wages an issue of political decision-making. . . . [P. 21]

Kuhnle added that, in the long run, the politicization of wage transactions should tend to equalize wages and standards of living and thus should narrow the present variations in the benefit standards of earnings-related social security systems.

Problems of the Welfare State

Even in the 1950s Titmuss (1958) found that a factor the welfare state planners had not taken into consideration was *occupational redistribution,* that is, employee fringe benefits, and *fiscal (tax) redistribution.* They had mainly considered direct public provision of services and cash. He saw these two submerged redistributive welfare systems having a remarkable expansion in Britain in the first twenty years of the postwar welfare state. Fiscal welfare had allowed some to pay less in taxes and have more income because of such things as home mortgage tax deductions.

Saville (1968) said three factors had developed since 1945 for the upper class that increased the inequality of incomes: expense allowances for high-level employees (fringe benefits), tax evasion, and capital gains. He said that what was happening now under welfare state policy was that the state saved for the working class and translated the savings into social services through compulsory contributions and a high level of direct taxation.

Occupational welfare, that is, fringe benefits given with a job, also benefit the middle and upper classes more than the working class; they include pensions, severance pay, death benefits, and entertainment and travel expenses. Such occupational welfare is likely in fact to be redistributive in the opposite direction from the public system, that is, benefiting the higher-level employees, such as managers, more. A problem above all with occupational welfare is that it is tied to the job—and thus is insecure, as the job itself is insecure—and does not even exist for the self-employed and the temporary worker.

Other problems of the public welfare state relate to the amount of funding. For Britain, provision was first seen in terms of decreasing *absolute* poverty; some, like Titmuss, by the 1950s were demanding more attention to *relative* poverty, meaning upping benefits to keep up with the affluence that came in. Britain in 1971 spent only 3.55 percent of GNP on pensions, compared to the 7.59 percent that Germany spent; Britain ranked sixth, with the United States (at 3.42 percent) trailing behind. On public health Britain spent 3.69 percent of GNP, more than the United States, but again far below Sweden's 6.44 percent and Holland, West Germany, Canada, and France. (See Table 4-1.)

The slowing of economic growth in Britain, coming earlier than on the

Table 4-1   Expenditures for Specified Social Welfare Programs as a Percent of GNP, Selected Countries, 1971

Country	Old-age, survivors, and disability insurance	Public aid and other social welfare	Public health care programs
Belgium*	4.97	1.03	3.96
Canada*	2.36	2.12	6.63
France	4.22	(†)	4.54
Germany (Fed. Rep.)*	7.59	1.00	4.66
Japan*	0.31	0.64	3.44
Netherlands	6.32	1.03	4.66
Sweden	6.03	3.50	6.44
United Kingdom	3.55	1.95	3.69
United States*	3.42	2.52	2.66

*Some public expenditures for health care are included under public aid.
†Public aid expenditures are not separately identified.
Source: U.S. Department of Health, Education, and Welfare, Social Security Administration, *Research and Statistics Note,* October 1974.

European continent, meant a starvation of the social services in a period of increasing unemployment and economic crisis. There was a turn back to some use of the means test for certain health services. Of course, even in the early days of the welfare state under the umbrella of universalism, some selectivity (service to those in hardship and special need) was envisioned and did exist, such as the supplementary benefits for the very poor (benefits that did rise with inflation).

Another major problem was that contributors to the public insurance system felt overtaxed; if they were recipients of private occupational benefits they often felt they didn't need the public benefits.

There was a decreasing number of workers to contribute payments to the public insurance system, as the birthrate went down, while there was an increasing number of recipients, due to a higher life expectancy and a broadening of coverage. New taxation methods were needed to support the system so that these workers did not feel the burden rested so heavily on them. In Holland and Sweden, where taxes on income and social security contributions took over 30 percent, on the average, of total personal income in 1977, there was some grumbling by workers (and in Denmark an actual tax revolt), although in all these countries people still wanted the services. For example, Kuhnle (1978) reports that the contemporary younger generation in Scandinavian countries had high expectations of welfare state services, taking for granted the welfare state provisions that they had grown up with, although they did not like the high taxes; these attitudes were tremendously different from those of earlier generations, who regarded the welfare state as utopian and unimaginable.

Another problem of the welfare state in many countries was that some services were overcrowded and in short supply and not working as efficiently as hoped. In the health service there were long waits for nonemergency operations; such conditions prevailed in Sweden and to a crisis level in Britain. There were waits for day care places in some urban areas of Sweden and for places in residences for the elderly in Holland.

Some British scholars felt that another problem was the fact that the early British welfare state planners had emphasized equal opportunity rather than equality of results or outcome; the former policy had not produced the leveling of incomes they had hoped for. Titmuss (1962) warns that we should not be deluded into thinking we can equalize social distribution of life chances by expanding educational opportunities. He felt that the middle class knew better how to use the educational system and the National Health Service. He said, "We now have to study ways of extending the welfare state to the poor." He said, regarding the access problem, that one needed to study how professional people (doctors, teachers, social workers) discharge their roles in selecting or rejecting patients, clients, and students for this or that service; they are the ones who hold the key to equality of outcome; they help to determine the pattern of redistribution in social policy.

In conclusion, there are problems in the welfare state but it is a dominant philosophy in many industrial countries today. In the future the welfare state is sure to change, but only by adding on some aspects of the older welfare philosophies. In fact, in the United States, social policy as expressed in legislation indicates we mix a little of each philosophy.

THE EFFECT OF AMERICAN VALUES ON SOCIAL WELFARE POLICY

The variety of philosophies and values mentioned in this chapter all weave together in the United States to shape the type of social service programs we have. In some programs, especially those for groups that are classified as the deserving poor, we follow the welfare state philosophy. Axinn and Levin (1975) call the Social Security Act of 1935, which brought in the OASDHI insurance program, the birth of the welfare state in America; this program was the watershed in American welfare history, bringing a new orientation toward people as social and economic beings. The effects of this insurance program sound very much like the goals of the British welfare state philosophy: it established societal protection for all as a principle; it established federal government responsibility for the worker's income security; it produced institutional reforms aimed at meeting universal needs which guaranteed permanent economic stabilizers for the society. Axinn and Levin also add that the Social Security Act was a "landmark in American political and social history, reflecting a shift from public governmental concern for property rights to a concern for the rights of people and, consequently, extending federal responsibility for social welfare" (p. 183).

Our problem in America is to accept that we have universal programs given as a right, such as education and pensions. As Kahn (1975) says:

> The United States has some social services for all people; we need to become more comfortable in facing *their normalcy* if we are to improve and expand the components. Certainly such services for members of all social classes are no less essential to a society than more traditional public welfare underpinnings for the poor and the deviants. [P. 171]

Americans have a universal public education system and consider it an accepted goal. And in the health care field, Americans accept a universal health coverage program for the elderly, Medicare, and many Americans favor a national health insurance program, a program Edward M. Kennedy has long proposed. Yet in many areas of social services, Americans are unwilling to support universal programs, which merge aid to the poor and aid to the nonpoor together. Briar (1969), Schorr (1966), and others have pushed for universal children's allowances like those that exist in every other industrialized country, but instead we have AFDC for the poor children and a child-dependent deduction for the better-off taxpayer.

We fear the welfare state terminology. As Kahn (1975) says, "The word welfare is often reserved in the United States for the public assistance recipients, the welfare poor" (p. 179). Elsewhere, he adds, the "welfare state" context has a deeper meaning. Kahn says, "Most Americans are afraid of words such as these and are often turned away from needed programs by them. But we, too, have needs: homes, income, services, problems, loneliness, community . . ." (p. 179).

The mixed value system Americans have is shown, Kahn states, by the fact that "we believe in public education, yet we somehow cannot give public support to high quality community living and care arrangements for the aged" (p. 171).

In "welfare state" European countries these mixed ideological positions seem less evident; there, people want the government to do more for all individuals, Kahn says. He also points out that

> . . . history and ideology [in America] have caused us to take one attitude toward public or private welfare services for the poor, another toward subsidy for the affluent, and still another toward public social utilities, or social infrastructure for everyone. *Society masks realities* by distinguishing among what it calls public welfare and social services for the poor and troubled, education and public health protections for everyone and benefits for the affluent. [P. ix]

One could also say the American public still has the frontier values, those values that originated in Europe with the Protestant Reformation and laissez faire economic policy, so ingrained into its thinking that most cannot understand that these values are somewhat out of step with twentieth-century developments. Values of individualism, hard work, personal success and achievement, and private enterprise still shape American social welfare legislation, even though the conditions that made such values viable have greatly changed. Theobold (1969), pressing for clarification of our directions in the twenty-first century, said:

> It is my firm conviction that most futurists in our society are still justifying obsolete industrial age values rather than trying to clarify the minimal requirements for our survival as we move from the industrial era based on power competition, production and transportation to the cybernetic era based on cooperation, process and information movement. [P. 60]

Sometimes traditional values are applied by politicians even though they themselves know the situation has so changed that the values will no longer work. This is especially true regarding values concerning work. In the last decade "work and welfare" programs have been proposed and enacted to an unprecedented degree, even though there has been an abnormally high unemployment rate and unskilled workers, such as those on welfare, are no longer required. The latest welfare reform proposal at this writing, that of President Carter, is in fact called the Program for Better Jobs and Income, sounding more like a works program than a welfare program, as the National Association of Social Workers (NASW) complained.

Yet many of the politicians and administrators involved know work for most welfare recipients is unavailable. For example, when the 1967 amendments to the AFDC welfare program came in, emphasizing a "work incentive" program, Howard (1969) reports, the department knew it would train more people for work than would be able to find jobs. Howard feels the policymakers saw the training program as an end in itself—not a means to obtain a job. The act of training meets the self-help criterion, the work-ethos orientation of the American public. To some of the public, compulsory training is seen, Howard feels, as the price to be paid for receiving assistance from the community, which, he adds, has almost a Pauline flavor of "he that will not be trained, neither let him eat."

Knowledgeable legislators put such provisions in the legislation simply to make it more acceptable to a middle-American public. As Weil, in his book on the Carter welfare debate (1978) reported, "The jobs component was designed to attract the support of those who believe that many on welfare should work." In the Nixon welfare proposals, statements strongly echoing the work ethos were used to push the bill. Nixon said, "No able-bodied person will have a free ride," meaning there would be no help for persons who choose not to work. In both proposals, those deemed employable had to find private jobs or take public jobs or training; these provisions were put in even though a number of studies, known to politicians, showed that most of the welfare recipients were barely employable on account of their lack of education and skills. One study showed that, of all those receiving AFDC who did not work, only 18 percent were fit for work.

To many politicians it was the voters back home with their Protestant ethic values who influenced their ideas on the shape of the welfare legislation. Weil (1978) reports for the congressional action on the Carter welfare proposals "that any member [of Congress] could be subject to withering criticism about an individual vote on a bill that might seem to have poured more money into welfare." It was no wonder, Weil reports, that "many in Congress, probably a majority, now believe that a jobs program as part of overall welfare reform is an idea whose time has come" (p. 27). Yet this was in a period of 7 percent unemployment rate.

Since 89 percent of the American public was found in a 1976 Harris poll to think that "too many people on welfare could be working," congressional representatives were certainly reflecting their constituents' wishes. On work incentives, 72 percent of the public in a 1977 poll said the Carter welfare plan "would give people an incentive to work, instead of just taking government handouts."

Yet this desire to have work values applied to the welfare program is tempered by both public and legislators. Howard (1969) points out that while the stress is on self-help (still the main American value), the society often exempts certain groups from the usual expectation that "every man must stand on his own two feet" and instead underwrites the requirements (or needs) of those whose efforts to "do it themselves" would be "too hurtful" to either themselves or others. The elderly, disabled, and ill are usually exempt, as are mothers of preschoolers.

Another fact is that, while traditional values of work dominate major aspects of these recent welfare reform proposals, whether Nixon's or Carter's, other sections of the bills have supported welfare state ideas, such as a guaranteed level of income assistance to the poor, almost as if they could be called a right. Even though in an early 1965 Gallup poll 67 percent were opposed to a recommendation that "instead of relief and welfare payments, the government should guarantee every family a minimum annual income," in about the same year a Harris survey found 68 percent of the American public felt government must see that no one is without food, clothing or shelter.

The Nixon welfare reform bill reflected this very definite mixture of values, with its work provisions and its minimum income floor as a rights provision. The editors of *Social Work* called it "guaranteed Protestant Ethic," saying its authors are "determined to mix one small part of social breakthrough, several parts of status quo and a good portion of reaction and then to proclaim this as 'a new departure.'"

A dominating value Americans have that plays into any welfare legislation is a dislike of the poor in general; they still feel that the poor are lazy and that they, not economic factors, are to blame for their own situation. Any social welfare program needs to cover other groups and to have the support of powerful special interest groups to succeed. The American public has felt we spend too much on welfare, 45 percent having said so in a 1975 poll. Although many among the public and in expert circles concede the nation's money income distribution is still very unequal, the value of redistribution of income, even to a minor extent, is hardly supported.

To date, the equal opportunity value has been stressed. The OEO poverty program, including the Head Start program, very much emphasized improving opportunities and access of the poor, through training, paraprofessional jobs, and citizen participation.

The values of private provision rather than government provision, and voluntary agency provision rather than government provision, both values considered desirable in the 1800s, are still expressed in American social legislation. Much housing legislation supports the use of subsidies by private developers or nonprofit ones; subsidies for medical care, it is felt, should go through a private intermediary, as in having Medicaid bills for low-income persons paid out through Blue Cross–Blue Shield's private health insurance company.

The value of efficiency is also still inserted in social service legislation. The required evaluation of programs is done in terms of economic efficiency.

CONCLUSION

In this chapter the major value orientations that affect social policy, especially policy toward the poor, have been discussed. These include the very early attitudes from Judaism and Christianity, from the Protestant Reformation, and from the poor law days in Britain. Attitudes discussed include not only the Protestant ethic on work and the Social Darwinism ideas on the survival of the fittest, but also Adam Smith's laissez faire economic policies, Freudian psychology, and finally the welfare state philosophy. It was pointed out that the frontiers in America in the 1800s encouraged certain value themes, such as work, individualism, economic activities with little government intervention, personal success and achievement, and equal opportunity. The American situation in the early 1900s and during the Depression, however, led to a questioning of these value bases and actually caused them to be rejected for some people. Still, many Americans hung onto the old values in the new situation or mixed the old and the newer welfare state values. Even social workers did this. As Axinn and Levin (1975) say for the 1930s, "Despite the frequent reference in the social work literature to a 'right to assistance,' this view was inconsistent with the philosophy that had impelled the development of voluntary social work. The latter had begun with an assumption of a character flaw. . . ." Axinn and Levin do point out that the Depression showed social workers people could be out of work on account of factors other than their own fault, yet, they also say, with the widespread dissemination of Freudian theory, voluntary family agencies moved to the further development of highly skilled "casework treatment to assist individuals in removing their own handicaps" (p. 193).

Today, social work is still accused of having a fixation on individual therapy to the neglect of social reform, although, as Romanyshyn (1971) says, there is more recognition in schools of social work that social problems come from system defects as well as individual maladjustments and the schools do prepare social workers to be change agents.

Like the public, social workers also still support the old work ethic in legislation, as in Carter's welfare reform proposal, even though they realize the postindustrial society does not need these low-productivity, poorly educated recipients in the work force.

This chapter also mentioned the effect these values have on legislation, especially welfare reform proposals. Here again, we see examples of the process of political policymaking. In considering policy alternatives for solutions (stages IV and VI of the stages of policymaking in Chapter 1), there is no question but that politicians take into account the values of their voting constituency and the values of the lobby groups pushing for legislation (stage VI) in both the narrower strategy-making stage (stage V) and the broader policymaking stage (stage IV). Members of Congress favor work proposals in the welfare reform bills because they know their constituents favor them.

As the year 2000 approaches, one hopes American values will fit the needs of a changing postindustrial society. Will they be the humanitarian values that provide services to all in a dignified way, or values closer to a laissez faire–oriented society, where everyone is self-serving and the "needy" get "handouts"?

Part Two
Social Policy Strategies

Part Two discusses the essential strategies of social policy formulation. It covers the core issues given in the framework for social policy development in Chapter 1. In other words, it is concerned with technical issues instead of a description of policies in a particular social service field.

Chapter 5 discusses the all-important eligibility questions on who gets what, or to what groups resources are allocated. This chapter centers on a discussion of services for all versus services for the poor, or universalism versus means testing or other selectivity techniques. Other criteria for eligibility include the insurance system, employment status, and diagnostic testing.

Chapter 6 considers the types of provision, such as cash versus in-kind benefits, and the advantages of each. Provision in the form of tax credits, assistance to the building, services, and even opportunities is also discussed.

Chapter 7 centers on such system issues as staffing and the structure of the agency. The role of voluntary agencies in providing social services is described. Then, coordination functions are discussed. Finally, the issue of level of staff is dealt with, including the role of the paraprofessional and citizen participation.

Chapter 5

Allocation Strategies: Determining Eligibility

INTRODUCTION

In our society, social services include many programs and activities, ranging from educational services to health to day care to housing. Chapter 2 indicated that many people, including both the rich and the poor and certainly those in the middle-income range, need these services. In most industrialized countries, some groups of citizens, such as the elderly, receive these services free from the state or from voluntary agencies because they fit into certain categories, while other citizens may not receive these services because they do not fit into that category. Also, in some countries, services of various types are available free to all, while in other countries they are provided only for the poor.

The question always is, Who gets what social service? What method of allocation should be used for these often expensive services to people? One major question is, Should *all* people get a service, or *all people in a certain category,* or should only people with a *certain level of need* in that category get help, or, regardless of need, just the *poor* people in that category? With the present health service system in the United States, many middle-class people complain that only the rich and the poor and the elderly can fully avail themselves of expensive health care. The health expenses of the poor and the elderly are paid for by the state, but those nonelderly slightly above the poverty level must pay their own expenses, and these costs may financially cripple these people for many years. Again, the question is, Whom should the state cover?

Education is another good example. In the United States we assume one will receive free education through high school. In many developing countries one gets only free elementary school education. On the other hand, in some European countries, such as Britain, all those who qualify for university education through certain tests are admitted and receive local authority grants to pay their college expenses. In many states in the United States there are tuition-free community colleges. One could ask, How much free education should the state provide (whether it be the local, state, or national government)? Should there be criteria attached, so that the state helps only those who, for example, pass certain exams, as in Britain for college students? Or should there be help only for poor students? How is the help given? At the high school level, is it given as a free voucher for students to go to a private high school, or does it take the form of a whole free high school system or just free schools in poor areas?

In the provision of each social service these and other questions are asked, and different approaches are used in different places. The answers are often furnished by historical perspective, value system, political expediencies, and, above all, availability of funds. Because of both your value system and historical developments you probably would say, Naturally, someone in America should have a free high school system; while again, because of the prevailing value system and historical precedent, you might be inclined to say there shouldn't be a free health system available to all. On the other hand, if you were a 20-year-old in Sweden you would take for granted there would be health care, day care, and student grants to all, for such a scheme of things has long existed in Sweden.

THE INSTITUTIONAL VERSUS THE RESIDUAL APPROACH

In any industrialized country there are many public utility services that are part of the community's or society's infrastructure that we assume should be provided by the state simply because all or many need or use them and it is more efficient for them to be communally provided, and possibly because private enterprise does not want to provide them where the expense is great and profit low or nonexistent. Sewerage and water services come to mind first, but in most cities we would include the library, transport and highways, hospital, school, and cultural center. These are available to all, possibly at a low fee, and are part of the community's infrastructure.

In the institutional concept of social welfare there is, along with the economic, religious, and political institutions, a social welfare institution that provides a social infrastructure for the community. Social welfare is seen as a normal, ongoing function of society. The industrialized urbanized society is continually developing lags and leaps in different areas of life that cause new needs. A continuing, many-pronged social welfare institution is needed to make provision for these needs, whether they be for day care, family counseling, services to the elderly, foster homes, medical services, job retraining, or whatever. In this view of society, as already mentioned, the dynamics of the industrial and technological system cause strains on the person and on different institutions, such as the family and the economy. New automation may cause unemployment and a mismatch of needed skills and existing worker skills; high productivity may mean early retirement; increased employment of women may mean a need for day care. These social service needs are seen as requiring a major ongoing institution in society to meet them so that progress is not held back by tensions and personal dislocation and disorientation. Second, the social service system in such cases is seen as providing a social *investment* in human beings that will benefit the industrial system, as may be true for such programs as job retraining and services to alcoholic executives and working women.

Opposed to this institutional concept of social welfare is the idea that social services take on *residual* functions: they are a temporary aid to those who through their own failure cannot make it in the system and whose needs are not being met by normal institutions. Here the idea is that a need for social services not only is temporary but will "wither" away. The residual approach assumes that individuals are out of tune for a short time with the ways of the society and need above all to be rehabilitated on an individual level; they have an illness that temporarily stops their normal functioning. The residual approach places emphasis on the disorientation of the individual, while the institutional approach places emphasis on changes in the industrial society itself. The residual approach would stress casework and diagnostic treatment. Gilbert and Specht (1974) suggest it would lead to a selective, means-tested service. The residual approach is the one historically stressed in the American value system.

UNIVERSAL VERSUS MEANS-TESTED SERVICES

It is unquestionable that the institutional approach, with its permanent infrastructure, is likely to lead to the existence of a number of social services that are of a universal nature, that is, are made available to all, or at least all persons in a category. For the institutional approach carries with it the idea, as already mentioned, first, that services are a *right,* a guarantee to a social minimum below which no member of the industrial society should fall, and second, that minimum-level assistance should be given to all in need as a compensation for the fact, as Titmuss (1969) says, that they are a casualty of the progress and technological advances in the industrial society.

What is meant by "universal" services? These are services made available to everyone in the community, whether rich or poor, young or old; or they can be services made available to all those of a special-status group, or *demograt,* such as a certain age group or families with children—in other words, those having certain demographic characteristics. Public high school education is one example, for it is free to the rich and to the poor in a town, but as with all such services the better-off are really paying for it through taxes or other revenue sources. Our social security system is the most important universal social service in the United States. During your or your spouse's working lifetime, amounts are taken out monthly from the paycheck as contributions to this old-age, disability, and survivors pension (OASDHI). When you reach 62, if you stop working this government pension starts and you receive it the rest of your life. This government pension goes to the rich as well as the poor. It is considered a right, a social minimum income to live on that the government owes you to compensate for your many working years. You have contributed to it and now it is your due. Medicare for the elderly is also a universal service, a demograt service available to all elderly, rich and poor. It pays most of their hospital bills, and the optional part (for a small fee) pays doctor bills. Since Bismarck's time in Germany some such insurance programs have been in place in industrial countries.

In many European countries major-priority services, such as government pensions, health care, day care, and family allowances, are universal services available to both the rich and the poor, although with the economic recession some means testing is creeping in.

Family or child allowances are one universal service that exists in over sixty countries of the world but not in the United States, although many have argued it should have such a program. If you move to Canada, for example, you will find you get a check from the government each month, giving you so much money per child. The check comes whether you are rich or poor. It was a program adopted in many countries before World War II for a variety of reasons, one being to encourage larger families. The allowance has had little effect on family size but has been a useful mechanism to help large families, one group that is in special need.

Unemployment insurance and workers' compensation are universal programs for specific categories that use contributions that have been made into the program.

In opposition to *universal* services are the so-called *means-tested* services, those using a selective system of allocation. Historically, the term opposed to universality as an approach to provision, has been *selectivity*, which has implied a means-tested service. For example, Blaug (1968) says, "Selectivity . . . is the principle that social benefits should be distributed in relation to needs, needs being revealed by some form of income assessment or means test" (p. 1). Gilbert and Specht's definition (1974) of "selectivity" is that it "denotes the idea of benefits made available on the basis of individual need, determined by a means test" (p. 55). Kahn (1973) defines "selectivity" as a system whereby people become eligible for services only if they are below a specified income—that is, meet a means test. However, Titmuss (1969) broadens the word "selectivity" to cover selective services not requiring a means test.*

Historically, means-tested selectivity services have been the dominant type, from the British poor law days of the 1600s onward. In means-tested services, one must prove poverty to be eligible. Those seeking assistance must list their assets on an application to allow the agency personnel to judge whether they are poor enough to qualify for the program. Different programs have different means tests, and so one person's assets may be too high to qualify for public welfare (AFDC) but not for the food-stamp program. Applicants for one program may have to include their children's income as assets while those applying for another do not. The basic premise in means-tested selectivity services is that they are for the poor. It is related to the residual concept of social welfare services, under which the poor are temporarily helped until they are able to muster a higher income.

*Reddin of Britain has further complicated the terminology in his book *Universality and Selectivity: Strategies in Social Policy* (1969); he says, "The presence of a means test does little to demonstrate the selective nature." What Titmuss was looking for is a non–means-test type of selectivity, hoping to employ instead a needs test applicable to specific groups or territories. In one essay Titmuss asks, "What particular infrastructure of universalistic services is needed in order to provide a framework of values and opportunity bases within and around which can be developed socially acceptable *selective* services aiming to discriminate positively, with a minimum risk of stigma, in favour of those whose needs are greatest?" This broad definition of selectivity, as Gilbert and Specht point out, really involves the selective allocation of benefits and thus would even include the universal-type program of children's allowance, selective because it goes only to children. Gilbert and Specht (1974) reject this broad use of the term "selectivity." We instead use the term "means-tested selectivity," as Kahn (1973) occasionally does, or "means-tested," in order to make clear our meaning. However, the student should be aware that the term "selectivity" is the one often used.

Gilbert and Specht argue, "Up until now we have used selectivity in the narrow sense to designate only means-tested allocations. Yet, as Titmuss points out, selectivity may be based on differential needs without the requirement of a means test. The dilemma, however, is that once the concept of selectivity is pried loose from strictly economic means-tested considerations, its definition may be expanded to cover innumerable conditions, even some generally interpreted as universalistic, in which case its meaning is dissolved" (p. 66).

Services are given here in terms of individual need instead of going to a whole group, such as *all* families with children. Here only poor families with children qualify, and in fact that is how AFDC, the major public welfare service in the United States, operates.

In the United States we think of our major social programs as means-tested selectivity services for which financial need is the main criterion for assistance, but this is not entirely true, since some programs are not means-tested but universal, for example, Medicare, OASDHI government pensions, workers' compensation, and unemployment insurance. However, AFDC is means-tested, as is aid to those elderly who are too poor to survive on their pension (OASDHI) alone and need more funding under the Supplementary Security Income (SSI) program. Besides these cash programs, we have nonmonetary programs meeting certain specific needs, such as the public housing program and now the Section 8 leased public housing, the food-stamp program, some day care programs, Head Start in some areas, student assistance, and, in some instances, casework assistance and job training, that are means-tested. Usually the means testing consists of allowing one group, such as the elderly, with an income below a certain level to use the program and declaring anyone above that level ineligible, but in some cases a sliding scale is used.

A few programs lie between the universal and the means-tested types, and they represent a case of using selectivity but trying to get around the means test while still helping mainly poor families. They help categories of people considered poor and in need. Some provide a program in a *poor area,* with the assumption that most who will benefit are poor; these include the Model Cities program; urban renewal programs; community health clinics, although in some cases these may require means testing for use; and some parts of the antipoverty program in target areas in the 1960s. (See Table 5-1.)

CATEGORICAL PROGRAMS

Note that the word "categorical" is used in describing some universal programs, such as family allowances and even Medicare. Among means-tested programs, SSI and AFDC could be considered categorical; this means that the program is directed toward a category of people who are in special need and in financially poor circumstances. Of the universal services, it can be said they became universal because there are so many in the category to which they are directed; some would suggest this regarding Medicare, since many elderly have major medical needs and lack the income to cover them.

Categorical assistance may also be given to provide *compensation to a group* that has done special services for society in the past, such as veterans

Table 5-1 Types of Assistance to Those in Need

Universal				Means-tested assistance	
For all	**Categorical (for specific groups)**			**In kind**	**Financial (cash) assistance**
Proposed national health insurance	**Specific contribution required**	**No contribution required**			
		By group	**By area**		
	Social security (OASDHI)	Family allowances	Model cities	Food stamps Medicaid Public housing Some day care programs Head Start	AFDC SSI
	Unemployment insurance	Veterans– GI college assistance	Urban renewal		
	Workers' compensation				

or even elderly, or a group that has been badly treated in the past, such as the American Indians. Some of these groups might fall into the category of *deserving* poor, whom the society is willing to help and to give fairly high benefits without means testing; this is the case for veterans and elderly. The society may consider other groups undeserving, such as single males out of work and some alcoholics, and these groups are given little help, often put on the low-paying county general assistance only after stringent means testing and the demand that they appear repeatedly at employment offices. AFDC mothers in the early days of the program, when they were mainly widows, and their children were considered the deserving poor, but as the group changed to consist more and more of young female heads of household divorced or deserted by husbands, often women from minority groups and, in some cases, deviating from middle-class morals (or at least rumored to do so), the AFDC group lost public support as a categorical group and was considered undeserving poor.

One problem in dividing those in need into categorical groups is that some people fall between groups; for example, older but nonelderly women without children must apply for the stringent means-tested general assistance doled out meagerly by county governments to those eligible for no federal programs.

NEED AS AN ELIGIBILITY CRITERION

Some services, of course, neither are offered to the whole population or a particular demograt or category nor are means-tested. In this case the criterion is *need* but not financial need. Thus, in Britain after the war, council (public) housing was offered to citizens on the basis of *housing need,* as judged by a complex application form, and on the basis of time spent on the waiting list and living in the community. In Holland, applications for places in homes for the aged now is judged in terms of *health need* by a local criteria board (after being admitted a person may also apply for financial assistance to live there, as 80 percent do, but financial status does not affect eligibility for admittance to the home).

Need as Determined by Diagnostic Testing

The criteria for eligibility for some services require diagnostic testing. For example, blindness as a criterion requires determining whether a person's sight is impaired to the point where he or she is classified as blind; optometrists' tests provide the necessary diagnosis.

ADVANTAGES OF UNIVERSAL SERVICES AND MEANS-TESTED SERVICES

Many societies offer a mix of universal and means-tested types of services and even some in-between types. Certain services, such as strictly financial assistance, will often be means-tested while others, such as public education, in most societies will not. Some services justify one approach more than the other. Yet for many services there is a question whether they should be universal or just for the poor. Let us look at the arguments both sides use.

To many social reformers, including the early ones in Britain who wanted to change the poor law system, a universal service has been seen as one leading to social justice and equality of opportunity, as a democratic kind of service. The same service will be used by all as a right guaranteed them by the state. The poor are not to be segregated. Provision of the service is through a long-term, accepted institution.

These reformers have felt that where *means-tested* services exist they segregate the society into the haves and the have-nots, the givers and the receivers, the second of each pair being looked at as "charity cases." The reformers, first of all, have seen the provision of *universal* services as a function that helps to keep an industrial society going. Universal services are seen as a social investment. Second, the provision of such universal services as a national health service takes certain vital functions out of the marketplace, functions some considered unsuited to the marketplace.

Reformers also thought that many needing services would not seek help if the services were means-tested, simply because if they accepted help, they would be looked at as charity cases. Many abhorred the stigma or negative labeling that went with a means-tested service: both in applying and in using the service one could feel like a beggar, a person of no consequence, who could be told by the social worker how to live and how not to live. That is the position of a welfare recipient in the United States. Such a person is considered a second-class citizen, to be denied rental units by many landlords, to be denied credit by stores and banks, and to have one's children ridiculed in school. Similarly, being on a means-tested free school-lunch program might mean a child has to stand in a separate lunch line, to be negatively labeled, to be set apart.

Another objection reformers have had to means testing is that if a service is means-tested some will not apply because they feel they won't be eligible; some, in fact, may not be eligible for a means-tested program simply because they are slightly above the very low poverty level for that service. The reformers have felt it is better to have some use the service who do not need it rather than have many *not* use the service who do need it, as is the case with some means-tested services.

Some argue it is too costly to use a means test for a service if very many persons are in the category the service is directed toward. Administrative costs *per recipient* of means-tested services usually run high compared to universal services. For example, in the early 1970s in California it was estimated that 18 percent of the AFDC funds went to administer the AFDC program, while for the national social security OASDHI program administrative expenses equal only about 3 percent of the total benefits.

Proponents of universalism argue that the cost of providing a service to many better-off citizens in a category is mitigated by the fact that better-off persons are actually paying for the service through their taxes. In this situation, all receive benefits from the program, including the poor, while the better-off pay for it indirectly by taxes or a contributory system. Some argue that the fact that middle-class persons are getting benefits means they will be more likely to support the program politically; they are less likely to vote it down or to want it cut back as they might for a program that is seen as a program only for the poor.

A major argument many give for a universal service is that it is a better-quality service. As Titmuss (1971) points out, middle-class people demand quality, while services only for the poor may degenerate into poor service. We have seen this happen with community general hospitals that are used by the poor only.

Last, a universal social service may be able to substitute for a service that employers otherwise need to provide as a fringe benefit, whether it be health insurance, day care, or workers' compensation (of course, the employer does pay for part of these services even when they are government programs). Such a program could be said to be part of the "social wage."

The Social Wage

If social welfare services are thought of as a social wage—that is, if the
state is considered the provider of certain benefits to workers, past,
present, and future, that employers would otherwise have to provide
individually to keep a content and well work force—this may be a
justification for a universal service. In Britain in the last few years
constraints on wages have been justified by the presence of exactly such a
social wage: the worker receives health services and, in many cases,
housing from the state. A good part of the British working class lives in
local-authority–provided council rental housing or new-town housing,
which can be considered a type of social wage. Adams (1978) says, "The
concept of the *social wage* draws attention to the fact that social security,
education, health programs and welfare are as much part of the real
income of working class families as the paycheck." He defines the social
wage as not including all public expenditures but as something that covers
"those costs of labor which take the form of benefits and services provided
by the state and is distinguished from . . . other types of state activity"
(p. 50).

The state's social wage function is to provide real benefits to workers
and their families that improve their standard of living. It can be called a
socializing of the wage system in the sense of taking over from individual
factory owners part of the task for providing for the production and
reproduction of labor. One of the former Labour government's top
ministers, Barbara Castle, explained that workers' standard of living
depends not only on their paycheck but also on the goods and services they
get from the state. Adams (1978) reports that Castle said 60 percent of
public expenditure goes to the social wage.

The author, during several years of research in Britain, noted that
when wage negotiations came up the fact that the government is providing
council housing or new-town housing—and thus that worker housing costs
are very low—is mentioned. In the United States a firm such as General
Motors would have to negotiate with workers and their unions about
helping to pay for such costs as health benefits.

Arguments for Means-Tested Services

There are many arguments put forth for means-tested services and against
universal ones. First, many feel that universal services are too expensive
and that if universal coverage is provided to many who do not need it there
will be money wasted in collecting the taxes to pay for it and in the high
administrative cost of giving the service to so many. The provision of some
universal services may not fit the priorities of the middle class, and so the
middle class will be given services it doesn't need and find itself left without
some it does need. Middle-class persons also may not like the idea that

some things are kept out of the marketplace; they may not like the government monopoly on the service and may prefer competition among suppliers and a free choice of what source they use. For example, some affluent persons in Britain say they want to use private hospitals and have a free choice of doctors. Even on the subject of education we hear middle-class people say they prefer a voucher system under which they have freedom of choice of what kind of school, public or private, they put their children in.

Liberals complain that a universal approach can mean "creaming," whereby middle-class users make more and better use of a service, such as hospitals under a national health insurance plan, and get more of the attention and benefits than the poor. If the service is a scarcity item, as when there are only so many places in a hospital or so many housing units to allocate, the middle class may take places the liberals would like to see go to the poor. For some universal services, such as libraries, community colleges, and mortgage subsidy schemes in housing, the middle class, with more inclination to use the services, may be the main benefactor. As Kahn (1973) says, if one has a universal service one must see that the poor have information about it and access to the service.

Some liberals also argue that in a means-tested service there is little "seepage" of the funds; most of the funds go to the target population in the greatest need and so there is more redistribution than with a universal service.

Some argue that the stigma and disgrace of the means test itself can be avoided by simpler forms, nicer application offices, more courteous staff, and, above all, more confidentiality.

Some actually praise the means test method because it keeps down the number of recipients while a universal service includes users who have only minimal need. These people also argue that total administrative costs are higher under universal services because even though costs *per user* may be low—because there is no eligibility check and instead the user is often simply mailed monthly checks or simply put on the program—the number of users is so high that total administrative costs will be high.

The whole matter may vary from program to program; some programs are so near to being a public utility or an institutional necessity for the functioning of society that they should be of the universal type. Others should be means-tested, since they provide the necessary extra financial help to the very poor, who, even when they have many universal services available, need extra money.

THE CONTRIBUTORY OR INSURANCE SYSTEM

Eligibility can take another form: it can be based on a contribution made to an insurance system, as in OASDHI, the pension system for the elderly and their families and the disabled and blind. The amount one receives is determined partly by the number of quarters in which one has been a contributor to the system, or by what eligibility category one fits into, or by the amount contributed. However, payments are also set by Congress in terms of the cost-of-living index and represent an acceptable minimum standard of living at the time.

Thus, although OASDHI is an insurance plan, the payments are based on *attributed need,* that is, an adequate standard of living for persons and their dependents. As Gilbert and Specht (1974) say, "While the program seeks to some extent to compensate the retired worker for his contributions to the system, it also seeks to provide a level of adequacy for the low-income worker whose contributions were minimal" (p. 73). As Hohaus (1960) explains, "Social insurance aims primarily at providing society with some protection against one or more major hazards which are sufficiently widespread throughout the population and far-reaching in effect to become 'social' in scope and complexion" (p. 61).

Employment Status

One's employment can be a criterion for eligibility. A number of benefits are related to past work status. OASDHI is a pension for workers and their survivors, although it also is for the disabled and blind. Unemployment insurance and workers' compensation are obviously related to a person's work status. So are services like job training.

Work status has opposite effects for different programs; instead of making persons eligible, being employed can make them ineligible or cause problems in their eligibility. For example, in twenty-four states, at this writing, there is no AFDC-UF program, whereby the household can get AFDC (Aid for Families of Dependent Children) if there is an unemployed father in the house; in these states families qualify for AFDC only if the man is absent from the house (this may be changed shortly by Congress).

A proportion of the poor households in the United States are assumed to be working poor; the proportion may be as high as 40 percent. Yet our present major welfare program, AFDC, does not, in most cases, cover them. In the welfare reform bill President Carter proposed in 1978, the working poor would have been eligible for benefits; in some states, such as Mississippi, this would have meant 35 percent of the families would have been covered.

WORK INCENTIVES

Work incentives have been built into the AFDC regulations in recent years to encourage the AFDC mother to work, and they have been included in the Carter plan. The idea of work incentives has been to ensure that the working poor always receive a higher payment than the nonworking poor. With AFDC mothers the way this has been done is to allow the working person to keep a part of her earned income and reduce the welfare payment by less than the amount of the additional income. Thus for each extra dollar the mother earns she can keep a part of it over her past AFDC payment. Of course when her income goes up to a certain amount her family is no longer eligible for welfare, and this often also disqualifies her from such other benefits as Medicaid, the health assistance for the poor paid for by the federal government.

That work status can make the family ineligible for welfare has always been a worry to the AFDC mother who does not understand how work will affect her eligibility status. She worries that if the income from work is great enough to disqualify her for continued payments she may not easily get back on welfare when work gives out, as it often does for unskilled workers. Opton (1971) says:

> Most AFDC mothers do not know with any degree of clarity how much of any earnings they would be allowed to keep, and how much would be deducted from their welfare grants. The complexity of the computations required by welfare regulations make it impossible, for all practical purposes, for anyone but a professional caseworker to estimate the financial consequences of taking a job.

CONCLUSION

A major policy issue concerns who should be eligible for a service deemed necessary. A decision in this area determines who gets what social services. Methods of allocation of services vary. The foremost allocation or eligibility question is, Should the service be available to all (be universal), or should it be for low-income persons (that is, means-tested)? The advantages and disadvantages of each type of allocation have been discussed here. Another question is, Should a service be only for certain categories of citizens, on account of need, to compensate for past services, or for other reasons? Need can be based not only on income but also on the person's health condition or the lack of a scarce good, such as housing. Eligibility can also be based on whether one has contributed into the program or has a certain employment status or is willing to undergo job training or educational improvement. Eligibility can be based not only on individual attributes but instead on living in a certain locale, such as a poor neighborhood or an area slated for urban renewal or a rural community.

All these criteria and more are eligibility questions of major concern to policymakers.

Chapter 6

Types of Provision

INTRODUCTION

A major social policy decision is which of the many forms the provision of assistance takes. The most obvious choice is between *cash* assistance and its equivalent *benefit-in-kind*. A benefit-in-kind is an actual good or service, such as housing or food, rather than the cash to buy food or pay the rent.

One form of provision is *insurance or contributory programs,* whereby persons or their relatives or employers contribute into the system, usually in relation to work. Recipients collect from such programs, usually in monthly payments, at some future date.

An indirect type of cash provision we use in the United States is *tax credits and tax exemptions.* Homeowners receive a tax subsidy; families get a deduction for dependents on their tax returns. These indirect subsidies amount to billions of dollars the federal, and in some cases the state, government would otherwise collect in taxes.

Assistance to the *building* rather than to the *person* is a form of in-kind provision. In the housing subsidy area, the poor have often been provided with housing rather than cash to be used for housing.

Another question is whether to provide funding for *area programs* rather than to individual persons in the area. While programs to benefit areas often take the form of benefits-in-kind, they also lead into another area of discussion: assistance in the form of social services.

Social services, a major category among types of provision, consist of certain kinds of professional assistance, such as counseling, information and referral, recreational programs, training programs, and many others; they are quite distinct from both cash and its benefit-in-kind equivalent. Many professional social workers are oriented toward provision of services. Such provision gives needed assistance to the middle class as well as to the poor. For persons with certain types of problems, counseling is the basic need and not money.

The last type of provision this chapter will cover is of a very different nature: the provision of *opportunities.* Here one is trying to compensate for past discrimination to various minority groups and assure the end of barriers to their participation in the employment and educational areas as well as equal treatment in purchasing or using a variety of goods and services, such as housing and credit facilities. Provision of this type is in the form of such things as affirmative action programs, which may follow from court decisions and legislative action.

CASH PAYMENTS AND BENEFITS-IN-KIND

Advantages of Nonmonetary (In-Kind) Services versus Cash Payments

A major issue in the discussion of how to provide services is whether the state should make a cash payment or whether instead it should provide a benefit-in-kind, such as housing or health services. In other words, the state can give persons checks and tell them to pay for their own health services, or it can provide a benefit-in-kind service, whereby they must go to government-supported hospitals or hospitals where their bills will be paid by the government. In the latter case they never receive cash.

An in-between system is where the person gets a voucher that may be used only to buy a certain good; this system also specifies how the funds will be used. Food stamps can be thought of as a voucher-type service; some suggest we should use a voucher system for education, whereby parents can shop around for the private school they want to use and then pay for the service with their voucher. The certificate obtained under the Section 8 housing program can be thought of as a voucher; here the government says it will pay part of the rent (an amount roughly equal to the difference between the actual rent and 25 percent of the household income) for a unit that meets certain qualifications.

The major argument for cash benefits is that they give the recipient consumers sovereignty and freedom of choice to budget their money according to their own idea of their needs, while benefits-in-kind are a type of social control that greatly inhibits their choice, making them use services and goods the government provides. Many would say that if the poor are to be made independent, to have confidence in themselves, they should be allowed to make expenditures for their families as they see fit, using the monthly payments the government gives them. They should be treated as competent persons who can manage their own funds.

Another reason for giving cash, some would say, is that poor households should not be treated separately as persons who must take what is given to them. Using benefits-in-kind can be stigmatizing, as is standing in a food commodity line. The distributed items may not meet particular persons' needs, as heavy provision of soybean flour, butter, and other surpluses in the food commodity program has not met people's nutritional needs; the poor still need money to supplement their diet. It may be also that the poor family's need is for new clothes while in-kind benefits are given for food commodities and for housing units, which the family may not need as much because it has a standard unit at a cheap rent.

Another reason for cash benefits is that a number of purchases not only are pragmatic choices, involving a decision to deprive oneself of goods in one area to acquire something one needs in another area, but also may be items with a personal meaning that are bought to bring happiness. One may want to skimp on other items to get a daughter a special graduation dress, for example.

The major form of assistance to the poor in the United States is through cash programs, whether means-tested or universal, such as the means-tested AFDC, the universal OASDHI social security pension, and the means-tested SSI supplement for the elderly.

Yet there may be reasons that some services should be benefits-in-kind. Public utility services used by the whole community, such as sewerage and libraries, we assume will be benefits-in-kind. There are other services which under certain conditions the public finds hard to take care of in the marketplace even if given the money to do so. For example, low- and moderate-cost housing could not be produced by the private market in many countries after World War II; the government had to step in and provide it. In some places good-quality modern hospitals have had to be built by the state; private enterprise has not been able to do it. In many areas one cannot buy good school education if a cash payment is given to do so; the expense is too great and the government has to provide it.

As Kahn (1973) says, "The presence of potential consumers, even consumers able to pay fees, is no guarantee that enough schools or hospitals of the required *quality* will be made available. The technical adequacy of a parental budget does not assure that their children will purchase nutritious school lunches. By creating a benefit-in-kind, some level of standards and some degree of sufficiency of supply, say of low cost housing, might be assured; access might be improved" (p. 96). In addition, as Kahn says, the program may be organized to achieve integration of population elements and lack of divisiveness (for example, if *all* children eat in the school lunch program).

Nursing home care represents a service we have left to private entrepreneurs in the United States, and the result is, in many areas, that there are waiting lists, so that many cannot get in regardless of income; the elderly poor on Medicaid, especially, find the doors closed to them in many nursing homes. There is also the problem of finding a high-standard nursing home, regardless of income. This is clearly an area where the state should intervene and provide an in-kind service (instead it simply pays the cost for a number of patients through Medicaid and Medicare subsidy).

Another reason the cash payment may not provide a good-quality service is that the consumer has some trait, such as being from a minority or being a female head of a household, that makes it hard to get a commodity, as happens sometimes on the open housing market. Access may be closed to such a person. A benefit-in-kind would be nondiscriminatory.

Some say that giving clients cash may allow them consumer freedom but they may not be knowledgeable enough to use it wisely. Their choices of expenditures may be influenced by advertising; their low status and lack of education may subject them to fraud or misrepresentation, as well as high cost and high interest rates, at furniture stores, local grocery stores, and automobile salesrooms. Last, their choice of purchases may give them individual satisfaction but be against the public good. The major argument conservatives give for benefits-in-kind is that the benefits go for what they are intended. The funds are spent more effectively because they hit the targets for which they were meant, whether housing, health care, or day care. The conservative does not trust the poor to spend their cash allotment on the expenditures the conservative feels are the essential ones. Thus the conservative prefers benefits-in-kind because they offer better assurance of where the money is going.

In political terms, there may be some advantage to having some services given as benefits-in-kind, simply because the conservative bloc will sometimes, though not always, vote for services in this form while they most likely would not for cash payments. Therefore, the separate benefits-in-kind program is a way of getting conservative support for a higher level of help to the poor. Also, certain business lobbies may support specific benefits-in-kind because they will receive business from it, as the National Home Builders Association does from subsidized housing.

Certain benefits-in-kind are also more likely to be utilized by those citizens who will not take cash benefits because they consider the latter too stigmatizing, thinking they label them as welfare cases.

Some benefits-in-kind, especially universal ones, but even some means-tested ones, have the advantage of mixing the poor with the better-off groups. Some moderate-income housing programs have been able to do this; they have been able to site housing projects in middle-class or better working-class areas. On the other hand, a major criticism of the conventional public housing program is that it does just the opposite—lumps the poor together in many cases in the worst slum—and therefore a housing allowance or Section 8 leased housing, whereby the poor receive financial help to pay the rent in private units, is better. If the benefit-in-kind provision is a hospital, this again may lump all the poor together, as in a general hospital.

Thus, one comes back to the advantages of a cash payment over benefits-in-kind assistance in the American setting, where in-kind services are usually only for the poor. It would seem that only for the provision of certain services, such as health care or housing, should a benefit-in-kind service be used, and even then the in-between type, the voucher system, seems best.

Insurance Programs (Contributory Systems)

Insurance, or contributory, programs are a type of provision where recipients or their families or their employers have paid into the program in the past, often in relation to employment. The best example is the OASDHI program, under which workers and their employers pay in over the years. Under this program, when workers retire they collect social security; when a male worker dies his widow and children collect; and when a worker becomes disabled or blind he or she is eligible for an OASDHI payment. Since payment is based on past contributions, many people feel they have a right to collect this insurance. Their families, if collecting it as survivors, may likewise see it as the same type of benefit as a normal insurance policy, since the recipient's spouse or parent paid into it. Rich and poor alike collect payments.

Other insurance programs include unemployment insurance and workers' compensation. In both programs, employers must pay into the program for each worker and workers collect when they qualify according to criteria set down by the federal government.

Part B of the Medicare program for the elderly, the voluntary part of this universal medical assistance program, is a contributory program, whereby the elderly pay so much each month for coverage of doctors' fees.

Tax Credits and Exemptions

Tax credits and tax exemptions are an indirect type of cash provision of help. One major part is the tax exemption of $1000 of income per child a parent can claim in filling out the federal income tax form. Schorr (*Poor Kids*, 1966) has seen this as a type of children's allowance; he himself has favored a regular children's allowance, like the ones that exist in Canada and northern European countries, over the present American system of tax exemption for each dependent. Some feel this per child tax exemption favors the wealthy, who can make better use of it; the large poor families in need of help just because they are poor do not benefit from a tax write-off on income they do not have.

Other areas where tax deductions or credits are used are housing and day care. The American middle-class home-owning household receives substantial housing subsidies from the federal government each year in tax deductions; the household is allowed to deduct on the federal income tax form all interest on the house mortgage, as well as the property tax.

Working families with children in day care can deduct this cost from their gross income before calculating taxable income.

Why does one call the tax exemption provisions of the federal government social service assistance? It is because the federal government is giving certain taxpayers an indirect subsidy, i.e., a $1000 exemption from taxable income for each dependent child. The government is allowing these groups to retain billions of dollars it would otherwise receive in taxes. In regard to tax deductions and credits for homeowners, Aaron (1972) calculates that "homeowners paid $7 billion less in taxes in 1966 than they would have if they had been governed by the rules applicable to investors in other assets. This amount is 16.7 percent of the $42 billion collected from homeowners under the personal income tax in 1966" (p. 55). Thus one can say that tax credits and deductions are indeed an indirect subsidy.

Assistance to the Building

Assistance to the *building* versus assistance to the *person* is one area of choice between cash and benefits-in-kind. Here the question is whether to provide housing per se, that is, to build either conventional public housing or Section 236 nonprofit housing at below-market interest rates, or to give a housing allowance to the household and let the household find its own housing. The latter could be said to be a type of *voucher* or certificate.

Assistance to the Area

Another debate is whether to assist the *person* or to assist the *area*. In the Model Cities Program and in the CAP part of the OEO poverty program, much assistance went to programs to improve the area, such as better playgrounds and community facilities. Assistance under these programs also went for *services,* on a non–means-tested basis, to all people in the area. This leads to a major question, whether assistance should be given in the form of *social services* or as either cash or the in-kind equivalent of cash.

SOCIAL SERVICES

The *social services* take a variety of forms: casework or group counseling, personnel training, recreational programs, physical therapy, and information and referral assistance. Kahn (1973) gives a list including practical, general social services, such as day care; therapeutic or guidance services, such as child treatment services; social services related to information and referral; and general social services at the boundary of other service systems, such as school classes for disturbed children.

A shared attribute of these services is that instead of giving a cash benefit or an in-kind equivalent, the program is providing some type of professional assistance to the person, whether it be a caseworker, a job trainer, or a day care teacher who is providing it. Romanyshyn (1971) says that "social services . . . are essentially people-changing institutions designed to equip individuals with the competence and resources essential for effective social participation or to control those whose participation is defined as a threat to society" (p. 52).

Some social policy experts criticize social work personnel for placing too much emphasis on services, especially on casework services, and too much focus on rehabilitating people to fit into society. In welfare reform circles, Morris (1973) says, "The narrower usage of the term . . . 'social services' . . . deals with the question: what should be done to handle the problems of social and personal disorganization that are believed to create the economic dependence and thus call into being much of this public income maintenance program" (p. 516). Many social policy experts feel such emphasis on rehabilitation distracts from giving the poor what they really need first of all: money.

Social policy experts have an even stronger criticism of the services orientation, saying it leads social workers away from the basic need to change the institutions of society to work better for the citizens.

Romanyshyn (1971) says some critics see "social work as a fixation on individual casework and therapy to the neglect of social reform" (p. 57). This gets us beyond the issue of the type of provision, services or cash, to a larger issue of changing the basic institutions in society, such as the economic system, rather than giving a certain type of help to those who are the victims of the present problems of institutional functioning, such as unemployment. Since social policy analysts are by nature change-oriented and reformist while those in the social work–therapy position have a more status quo or "adjustment" philosophy, as Titmuss (1969), Katz (1978), and Galper (1975) point out, social policy personnel are more likely to be interested in making adjustments and changes in institutions *themselves,* not just assisting the victim: they worry that those professionals providing social services are "blaming the victim," are concentrating on individual pathology and ignoring either (1) the victim's immediate need, money, or (2) the more long-run need, changes in society's institutions to give employment or other essentials.

However, one should not disregard services on these grounds; one can argue that many people do need counseling, information and referral services, recreational programs, and many other services. One can say even for a number of middle-class persons in our society that there is a major need for counseling, information and referral, recreational, and a variety of other services. These people can often afford to pay some part of the cost of the service but do not find the services available on the private market. Whether it be an information and referral center for the elderly, a single parent program of the Family Service Agency, a homemaker service, or child abuse assistance through Parental Stress, the program provides a useful service that money alone often cannot buy.

Human Investment

Some services may have an *investment* goal. Thus manpower training may be seen as an investment that salvages certain unskilled from the unemployment ranks and makes them more of an asset to industry. Educational services in general can be seen as an investment for our economy. Kahn (1973) points out that historically "many of the pioneering settlement [house] leaders spoke of the services as facilitating more rapid Americanization, promoting community adjustment and harmony, encouraging self-support, and decreasing deviance." He also says, "Many of the proponents of stronger social service programs began in the 1950s and the 1960s to talk of investment in human resources, and they advocated social service programs as good development strategy" (p. 96).

Kahn does point out that a social policymaker must be careful in using the criterion of whether this service or that is a "better" investment, a market question. The investment criterion, if carried too far, may mean less emphasis is given to programs where the investment payoff is low, such as services to the elderly in nursing homes. Also, stressing the investment payoff, while it may increase public support for a program, may mean the public will look for a large, tangible payoff, something that might be hard to document, for example, in the case of service provision to AFDC mothers. In working with this investment criterion, as Kahn says, the investment notion should not be "tied only to narrowly conceived productivity payoffs."

The provision of services, especially casework and group work services, has in recent times, especially in the early 1970s, lost some public support, although it regained some in the mid-1970s. Many think this decreasing support was partly due to the difficulty researchers have documenting that social services actually help people in the ways they ideally are meant to. For example, Fischer (1973) reviewed eleven controlled studies and concluded that social casework services, which he broadly defined as services provided by professional caseworkers, yielded no greater improvement among a variety of client populations than did no intervention at all. Berger and Pillavin (1976) later reviewed one of the studies, that of casework to the elderly, did research, and came to a slightly more positive conclusion.

One major reason social services were criticized in the late 1960s and early 1970s was that they were not making people economically independent, a goal assigned them by Congressional policymakers. As Mildred Rein (1975) reports for AFDC services provision, "From 1956 to 1967 the competing goal of strengthening family life gave primary importance to rehabilitating the AFDC family, a process that, it was hoped, would lead to economic independence" (p. 515). Social services were seen by Congress in the early 1960s as a means to prevent and reduce dependency; in the 1956 amendments and in the 1962 amendments to the Social Security Act, approval was given for the first time to the states for reimbursements for social services. Reports at this time, such as the Wyman study, pictured AFDC recipients with incapacitating disabilities who could be helped in many instances by casework counseling to move to self-sufficiency. As Mildred Rein says, "The professionals were instrumental in the formulation and passage of both the 1956 and 1962 amendments. They believed that public assistance recipients did not work because their personal competence needed to be increased; they were temperamentally and intellectually incapable of adjustments to the demands of our complex society" (1975, p. 516). Rein adds that the goal was rehabilitation and the method, casework; Congress accepted this policy as a means to encourage economic independence and so to constrain the AFDC caseload.

Thus the casework services had the goal of creating economic independence; in other words, their primary task was to get welfare recipients off the welfare rolls. By 1967 it was evident that these services were not doing that particular job; AFDC rolls were dramatically increasing, not decreasing. Therefore Congress in the 1967 amendments tried to move to strictly work-oriented services. As Rein (1975) says, "With the passage of the 1967 amendments, work for the family heads became a dominant objective to be achieved by direct work-related social services. . . ." She later adds, "Personal competence, which was the aim in 1962, now [in 1967] became skills competence and was to lead less circuitously to work" (pp. 515, 517).

Morris (1973) asks lamentingly whether services in an American society set up in the present way can ever bring welfare recipients to this goal set for them of self-support or a job, and whether one should use this narrow goal to judge whether these services are useful or dysfunctional in our society. He says for example, that it is doubtful that "reorganization [of services] will work well as long as the avowed purpose is to accomplish things that these services cannot possibly accomplish . . ." (p. 516). The inconsistency of purpose lies in regarding *economic independence* and *functional competence* as the same thing, Morris says; he adds, "In fact, it is possible to be functionally competent and economically dependent."

In the section of Chapter 8 on AFDC mothers this very fact will be pointed out. Morris is saying that services can help people with their emotional problems or assist them in moving from deviant to nondeviant behavior or aid them in coping with being handicapped or in raising their children in a variety of ways, but services may not be able to give them jobs in a society that has too few. Morris (1973) states:

> If jobs are the desired end, it is clear that none of the services now being offered . . . can produce jobs for workers with few skills; there are no extensive day-care programs for children of working mothers at a cost comparable to the mothers' own care at home; counseling and therapy do not help the mental patient nor the ex-convict overcome community prejudice against hiring; physical rehabilitation does not reduce the reluctance of industry to accommodate to the requirements of the severely handicapped; neither job referral nor counseling has significantly affected motivation when suitable jobs are not available. [P. 516]

Many in Congress and HEW have themselves, in reality, even after the 1967 amendment, looked toward social services to fill functions other than relieving economic dependency. Mildred Rein (1975) documents that there was an opposing professional group fighting for social services to strengthen family life and to keep families intact through supportive, substitutive, and supplementary services. In looking at services offered from 1967 on and the groups to whom they were offered, she concludes there was actually a social service explosion. She says the laws of the early 1970s allowed open-ended funding, loosely defined services, permission to purchase services from other agencies, and a broad clientele including former and potential welfare recipients who could be eligible on a "group" basis. She also points out that the 1974 amendment changed the goal for services from the narrow 1967 one of eliminating economic dependency; the 1974 goals extended beyond those of self-support and expanded eligibility to the middle-income population, created a structure for infinite kinds of services, set up exacting child care standards, and made possible the public support of private agencies. She adds that "the 1974 amendment appeared to be a step on the road to universal social services, to broad coverage of several income classes regardless of need." At the end of the 1970s, one sees an increasing variety of social services offered to different groups, without a means-test, with services offered under Title XX of the Social Security Act.

PROVISION OF OPPORTUNITIES

Provision of opportunities deviates considerably from the types of provisions mentioned above. A person is not given cash, an in-kind benefit, a voucher, or a tax credit; nor does the recipient get a traditional type of service, such as counseling. Instead, the effort is a civil rights one to ensure in various ways that a minority person, whether someone from a mistreated racial or ethnic group, a woman, or a gay person, or a member of such deviant groups as ex-convicts and ex-mental patients, has the *opportunity* to use available programs and services. In other words, here the emphasis is making sure that these groups are not denied opportunities because of their minority status.

The provision of opportunities may be enforced through a civil rights commission, an affirmative action division, a fair housing group, or a legislative action or court decision. The opportunities themselves may consist of:

- Positive action to open more positions to minorities in employment, in medical schools, or in other professional schools
- Such specific measures as quotas, a type of measure tested in the Supreme Court in *Bakke* in regard to medical school entry (see Chapter 13)
- Busing children from one school to another to achieve racial balance in a school district
- Opening up equal credit opportunities for women

Opportunity provision can also take the form of offering greater access to services by establishing or strengthening agencies or community groups that have the prime job of providing information and advice on services, usually on a neighborhood basis; providing advocacy services, as the welfare rights groups have done; providing a complaint machinery, as Ralph Nader's consumer groups do; or providing legal services to open up opportunities, as Legal Aid centers have done.

As was mentioned in Chapter 4 under "Equal Opportunity," opportunities are not the same as redistribution of income. They open up greater *chances* for personal mobility, for example, through greater availability of higher education or of beginning-level jobs, to groups who have been discriminated against. However, providing opportunities does not ensure that the majority in the discriminated group will have a more equal share of the country's assets. Certainly, when one notes that over the last twenty years the black male has continued to have an average family household income less than half that of white family incomes, one can say that the legislation, court orders, civil rights commissions, and the like that supposedly have provided greater opportunity for the black population in the last ten years have had limited effect.

CONCLUSION

Different types of provision have been covered in this chapter. The major kinds of material provision are cash, benefits-in-kind, and the in-between voucher system. Opposed to these is provision of social services. Each fits certain needs and situations and has certain disadvantages. Minor variations on these types are tax deductions and credits, insurance, assistance to the building rather than the person, and help to the area rather than the individual. A still different type of provision is that of providing opportunities or access to present programs.

Policies on Structuring and Staffing the Delivery System

Chapter 7

Policies on Structuring and Staffing the Delivery System

INTRODUCTION

An issue to be resolved in providing for those with social service needs is how the community is to deliver these services to them. The primary question concerns the structure of the service organization. Should it be a nonprofit voluntary agency or a public agency? Should delivery be through a multiservice agency that meets many of the varied needs of the clients, or should there be a number of specialized agencies?

Related questions concern the coordination of services in the community. How much duplication of services should be allowed, and, on the other hand, how should the gaps in providing service be filled? These issues are also related to the question of how the community makes service delivery efficient and effective.

Another question concerning delivery of services is on accessibility of the services. Should there be a special information bureau and should agencies broaden their means of reaching those in need? How can the agencies cut down on the red tape and other bureaucratic barriers to reaching quickly those in immediate need?

Another major aspect of delivery of services is staffing. Should the staff consist mainly of professionally trained people, or should there be more room for persons with only a bachelor's degree or for paraprofessionals? In what ways do professionally trained personnel have trouble in practice filling such roles as probation officers and welfare eligibility workers? Are they trained in such a way that it is hard for them to meet the less therapeutically oriented demands of the bureaucracy and the public?

The whole issue of citizen participation in delivery of services is an important one. In what ways should the clients themselves take part in the provision of services? In some cases they work in the agency as paraprofessionals and in others they are on the board of the agency. An example of these delivery issues is the following:

> An alcoholic drying out and rehabilitation program was run by nonprofit agency X. Some federal funding came through, but under the terms of that funding the agency had to serve all those who at one time would have been put in the local jail. Then the county started its own rehabilitation program, with the aid of federal funds. It made few referrals to agency X. Now there was a duplication of service. At the recommendation of the local Community Chest the two programs got together and planned how to divide the work and the clientele. This coordination effort was lauded.
>
> Staffing of agency X was also a problem. The local Alcoholics Anonymous group felt that some of its leaders should be employed as paraprofessionals in agency X's rehabilitation program. Second, it felt that one of its members, as an ex-alcoholic, should be on the agency's board to represent the users of the service. It also felt that agency X should have more of an outreach program, since at present it was accessible mainly to the middle class. AA suggested that one worker be stationed in an office in the local multi–social service agency center, which housed a welfare office, a social security office, a health office, and a senior citizens' program, since some of the users of these services had an alcoholic problem.

This example illustrates several of the problems in delivering services.

VOLUNTARY AGENCIES VERSUS PUBLIC AGENCIES

A major social policy question is whether to use nonprofit voluntary agencies or public agencies to provide services. Even federally funded programs can be carried out by nonprofit voluntary agencies; in one study, for example, it was found that over 70 percent of the voluntary agencies in an area received some federal funding.

When one speaks of nonprofit voluntary agencies one thinks first of those affiliated with the Community Chest, United Crusade, or United Way, whatever the coordinated fund raising body is called in a particular community. Some of those so affiliated that are known nationwide are the Family Service Agency, the Children's Home Society, the American Red Cross, the Salvation Army, the Catholic Charities, the Urban League, and the YWCA and YMCA, to name only a few. However, there are also newer, more unstructured, and sometimes nonconformist, small agencies, as well as some minority organizations, that may not belong to the Community Chest.

History of the Role of Voluntary Agencies

Before discussing the issue of whether to depend on such voluntary agencies for new social programs, it might be useful to examine the role of nonprofit voluntary agencies in American history. Assistance to the poor and other groups in need was to a large degree carried on by charitable voluntary agencies up to the 1930s, when the Depression caused the federal government to take the leading role by introducing national social insurance and public welfare programs. Americans had a laissez faire attitude that saw government intervention in a negative light, especially in regard to social welfare needs.

Although local governments, following the example of the poor law methods in England, did grudgingly provide some help (usually with a stigma attached) to those they called "paupers," mainly through the ill-suited almshouse, much work was left to local charities. After the Civil War these charities greatly increased in number and type as the great period of American industrialization, urbanization, and immigrant influx brought increasing needs. Such groups as the New York Association for Improving the Condition of the Poor arose.

In many cities a Charity Organization Society (COS), based on the British one, was organized by lay leaders, the earliest one being established in 1877. Such groups at first used volunteers, gave advice through friendly visiting, and after social investigation frugally gave out funds to the poor considered deserving and in need. Individual help rather than financial aid was stressed; recipients were considered to have fallen on hard times due to their own misdeeds. Settlement houses, such as Jane Adams's Hull House in Chicago (1889), were organized to meet many of the needs of slum dwellers, from education to day camps, nursery schools, and social clubs.

Specialized agencies, such as the early orphanages and the Children's Aid Society of New York, sprang up just before the Civil War to deal with abandoned children of the tenements. Other agencies dealt with the aged, with widows, with the deaf, and so on. The NAACP came into being to deal with the problems of blacks.

Many of these agencies were small, operating in just one community and often duplicating each other's efforts without any coordination. Some were run by church groups. Some seemed to exist mainly to glorify the "lady bountifuls" from the upper class on their boards. Most of these nineteenth-century organizations were paternalistic in their approach, considering the poor a class apart, individuals who should be guided by their betters.

There was a growing feeling these charitable agencies should be directed, and in Massachusetts in 1863 the Board of State Charities was formed, followed by similar boards in many states. Voluntary agencies today are usually controlled by the state and also accredited by their own national professional group, such as the CWLA (Child Welfare League of America), and their local Community Chest. Such national coordinating associations sprang up as early as the 1870s; an early one was the National Conference of Charities and Corrections.

The national government slowly started to provide social services and share some responsibility with charitable organizations, even though the philosophy of the federal government up to 1935 was that providing social services was not its job. For example, Dorothea Dix, crusading on mental illness, was unable to get some states to act but got Congress in 1854 to give land for institutions for the care of the deaf and mentally ill, only to have President Pierce veto it on the ground that charitable activities were not specially delegated to the federal government and therefore were reserved to the states. Even in the early Depression years President Hoover still could preach this philosophy, saying, "It is a question of the best method by which hunger and cold shall be prevented. It is a question of whether the American people will maintain the spirit of charity and mutual self-help through voluntary giving and the responsibility of local government, as distinguished from appropriations from the Federal Treasury."

Yet the federal government did at an early point provide certain minor benefits to Indians and to veterans, with a national pension system for physically and mentally disabled veterans by 1833, and in 1908 the Congress passed a limited Workmen's Compensation Act.

States were also gradually taking on more responsibility; Ohio and Illinois by the early 1900s had statewide aid to the needy blind, soon followed by other states. Various states enacted laws providing pensions for the aged, although in some states these laws were knocked down by the courts as unconstitutional. Most states in this period also added legislation on assistance or pensions to widows with children or deserted mothers. However, as Smith and Zietz (1970) state, "In this movement toward government intervention on behalf of the citizens, the United States proceeded at a much slower pace than the industrial nations of Europe, . . . making piecemeal attempts to come to grips with the new society" (p. 54).

The shockwaves of the massive poverty of the Depression changed this situation. With thousands of people on breadlines, many families poverty-stricken, and millions unemployed, the charitable organizations could not handle the situation. Their focus on individual help and on friendly visitor counseling to rehabilitate the wayward poor person did not fit the needs of the 1930s. Massive financial assistance (in the millions of dollars), work programs, and the like were called for, and the government finally stepped in to provide social insurance and other programs.

The Voluntary Agency Today

The great increase in government involvement does not mean that voluntary agencies died away. They increasingly left cash and material assistance to public agencies and concentrated even more on their early concern of providing services to individuals and families. Thus we still have settlement houses, family service agencies, child welfare agencies, services for the aged, church-based social services, and institutions caring for many categories of people, including emotionally disturbed children, unwed mothers, the mentally retarded, the blind, the aged, and the mentally ill. In addition, there are agencies dealing with such deviants as the delinquent, the alcoholic, the drug user, and the ex-convict, and other organizations devoted to improving the situation of minorities and new immigrants and providing access services and legal aid to the poor. In addition, there is a whole array of recreational and educational programs, from the YM-YWCA, the Girl Scouts, and the Big Brothers to day care and camping programs.

A number of these agencies are not wholly outside government; they often receive government funding, either as a contractual payment per case or as a block grant for some particular activity or some experimental program, whether from the county social service department or from a federal agency. For example, counties pay private agencies for the care of emotionally disturbed children. Kahn (1973) reports that public funds are increasingly expended through nonstatutory or semipublic programs and that "of $1.6 billion for social services under the Social Security Act of 1972, one-third was for purchase through the voluntary sector or other public programs" (p. 41).

In the late 1970s the 2300 or more community fund raising bodies—the United Funds and Community Chests—for the volunteer agencies raised over $1 billion a year, according to *Giving U.S.A.* Thus, while acknowledging these voluntary agencies' much weaker financial position today in contrast to government expenditures, one still must realize they are a major provider of services.

Coordination: Fund Raising, Troubleshooting, and Planning

The community fund-raising bodies were established to provide an alternative to separate fund raising by individual agencies, which caused not only annoyance and confusion to the potential donors in the community but also expensive duplication of fund raising efforts. A single drive, usually for a whole region and its agencies, enhanced the opportunity for an appeal to ordinary workers through their employers and assured them that there was efficient planning and budgeting of "approved" services backed by the stamp of community leadership. However, traditional agencies still have a separate fund raising event of their own.

The community funding body has been a centralized policymaking power in the voluntary sector of the community, since it budgets out funds not only in accord with agency budget requests but sometimes according to priorities it sees itself, as the author knows from working with such a body. The community leaders on its committee, usually middle-level members of the local power elite who represent the community's main businesses, often have a conservative view of social welfare and are inclined to support the more traditional and sometimes more middle-class–oriented social agencies, those espousing traditional social policies. The innovative organization, the new street-corner agency, the less formalized group using paraprofessional staff and possibly serving deviants, may find it hard to be included in the list of funded organizations or to receive substantial funding. In recent years, however, as a result of protests against the prevailing funding practices of community fund raising bodies, especially on the West Coast, such groups have been more likely to be included among the funded organizations.

Closely allied to the fund-raising agencies but now often a separate agency are the community welfare planning councils or welfare federations, which bring together social welfare agencies and often welfare and health agencies. These policymaking coordinating bodies have a research and planning staff. They not only call meetings to bring together agencies in similar work, recruiting their professionals and lay leaders for joint consultation, but in many ways also act as the social policy instigator, the community planner for these voluntary agencies. They gather statistics on unmet needs and on the amount and type of service given by agencies, as the author once did. They try to detect gaps and duplications in service and take on many of the jobs mentioned in Chapter 1. They promote public understanding, and channel lay expressions of concern and need back to agencies; they often include an information and referral office. From all this work they may help plot out community priorities for funding and recommend them through budgeting decisions passed on to their close affiliate, the Community Chest or United Way fund-raising source.

Another factor that sometimes leads organizations to change their focus in accordance with unmet needs is consultation with their own national coordinating body—the CWLA or Planned Parenthood or the national Girl Scouts organization. The national organization may provide direction for its affiliates to shift to a new role on account of need or the takeover of the old role by a government body. For example, the Family Service Agency (FSA), with its many local affiliates, lost interest in providing income relief to the poor after the 1935 Social Security Act pushed the federal government into that role. It then centered on family casework services, mostly requiring the one-to-one relationship of a highly trained social worker to a client individual or family. By the mid-1960s the FSA was again reassessing its role. First, it had been criticized as an elitist organization dealing mainly with middle-class problems; some pointed out that because of its reliance on the casework approach, the poor, less able to verbalize and more concerned about money than about middle-class family problems, were not its main clientele. The FSA started to move into community organization work for neighborhood improvement; it started to seek out ways to work in slum neighborhoods rather than have clients come to it. Some of the member agencies moved more into social advocacy. Their staffs and their boards began to include minorities. In the 1970s, faced with changes in the family, they again innovated, introducing divorce counseling and programs for single parents.

Advantages and Disadvantages of Voluntary Agencies

The example of the history of the FSA leads to the question of the advantages and disadvantages of running programs through voluntary agencies. The most frequently cited advantage of these agencies is that they can be more innovative and experimental than the large, public bureaucracies, which are usually dependent on political support. They can more easily change with the times and the needs, because of both their smaller size and, in some cases, their more informal structure. New agencies can arise as new needs appear or alternative approaches to handling needs seem more appropriate, as we have seen recently with alternative programs for delinquents and drug abusers. They can be in the vanguard of new causes, such as assistance to homosexuals or battered wives or abused children, taking on these needs long before government agencies are established to deal with them. In other cases they can highlight a problem. Some of these agencies may fill gaps in government provision; for example, to the older divorced woman who does not qualify for AFDC and may have trouble getting the county's general assistance.

Many of these new programs and less orthodox agencies start from the efforts of volunteer lay staff and of those who have had the problem themselves. At most, they may move on to a stage where they can afford paraprofessional staff, including those employed under the Comprehensive Employment and Training Act (CETA). Thus, this type of voluntary program harnesses the talents of eager volunteers and paraprofessionals to address an urgent social need, something the government bureaucracy usually cannot do. These agencies also offer a place for concerned citizens, whether idealistic students or service-oriented housewives, to provide service to the community; for the student they also offer the first step in a career of social service; to the ex-alcoholic, ex-addict, or ex-convict, they give a chance to help others.

All this, however, should not be taken to mean that all voluntary agencies are staffed by paraprofessionals and volunteers. On the contrary, the older traditional agencies, such as the Children's Home Society, the Family Service Agency, and the American Red Cross, are likely to have some of the best-trained social workers in the community. First, these agencies have had the long-time tradition of requiring more training, including an M.S.W. degree, than such public agencies as the welfare department, although this contrast is decreasing. Second, these agencies are known for having highly skilled caseworkers, including psychiatric social workers. In fact, for this reason some say that private agencies should provide casework services while public agencies provide cash or income maintenance.

Another advantage of voluntary agencies is that they are often community-based and that even when they are an affiliate of a national organization, such as the Family Service Agency, they have a local board they must respond to. This means they are more in tune with local needs and are shaped to their own community's situation. One could say that private agencies are humanitarian while public ones stick to regulations. Added to this is the feeling that private agencies can better respond to urgent emergency needs, the way the Salvation Army commonly does with its help to destitute persons.

The more traditional agencies—those funded by United Crusade or United Way or whatever—are also backed by the local power elite, who are often members of their board, which can increase the communication with local political forces and elicit more community support and understanding, although often this greater communication also ties them to this power elite's more conservative view of the poor and deviant groups and its policies to deal with them.

A number of voluntary agencies meet the needs of the middle class more than those of the poor, either because of their casework approach, as mentioned for the Family Service Agency, or because of the type of service they offer, as in the case of the Girl Scouts; many are trying to broaden their constituency to include the poor and minorities through advocacy and the restructuring of their approach. Is there a social policy advantage to having these voluntary agencies that serve the nonpoor, often charging them on a sliding scale? Certainly there are many services the middle class needs, such as family counseling and services to the elderly; often they are barred by the means test from receiving them from public agencies, or they may be turned away by the stigma attached to public programs. However, a further question would be, Is it not better to provide *one* nonstigmatic *universal* program for all, charging on a sliding scale, than to provide one for the middle class and one for the poor?

Another reason for providing voluntary services, some would say, is that they offer a choice. Today, as federal national health insurance measures are proposed, we hear this reasoning regarding this type of service.

Government Purchase of Private Services

Using a voluntary agency with federal funding is good for a program for a small group, especially an experimental program, because it helps start a government program quickly without the need to comply with federal bureaucracy requirements, including those related to civil service. For a voluntary agency accepting such government funding there can be disadvantages, of course, such as losing some of its autonomy and finding itself less able to innovate. A disadvantage for the client of a government-funded program of a voluntary organization is that there may be less accountability to the public than when the program is carried out by a government organization; the voluntary agency still must respond to its own power elite, its board or whatever and may inadvertently, on account of its past image, or intentionally exclude minorities, those it considers the less deserving poor, and more deviant users.

An example of the problem of this mix of government and private assistance is given by Mildred Rein (1975) in regard to providing day care services for AFDC families and others under the 1967 amendments to the Social Security Act. By 1972 a large proportion of the federal child care expenditures were through private purchase. She says, "Provision of such child care services runs into the danger of being discretionary not only in methodology but in the selection of the client body. This may be not an approach to the ideal of universal social services after all, but an attempt to select out for services a group other than the poor" (p. 534). Rein also says that child care "purchase from private organizations, which was nowhere as important monetarily as purchase from public ones, turned out to be very important politically" (p. 530).

Yet for some services this relationship of voluntary agency and federal funding has an important advantage in that it encourages public support for a program in a country where there is suspicion of any public programs and a more positive attitude to voluntary agencies. Such arrangements exist in several northern European countries for services for the elderly and for housing. For example, Denmark has nursing homes managed by nonprofit voluntary organizations but built with the help of municipal government subsidies. In Holland the various housing associations get all their building funds from the national government. In both cases there are strict government regulations on design, rents, and other matters, such as staffing in the nursing homes.

Duplication of Services

A major issue may center around duplication, already mentioned in connection with community fund raising bodies and national coordinating organizations. Some church-based and ethnically based voluntary organizations also duplicate services provided by other groups. While such organizations can better tailor policy and practice to a cultural or ethnic group's needs and customs, the duplication means greater expense. Since there is evidence that some private agencies with casework services are already more expensive than their public counterpart, the fact that there are several private agencies duplicating each other only further exacerbates the situation in a field where money is scarce.

Some experts also complain that this pluralistic system in which several agencies, religious and ethnic, offer the same service hurts social equality, since it means that the service is not equally available to everyone but only to special groups, even though the funding behind it may be government monies. In Holland this very situation exists. A major program for the elderly there is residential homes for the aged. These are built by religious groups, mainly Catholic, Dutch Reformed, Humanist, and "neutral" foundations; the subsidy for the building comes indirectly from the national government; the subsidy to the individual who cannot afford the monthly fee, as 80 percent can't, is also from the national government. While most of these homes admit some persons not of their religious affiliation, the situation is obviously awkward. One can be Dutch Reformed and find that the only opening in one of the community's four residential homes is in a Catholic one; since there is a long waiting list for all, one feels compelled to take the opening, if accepted.

In conclusion, most would agree there are benefits to having private agencies. The question is, How many and what kind of services should go through them? Certainly most income maintenance programs should not. Possibly most universal programs of the welfare state type should not.

COORDINATION OF SERVICES

Coordination of fund raising and of service planning in the voluntary sector has already been described. Let us elaborate on this and look at some of the problems of coordination found in the government sector. Coordination can mean bringing together all agencies dealing with certain types of programs and problems. A Community Chest or United Way encourages this through financial planning; a separate or affiliated social planning council may also do this. In addition, one or both of these types of coordinating bodies may bring together a wide range of agencies on a problem basic to all of them, such as the use of Title XX money or the distribution of revenue-sharing funds. A coordinative group may get these many community agencies together to find the gaps in services and to decide who should fill the gaps, or to discuss services to various groups, such as minorities, and to various areas of the city.

It may also be desirable to coordinate certain kinds of services on an areawide basis. Today most areas have health coordinating bodies, which try to limit the duplication of special equipment in hospitals and try to determine areawide medical needs such as hospital beds and make the best use of present facilities. Other kinds of area coordination include organizations of local governments to deal with such regional issues as federal housing subsidy distribution, transportation systems, and distribution of parks.

Multiservice Agencies

The delivery of services can be made through multiservice agencies and centers. Should one agency have a number of different divisions that deal with a variety of problems? Will this provide the integration of the service delivery mechanism that, as Katz (1978) says, most workers find necessary because they are now incapable of providing all the services a client needs?

One can say that county social service agencies often have such divisions; they have divisions dealing not only with cash assistance, such as AFDC and general assistance, but also with child protective services for neglect and abuse cases and a foster home division.

Another way to provide a variety of services in one agency is through a multidisciplinary team, but as Katz says, this may become costly. The opposite to this is many very specialized nonprofit voluntary agencies with staff highly trained for its own type of work, whether adoption procedures, drug abuse work, or mental health counseling. In some cases, for the multiproblem client an agency giving a variety of services can be of much greater help.

Multiservice Centers

A multiservice center is one that houses a number of agencies for the neighborhood or town in one location. Katz says the multiservice center is like the one-stop shopping center for social services. One way it is created is to have the different agencies assign staff to the center. Thus, the welfare department, the Social Security Administration, and the health department may each have an office in one building. The client with multiple problems need not run about town to find each service. Because of these agencies' easier accessibility some clients who need health programs, for instance, may make use of such services. These cooperating agencies may also be better able to work together to take care of the needs of the multiproblem client. One staff member may have primary responsibility for the client; the worker knows the details of other agencies' programs and eligibility requirements and sometimes can even sign the person up for the other services. By having cooperating services together, one can prevent clients from overutilizing the resources of different agencies. Jones (1975), however, has documented for Contra Costa County, California, the problems of getting agencies in a multiservice center to cooperate with each other and jointly serve the client. As Katz says, agency staff still respond more to their central office than to local needs.

Centralization

Centralization of services in a city is another issue. The multiservice center often represents an attempt to decentralize services to the neighborhood level, thus making these services more accessible to users. Some argue, however, that decentralization is inefficient, since it is hard to supply specialized staff and equipment, such as for health programs, to all the centers. Second, it may mean more administrators and more office space, and thus these decentralized centers increase costs. Whether one chooses a centralized or decentralized approach may depend on the type of service given. Decentralization through a multiservice agency, as Katz points out, can get around inaccessibility and fragmentation of services, and it can be more humanized and respond better to individual clients' needs. Katz says this is especially true if the multiservice center is run along the lines of a client-centered model with neighborhood residents on the board, doing outreach and even working in the agency. This way changes in the demand for services can be met.

Agency Regulations

Agency regulations are another aspect of service delivery. The inconsistency of eligibility requirements for means-tested programs is considerable. One may find oneself eligible for food stamps but not AFDC, or even for Medicaid and not AFDC. Certain assets, such as a house or a car, may not be considered in calculations for one program while, if they are over a certain value, their value may be included in calculations for another program. In Chapter 8 an illustration is given of the number of forms one must fill out before being accepted for the AFDC program. The Section 8 leased housing program demands extensive apartment hunting and agency contact before the subsidy is given.

Research on such regulations also illustrates the gaps in provision for some groups. For example, the poor divorced woman of 55 without any children may find that regulations make her ineligible for many services even though her income is below poverty level. The different programs have specific regulations about whom they can serve; some groups, such as non-aged single adults and non-aged childless couples, do not fit into most programs.

LOCAL AUTONOMY

Local autonomy is another issue in the delivery of services. For example, in financing and decision making in the public schools we have seen strong support for local control, even though the states and the federal government provide funding to the schools. Also, in the debate on national health insurance one question is the degree to which local hospitals will remain decision-making bodies.

Some programs, such as veterans' programs, have been run quietly by the federal government while in others that have been mainly federal government–sponsored there have been major fights over what levels of authority and what type of agency should deliver the service. When the OEO War on Poverty programs came in under President Johnson, the CAP part (the Community Action Program) was controlled much more by Washington than were many of the other social service programs; normal local agencies were bypassed in some cities. Mayors' offices in some cities complained that the funds went directly to local poverty boards and they had little part in delivery. Long fights were waged between groups representing the poor and the mayor's office over control or delivery of services in such places as Oakland and San Francisco, California.

ACCESSIBILITY

Accessibility is another issue. One side of this question is whether the service is accessible or available to certain groups and not others, as was mentioned in connection with agency regulations. Besides regulations, inaccessibility can be due to informal agency policies. In the past many voluntary agencies and even some public ones had an informal "whites only" policy. For example, blacks were discouraged up to the mid-1960s from applying for FHA-insured mortgages. In general, many lower-class citizens felt unwelcome in some voluntary agencies, as has been shown. Today groups like the Family Service Agency and Planned Parenthood have developed advocacy programs to reach the lower classes and minorities and have often set up offices in poverty neighborhoods.

Accessibility can also mean the knowledge of a program's existence and the means to use the program. Today many agencies have minibuses to bring clients to their programs, as do meals programs and health programs for the elderly.

The existence of programs is now sometimes advertised in the newspaper and on radio, and posters are distributed to announce it. This has long been the practice in Britain, but in America, where it has been customary to keep the number of users to a minimum, we have often not publicized programs in the past.

A means of heightening the knowledge of available programs is to provide an information and referral service. Many local councils or committees on aging do this for seniors. Some social planning councils have a staff member who performs this function. In Britain there are citizens' advisory bureaus and even housing advice bureaus.

While one can see the advantages, Gilbert and Specht (1974) point out that one disadvantage of providing an information and referral agency is that it provides one more step a client must go through to get service. Of course, such a preliminary screening means the person is more likely to be sent to the right agency. Gilbert and Specht also complain that "the addition of an access agency suggests that other service-providing agencies will diminish the access services they previously offered as a marginal function." However, Gilbert and Specht as well as Kahn (1973) would strongly agree that there is a great need for making services more accessible to various groups in the population.

Stigmatization also makes certain programs less accessible, in that it causes many in need not to use the service. They feel that use labels them as charity cases or paupers. A major reason the poor law assistance in Britain was so abhorred was the stigma attached to its use. Most would agree that the delivery of services should be made in such a way that stigma is kept to a minimum; that is, there should be more confidentiality, simpler forms, and an agency that is not itself stigmatized as an agency for the poor. For example, in the past the elderly poor regarded the OAA (Old Age Assistance) program, run out of the local welfare office, as "charity" for paupers. When in 1972 the delivery of service was moved over to the acceptable federal Social Security Administration office, and the name was changed to SSI (Supplementary Security Income), many more of the elderly were willing to apply. Public housing complexes, so very visible, were always considered stigmatizing housing for the poor; many who would never have moved into them because of stigma are now willing to participate in the Section 8 program, under which they live in private, standard rental units without being set apart but have part of their rent paid by the public housing authority or a similar agency.

STAFFING

While in the early years of social service provision in voluntary agencies volunteers were used widely, in the last few decades the agencies have generally had professional staff. In the prestigious voluntary agencies, such as the Family Service Agency, the Children's Home Society, and the American Red Cross, often these are personnel with a master of social work (M.S.W.) degree. In public welfare agencies and probation departments in the more industrialized states the agency workers have been persons with at least a bachelor's degree. However, by 1970, with the addition of the "eligibility worker" category in public welfare, a number of workers had fewer than four years of college.

Professional staff, especially those with the M.S.W. degree or even a bachelor's degree in social work, learn certain therapeutic-casework skills and certain social science theories, learn the professional role in relation to the client, and learn the standards and ethics of the social work field through their schooling.

Paraprofessionals

In addition to professionals today there are various types of paraprofessional workers. Their inclusion in the agency staff may be to cut costs or to take advantage of the availability of federal public works aides or to purposely include area citizens in the agency work force. Professionals often feel threatened by such additional staff, as their use may take away some of the professional positions. Also, the inclusion of paraprofessionals may lower professional standards, since these paraprofessional staffs are not skilled in clinical therapeutic methods but are more likely lay dabblers in counseling; paraprofessionals may not be attuned to the ethics of the social work profession since they have not taken college social work courses or in fact have usually not had any college work.

On the other hand, many lower-class and minority clients may feel more at home with the paraprofessional worker. The paraprofessional speaks the same language as the client and has somewhat the same world view and attitudes and the same cultural background. The professional worker often has communication problems due to the lack of some or all of these attributes. Another advantage of using the paraprofessional is that this person can free the highly skilled worker from menial tasks. If provided under a federal program such as CETA, he or she can be an additional worker the agency could not otherwise afford.

Another advantage of paraprofessionals is that they may be better in tune with their own community's needs than middle-class agency personnel. Today there are many new and informally structured agencies founded by community people or people who in the past experienced the same deviant situation as the clientele; they feel they not only know the problems but also have good rapport with the clientele, since they have had the same experiences. These self-help groups include the Delancey Street Foundation and Seven Steps, for ex-convicts; Alcoholics Anonymous, for alcoholics; OEO target-area groups; and various neighborhood associations.

The question comes up whether these self-help groups do a better job of helping their clientele than professionally staffed agencies. For in-depth counseling, including that in mental health clinics, it seems that professional staff are needed. For group counseling a professional staff member may prove the best leader, although for programs to such deviants as drug addicts this may not prove true.

A college degree seems necessary for Social Security Administration and county welfare office programs because of the complexity of the regulations. Certainly personnel dealing with foster children or adoption cases should have professional training. This applies even more to those carrying out the very delicate family intervention protective service, with its legal aspects. Any agency dealing with psychiatric care, whether for adults or children, needs professionally trained social workers.

On the other hand, some community programs benefit greatly from the use of paraprofessionals, although the lack of organization and standard financial record keeping found in some such agencies may be due to the lack of any college-educated staff.

Which of the types of staff—each with its own value orientations and level of skills—is used has a major influence on how the service is delivered and so the issue merits great consideration.

CITIZEN PARTICIPATION

Paraprofessional staff may be employed by an agency to give users a chance to participate in the running of the agency and to avoid the "colonization" image of an agency with only outsiders, usually more powerfully connected whites, who dictate programs for local minority poor. Today many public housing agencies employ residents as agency maintenance and clerical workers. Other agencies use locals as receptionists. The Head Start program for preschoolers uses mothers in paid paraprofessional positions and as volunteers.

This is just one type or level of citizen participation. Broadly speaking, citizen participation means a greater role for local citizens, especially the users, in the decision making and functioning of the agency. It is related to the question, Who has the right to do what to whom, on what grounds? The traditional social service approach was a paternalistic one whereby middle-class social agency personnel thought they knew what was best for the poor and usually were the ones who represented the poor before the mayor's office and other groups. Decisions were made behind closed doors and often informally among the elite. Hayes (1972) gives a good example for Oakland, California, where the community's industrial and business elite, in a private, nonofficial group called "OCCUR," held private breakfast meetings in the 1950s to decide on urban renewal plans without the participation of the poor or minorities:

> OCCUR rapidly became the contact point for business and governmental groups involved in the process of urban renewal. . . . The main feature of OCCUR's activity has been a weekly breakfast meeting. . . . it should also be noted that access to such information was restricted to a select group. All of those in attendance at the meeting attended by this writer were either local businessmen, property owners, or officials of local government agencies. There were no community blacks, small businessmen, or wage earners . . . in 1959. . . . [P. 112]

After long protests in 1969 a few representatives of the poor in the area where urban renewal was in progress were included in these meetings. Hayes gives a similar example on how welfare policy was made in Oakland. This elitist approach has also been labeled "colonialism," whereby the white outside power structure dictates the treatment of the minority group and uses its own people as enforcers or regulators, whether social service personnel or police.

Public works assistance, often federal "pork barrel" money, has usually been tied to such elitist politics: money is distributed by city hall to the faithful ward heels and other politically useful groups. The OEO poverty act of 1964 included in its wording that there should be "maximum feasible participation of the poor" in the Community Action Program. As Sargent Shriver, administrator of the program, said:

> At the heart of the poverty program lies a new form of dialogue between the poor and the rest of society. . . . there is a legislative, and ethical, and, for those of us involved in the program, a personal commitment to insure that the poor themselves actively participate in the planning, implementation, and administration of the programs. [In Dunne (ed.), 1964, p. 9]

Shriver then stated, "Involvement of the poor will mean giving them effective power, a respected and heeded voice and genuine representation in all stages in the significant decision making process."

This call for action on the part of the poor was taken up in some cities to a greater degree than had been expected because former civil rights activists and those calling for "power to the people" saw the CAP as a program for carrying out these policies. Here was millions of dollars coming in to big cities for assistance to the poor. In San Francisco, Oakland, and many other cities leaders of the poor fought to keep the decision making out of the mayor's office, by seeing that representatives of the poor were on both the CAP poverty councils and the neighborhood target-area councils.

In some cities, the neighborhood poor themselves elected the CAP representatives. These community representatives were often the more ambitious, upwardly mobile leaders of their community, yet in many areas they lived in the community and represented community demands and protests rather than being coopted into the city's elitist leader group. In some places, of course, some had little popularity in the community they were supposed to represent but were considered "Uncle Toms."

Kramer (1969) saw a range of variance in CAP citizen participation, from complete control of the councils in some places, to joint participation with the traditional citywide leaders in others, to some advisory role. They could be council members or program workers.

Moynihan (1969) said the program was really a method to recreate the urban ethnic political machines. He thought that one problem with the program was that it created considerable infighting within groups that distracted participants from the goal of providing services to attack poverty.

While most observers agreed this infighting existed and detracted from carrying out service efforts, they also thought the program was a step forward in citizen participation. One could say that out of this major participation effort came a norm of future decision making in social service organizations. The Model Cities program again incorporated citizen participation into its structure; most urban renewal and redevelopment groups include active citizen participation in their planning structure. Most social service agencies put users on their boards and employ users in their agencies.

Some of this endeavor is, of course, tokenism and in a number of cases cooptation, whereby the few user-representatives are persuaded to agree with the power elite's decision to the detriment of their own community's interests. In other cases, however, the community group, now informed of city hall decisions, fights against them, whether they are for a new expressway, an urban renewal project, or the use of public funds for a nonessential facility. At the many hearings now called on such matters as the use of revenue-sharing or block grant funds, neighborhood groups are vocal and receive newspaper and television coverage. Yet, most experts feel we must not be deceived into thinking we have reached the point where we have given the poor real power over their lives. The professional expert and the political machine of city hall still are quite important in making city decisions, although they may respond more to protests from neighborhood and ethnic-racial groups in the community than in the past.

In some areas citizen participation has turned into ethnic-racial political activism.

Why should one give the poor power? With the welfare office, the police, the urban renewal agency, the landlord, and even the local grocery store owner making major decisions for them, the poor have traditionally been powerless. They have had to go begging to many of these sources of power to get any assistance. Their lives could be disrupted when the landlord evicted them, the urban renewal agency relocated them, or the grocery store owner stopped their credit. This feeling of powerlessness meant loss of confidence, a feeling of being a second-class citizen, and a feeling of being an outsider. Haggstrom (1964) maintains that giving the poor some part in making their own decisions builds their confidence and makes them feel they are in the mainstream in their community rather than outsiders. Participation in OEO or service organization boards gives them the feeling of helping to make decisions; work in the agency gives them a purpose and confidence. This may all be only therapeutic, but even that, some experts feel, is useful. But to some degree there is power, at least that of the occasional veto of city hall plans.

The policy issue here is how to maximize this citizen participation in a meaningful, nontoken way and to use the knowledge these community leaders have to better plan any community action so that it is in tune with the real needs of the community. At the same time, one must not ignore the professional expert and one should not let situations develop where community leaders get into a meaningless fight with city hall that halts useful programs, nor should cooptation be allowed to become the normal way of doing business.

COST AS A POLICY FACTOR IN STRUCTURING THE DELIVERY SYSTEM

Costs are in reality a major determinant of the structure of the delivery system, just as they are in the choice of programs and in eligibility for these programs. Kahn (1973) points out this reality when he says that a debate about income maintenance strategy is often resolved on the basis of expert research that shows where the greatest economic efficiency is, that is, which program has the highest possible proportion of money reaching the "target population," the poor, in relation to the seepage to nontarget groups. Little consideration is given to the fact that the program, with its means-test approaches, may stigmatize.

Cost-effectiveness studies can be used in a variety of decision-making areas. Analysis of estimated cost can indicate the costs of centralized versus decentralized services and of a separate information and referral office. Cost studies can easily give data on the relative costs of professional and paraprofessional staff.

These systems analysis–cost benefit studies usually have a "specification of goals, careful attempts at quantification, specification of alternatives available, clear definition of criteria, and the employment of either 'best buy' for a given expenditure unit or 'cheaper price' for a given desired effect as the decision-making base" (Kahn, 1973, p. 126). Gilbert and Specht (1974) say of cost effectiveness:

> When applied to the basis of social allocations (who gets what) it is measured by the extent to which each dollar of benefit is allocated to those who are most in need and could not otherwise command the benefit on the open marketplace; the guiding thought is that there be no waste of resources. [P. 44]

They add that with the cost-effectiveness criterion, a high degree of selectivity is employed in determining who is eligible for benefits.

The cost-benefit experts are good at determining the cost of a program if certain groups are included or excluded, for example, if the working poor are included in a welfare reform proposal or, on the other hand, if survivors aged 16 and over are no longer covered by OASDHI. As Rivlin (1971) points out, these cost benefit studies can determine "who benefits and who pays." Kahn (1973) adds to this, saying, "The efficiency approaches may sometimes shed light on the consequences of choosing decentralization or centralization; vouchers or benefits-in-kind or cash; universal or selective strategies. They can specify the costs or benefits of funding voluntary programs, as opposed to public operations" (p. 127). Yet even in these areas efficiency experts may leave out certain hard-to-measure effects related more to social costs than to economic costs. It will be hard for them to choose a delivery system on whether it is more or less stigmatic. Yet stigmatization has an effect on the number of users and thus the costs.

Cost-benefit studies can give some indication of the degree to which certain "investments," such as expenditures for manpower training to increase employability, pay off, if the idea of return on investment is used as a criterion. Kahn (1973) gives some examples of this type of economic analysis from studies, saying:

> The same analysis argues against expanded public day care as part of a reform of public assistance on the grounds that the payoff was too small—it would cost more to provide good day care than the mothers could earn. Family planning services, on the other hand, yield high cost benefit ratios and were readily recommended for expansion in another study. [P. 126]

Kahn thinks the cost-benefit strategist is limited in the ability to make decisions between major program options. He says, "The system analyst cannot help one to decide between more elementary school educational support or more investment in manpower programs. After a selection is made, he can help choose among programs or specify details within the selected field."

Political considerations and value orientations in many cases play a more important part than costs in deciding on programs and delivery systems. Historical factors may also be important; for example, one welfare program, the food-stamp program, is delivered through the Department of Agriculture on account of historical accident. President Carter's 1977 suggestion to combine the food-stamp program and AFDC and thus save administrative costs has so far not been taken up, to some extent because federal departments tend to preserve their autonomy.

Political considerations have continually acted as a damper on cost efficiencies. For example, it may be that a central administration for a program is less expensive but neighborhood groups demand a decentralized program. It is generally more cost-efficient for a state to provide all the costs for local schools rather than pay part and let localities, through property taxes, provide the rest, but this is not considered politically advisable if local control is given a high value. Finally, it is more cost-efficient for the federal government to run a health insurance program with payout directly to the provider, but the political strength of the AMA (American Medical Association) makes this an ill-advised strategy to get a health insurance program through, as Edward Kennedy has found.

Values have sometimes led to support for more expensive programs; for example, many conservatives, though generally considered cost-conscious, have been in favor of correctional facilities rather than probation for delinquents because they feel offending youth shouldn't be out on the streets. (In recent years legislators and judges in California and other states have seen the high cost of this approach and have moved in the direction of probation-diversion programs for this and other reasons.) Legislators have generally centered on programs to assist those who are already seriously affected by a condition such as chronic illness, instead of providing preventive programs that could lessen the need for the much more costly treatment programs.

The most scandalous example of this kind of wastefulness is the form of assistance given to the elderly. Many elderly could be kept out of nursing homes if there were a day care program, a congregate housing development (with common dining room and some personal services), or even a public visiting nurse or homemaker. All these programs have been severely underfunded while billions are paid out through Medicaid and

Medicare for nursing home care of the elderly (one-half to two-thirds of all nursing home patients have their expenses paid by the government). In addition, a profit-making private delivery system has been allowed to exist instead of nonprofit nursing homes like those found in much of Europe.

One Broad Program versus Several Narrow-Focus Programs Costs play into all levels and parts of providing social services. Yet political considerations override costs in many cases when a decision is made whether to have a broad program or a number of narrowly focused ones. Legislators may feel that one large income maintenance program will not get through Congress, because of its costs and size; they may feel that three separate programs, AFDC, food stamps, and Medicaid, each with its own political supporters, will do better. Grocer associations and farmers will back the food-stamp program; some medical personnel will back Medicaid. The costs of the three will be looked at separately by the public and by Congress. Thus, while it might be more efficient to put all three together, since they all target mainly (though not entirely) on the same group, it is politically easier to get the measures passed separately. Another reason for three separate programs is that some who will not use AFDC (or even SSI) will use the other, less stigmatic programs, and thus some poor will get the help they need.

CONCLUSION

Policy options concerning the delivery of services have been described in this chapter. The most important one is whether to deliver the services through a public agency or a private one. This involves the issue of government purchase of services through private agencies. The advantages of each delivery option were listed. The benefits of delivery through multiservice centers and multiservice agencies were also discussed.

The type of staff that delivers the service can also vary; the use of paraprofessionals was covered. A larger issue of user or citizen participation in both staffing the delivery system and making decisions regarding programs was covered. Last, these alternative delivery possibilities were related to cost, and the issue of cost-effectiveness was explored.

Part Three

Social Policy in Specific Social Service Fields

This part of the book covers policy in particular areas, such as income maintenance or welfare assistance, child welfare, services to the elderly, housing and the environment, juvenile justice, and policies to end discrimination against racial and ethnic minorities.

For each area the needs and the goals are given, following the outline in Chapter 1. Present programs are described and then policy issues discussed. In each of these policy areas we can ask, as we did in Chapter 1, what the eligibility requirements should be for using the service. We find we might answer this differently for housing and for services to the elderly, for example, and if we look at the way services are provided at present we find even in each area a variety of eligibility requirements for different programs. Then we can ask what types of assistance, cash or benefits-in-kind, tax credits, or whatever, are and should be used in each social service area. We also look at the present type of delivery system, including staffing, and then look at problems in it and improvements that have been suggested. For example, should we use more paraprofessionals?

In each of these areas, but especially in regard to welfare reform policy, we discuss the values that help shape the type of provision. We also mention power bases and their part in implementing or obstructing a certain course of policymaking. In these chapters we also mention the costs involved in using different alternatives.

As one reads each chapter one should keep all these issues in mind. At the end of each chapter they are summarized.

Chapter 8

Social Policy for Income Maintenance

CHARACTERISTICS OF THOSE IN NEED OF CASH ASSISTANCE

It is always astounding that the public image of the poor is one of lazy, carefree males who are able to work and are in a two-parent household. Any intelligent student can easily guess that some of the types of people most likely to be in poverty are the disabled, the sick, the elderly, and members of female-headed households. Almost one-fourth of the elderly live below the poverty level, and most of the rest live only slightly above it. Nearly 2 out of 3 poor persons 16 years old and over in poverty in 1976 were women. This amounted to 10 million women.

Female-Headed Households

In 1976 half of all poor families were headed by a woman, while in 1950 only 24 percent had a female head. This increase was related to the general increase in female-headed households in the population. In 1950 only 10.1 percent of all households were female-headed, but by 1976 14 percent were, a 40 percent increase in the rate, which was due in part to the great increase in divorce rates.

Many of these new female-headed households became poor because husbands did not meet child support or alimony payments. The Urban Institute in 1976 found that 40 percent of the absent fathers contributed nothing while the average payment of those who did contribute was less than $2000 a year.

Many of the women heading these households were poor also because the jobs they were in paid very little. Over half the occupations dominated by female workers in 1970 paid poverty-level wages. For example, apparel manufacture, in which 81 percent of the work force was female, paid an average weekly salary of $93 in 1970. In the same year 6 million women worked full-time, year-round, and earned less than the current poverty level for a family of four. If she had to deduct child care costs from this income, the woman and her children had barely enough to subsist on.

An example of need is the case of Mrs. Jones.

Mrs. Jones had been married for six years and had three children. Her husband was a salesman for a farm machinery company and traveled widely. When his sales region was changed from the West to the Midwest, he moved to temporary quarters and planned to have his wife and the children come to the new area as soon as he got settled and found a place for the family to live. However, business was not very good and he kept putting the move off. Letters became less frequent, and he often was out of town when she called his hotel. Finally, he wrote that he had another "friend" and wanted a divorce.

In the divorce case Mrs. Jones's lawyer did a poor job of fighting for adequate child support and alimony. By two years later she was receiving only sporadic payments and had no current address for her husband. After using up her small savings, she made such economy measures as moving from the family's pleasant rented ranch house to a small apartment in a poorer area.

She tried at first to find a clerical job, but the pay of $120 a week barely covered expenses, including private day care for the 4-year-old, and furthermore, she hated to be out working when the 6- and 7-year-old girls came home from school. Last year she instead turned to welfare for assistance and now gets $493 a month from AFDC, an amount that barely covers rent, food, and clothing for the children. Mrs. Jones seldom goes out except to shop; she has little money for movies or for a baby-sitter. She is reluctant to see her old friends because she has no decent clothes and her friends are far from her new neighborhood and might not accept her without her husband; she has made few new friends.

Poor Children

Female-headed households involve not only poor adults but also poor children, as do poor male-headed households. In 1970 almost one-fifth of all American children under 18 lived in poor households, and almost another 10 percent lived in "near poor" households. Nearly 1 out of 8 of the nation's children were on welfare.

If one looks only at black households, far more than half of the children lived in poor or near poor households.

Large Families

One reason so many children live in poverty is that large families are more likely to live in poverty. In 1970 over a third of all families with six or more children were living in poverty; over half the black families with six or more children were living in poverty.

Minority Families

Minority families are much more likely to be living in poverty than white families, just as black male household heads are twice as likely to be unemployed as white household heads.

In 1970 over a third of all nonwhite persons in the United States were poor persons, while only around 10 percent of white persons were poor. In the South, the proportion of blacks who were poor was much greater.

The Working Poor

One large group of the poor that most people are unaware of is the working poor, those people who work full time for a good part of the year but make such low wages that the yearly total comes to below the poverty level. Many women and some males are in low-paying jobs, perhaps as farm workers and laborers. Such low-level workers can be found in places such as the South, the Appalachian area, the barrios of the Southwest, or the Chinatowns of the United States. Some are seasonal workers who cannot find work during the off-season, whether in farming, lumbering, or construction. Many work at the minimum wage level.

In 1975 the Bureau of the Census reported that of the 3 million male-headed households living below the poverty line, almost 2 million of the male heads were in the work force. Far over half these households were white. Ten percent of the 2,430,000 female heads of poor households, including 26,000 retired, were in the work force forty or more weeks in 1975.

In the South, there is a high concentration of working poor, so large that if Nixon's welfare reform bill, which gave assistance to the working poor, had passed in Congress, as many as a third of the households in some Deep South states would have received welfare payments.

Today, most of the working poor, especially males heading house-holds, are not covered by welfare programs.

The Magnitude of the Problem

As important as the categories of people most likely to be poor is the magnitude of the problem. In 1975 almost 26 million people were living below the very minimal government-set "poverty level," which in that year was $5500 for a nonfarm family of four, far below the 1975 median family income of $13,720.

Various experts point out that the *proportion* of the American population that is in poverty has been decreasing; this was true through 1974. In 1959, 22.2 percent of the population was in poverty, and by 1974 only 11.6 percent was, although some say this was partly due to the fact that the poverty line was not adequately raised during that period, meaning that only the very, very poor were counted as being in poverty in 1974. Since 1974, even the proportion of Americans in poverty has risen slightly; by 1975 it was 12.1 percent of the population.

For female-headed households the decrease in the proportion below the poverty level between 1959 and 1974 was much, much smaller than for male-headed households. (See Table 8-1.)

Inflation in 1975 caused buying power to be at its lowest level in five years and more people to be in poverty. This brings up a major issue. Is the poverty level set by the Department of Health, Education, and Welfare (HEW) a realistic one or a very, very low level? Would there be many more people and a higher proportion of our families in poverty if it were at a more realistic level? By measures other than this poverty level, such as that of the U.S. Department of Labor, many more people might be said to be living without adequate cash to exist. Thus there was a very great gap between the $5500 poverty level and the median family income of $13,720.

Table 8-1 Families Below the Low-Income Level, by Sex of Head, 1959, 1967, and 1974, by percent
(Families As of the Following Year)

Year	All families		Families with male head		Families with female head	
	Black	White	Black	White	Black	White
1959	48.1	14.8	43.3	13.4	65.4	30.0
1967	33.9	9.0	25.3	7.4	56.3	25.9
1974*	27.8	7.0	14.2	4.9	52.8	24.9

*Based on 1970 census population controls; therefore, not strictly comparable to data for earlier years.
Source: U.S. Department of Commerce, Social and Economic Statistics Administration, Bureau of the Census.

Fuchs (1967) argues that the poverty level should be set at not less than half the median family income, or in 1975 at $6860. The Department of Labor's Bureau of Labor Statistics has an austerity, or lower standard of living, budget that again is considerably higher than the government poverty level figure. For example, in the fall of 1975 this was $9800 for a family of four, much higher than the $5500 government-established poverty level in 1975.

The underestimation of the number in poverty, as stated above, may be due to the fact that the government poverty level has not been raised adequately since 1959. Orshansky (1968) points out that "the average income of four-person families increased by 37 percent between 1959 and 1966. In the same period, the poverty line was upwardly adjusted only 9 percent; it took into account the changes in cost of living but not the relative increases of income going to the non-poor."

Being in poverty is, of course, a state of relative deprivation in comparison to others. In 1975 there were 25.9 million people in families that needed two-and-a-half times their income to reach the median family income in the United States that year; these people consider themselves much worse off than the rest of the population.

The income distribution for the nation in 1975 shows that the bottom 20 percent of all households falls far below the rest of society in the proportion of the nation's aggregate income it had (only 3.5 percent).

Malnutrition is, of course, an extreme indication of poverty in *real* terms in any part of the world. *Hunger, U.S.A.,* the report of a 1968 citizens' board of inquiry, reported, "It is possible to assert, with a high degree of probability, that we face a problem [malnutrition and hunger] which, conservatively estimated, affects 10 million Americans, and in all likelihood, a substantially higher number" (p. 32).

Hunger for children can mean long-term physical problems, including brain damage. A black, female-headed plantation family in the South was described in U.S. Senate nutrition hearings as having thirteen children, with the mother a woman whose flesh was so shrunken she could not have weighed more than 100 pounds, and children with dull eyes who were totally inactive.

In describing poverty, one should not deal with statistics alone, because the real tragedy is that of families and elderly who each day try to cope with a lack of money in a society where it is hard to do anything without money. In the case of the Mary Ames family, the father took off for Alaska two years ago, leaving behind a wife with only a tenth-grade education and three children and little income. Mary moved from a comfortable house to a trailer camp. She is now on AFDC, the public welfare assistance for families. Mrs. Ames says the hardest time is the last week in the month. Her one daughter was graduating from junior high this past spring and she needed a special dress and new shoes. Mrs. Ames had to borrow the money from a relative. She said, "It's hard to say no to the children and tell them they are different from other children and can't have money for these things, even little things like going to movies." She added that as things stand they might not be able to meet the next month's rent.

In Washington, the author, working on a Howard University Community Action program in a poor area in 1962, heard of people who didn't have enough money for heat and substituted a fire of newspapers and odd wood in a pot in their living room. People in this area, including newcomers from the South and families evicted for lack of rent, had emergency housing needs. Some families literally had no place to rest their heads some nights.

Elderly urban poor, especially men, can be found in any skid row area, living out their last days on an insufficient SSI monthly check in transient hotels that years earlier should have been condemned.

With this account of the poverty situation in the United States, we move on to the policy issue of how to help the poor to have a decent income. We center on the most controversial income maintenance program, AFDC, rather than all such programs; in other words, we will not cover SSI or OASDHI, the other chief programs.

THE PRINCIPAL EXISTING MEANS-TESTED CASH ASSISTANCE PROGRAM: AFDC

The largest means-tested public assistance program in the United States is AFDC, Aid to Families with Dependent Children. This is the program that everyone associates with "welfare," even though there are many other cash assistance programs. In 1977 there were over 11 million AFDC recipients, the majority of them children, in 3.5 million families.

Benefits depend on need and are meant to cover the minimum costs of food, shelter, clothing, and other items of daily living. Recipients must prove lack of financial means to take care of these needs. The goal of the assistance is to provide for needy dependent children and, since 1950, their caretakers. Such children must be deprived of the support of at least one parent by reason of death, desertion, or incapacity or disability; in certain states since 1962 these children can also be in homes where a father is unemployed (under AFDC-UF). Benefits are paid directly to the children's parent or caretaker-relatives and in the form of cash with no restrictions on use. The goals of the program have been to keep the child in the family and support family life; the program was originally meant for widows and their children. However, today most widows and their children receive high enough payments under the survivors' provision of the universal social security payments (OASDHI) that they do not need to turn to the AFDC program.

Deserted or divorced women and their children make up the largest group on AFDC. In only half the states in 1979 are families with an unemployed father eligible, even though the federal government has allowed states to include this group since 1962. Even in states with AFDC-UF, few of the cases are families with an unemployed man, partly because of strict requirements. However, this may change, and the federal government may make AFDC-UF mandatory in all states. In 1973 in reality half the relatively few men in AFDC families were incapacitated and half were middle-aged or older.

In the AFDC program, payments are set according to each family's countable income and needs as determined by state law. They are paid by the local administrative unit, usually a county, and application is made to this local administrative unit. Benefits are funded by complex formula grants to state welfare agencies. Each state contributes a certain amount to the cost of assistance, varying from 17 to 50 percent as calculated in terms of that state's relative per capita income. Each state also contributes to administrative costs. States with low per capita income receive a higher federal contribution.

Many state governments have not brought their payments up to the amount they themselves recognize as being necessary for the basic needs of the family. In general, of poor female-headed families with children that get AFDC or OASDHI benefits or both, 61 percent were still poor *after* receiving these payments. The payments have not increased greatly over time and are lower than for the deserving poor under SSI. (See Table 8-2.)

For the amount of payment and many other criteria the state sets

Table 8-2 Average Monthly Public Assistance Payments per Recipient, by Program: 1950 and 1975 (Current Dollars)

Year*	Aid to families with dependent children (AFDC)	Supplemental Security Income (SSI)† for the—		Permanently and totally disabled	General assistance	Emergency assistance‡
		Aged	Blind			
1950	20.85	43.05	46.00	44.10	22.25	(X)
1975	71.50	91.00	147.00	141.00	103.55	158.17

X= Not applicable.
*Data relates to December of each year.
†SSI for the aged was Old-Age Assistance until 1974: SSI for the blind and disabled was Aid to the Blind and Aid to the Disabled until 1974.
‡Program begun in 1969; data relate to family units, not to individuals.
Source: U.S. Department of Health, Education, and Welfare, Social Security Administration, *Social Security Bulletin*. April 1976, and *1976 Annual Statistical Supplement to the Social Security Bulletin*.

down the rules. However, in some cases the Supreme Court has overruled the state or HEW has vetoed a state rule. This has been true of rules for a man in the house and on illegitimacy, among others.

Trends in AFDC

Changes in Regulations   A number of court decisions have cut down on the punitive aspects of AFDC. AFDC, serving mainly divorced and deserted women, had a very bad name in the 1960s. There were numerous stories of the promiscuous behavior of the women. The many illegitimate births in AFDC households only further inflamed the issue. "Man-in-the-house" rules became common, whereby an AFDC home was considered ineligible if a man was found to live there. While the welfare department threatened to take the children out of the home, in reality it was more likely to cut off aid. In fact, behind the community's moral indignation was a desire to cut down on the number of welfare cases. Welfare department personnel raided recipients' homes at midnight or 6 A.M. without a warrant, looking for signs of the presence of a man. Even a suit in the closet was excuse enough to cut off aid. In one case, an investigator climbed into a tree at two o'clock in the morning to look into a window of a welfare family's apartment to see if a man was there. However, in 1968 the Supreme Court struck down the man-in-the-house rule in Alabama and later strengthened its decision in regard to a California case. Second, HEW warned the states to guard against violations of constitutional rights, such as illegally entering a home. However, such interest in moral behavior has never stopped. Even rules on dating existed in some states; one woman asked how she was to get a new husband if she couldn't even date.

Residency Requirements   Residency requirements were also struck down by the Supreme Court in 1969. Before that time welfare departments had used these residency requirements as a way to keep applicants off the rolls; the welfare department instead often gave applicants a bus ticket back to their home town. States such as New York thought that the Supreme Court residency decision would greatly increase their welfare rolls, with people flocking to those areas with high AFDC payments. However, Lourie (1970) showed that after this decision states with relatively high AFDC payment levels did not attract a disproportionate number of nonresidents.

Liberal Interpretation of Eligibility by New Workers   In the late 1960s there was evidence that more applicants were being accepted for welfare than in the past. This was partly due to young workers' feeling during the time of civil rights activism that in some cases "welfare was a right" and their feeling sympathy for the poor rather than the bureaucracy. Some understood, as Charles Reich (1963) did, that "it is closer to the truth to say that the poor are affirmative contributors to today's society, for we are so organized as virtually to compel this sacrifice by a segment of the population. Since the enactment of the social security legislation, we have realized they have a right to a minimal share of the common wealth" (p. 1347). This attitude was more common in large Northern cities, and this was the place where more recipients were now residing on account of the northward and urban movements of the population. In 1968 in some Northern urban areas, such as Cleveland, 80 percent of applicants were accepted, while in many Southern and rural states applicants were discouraged, with only 30 percent accepted in Houston, according to Komisar (1977).

Citizenship When citizenship was outlawed as a qualification for welfare, in a 1971 Supreme Court decision, there was again an increase in the number of applicants.

The Welfare Rights Movement The movement for welfare rights that started in 1963 in several parts of the country also was an instrument for increasing the number on the welfare rolls. One of its interests was informing the poor of their eligibility for welfare; hospitals, working with Medicaid patients, performed a similar service. Romanyshyn (1971) points out that "a change in the political climate accompanied by the development of a militant welfare rights movement encouraged the acceptance of a citizen's right to social provisions established by law. As the stigma of assistance is altered, more of the poor are prepared to apply for aid. As the right to assistance is emphasized, fewer applicants are turned away" (p. 235). The movement's members also protested changes in eligibility requirements that would lead to cutbacks in the number of eligible recipients. For example, at the time of its annual meeting in Nevada in 1970, its members picketed casinos in Reno and Las Vegas to protest a proposed new set of eligibility rules that would have cut off 3000 recipients. Piven and Cloward (1971) gave another reason for the increase in welfare rolls: seeing welfare as a means to quiet political unrest, these authors thought the increase followed the historical pattern of reasons authorities allow the welfare rolls to increase, in this case in answer to racial turmoil and disturbance.

The Increase in Number of Recipients The increased number of welfare recipients, due to all these reasons plus a high unemployment rate in the 1970s, was the most bothersome trend in the minds of the public. The number of AFDC families jumped from less than 1 million in 1962 to 3.5 million in 1977.

The Provision of Services to AFDC Families　　Social service counseling has been considered part of the AFDC program; special funding has been added for this purpose from 1962 on. The idea behind it was that welfare recipients needed individual counseling to help them readjust their attitudes and behavior so that they could fit into society and hold down jobs. The assumption was the traditional one, that persons on welfare were there because of some defect in their personality and not because of structural problems in the economy. As time passed, social workers found that the 1962 provision meant only more paperwork in classifying the causes of problems rather than time for individual rehabilitation. Some questioned whether one-to-one casework techniques worked for low-income AFDC cases. By 1967 the service requirement was redefined as specific job assistance.

Since 1972, the main function of the AFDC administration, providing cash assistance, has been separated from the social service function. Earlier one worker had to carry on both jobs. Now there is an eligibility worker and a separate social service officer. The eligibility worker determines whether the family qualifies for the program, in terms of both income and other criteria, such as whether the husband is absent from the home. This worker also reexamines the recipient's eligibility. The eligibility worker does not do social work counseling but instead refers the person who needs it to the appropriate division of the agency. Unfortunately, this means that recipients have used the social services less since this split in functions took place.

Workfare　　Congress, by 1967, was increasingly unhappy with the AFDC program, since the number of cases seemed to soar upward instead of decreasing. They increased more than threefold from 1962 to 1979. Stories of fraud, immorality, and living a life of ease on the dole, stories especially prevalent as the black proportion of the clients increased, made Congress turn to punitive measures.

The 1967 amendments to the Social Security Act in regard to AFDC are said to have turned welfare into "workfare"; the main goal became getting people off dependency on welfare. The 1967 amendments said welfare could be terminated for any individual deemed employable by a case plan who refused to accept work or training.

A work-incentive program called "WIN" was brought in to provide training and employment in coordination with the Department of Labor for all welfare mothers considered suitable for work, including mothers with school-aged children (it excluded those with preschoolers). Day care provision was authorized. Mothers were also given the work incentive of being allowed to keep the first $30 of monthly earnings or the training money plus having one-third of the remainder exempt from consideration in determining continued eligibility for assistance.

The Characteristics of AFDC Recipients

A major question on income maintenance policy is who should be covered. A criticism of welfare reformers is that the present means-tested AFDC program only partially covers the group in need. Second, the public has an inaccurate and stereotyped image of the recipients. It sees them as lazy, as able to work but without work interest, as newcomers to the area, and as male-headed households.

AFDC recipients differ considerably from this image. They also represent only a very small segment of the total poor. There are few male-headed families on AFDC. In very rare cases (4 percent) does the family include an unemployed adult male and certainly never an employed male. Even in half the states with AFDC-UF, only about 10 to 15 percent of the AFDC households have an unemployed male head. The majority of AFDC recipients are children; 1 out of 8 children in the United States in 1975 was on welfare.

In 60 percent of the households headed by females on AFDC there is at least one child under 6. Seldom is the woman widowed; only 5 percent are. In half the cases she is divorced or deserted; in almost 1 out of 3 cases the mother is not married to the father of the child. In one-tenth of the cases the father is disabled or ill. The large number of divorced women receiving AFDC is due to the fact many are not receiving child support or alimony payments; only a small minority of the spouses were fulfilling their obligation.

A large proportion of AFDC women are minority women, especially black women; 46 percent of the total are. Yet, white households still make up the majority.

About 15 percent of these AFDC mothers work full- or part-time, mostly full-time. Williams (1975) figures that if one adds in those getting training or awaiting training or work, the figure might be up to 25 percent. Williams found that only a third of his studied recipients were dependent solely on welfare over a 37-month interval. Fully three-fourths of these recipients had worked full-time at a regular job some time in the past. Like Mildred Rein (1972), he found some in and out of work and some combining work and welfare.

In Mississippi, welfare recipients were encouraged to work in the fields. The low AFDC payments in Mississippi and the availability of low-paying jobs made this combined source of income more necessary.

Lack of education was considered a serious problem concerning the employability of this recipient group. Only 1 in 4 AFDC recipients nationwide had finished high school.

There are, of course, variations among recipients in their potential for employment and their chances to get off welfare. In one review of studies, Friedman and Hausman (1975) report:

The turnover in the welfare population is high. Estimates of the average number of months spent continuously on AFDC vary from under two years to over three years, reflecting regional variations. The length of spells on AFDC are associated with differences in family structure and labor market experience. Male-headed families and families with a head who had a good chance of becoming employed are more likely than female-headed families and families with limited employability to leave welfare. Whites, those with higher non-wage income, and those with better labor market opportunities, all have better prospects of leaving welfare. [Pp. 28–30]

The average period on AFDC is two years, but in 1969 forty-five percent had been on it over three years. For white households the period often is much shorter. Burgess and Price (1963) found the median number of months for white recipients to be fifteen and for black recipients, twenty-two. With minority households Friedman and Hausman point out, "Once off welfare, non-whites and those whose expected wage is below the legal minimum are more likely to return to welfare. . . . [Fluctuations in] unemployment or other small changes frequently result in their return to welfare" (pp. 28–30).

Secretary of Health, Education, and Welfare Joseph Califano in 1978 said the fluidity in and out of welfare was considerable and used this as a point for his reform proposals to move people off welfare and into jobs. Califano said, "This country is not full of people that have been sitting on welfare for three generations. This is a really pernicious myth. . . ." Other data show that only a small proportion of the AFDC caseload is a second-generation group. Greenleigh Associates (1969) in New York City found that about 10 percent of the AFDC cases had received welfare assistance as children.

Some female welfare recipients, Pearce (1978) reports, may be long-term users, because even when these women find jobs, their pay is so low they usually must also stay on welfare.

Some AFDC families may be long-term users simply because of the physical conditions of the household head. In 10 percent of the cases the father was disabled or ill. In the New York City study it was found that nearly a third of the female heads of AFDC households with children under 18 were beset with social problems, the most frequent being chronic physical illness and child care needs.

Contrary to myth, AFDC families are not typically those who have migrated to an area, especially Northern cities, to get the supposedly high AFDC payments. Study after study shows the opposite, that most recipients have lived in the area several years or more. In its battle in the Supreme Court to overturn residence requirements, which it won, the American Civil Liberties Union (ACLU) pointed out that less than 1 percent of the people who were receiving benefits had been in New York less than a year. Ostow and Dutka (1975) in their New York study found that many recipients were immigrants, mainly Puerto Ricans and blacks, but their median preacceptance residence period in New York City, that is, the period before they started receiving welfare, was three years. The authors said this suggested a failed attempt at self-maintenance rather than immigration for the purpose of gaining prompt access to the state's liberal welfare system. In the famous Newburgh, New York, case in May 1965 regarding attempts to cut people off welfare, the city fathers found that the majority of the relief recipients were white persons, often long-time residents, not black newcomers.

One other myth is that AFDC mothers have more children in order to get higher AFDC payments or to stay on welfare. A number of studies show that most AFDC mothers are not so calculating. As Kriesberg (1970) points out, "If children were born in order to maintain and increase assistance benefits, then one would expect husbandless mothers to remain on the welfare rolls for a very long time. . . . however, the median length of the time payments were received was less than two years" (p. 147). His and other studies conclude that there is little evidence that this is the reason AFDC mothers have illegitimate children. Cutright (1970) found, in fact, that women were more likely to use contraceptives when they were on welfare.

Illegitimacy There are, however, many welfare children who are illegitimate. In almost half the AFDC cases, there is at least one illegitimate child. Unwed mothers make up about a third of the total AFDC caseload. The reasons for this situation are many. First, knowledge of the use of contraceptives is low among this poorly educated population, even though in the past few years, in a departure from earlier days, the AFDC administration has strongly encouraged welfare mothers to avail themselves of family planning. Second, until the Supreme Court ruled abortions legal and Medicaid stepped in to pay for them, most welfare mothers did not have this recourse; even after these changes, abortions were difficult to obtain in many states. Third, a number of AFDC mothers are living in a nonmarital relationship with a man, often without the AFDC administration's knowledge, either because they cannot afford a divorce from the first husband or possibly because they fear they will lose AFDC funding if they do remarry. Some enter into such a relationship just in the hope of getting married and getting off AFDC and instead get pregnant. Griswold et al. (1967) found that most of these relationships were long-term; only 2.6 percent of the children in this AFDC sample were the result of casual, short-term relationships.

Problems in AFDC

Politicians, the American public, and policy experts all have long called for reform of the AFDC cash assistance program. Although the public's concern has been with the size and cost of the program, to the policy-makers concern has been with the eligibility regulations, which they find a carryover of the poor law philosophy, with its means testing, stigmatization, and division between the deserving and undeserving poor. The delivery system they consider restrictive, inhumane, and unfair in its treatment of clients. The accompanying example of the teenager in the welfare family represents a case of this humiliating treatment.

The Experience of Being on Welfare

One teenaged girl in a welfare family reported:

> To us, the welfare agency primarily meant restriction, regulation, and arbitrary authority. It appears that the rules varied with the public opinion of the time. If the "good citizens" were stirred up by a few stories of abuse of welfare and growled about the luxurious and comfortable lives that the recipients had, then we could expect that the regulations would tighten. Television sets, washing machines, and other appliances that most people consider necessary were forbidden unless we could produce signed statements from relatives stating that these items were gifts.

Our word was not good enough. This teenage girl added:

> When the "good citizens" worry about the morals of the recipients, the agency makes an attempt to regulate the personal life of the recipient in ways that the ordinary citizen would not allow. If a child was born out of wedlock, the mother would be threatened with having her aid stopped. What the good citizens never understood was that a woman would allow a man to move in with her in order to have the little extra money he would provide. The man would move out when the woman got pregnant and leave her worse off than before, but she could always hope that he wouldn't leave her and that he might consider marriage.

The degrading aspect of welfare is another problem. This same girl reported:

> By the time I was in high school, the problem of being a welfare child took on new dimensions. There was always a concerned teacher who

---

caused me many embarrassments. I was, frankly, a good student, and the teachers noticed me, but I could have done without some of the notice that I got. . . . when the subject of "What does your father do?" came up, I was unable to answer with any confidence. . . . Finally, I had no other alternative than to admit that our family survived through AFDC checks—especially after the public worker started calling the school to inquire about grades.

The phrase "your caseworker called the office today" was the beginning of many patronizing and personal talks with the teacher that I could have done without. Being singled out as a welfare recipient by the caseworker's "concerned intervention" all but ruined my social life, since the stereotyped view of the welfare recipient overrode whatever impression I had made on people as a person in my own right.

This teenager put in a plea for understanding of the welfare recipient's position and the need for dignity when she said:

I finally accepted being poor, and the fact that I did not have a really good coat for winter, or shoes or carfare could be endured. What I object to most and what I could not endure without hurt are the suffering and degrading effects on our fading pride. We were emotionally broken simply because we were poor and could not survive without aid. I object to being ragged and treated like a beggar simply because I am poor.

What we do, plainly and simply, is to survive the best way we know how. If only people knew how hard the welfare system, which is supposed to help us, makes it for us to survive. Inconvenience and embarrassment were constant symbols of our relationship to the welfare system. We were always afraid, when we had friends in, that we would be interrupted by the knock at the door. Our public assistance worker would never think of coming back some other time. . . .

Source: Charles Atherton, "Growing Up Obscene: The By-product of Life on AFDC," *Public Welfare*, October 1969, pp. 371–374.

Degradation   The degrading aspects of public assistance are major problems to users, although they are sometimes purposely used by an administration to keep welfare rolls down. Since the poor-law days the stigmatizing aspects have caused many poor to shrink from the use of public assistance. Even today many poor eligible for certain programs do not use them for this reason; a University of Wisconsin Institute of Poverty study (Barth et al., 1974) found that 17 percent of poor female-headed families with children did not receive any benefits at all from either social insurance (OASDHI) or public assistance; for other groups the proportion runs as high as half.

Lack of Rights   In practice, the welfare client does not have the rights to privacy that other citizens have. While the man-in-the-house regulations have been ruled out, social workers can ask many personal questions of recipients and in many ways intrude into their personal lives, whether by making an unexpected visit, asking about intimate matters, or giving moral conduct advice, or job counseling or childrearing suggestions, or even consumer choice restrictions. Although the Supreme Court in 1966 ruled that the receipt of welfare benefits was not conditioned upon a waiver of Fourth Amendment rights and HEW has warned the states not to carry on practices that violate the person's privacy and personal dignity, many examples of just that occur.

There is a punitive nature to many welfare department rules and activities; acting as an authoritarian figure, the agency and its workers often give clients "thou shalt" or "thou shalt not" instructions.

Second-Class Citizenship   A feeling among welfare clients of being the outsiders in an affluent society is the result of such policies. It makes the welfare recipient feel like a beggar living unworthily on the backs of others. The recipient seldom realizes that other, "upright" middle-class citizens often receive much more money in welfare benefits. If the word "welfare" is used in a broad context, then the middle-class recipient is receiving considerable benefits. Whether it be subsidies for higher education, veterans grants, tax deductions, or soil-bank refunds, the amount may greatly exceed the AFDC recipient's check.

Red Tape and Bureaucratic Hostility   Another problem in regard to the delivery of AFDC benefits is that there are complex eligibility requirements that change regularly. Many forms must be filled out, usually in inhospitable offices after long waits. The filling out of endless application forms and the need to provide numerous verification documents is degrading, especially in the brusque manner in which the application procedure is conducted.

To many on AFDC these actions make them feel that the agency is all-powerful and they powerless. Wiltse (1963) reports that his sample of San Francisco AFDC recipients had "a feeling of vulnerability to the structure of society in which AFDC parents felt themselves to be pawns of the agencies of the community and of the authorities in those agencies, i.e., the public welfare agency, the county hospital, social workers, doctors, the police department, and the court" (p. 812). He felt this situation led to a "pseudo-depression syndrome" for many.

The evidence required with an application invades one's privacy. One especially disliked requirement dating from 1950 was that where a father had deserted, the mother had to cooperate with law enforcement officers by furnishing information that might help locate her husband. If she didn't do this, she could be taken off AFDC. Though this regulation had only modest success, there was a new push in 1974 largely due to the fact that by 1974 half of all children on AFDC programs had parents who were separated or divorced and most of the fathers of these children paid no support. One HEW study estimated that of the 2.8 million AFDC parents absent from the home, about half of these were financially able to contribute to their children's support. In 1978 HEW tightened its rules requiring a mother on welfare to identify the father of her child, thus increasing the effort to locate the father and get him to reimburse welfare costs.

An example of the problems of applying for welfare in the main San Francisco welfare office is reported by a local reporter in 1976:

Hoping for a Little More

The waiting room of the welfare office was becoming more and more crowded; there weren't enough chairs. People were pushing up against the wall and little kids were sitting on the dirty floor. . . . one lady sat in a chair munching on a peanut butter sandwich. With peanut butter glued to the corners of her mouth, she said, "I always bring these down here because I know it's going to be a long wait." She got up to stretch and her chair was gone.

Applying for AFDC is tedious and degrading. . . . You fill out a form stating your name, your children's names, marital status, list of possessions, bank accounts, number of cars, home ownership or rental, and means of support. After these forms are completed you are screened to determine whether you qualify to apply. In one recent month, 200 of 822 applications were screened out because they didn't meet the basic requirements.

If you pass, you are scheduled to come back in two or three days for the longer, more grueling group interview.

If you return you must bring appropriate proof of your status— pregnancy verification, birth certificates for each child and proof that they are in school full time if they are over sixteen, rent receipts, utility bills, wage stubs, death certificates, health and life insurance policies when necessary, and so on.

You are given a cumbersome ten-page form in minuscule print called the "Statement of Facts Supporting Eligibility for Assistance" or the "WR-2." Among other things, it asks you to list all personal property you may own: the purchase price, date purchased and amount owed on such things . . . as gardening and cleaning equipment, stoves . . .

At the group interview, if all is in order, you are escorted along with fourteen or eighteen other applicants to a second floor room by an interviewer. Once again you go over the "WR-2" page by page, you fill out more forms such as a monthly income report called "WR-7." The "WR-2.1" asks you to give information about the absent husband. You are then given a "MA-595" to take to the employment office to register for work if you have a child over six years old.

After this ninety-minute paper extravaganza you are given your eligibility worker's identification and phone numbers and are asked to call him. He ultimately determines if you are really eligible, computes your budget and issues MediCal cards and food stamps. If you are desperate, he might even issue an emergency check the same day.

Source: Joann Klein in *California Living* Magazine, August 1, 1976, pp. 19–21.

Administrative Costs   The San Francisco welfare office example illustrates high administrative costs of this complex program, with its individual budget preparation and many checks on applicant statements. In the early 1970s in California administrative costs came to over 15 percent of the AFDC program costs. If one calculates the staff time required—to interpret the numerous, always changing regulations, to verify income, to check eligibility requirements, to do periodic reverification, to draw up individual budgets, to meet requests for special needs (such as children's clothing), to readjust budgets when incomes go up or family composition changes, to refer persons to help in other agencies—then one can see why there are high administrative costs.

In programs where forms have been simplified, individual budgets have been dropped, and only minor verification is done, such as the means-tested SSI for the elderly, disabled, and blind and the universal social insurance (OASDHI) program, where no income verification is necessary, the administrative costs are much, much lower. Everyone is simply mailed a monthly check from one central location.

The Commission on Federal Paperwork in 1976 reported that $6 billion could be saved in welfare costs every year by simplifying and cutting down on the forms used by welfare recipients.

Fraud   The complex eligibility requirements and the paperwork help cause fraud, although the problem is greatly exaggerated. The Commission on Federal Paperwork report (1976) said that simplified forms used uniformly by all agencies would cut fraud, since checking would be easier and welfare applicants would be less likely to err in filling them out. Today, people who often have only an eighth-grade education and low reading ability are asked to correctly fill out forms even social workers have trouble dealing with, causing some unintentional misrepresentation. Another problem is that many eligibility workers are new to the job. They are faced with thick books of ever-changing regulations. It is not surprising they sometimes make mistakes. A 1977 HEW study of fraud found that 51 percent of the errors were made by welfare agencies or social workers. Commenting on this, it added, "How much represents actual cheating never has been determined, but fraud prosecutions represent less than one percent of all cases." The report said that 5.3 percent of the 11.2 million AFDC recipients at that time were ineligible, 13.1 percent were overpaid, and 4.9 percent were underpaid.

Other studies have shown that many errors in individual recipients' benefits are overpayments of under $5. Some are due to recipients' not reporting changes in some aspects of their position, such as some minimal work activity.

Agencies, because their outlook is that the client is to be mistrusted, center their efforts on eliminating fraudulent claimants. One can question whether emphasis should be placed on discouraging the small potential number of fraudulent or unworthy cases, especially since, as Costain (1979) reports, "Studies of AFDC caseloads have repeatedly shown low ineligibility rates, low enough as to be expected in the administration of any such large-scale and administrationally complex program" (p. 156). She bases this comment on the HEW *Report on the Disposition of Public Assistance Cases Involving Questions of Fraud* (1970). Some wonder whether, instead of this focus on fraud, emphasis should be put on seeing that all in need do apply for help rather than going hungry and without shelter. Some, especially in Britain, would say that the good society should encourage use of public assistance by all those in need. In the United States, little attempt is made to inform people of their eligibility, as welfare rights leaders have pointed out; more concern is directed to cutting people off on legal technicalities or by new regulations.

Differences in Payments in Different States   Not only are eligibility rules not standardized from state to state, but payments are also not standardized. In 1977 the average payment per person was $14.50 in Mississippi and $114.83 in New York. For an AFDC family of four in 1975, the combined state and federal benefits were only $720 per year in Mississippi, as compared to $5954 in Hawaii. That was a year when the average family income in the United States was around $13,000. It is questionable whether any family of four could manage on $720. Many

Southern states made similarly low payments, far below the minimum amount of money the states themselves estimated a family could live on. Fewer than twenty-six states in 1977 made AFDC payments as large as two-thirds the poverty-level amount, a low amount in itself.

While the 1967 amendments to welfare regulations required that the welfare departments reflect rises in the cost of living when they set their need standards, few states raised payments (Komisar, 1977). Pearce (1978) reports that benefit levels have actually been declining. In 1960 the average AFDC payment per family was 26.4 percent of the median family income, but by 1975 it was only 18.9 percent, a considerable downward movement. Payments to AFDC families are always below those to groups considered more deserving, groups such as the aged and the blind.

The Overall Cost of Welfare   One reason the payments are kept low is that the overall cost is high and has risen sharply in the last ten years. Part of this is due to the normal rise in the child population over the years. Pearce (1978) says, in fact, that as a percentage of the population, the number of AFDC cases has remained stable over the years.

State and local governments, especially in core cities, have felt the problem of increased cost. In ten core-city areas in 1977 more than 10 percent of the residents were recipients of AFDC. Because core cities, such as New York, pay a part of the welfare cost, the very high costs have been partially responsible for their near-bankrupt condition.

By 1977 the number of families on AFDC was 3.5 million and the cost stood at almost $6 billion, including federal and state administrative costs. However, by 1977 veterans benefits had risen to over $8 billion and many other programs, such as Medicare, were much more costly; federal civil service retirement costs were at $10 billion and OASDHI at $87 billion. AFDC in reality was only a very small item in the national budget, equaling about 1.5 to 2 percent of GNP. Charles Schultze (1976), in fact, states that the real *increases* in domestic federal expenditures between 1955 and 1977, as ratio of GNP, were in the rapid expansion of retirement, disability, and unemployment compensation, which was responsible for slightly more than half the growth. The introduction of new low-income assistance programs providing food and medical and housing benefits also accounted for some of the growth. Therefore, one should be careful not to exaggerate the increased cost of AFDC. Furthermore, all these programs to help the poor, including social security payments of $87 billion, took only 8.4 percent of the GNP in 1977, far below the percentage in most northern European countries.

The Work Incentive–Job Training Issue   A major focus in the last decade, as has already been mentioned, has been to get those on welfare into jobs. As welfare rolls increased, it was felt that training programs, public works programs, and work incentives were needed to try to get persons partially or fully off welfare. However, problems arose. While study after study showed that welfare recipients had a positive attitude toward work and that members of the working poor group would not stop working, evidence also indicated that many recipients were unemployable.

The WIN experience has shown that welfare recipients are hardly averse to training for a job. A much higher proportion of them applied for training than expected; in California, 80,000 applied for 16,000 openings, and funding limitations meant many had to be turned away. Mildred Rein, in her study of AFDC recipients (1972), likewise found that many of the AFDC mothers were willing to work.

In the most generously funded work incentive research to date, the New Jersey Income Maintenance Experiment, findings showed that the sampled low-income two-parent households were not likely to stop work when they were given a welfare payment to supplement their wages to the point of bringing them up to an acceptable income level. However, there was some degree of work withdrawal for wives, mainly in Spanish-speaking households, due to this income assistance from the government. Hausman and Friedman (1975) report that even among the 3 to 4 percent of the participants who did not work, it was health problems, not distaste for work, that determined their employment status.

The more current Seattle-Denver Income Maintenance Experiment interim report (Keeley et al., 1977) on the impact of a negative income tax program on the working poor did show some work withdrawal following provision of benefits. Its data gave evidence that, overall, husbands reduced their labor in response to this government income assistance very, very slightly and female heads of households also only slightly.

A number of problems have arisen in moving welfare recipients into the work force. First, while politicians have indicated that many welfare recipients are capable of work, in case after case the opposite has been shown, that is, that many are unemployable. Second, while officials have hailed training as making many eligible to qualify for participation in the work force, in reality many are not trainable or are being trained for obsolete, dead-end, and low-paying jobs. Third, in some areas, the only work available is of the low-wage, stoop-labor type. Welfare recipients have long provided cheap labor for harvest work, and they receive little welfare money during periods when they are needed in the fields. Recipients have protested against this in several places, both because the pay has been too low and because the work, often stoop labor, very difficult. Costain (1979) states, "With ill-defined criteria for assessing what constitutes "suitable" work, the door was left open for racial discrimination and poor labor conditions for AFDC parents" (p. 171). Fourth, the work incentive of allowing workers to keep part of their pay rather than have it deducted from their welfare check has not always worked smoothly; if one receives public housing or food stamps, any earnings affect one's ability to qualify for these other services, which do not have work-incentive clauses and count all income in determining eligibility.

In the area of capability, there are many examples of problems. For example, in the early 1970s New York State passed a law saying that all able-bodied recipients should register for work. Of almost 2 million recipients in the state in 1971, only 38,400 were rated employable; of the 38,400 only 4 percent got jobs lasting any amount of time.

California fared little better in its "work or else" welfare experiment in the early 1970s. A State Employment Development Department official reports that the "work or else" package "did not prove to be administratively feasible and practical." During the program's peak year of 1974, it is reported that only 4760 individuals participated in program work assignments out of 182,735 persons available for assignment.

In the WIN program, the 1967 training and job program for AFDC cases, many were found unemployable. As of 1972 1 out of 4 recipients were not referred at all because of age or number of children; 1 in 7 were excluded because of illness, disability, or advanced age; and others were eliminated because of the lack of child care arrangements or because they were attending school full-time or for other reasons.

Even the Department of Labor, in working with the WIN program, admitted that with an unemployment rate over 6 percent many more were brought into training than could find jobs and, ironically, many trainees were men, not a true AFDC representation. One could see how these poorly educated, psychologically handicapped welfare recipients, many of whom were from minorities, might fare badly in any competition for jobs. Also, because of their very limited educational skills, the only jobs they could be trained for were often the unskilled and semiskilled ones, such as gas station attendant, file clerk, or beauty operator for which labor was already abundant. In a computerized, industrial world, many of these people did not fit in; as the Commissioner of Welfare in New York State in 1965, George Wyman, said, "It would be pointless, wasteful and cruel to try to prepare [financially needy] families for an economy into which they cannot be integrated because it can offer them no opportunities to become productive, self-supporting, and responsible citizens" (Howard, 1969, p. 198). To some work ethos advocates, the training was seen as an end in itself.

Yet the question persists, Who should be trained and what type of training should we provide? Is it futile to train those with only minimal skills or mothers with children?

Pearce (1978) says of the welfare WIN program that it has created a "workhouse without walls." By taking a group of women who are already handicapped by low educational levels, low skills, and low occupational status and giving them either no training or minimal training in fields that do not pay a living wage and forcing them to work, WIN has created for many women a no-win situation. "They cannot use welfare training programs to get decently paid employment, nor can they use paid employment to get off of welfare" (p. 20).

Smith (1975) verifies this, finding that two-thirds of the female WIN ex-participants who were working received supplementary welfare grants on account of low income and large family size. A 1971–1972 Census Bureau report showed that most in-training positions were in clerical and sales, private household, or other service work, mostly low-paying jobs.

If a mother on AFDC is lucky enough to obtain a job paying decent wages, above the welfare maximum, she faces dilemmas that may make her reluctant to take such a job. If taken off welfare she loses her Medicaid assistance, her food stamps, and possibly child care benefits.

Welfare recipients often do not know what is the breaking point in job income that will cause them to be taken off welfare, as Handler and Hollingsworth (1971) found in Wisconsin; their welfare worker is often not able to tell them accurately. In such cases the recipient errs on the safe side.

The Breakup of Families   The most serious problem with AFDC at the time of this writing has been left for last, because there is a chance that Congress by 1981 will mandate that states have AFDC-UF, in other words, that all states allow families with unemployed fathers to apply. However, even with such a mandate it is questionable whether states will easily admit such families to the program. At this writing (1979) most recipients are women and their children and the program can rightfully be accused of breaking up the family instead of strengthening it. In many cases the husband is forced to desert so that the wife and children can qualify. Even in the half of all states that have AFDC-UF, restrictions related to his work make it difficult for the family to get prompt aid if he is around. He must have a waiting period without employment before applying and a substantial recent work history. The quickest way to get assistance is for him to leave. Thus, it is not surprising that when Moynihan (1965) charted the desertion rate for black families and the AFDC application rate for black families he found the two lines to run parallel, with increases in AFDC cases following increases in desertion, and with increases in black male unemployment meaning increases in black AFDC cases. It is simple: you are unemployed, you desert, and your wife and children can get on AFDC. For example, take the case of Mrs. M., who said:

> We just couldn't cope anymore. Henry had lost his janitorial job. The rent was behind and the landlord was threatening eviction. The three kids all

needed new shoes. We were down to eating peanut butter sandwiches meal after meal or grits. Henry decided the only way was for him to leave and for me to apply to the welfare department. The lady asked where my husband was and I just said "gone to Alaska" and she really believed it. Henry doesn't even dare come back for a night because we heard of these raids where they come to bother you early in the morning just to see who you are sleeping with.

In another case of an unemployed husband, the woman said, "I went to the welfare office and the lady said the only way they could help me and the children is if my husband, Hans, left. I told them the children would die if they lost their father and the lady just shrugged her shoulders and said that was the only way."

Thus, as of 1979, without AFDC-UF readily available, AFDC can be called a program that actually breaks up families. In contrast to the counseling we give to the normal American family, where we consider it so important for the child to have a male figure present and particularly encourage divorced fathers to visit their offspring, we seriously discourage AFDC fathers from doing so. And, in the days of the man-in-the-house rule, we especially discouraged any suitors for the AFDC mother, threatening to cut off her welfare if such a man was found to live in her home. Many an AFDC mother has turned the other way, forming a relationship with a man she hoped might get her off welfare or pay some of the rent and other bills.

The AFDC ruling that disallows aid to families where an unemployed husband is present, which, in 1979, still holds in half the states and for practical purposes is in effect for some cases in all states, is especially ironic, since our economic system fosters such unemployment. The main victim of this AFDC ruling is the black male, who historically has been part of a pool of workers welcomed in industry and elsewhere during economic upturns but easily expended in times of recession. He is the last hired and first fired; he might be called the underbelly of the work force in a technologically developed society. Thus to deny welfare to his family when he is unemployed unless he leaves is to ignore the role the economic system has given him, that of a person involuntarily in and out of the labor force.

RECOMMENDATIONS FOR REFORM OF THE WELFARE SYSTEM

The problems of AFDC that have been covered include the breakup of the family, the lack of privacy for the user, and the degrading, stigmatizing aspects, the feeling of second-class citizenship, punitive control, the eligibility red tape, bureaucratic hostility, the administrative costs, the issue of fraud, the differences in payments between states, the overall cost of welfare, and the work incentive–job training issue.

Various suggestions have been put forth to remedy these problems. Some relate to revamping the welfare system, and others are broader policy measures. The broader ones fall into several categories. The first approach is to directly reduce the number of persons on the welfare rolls. First, government measures could be used to improve economic growth and decrease unemployment, to improve the economies of depressed areas, and to decrease inflation. All these measures could decrease the number needing welfare assistance. Other government measures that would reduce the number applying for welfare would be limiting the immigration of unskilled workers, many of whom arrive with large families; as of 1979 the increased immigration, both legal and illegal, of Vietnamese and other Asian groups and of Mexican nationals has helped increase the welfare rolls in such states as California. Measures to decrease unwanted pregnancies among young girls, including free abortions and greater family planning counseling, would again keep welfare rolls down. More provision of day care would also allow more mothers of young children to work.

Government actions to open up opportunities, including antidiscrimination measures and the provision of assistance to education, could also help certain of the poor.

Employers can also do their part to keep the welfare rolls smaller. They could be asked to expand their coverage of risks for their workers by increasing their contribution for longer periods of unemployment and making higher workers' compensation payments or paying them for a longer period and they could be required to provide health insurance. Employers could be forced to pay more to the group now called the "working poor" if the government increased the minimum wage.

Another strategy to take people off AFDC is to move more poor away from the means-tested welfare program to other, universal (or non–means-tested) programs. These could include such insurance programs as unemployment compensation or OASDHI, in the latter case by making more groups eligible. Veterans' benefits could also be expanded. Help could come in the form of a universal children's allowance that would provide a monthly stipend per child for all families, rich and poor alike. This means that large poor families would get extra help without having to apply to a means-tested program such as AFDC. At present the nonpoor who pay income taxes get a tax deduction ($1000 in 1979) for each child, which is an indirect type of children's allowance; a true, paid-out children's allowance would be a substitute for this tax assistance. Children's allowances exist in almost all industrial countries. The degree to which they help poor families depends on the amount of the allowance. Government help could also be in the form of housing subsidies or higher food-stamp payments. Government could also help the poor by decreasing their tax burden, including their sales taxes and their contributions for social security insurance.

All these measures would mean there would be fewer poor who would have to apply for means-tested welfare assistance, but they would by no means fully eliminate the need; some would always be so poor that general overall cash assistance would be necessary.

Other suggested policy changes in the welfare program are those getting people off welfare and into jobs:

1   Introducing job training programs in cooperation with the Department of Labor and having recipients on both training and welfare
2   Giving people incentives to work while on welfare
3   Providing public employment jobs and encouraging private industry to provide apprentice or trainee positions through tax incentives or payments for each trainee
4   Making it mandatory that those considered employable report to the employment office and accept jobs or training
5   Providing day care for those welfare mothers going into training or employment

A different set of proposals for reforming the welfare system involves expanding the coverage to include more categories of people. One major proposal in recent years is to include the working poor in the program. Other groups recommended for inclusion are families with an unemployed husband, which, as of 1979, are not included in half the states and because of rigid regulations are only rarely included in other states. The objective of family stability would be greatly helped by the inclusion of both these groups. Couples and singles under age 62, now excluded from all but local general assistance, are also recommended for coverage.

There are several recommendations for making the system both more equitable and more efficient. One is to standardize eligibility regulations among all the states and to standardize forms. A related one is to standardize payments for all the states so that the very large differences between such states as Hawaii and Mississippi are decreased or ended.

A major need is to simplify forms and the whole application procedure, including investigation and documentation of eligibility. This would decrease the degrading aspects of applying and the hostile atmosphere in the welfare office. This and administrative changes could lessen the feeling of second-class citizenship and begging for welfare. More adherence to standardized budgets and less individual budget treatment would also help. All this would lessen the paperwork for the staff and decrease administrative costs.

A very important move in the direction of simplifying forms, decreasing administrative costs, and decreasing stigma would be a negative income tax.

Negative Income Tax

The negative income tax is a general payment or allowance to all households in poverty. It would cover not only the groups now on welfare but also the working poor and others in presently excluded groups. To test this long-discussed idea, the government has run for several years an extensive demonstration, the New Jersey negative income tax (NIT) experiment, through the Institute for Research on Poverty of the University of Wisconsin and Mathematica, Inc., New Jersey. The experiment gave out an allowance to a sample of male-headed working households falling below a certain income level. This guarantee, usually expressed as a percentage of the poverty-line income, is the main characteristic of the NIT and what makes it a kind of guaranteed annual income (GAI); in other words, this is the allowance a poor family gets if other income is zero. Then there is a rate at which all other income, such as wages, is taxed; the rate on the dollar earned is set to give an incentive for the poor household to work (Pechman and Timpane, 1975). There can be different guarantee or allowance levels and different tax rates; several were tried in the New Jersey NIT experiment. Lampman (1971) gives an example:

> A negative income tax with a guarantee at the poverty line and a 50 per cent tax rate (hence a break-even point at twice the poverty line) would have cost at least $25 billion in 1967 in benefits and income tax forgiven over and above what we were then spending for transfers [government assistance]. These net benefits would go to some 80 million people, leaving the upper 120 million to pay the $25 billion on top of the taxes they are now paying. [P. 158]

If the discussion of this type of transfer (government assistance) payment sounds complicated it is because policies in this area, usually calculated by economists, are hard to work out. Payments to the poor household decrease as income rises, although not at such a steep rate as to discourage work incentive. When the family income reaches a certain "break-even level," the allowance or assistance is cut off.

As with an income tax, a pay or account period must be used. Instead of yearly income it can be a month's income, or a "moving average" year, taking into account the previous month's earnings. Decisions on all these factors can affect work incentive under the program, and this is what the New Jersey NIT experiment centered on.

The negative income tax is much simpler than the present welfare system, although there are a number of decisions to make, such as the percentage of poverty-line income, the tax rate, and the break-even point. Now let us look at the more modest but more widely considered Nixon and Carter welfare reform proposals.

Reform Recommendations in the Nixon and Carter Proposals

Some of the proposals for welfare reform that have been covered in this chapter have already been put forward in the legislation proposed by the administrations of Richard Nixon and Jimmy Carter. Both proposals are fairly similar. The Nixon one (the Family Assistance Plan or FAP) did not pass Congress, though parts of it were enacted; the Carter proposals, *A Program for Better Jobs and Income* (H.R. 9030), were not passed in 1979. A summary of the changes these proposals recommended follows.

Coverage for the Working Poor and Families with an Unemployed Husband   Both presidents' proposals would have given assistance to children of the working poor and, in *all* states, assistance to children of the able-bodied unemployed. The Carter proposal also included childless couples and singles.

Including this large group of working poor presents a number of problems and may be one reason Nixon's FAP bill (H.R. 1) was defeated. It is costly, because so many people are involved; it would cover the half of the poor families headed by a nondisabled and non-aged male who receives neither public assistance nor social insurance benefits today. The Carter proposal, in essence, would have been a supplement to the present wages of people earning minimum wage or below (in 1972 over 5.5 million Americans were working at less than minimum wage). If such proposals had been implemented, it was estimated that as much as a third of the population in some states would be getting welfare. Some critics complained that it turned too many into welfare recipients, dependent on a government dole. Others called these proposals a new Speenhamland Act (the 1795 English plan to have local authorities supplement low wages). This act was disastrous, since it induced employers to keep wages low and allow the government to bring workers' income up to an acceptable standard. Because of these facts, a *Social Work* journal editorial, on "Mr. Nixon's 'Speenhamland' " (Levi, 1970), asked, "Should we not further anticipate that an increasingly greater proportion of the combined income (wages plus benefits) of the working poor will be paid out of general tax funds?" (p. 8).

Unions have criticized both the Nixon and the Carter proposals for covering the working poor, by saying they would subsidize employers and encourage non-union factories in the South because they mean cheap labor. Yet the question arises, How does one help those families with a male head in the work force who is working full-time but whose wages are so low that the family is still poor? Since this group is largely white and in many cases Southern, giving help is of special interest to some politicians. An increase in the minimum wage is another way to help these families but one less appealing to politicians who are also employers or affiliated with them.

Providing Jobs and Job Training   Both the Nixon proposal and the Carter one were workfare proposals, with the stress on getting welfare recipients into jobs. The name of Carter's bill, *A Program for Better Jobs and Income,* indicated this. The eligible poor population was divided into those expected to work and those—the elderly, the disabled, and female family heads with young children—not expected to work. The group expected to work included, in two-parent households, at least one adult and, in single-parent households with children, the mother, if it did not interfere with caring for the children.

In the Carter proposal, it was assumed that public employment, at least, would be found for those expected to work or that training would be provided and then people would be pushed to continually apply at the employment office and hunt for private-sector employment. Interest in jobs in the private sector was encouraged and deduction incentives were given to make them more attractive than public-sector jobs. However, under the Carter proposals there was also a "Public Service Employment Program," with the wage rate slightly above minimum wage. The proposal was for creating 1.4 million public jobs (a large number of such jobs were actually brought in under the CETA program); these included jobs for people to aid the elderly and the sick, to provide child care, to serve as paraprofessionals in the schools, to work on recreational facilities, and to clean up neighborhoods. The National Association of Social Workers (NASW) commended these proposals as "a recognition of the importance of job opportunities and their correlation to the welfare system."

Work Incentives   Welfare recipients would have an incentive, in the form of having a part of their wages not counted in determining welfare payments, to take either private or public jobs or training, under the 1978 Carter proposal.

Working Mothers   Single parents with children aged 7 to 14 were expected to accept part-time work or, where appropriate day care was available, full-time work. It is this work condition that was seriously criticized as an imposition by welfare rights groups and social workers, because it pushed to the employment office, almost as a punitive measure, the mother of a number of children without after-school care who had very limited skills and no high school diploma.

This "willingness to work" emphasis of the Carter proposal is criticized by Northwood (1978), who states:

> The institution of a mandatory work requirement . . . would alter the primary goal of the AFDC program: that of strengthening family life. It would deny that all mothers have a *right* to income support to enable them to take care of their children themselves and should not have to go to work . . . [P. 552]

To what degree should women with children be asked to go into training or employment? Sixty percent of the AFDC families are women with children under 6. In most states that have established work regulations for welfare recipients, these mothers of young children have been exempt. Mothers with school-aged children are pushed more strongly toward the employment office and labor market.

Do we really prefer having the mother work rather than stay home and take care of her children, especially if the pay she brings in from the work is so low she must still stay on welfare? Shouldn't she at least be given a choice? If participation is compulsory, with referral for work or training a mandatory condition for continuing to receive assistance, there is insufficient latitude for AFDC mothers to decide whether being at work and needing alternative child care during the day is contrary to the welfare of their own families.

Johnnie Tillmon of the Welfare Rights Organization reported in the January 1972 issue of *Ms.* magazine:

> In this country, we believe in something called the "work ethic" . . . but the work ethic is a double standard. It applies to men and to women on welfare. It doesn't apply to all women. If you're a society lady from Scarsdale and you spend all your time sitting on your prosperity, painting your nails, well, that's okay. Women aren't supposed to work. They're supposed to be married.
>
> But if you don't have a man to pay for everything, particularly if you have kids, then everything changes. [P. 115]

Day Care The next question is, if we demand that these welfare mothers work, Should we see that enough day care centers are built, ones that serve children after school as well as preschool children? Under WIN we have not done this. Also, "the Carter welfare reform plan," as Parry (1978) points out, "unfairly discriminates against female involvement in the labor force by virtually ignoring the issue of child care, thus creating a major impediment to employment by female headed households. . . . combined with the provision requiring some mothers to work (approximately three in eight) [this] creates an untenable situation for many women."

A Job Program, Not a Welfare Program   The ability of the poor to fit into the job market, the main assumption of the Carter and Nixon proposals, has also been seriously questioned by NASW. They say of the Carter reforms:

> One of the basic philosophic stumbling blocks preventing association support of the Carter proposal is NASW's belief that a jobs program is an inappropriate mechanism for large-scale income transfers to the poor. Too many of the poor cannot work, but should receive adequate benefits—the current proposed benefit is only 65 percent of the poverty level. [Parry, 1978]

Standardized but Low Payments   What the Carter proposals recommended was a *standard federal payment,* a national basic benefit, rather than the present complex federal contribution formula to individual states; this would have been much higher than present AFDC payments in the many low-paying states, such as in the South. However, this payment would have been low for today's high-paying states. In addition, to create the incentive to work, the working poor had to be given more than the nonworking poor. Therefore, as Northwood (1978) says, "In one sense the Carter proposals represent a well-organized campaign under federal auspices to downgrade the standard of living of the welfare poor," and this would be especially true of the nonworking poor (p. 557).

One reason for the policy of keeping payments low was the problem that total costs would be up when the grants in low-paying states were increased and the working poor were included together with childless couples, singles, and families headed by unemployed men.

This standardized national basic benefit, with all its shortcomings, can, however, be looked at as establishing a *guaranteed annual income,* or "a minimum cash benefit level within a federalized income support system," as the NASW says and for which it positively commends Carter (Parry, 1978). It makes the right to a minimum standard of income more of a reality. It also would have greatly raised the level of assistance to those in the ten poorest states. Whether it greatly narrows the disparity between states in amount of payments is not certain.

In reality the Carter plan might have protected recipients' loss in high-benefit states by encouraging the states to supplement the federal contribution. On the other hand, political pressures make it imperative that recipients who now get high benefits not have them drop too much under such a new program; the federal government is not willing to allocate enough funding to provide this higher level of financial assistance (instead keeping it very low—for a family of four, at two-thirds of the poverty standard) and leaves it up to the states to bring the payment up. Some states will not.

Standardization among the States   Another positive aspect of the Carter proposals was a plan to substitute more federal criteria for state-determined criteria. The plan was for uniform application procedures and eligibility criteria.

Paper Work and Administrative Costs   The Administration also planned to cut the total amount of paperwork as well as standardize it both nationwide and between programs. This and many of the other measures, including standardization of payments and forms and centralization of financing, could cut administrative costs, as could another recommendation, combining programs.

Combining Programs   The Carter proposal was to combine the food-stamp program, AFDC, and SSI for the disabled, blind, and elderly and replace them with a single system of cash assistance, causing less administration. Since many poor do not get food stamps now, this move would change their situation. While many liberals praise this combining of programs, this author wonders how it would work for SSI recipients, who since 1973 have not had to go to the welfare office to receive help but have gone to the much less stigmatizing Social Security Administration office, where many middle-class people go to apply for their OASDHI benefits.

Division of Functions   One administrative aspect of the Carter proposals would actually have made bureaucracy costs higher, and that is the fact that the Department of Labor would be involved in the jobs and training part of the program, as it was in the Nixon proposals. NASW complained that the proposals would have divided administrative functions among three federal departments: Labor, the Treasury, and HEW. It pointed out that substantial mechanisms for coordination needed to be developed.

Social Services   The social service component in the Carter plan was also criticized by NASW, which stated, "The association is also disenchanted with the provisions, or lack thereof, for supportive social services to complement the cash assistance component" of the plan. And Parry (1978) of NASW added, "Unhappily, services presently performed routinely in public assistance programs for all recipients will now be unavailable to many."

CONCLUSION

Looking backward at our social policy strategies in Chapter 1, how did the Carter plan approach these issues? How does it answer the policy analysis questions? It could fill the income need for more groups and increase family stability. As for the choice between programs of a broad nature and those of a narrow nature, it is trying to broaden the program by linking food stamps with AFDC and SSI.

In eligibility or allocation strategy, the Carter plan is still a means-tested program, though income criteria will depend on whether one is working or not. The working poor may keep part of their earnings.

On the question of categorical assistance versus assistance to all, the program may be moving away from categorical assistance to more universal coverage, since it first of all covers all types of families, as well as singles and childless couples, and second puts SSI recipients in with families formerly receiving AFDC.

Cost-effectiveness is encouraged in a number of ways, such as by centralizing some of the administration, standardizing regulations and procedures, combining programs, and pushing present recipients toward work. However, the addition of a number of new categories of recipients will increase cost.

Concerning the type of provision, it will be cash; the program will even eliminate the in-kind, voucher-type food-stamp program. It will not be a contributory insurance system. It remains, of course, assistance to the person, not an agency, building, or area. Last, it comes closer to welfare as a right for all, because it both provides a basic federal assistance level and covers all types of poor, not just the narrow categories now covered. Whether stigma will be decreased is debatable, since there will still be a welfare office to go to, a declaration to fill out that one is poor, and a demand to meet stringent regulations or face punitive action; on the other hand, the program would no longer be only for AFDC recipients, mainly females, who unfortunately present a negative image to the public; the program would now cover the working poor, the elderly, disabled, blind, singles, and childless couples.

The delivery structure would still be a public agency but there would be a greater federal role and the Department of Labor would now be more involved. On three other aspects of the delivery system—whether there will be a multiservice agency, a coordinating agency, and a program stressing accessibility—the answer seems to be no. While there would be a new agency, combining the present ones, the type of staff is likely to stay the same.

In general, the Carter plan can be described in the way the journal *Social Work* described its predecessor, the Nixon proposals: "Mix . . . one small part of social breakthrough, several parts of status quo, and a good portion of reaction and then . . . proclaim this as a new departure" (p. 3).

Whether the political climate and value system in the United States in the present period, as described in Chapter 4, allows even this great a departure from current policy may be questionable, since the proposal has had very little support in Congress. As Northwood (1978) says, "Welfare reform has been the submerged reef on which many presidential administrations have floundered" (p. 547). (Former HEW Secretary Califano calls welfare reform the Middle East of domestic politics.) Moynihan (1973), the chief architect of the Nixon proposals, points out how difficult it is to get a proposal through a conservative, rural-oriented Congress. Work incentives and work requirements, often unrealistic, need to be included in any bill to get it passed by conservative members of Congress (even Nixon's FAP bill wasn't passed). Moynihan describes the heated confrontations and strong opposition within Nixon's Cabinet at the many meetings over the bill and talks of "battles raging." Similar battle lines were formed in 1978 on the Carter proposal, although this left out or softened some Nixon proposals that liberals opposed.

One can say these proposals are simply a patchwork of reform. They are neither a full-fledged guaranteed annual income (nor are they a *simplistic* negative income tax) nor a major measure to correct the employment problem for low-income persons. In the long run it is in the private market that more jobs must be provided, that decent wages must be paid for female-dominated occupations, and that successful training programs for the poorly educated must occur. Public employment is temporary; with its wages at minimum-wage level to meet unions' and private employers' opposition, and with promotion and fringe benefits unlikely.

Policy for Child Welfare Services

Policy for Child Welfare Services

INTRODUCTION

"To save the children" is a phrase familiar to all of us. An important value in our society is to provide for the well-being of children, to see they are not abused, neglected, abandoned, or otherwise mistreated.

One hears stories where a mother has left her young children unattended in a hot automobile for five hours; where a father has molested his teenaged daughter; where a mother is mentally ill and despondent and does not fix meals or dress her 3-year-old twins; where a family has its 12-year-old son working in its dry cleaning establishment; where a child has a large, open sore on her arm that looks infected and there is no indication of medical attention; where a family has a 12-year-old child stay home from school continually to take care of the 3- and 4-year-old children while both husband and wife work. In all these cases we say something must be done.

Child welfare services are the provision of professionals to deal with these and many other child-related problems. The child welfare worker is someone who attempts to help with social problems which come from deficiencies in parental responsibility or impairment of the parents' ability to provide for the necessary needs any child has. These services are given to correct the inadequacy of the parent-child relationship. They may be aids to support and supplement the family in meeting the child's needs. In some cases, the services must substitute for the family, such as when the child is neglected or abused, is dependent because a parent or parents are incapacitated, or, in some cases, is delinquent or physically or mentally handicapped.

Child welfare, in its broadest sense, incorporates the social, economic, and health services of public and private welfare agencies which secure and protect the well-being of all children in their physical, intellectual, and emotional development (Friedlander and Apte, 1974). Its clientele are not just the poor but all children; many middle-class children have emotional problems, are in need of protection from neglect or abuse, are physically handicapped, or suffer from many other types of problems. In this child welfare field the focus is on providing services, not just cash assistance. The service may be a supportive one, such as the Family Service Agency, which helps families function better, or a child guidance clinic, which uses therapeutic techniques to improve parent-child relations and the child's emotional state; it may be a protective agency working with cases of neglect and abuse; or it may be an adoption agency working with unwed mothers and couples seeking to adopt children. The child welfare agency may be working with children placed in foster homes for a variety of reasons. The agency may be an institutional setting or an outpatient clinic to serve emotionally disturbed or handicapped children. It may be a probation service or correctional facility for delinquent children.

The continuing changes in American society have put stresses on many parents that affect their ability to perform their parental responsibilities adequately, as was stated in Chapter 3. Most families are no longer extended families but isolated nuclear families without relatives close by to baby-sit, to give childrearing advice, and to be supportive in husband-wife relations. The high geographic mobility of families today means that wives must find new child care facilities and deal with new schools and health services after each move; this also impairs adequate parental functioning. The situation where more and more mothers work, even when children are very young, means stress from the dual role of mother and employed worker and the constant need to find adequate child care facilities for young children. The high divorce rate indicates that many families are suffering family breakdown and marital tensions before and after the divorce, and this has its effect on the child. The single-parent situation following many divorces means that the strain of 24-hour parental responsibility is placed on one parent, usually the mother, who often lacks financial means to relieve the burden or, if she works, must resort to the use of child care facilities for young children. Then there is the "blended" marriage, in which the child must adjust to a stepparent and stepsisters and stepbrothers, and later to half siblings.

Many children live in poverty; 1 out of 5 did in 1970. They often lack the basic clothing and the toys the better-off child has. They often live in crowded, deteriorated housing infested with rodents and roaches. They often live in slum areas, where the chances of lead poisoning and other health hazards are high, where violence and crime are prevalent, and where gangs and drug abuse are common.

Membership in gangs and illicit drug use now also occur in many middle-class areas where there is little planned recreation and where it is common for both parents to work or for the father to be out a great deal. The child in suburbia is not free of problems, although they may take some different forms than in inner-city areas.

There are a number of situations children may fall into. Some problem children, one might say, have fallen through the cracks; that is, no one has met their need or answered their cry for help and they have now become problem children whom we often shuttle away to unloving foster homes or institutions or let stand about as the unwanted school dropout, the unemployed youth, or the drug addict, who when reaching adulthood will drift into our skid rows and slums, our hippie retreats, or our correctional facilities.

"To save the children" means to some to provide preventive child welfare services to see that these situations never occur, as well as to provide services to meet crisis and family breakdown needs. An example to emphasize this is the case of John Paul.

John Paul was 4 when his father deserted the family. His mother had to work each day until 6 P.M. and had him cared for by a neighbor, who often left him alone while she went out shopping. Later he went to school but did not do well because his reading and speech were poor, on account of his isolation as a young child. The school did not give him adequate remedial work. When he was 10 his mother remarried, and his stepfather did not like him. His mother asked her sister, who had five children of her own, to take care of him, and three months later the mother and her new husband left town. They seldom sent money to the sister, and so she turned to the local social service office and asked that John Paul be put in a foster home. John Paul, because of his failure in school and lack of love at home, was now a difficult boy to deal with and moved from foster home to foster home. At the age of 13 he was put into a group home, but after he got into trouble with the law for the third time and after being put on probation twice, he was put in a correctional institution.

What preventive steps could have been taken to help John Paul? Would better day care have been useful? Would family support to his mother have prevented her abandonment of him? Could the school staff have caught his deficiencies early and lessened his school failure?

THE NEEDS OF CHILDREN

John Paul suffered because a number of his basic needs as a developing child were not satisfactorily met. All children have a need for parental affection, for emotional stability, for understanding, for personality growth, and for creative stimulation. They have a need for instruction to develop intellectual abilities and basic skills. They need health care to ensure normal physical growth. They need regular, nutritious meals; satisfactory clothing; and safe and sanitary shelter in a satisfactory, wholesome physical environment. They need stimulating and pleasurable recreational activities. They need basic maintenance, care, and protection during their minority and a parent or guardian who will act as an intermediary between them and the rest of the world.

Young persons must have adequate rearing so that basic socialization takes place. This must include inculcating in them a basic set of controls over behavior, teaching them societal responsibilities, introducing them to basic role performance, and in general training them to become contributing citizens in society.

PARENTS' RIGHTS, CHILDREN'S RIGHTS, AND THE STATE'S RIGHTS

The nation has a concern for its children because they are its future citizens. The needs of the child are left to the parents to fulfill with little interference from the state, but when the parents do not meet the *minimum* acceptable level of care, then the state is considered justified in stepping in to ensure the social maintenance of the larger order, the community, for it is the whole community that suffers if the parents do not carry out their responsibilities to support their children, to discipline them and socialize them to the ways of society and to protect them.

As Costain (1979) says, when parental care falls below a certain level,

> . . . the state has a responsibility to intervene, that is, to exercise the ancient law of *parens patriae,* under which the court, acting as a protector of the dependent and immature child, uses its power to require a better level of care or treatment for a particular child. This may result in removal of the child from his or her own home to a foster home or institution. [P. 8]

The state may also decide that for the benefit of society the child must use certain basic services, such as education and certain health services like immunization, or must meet certain basic requirements.

Parents' and Children's Rights

Rights have varied over time. While parents still have great independence and latitude in caring for their children, in this century in America the child's rights have been established in a number of areas.

The existence of laws protecting the child was hardly the case throughout most of history. The parent, especially the father, had complete authority over the child up to the twentieth century, and his treatment of the child was seldom a concern of the community.

Historically a low value was put on children. In ancient times, when the common people barely had enough food to eat in a normal year and had to go without in times of disaster—whether famine, economic upheavals, bad winters, or wars—infanticide was not unknown. It was justified on the grounds of lack of economic resources or lack of a mother to care for the newborn child. (Some groups buried the child with the mother if she died in childbirth.) Special categories of children, such as the illegitimate child in nineteenth-century Europe or the defective or deformed child in many tribal groups, were killed at birth.

Abandonment of children was also common throughout history. The child left on the parish doorstep by a poor mother was well known not only in nineteenth-century America but also in most historical periods. The church at an early point took on the role of providing for such children. However, many children were left on the roadside, and a large number died from exposure or starvation.

Children were also sold into slavery or contracted out as indentured servants in many countries. Such sales existed in the Roman Empire, and in China poor peasants sold daughters to rich merchants. Most black children in the United States before 1865 were slaves, liable to be sold with their families by their master; as Billingsley and Giovannoni (1971) say, "The very existence of slavery meant that child welfare institutions could develop in this country without concern for the majority of Black children; this factor alone ensured an inherently racist child welfare system" (p. 24).

Indenture of children was somewhat different. A family contracted for the labor of a child for a specific period of time, perhaps five to ten years, and then the child was free, usually at age 21. This was considered a way to provide for poor children. In colonial days many were recruited from the almshouses of London to come to the New World in this role.

In the early days of our country, especially during the early 1800s, another institution used for children was the almshouse, where abandoned or orphaned children too young to be indentured and poor children with families were mixed with a variety of others in need, including alcoholics, mentally ill, and criminal types. They were all crowded together in poorly maintained institutions where privacy was at a minimum and living conditions deplorable. Friedlander and Apte (1974) say that the almshouse was often called the "human scrap pile."

It was to rescue young children from such places that orphanages were established. In the early days of orphanages it was assumed that most children would go on to be indentured servants when they reached the age of 12. Actually by age 12 a person was no longer considered a child in those early days. In fact, even from the age of 7 on, Kadushin (1974) says, in the seventeenth and eighteenth centuries in both Britain and the United States some children were working in factories. But in the nineteenth century, there was a call for better care for the young child, and the orphanage, an institution where only children resided, was an answer. Religious groups and charitable organizations took up the call, establishing homes not only for orphans but also for those whose parents were too poor to care for them.

The next shift in child welfare policy was to the free foster home. One of the first child welfare agencies initiating this change was the New York Children's Aid Society, which from 1853 on moved city children to the countryside to work for farmers and rural merchants. The main purpose was to get the 10,000 or more vagrant children, many with parents, off the streets of New York City. The hordes of them were considered a danger to the citizens; the rural life, away from the tenements and vice, was considered a good environment for these children. A free foster home was provided by the farmer in return for free labor; some called it the indentured servant system in sheep's clothing, with an overlay of Christian charity. There was little selection of foster parents; those who were willing got the children.

Since after the Civil War, with the abolition of slavery, the indentured servant system was held in disrepute as something unacceptably close to slavery, the free foster home system became a popular alternative.

With the establishment of different voluntary organizations devoted to the care of children, there developed an interest in establishing rights for children. By 1883 foster homes were being selected on the basis of love and not economic use of the child. Agencies devoted to placement of children in a humane way arose, such as Children's Aid Societies in a number of cities and the American Education Society in Chicago, which later expanded to become the National Children's Home Society. For children in need of protection, it took a celebrated court case of the Society for the Prevention of Cruelty to Animals regarding a child to give rise to a Society for the Prevention of Cruelty to Children in 1875. Adoption was another area where the child had historically been at the mercy of adults, but by the mid–nineteenth century in America many states had enacted adoption laws.

At the present time a wide variety of regulations and acts exist to ensure children's rights, and a number of agencies have come into being to protect these rights, which even include the right to counsel in a juvenile court and in some states the right in a divorce case, if one is over a certain age, to determine which parent one will go with. Parents' rights have been amended to some degree to ensure the children's rights and to allow the community to intervene when necessary.

CHILD PROTECTIVE SERVICES

The call to save the child is very applicable to child protective services aimed at protecting the child in danger of abuse or neglect. For example, there is the case of Mary Ellen, aged 4.

A doctor reported to the county child protective agency that he had just treated a child, Mary Ellen, for multiple burns. He had treated the same child for a broken leg last month when she supposedly had fallen off a bike. He noticed she had several scars on her right arm.

A social worker for this protective service investigated the case. At first the single mother protested the interference from the social worker, but when the worker pointed out she would then have to bring the case to the attention of the courts, the mother agreed to talk to the social worker. She explained how she had three children, Mary Ellen the oldest. The other two were docile, but Mary Ellen was continually disobedient and mischievous. The mother said that without any baby-sitter to occasionally take over the care, this 24-hour supervision of the kids with no husband present got her down. She had only her AFDC check, and so she often had little money even to feed the three children, especially at the end of the month.

Mary Ellen was always jumping about, making noise and asking questions. Sometimes she, the mother, couldn't take it, and she decided she would teach the child a lesson and make her more obedient. That's when she burned Mary Ellen's hand. The time Mary Ellen "broke her leg" was when the mother found Mary Ellen taking all the food out of the cabinets and feeding different foods to the other children and the dog. The social worker started extensive work with the mother on these child care problems; she got the mother to join a group of other mothers who had such problems in group therapy sessions run by the Parental Stress organization. The worker arranged child care for the children in a day care center three times a week. The worker had debated about whether she should take Mary

Ellen out of the home, but she felt that the mother seemed eager to change her ways. Therefore the worker decided that Mary Ellen need not leave the home but the case should be closely watched. The mother seemed to respond well to the Parental Stress organization's group therapy programs.

Child protective services focus first of all on the child in danger. It is these services' responsibility to see that conditions improve in the family so that future neglect or abuse is unlikely; when they are fearful that the child is still in danger, they must take the child out of the home.

Child protective services are concerned with *abuse* of the child, usually physical abuse, such as burning a hand, breaking bones, striking the child to the point where there are serious physical effects, and anything more than temporary pain, scars, or immobility. Child abuse can also include molestation by the father. Some could add emotional abuse, such as continually locking the child in a dark closet for hours.

Child *neglect* is a broader and less severe situation. One considers child neglect to exist when parental care falls below a certain acceptable minimum for childrearing, for example, when young children are left alone frequently, not fed regularly, not dressed properly, and in general ignored. Basic food, clothing, and shelter may not be adequately provided. Children's medical needs, such as treatment of an open wound, broken arm, or bad ear, are not attended to. Essential educational needs, mainly attendance at school, are not taken care of.

In some cases the parents are considered neglectful because they demand long hours of work of their children; in other words, they exploit the child to work either for them or for others. An occasional type of neglect is that children are exposed to situations that society considers immoral, such as prostitution, bar life, and other scenes of deviant activity. The last type of neglect, one less likely to be detected, reported, or treated, is emotional neglect, where parents deprive children of affection and loving, express hatred for them, or pick them out for continual criticism and ridicule. This may happen to a child when other children are favored, when the child is the result of an unwanted pregnancy, where the stepparent resents the intrusion of this child into his or her family life, or when a single mother feels the child is continually depriving her of opportunities outside the home.

These situations are among the many forms of child neglect and abuse. Much neglect and abuse are caused by the stressful situations the parent or parents find themselves in, such as poverty, lack of a husband, lack of relatives for baby-sitting, or general marital tensions.

Sometimes neglect or abuse is due to the immaturity of a young parent and the lack either of willingness to take on parental functioning or of understanding what the childrearing role demands. Some parents do not understand the gravity of their acts of child neglect. They may never have been taught that leaving children alone for many hours is considered by community members a serious mistreatment of the children. The abusing parent himself or herself has often been neglected or abused as a child.

In some cases neglect or abuse may be due to different cultural norms. The parents may come from a culture where caning or otherwise physically abusing the child is acceptable. Many parents today are unclear about when hitting or spanking a child is so serious it is considered abuse. Keeping a child at home for long periods in his or her room is considered acceptable in many cultures; in fact, whether it constitutes child abuse or neglect in our culture is still debated and may depend on how severely it is carried out. Last, child abuse may be due to an unnatural situation in which a father is in too close, continued proximity to a teenaged daughter.

Interest in child abuse and child neglect began in 1875, when the Society for the Prevention of Cruelty to Children was founded, and for many decades after that it was centered in private agencies. Gradually public agencies stepped into this field, establishing a division of child protective services and taking on the dominant responsibility for services in each area. Investigation became a mandatory function. It also became mandatory for agencies dealing with children to report suspicious indications of abuse and neglect; this included schools, medical doctors, and police.

The child protective agency became an authority, investigating cases and counseling parents even when the parents did not want such interference, working with the appropriate judges where necessary, making responsible decisions whether children in danger should be taken out of the home, and—when the child was in the home—following the case until the agency deemed the situation had considerably improved. This kind of agency works under legal mandate.

The 1974 Child Abuse and Neglect Prevention and Treatment Act increased both the amount of reporting required and the amount of research being done on the subject. Individual states, under federal funding, have set up child abuse centers. Nonprofit organizations have received some federal funding and CETA workers.

Until recent years neglected or abused children were taken out of the home in many cases. They were often put in temporary group shelters, in some cases a county facility for neglected and dependent children and in some cases a detention facility also used for juveniles accused of crimes. In some cases jails were used. Then the children were moved on to foster homes, unless it was felt appropriate to put them back into their own homes.

Today this situation still exists in a number of places and in a number of cases, but there is much more of an attempt to keep the children in their own homes. There is a realization that it is possible to help the parents improve the home situation. Many parents unintentionally neglect or abuse their children. Many parents have stressful situations that can improve. Many, ashamed of themselves for this crisis behavior, could, with therapy, restrain themselves from such actions. Many could manage their child care responsibilities better with the help of such services as day care or baby-sitting.

In the 1970s more effort was made to help parents and thus to keep the children in their homes. Voluntary parental stress groups, often including ex–child neglecters among their volunteers, have sprung up across the country. They provide 24-hour telephone hot-line counseling for parents in crisis situations who are about to harm their children or for relatives or neighbors who want to report such activity. These agencies often have trained volunteers to intervene in a crisis or stressful situation and have group therapy sessions for potentially abusing parents in an atmosphere of confidentiality and self-help. These agencies also often provide temporary baby-sitting in the crisis situation and give out information on more permanent supportive services.

All these services make it safer to keep the child in the home but some experts complain the child is kept in the home too often. Goodhue (1976) asks, "Which takes priority in child abuse cases—the rehabilitation of parents or the welfare of children? One concerned minister says 'It's obvious the kid's safety should come first.' He doubts that it does. He adds, 'It's the thing within welfare and probation departments to give total lip service to the welfare of the child, but the way they're acting, their top priority is rehabilitation of abusive parents' " (p. 6). The article notes this minister has reasons to think this way, because "follow-up studies of children who survived battering revealed that 50 to 60 percent have long-time medical problems." Other experts say workers took the abused child out of the home and thought everything would be all right but it wasn't. Realizing that, officials are doing all they can to help troubled families solve their problems and stay together. Levin says, "Sometimes children have been endangered by being returned to their families" (Goodhue, 1976).

This all gives evidence of the delicate parent-child issues social workers must face. They must check on complaints from neighbors and agencies, must interfere with a normal, private family function—that is, bringing up its own children—and then must decide whether the child can stay in the home.

The American Humane Society 1978 National Symposium on Child Protection brought up other current issues in this area, such as the problem of emotional abuse and neglect—one of the most difficult ones for workers to deal with from the standpoint of diagnosis, treatment, and legal implications—and the problem of how to treat those family members involved in sexual abuse or incestuous relations. Workshops also centered on the role of the juvenile courts, the type of court evidence needed, and the social worker's performance as key witness in such cases. The social worker and the courts have difficulty in getting evidence on certain types of cases. Data show that middle-class as well as lower-class parents abuse or neglect their children but often in a very much more hidden way; social workers' attempts to intervene are very heavily resisted by middle-class parents, who fear that such knowledge may become public.

Gil (1973) looking at legally reported instances of child abuse, found for the country as a whole 9.3 cases per 100,000 children reported in 1968.

DAY CARE

A major supportive service to the family is day care. As more and more women with young children go out to work the need becomes greater. Second, as the number of single parents is increased by divorce, the need for day care increases. Almost one-third of mothers with children under 6 are in the work force, or, put another way, there were over 4 million mothers in the work force with children under 6 in the early 1970s. Many of these mothers even have infants and toddlers they must place in day care.

In 1975 the Child Welfare League of America estimated that about 33 million children up to age 18 needed some form of day care while their mothers worked; an estimated 7 million were under school age. The League estimated that about 1 million day care places were available to *preschool* children. In 1971 there were roughly 18,435 day care centers plus 55,366 licensed family day care homes. The largest proportion of preschool children of working mothers are taken care of by relatives or neighbors or private, nonlicensed family day care, that is, private homes where a nonrelated homemaker cares for one to several children. Less than 15 percent of family day care homes were licensed in 1975. Day care centers, that is, special centers with a regular staff and routine, served less than 10 percent of all those in care arrangements. Yet there has been a great increase in the number of day care centers and licensed family care homes in the last decade. There is a continuing effort to see that family care homes are licensed so that the state can inspect them and ensure a certain standard.

While one thinks of organized day care centers as a public or nonprofit activity, in reality half the centers are privately owned. In 1976, *U.S. News and World Report* stated that in recent years the number of commercially operated day-care centers has greatly increased but some might be closing because of rising costs. A number of these private day care centers are chains in which profit is a major motive. At the same time there are a number of cooperative day care centers, where the parents volunteer a day or a half day of work a week at the center and thus keep costs low.

There are also a number of public day care centers funded by the federal government, with Title XX funds, for example; in fact, a surprising number of government statutes, such as the Elementary and Secondary Education Act of 1963, provide day care monies. In some cases, the day care is especially for AFDC mothers or for those in manpower training programs or other programs. Because of this the federal government has had considerable influence on setting standards for all day care centers. One report was that the federal government paid out $1 billion for day care and preschool education in 1977.

In many cities there are public day care centers; in San Francisco in 1976 there were twelve centers funded from state, city, and United Crusade monies and forty-seven other children's centers operated by the school district. Churches and service groups often sponsor day care centers, as do colleges and universities. Some factories provide day care for their female employees, although many have found it not to work out when there are not enough users.

Some day care centers and preschool nurseries are open only part of the day and so do not fit the needs of working mothers. Others operate from seven in the morning until six at night, even though they may also have a shorter-day preschooler program. However, even these hours can present problems for the working mother, since she must be sure she gets to the center by 6 P.M. Many mothers use private family day care provided by neighbors mainly because it is closer to home and they can better work out the hours of care. Yet, family day care can be very unreliable: the baby-sitter may become sick, may decide to discontinue the service, and, most important, can not always be trusted to provide a decent standard of care. The baby-sitter may leave the child alone or take the child to places the mother would consider undesirable. Yet the bulk of day care in the United States is done by these private, unlicensed family day care persons. Many prove unsatisfactory, and children are thus moved from one family day care home to another. There are days when the mother has no family day care person; sometimes she even keeps school-aged children at home to do the babysitting. An example is Mrs. K:

Mrs. K. is a divorced woman. She has a year-old girl and a 4-year-old boy. She works from 8 A.M. to 5 P.M. and must travel thirty minutes each way by bus to work. She leaves the 1-year-old with a neighbor one block away from her home, but this neighbor will not take the 4-year-old. Mrs. K. has had the boy in three different homes in the last two years, all unsatisfactory, but now is lucky to have him in a public day care center that allows her to pay on a sliding scale according to her income. This means Mrs. K. pays $40 a week to the neighbor and $15 to the day care center.

The neighbor taking care of the 1-year-old has a poor heating system in her home and so sometimes the child is cold. Last month the neighbor got the flu and could not take care of the girl for a week. Mrs. K. stayed out of work two days and then found a teenaged baby-sitter to come in the other three days.

Mrs. K. also has had troubles with the day care center. It reprimanded her for not getting there by 6 P.M. to pick up the boy one night. Second, it was closed on a public holiday when Mrs. K. had to work, and so she had to get a baby-sitter. Third, the center wants her to come in to a parent session one night a month.

Many licensed day care centers have long waiting lists, especially those publicly funded, in which payment is on a sliding scale and standards are high. For example, in 1976, San Francisco School District day care centers had a waiting list of over 1000 places.

Day care is not cheap, often running $40 or more a week in 1977, or over $2000 a year for the working mother, unless the center is a publicly funded one, a cooperative one, a church or college group, or an employer-sponsored center. While the mother can write off some part of the day care cost as a deduction on her income tax form, cost is still a problem. Because many single parents cannot afford expensive care, private day care centers try to economize on meals and services to keep costs moderate.

Federal standards of quality are considered high, requiring a large staff, good equipment, and a decent space-to-child ratio; they have been widely debated. (States also have standards and licensing personnel; however, a number of states are lax in enforcing their standards.) Standards are one of the major issues in day care; the Federal Interagency Day Care Requirements (FIDCR) groups have had continual debates over the years about staff qualifications, the number of staff in relation to the number of children, the degree to which services should exist, and space requirements. High standards mean high costs that neither the parents nor the government are willing to pay.

In 1976 the real total costs per child for the San Francisco–state financed programs were $3400 a year, even though the parents paid much less. The 1976 child day care bill was vetoed because of its high staffing ratios (1 adult for every 4 children aged 6 weeks to 4 years) and thus high costs.

How to license family day care homes should be an important policy issue. Under such licensing a study is made of the home to be sure standards are met, and later, revisiting is done. When standards are too stringent some very much needed family day care homes will be rejected, as happened, for example, in San Francisco's Chinatown, where there were 3400 children under 5 in 1976 but only two licensed homes. Most lacked a backyard and other requirements.

The problem in licensing family day care homes is that the nonrelated person taking care of the children is reluctant to submit to the licensing process, fearing it will up the cost of care. Some states are experimenting with simpler methods of self-evaluation and reporting on a form sent to the family day care person, to be followed by random checks among those returning the mailed forms. This is also cheaper for the licensing body than the full licensing process. The horrors that exist in some private family day care homes and even in private day care centers mean that some level of standards is necessary; but if they are too high, costs are too great and therefore bills are vetoed. The resulting lack of funding, some politicians argue, then means that day care centers are closed and working mothers will return to the welfare rolls.

The reality of the situation today is that there are many mothers, often without a husband present, who are forced to work and have little choice but to turn to some form of day care. The question is, How do we make it a service that will encourage the normal emotional and physical growth of our society's children?

FOSTER HOMES

Since the 1909 White House Conference on Children, the dominating principle has been to keep the child in the home whenever possible. It is understood that even the family that seems to be disorganized, deviant, or living in a deplorable environment, if it even minimally provides the child with love and care, is better than a substitute arrangement. The blood tie with the natural parents has great psychological meaning for children, and to tear them away from this relationship makes them feel rejected and abandoned. Also, the most likely substitute, a foster home, in reality can seldom be an adequate permanent substitute for the natural parent or parents. It gives the child only a temporary "parent" under agency supervision, and it creates a dangerous illusion of a satisfactory alternative that may lead to the natural parents' complete withdrawal of love and responsibility. It involves the child in a triangle relationship—a social work agency, a substitute parent, and a natural parent—that often does not work.

Yet every year in recent years well over 250,000 children have been in foster care, mainly in boarding homes, that is, private homes in which the family has agreed to care for the child as a full-time substitute family, under agency supervision and with an agency payment for each child. Billingsley and Giovannoni (1971) state that the twentieth-century idea is that families should stay together but the twentieth-century practice has been to take children away from their parents. Child welfare divisions or agencies have this as one of their main areas of service, along with adoptions. Children in their own home have received mainly cash, not services; only a small number have received such supportive services as day care and homemaker services, and even then they were not handled by these traditional child welfare agencies.

While the trend is to try to provide more supportive services to the family and to the child in the home, the need for foster boarding homes is unlikely to disappear. In fact, in the last decade it increased. What are the extreme circumstances that force the family or the social workers and a court judge to decide to give the social work agency custody of the child?

It may be that the mother is mentally or physically ill and is in the hospital or bedridden and the child or children must be temporarily removed until maternal care can be restored. The mother may be an alcoholic or drug addict who cannot responsibly carry on her care of the children. The mother may prove unfit to cope with the special needs of a handicapped child.

Neglect or abuse of the child are common reasons for temporary or long-term removal of the child. It can be physical neglect, that is, grossly neglecting basic physical needs. Abuse is even more serious, as in cases of beating the child. The parent may abandon a child, especially an illegitimate child. These are all parent-related problems. Sometimes there are child-related problems. For example, the parent can ask that the child be removed from the home because of violent, aggressive acts, eccentric behavior, or uncontrollability.

A child awaiting adoption may also temporarily be put in a foster home, again a private home where the foster parent receives a payment for care and maintenance of the child rather than a salary.

After the social welfare agency—either a public agency, such as the child welfare agency or the family and child division of the public social services agency, or a private agency, such as the Catholic Charities or the Children's Home Society—finds a need for a foster home (and in certain types of cases, after the court prescribes it or assents to it), then the placement process begins.

Any foster home service usually involves two or more divisions: the division called the home finder division, which searches out suitable foster homes, and the division that places the child in the home and supervises the child while he or she is in the home.

The placement of a child in a foster home is always a difficult thing.

Many times children are not ready to give their affection to substitute parents and are emotionally upset about removal from their own home and often unsure why it has occurred. Even children who were badly treated or rejected may have a strong desire to be back with their natural parents. In some cases a temporary foster home is used while the child is sorting out the situation mentally. Foster parents must try to work with children to make them feel wanted in their new home.

It is the social worker's job to try to make the foster parents understand the child's background and emotional problems. The social worker may also explain to the foster parents their responsibility for the health care and education of the child and how they must share these with the agency, which has the ultimate legal responsibility for the care of the child. The social worker must also make them understand that they cannot play the role of natural parents, as in an adoption case, and that they must be willing to let the natural parents visit the child.

The social worker must also, in monthly or bimonthly visits to the foster parents, check on the job they are doing and on the well-being of the child, often by talking to the child separately. In actuality, in carrying out these tasks the social worker has a minimal degree of real authority over the foster parent, because the foster parent is paid only a low-level monthly payment for the child. A foster parent who is generous with birthday and Christmas gifts, clothes, treats, and recreation money may actually be paying out more for the child (especially when the child is a teenager) than the agency is reimbursing. Thus the foster parent is not a paid employee of the agency.

While the agency personnel can take the child away from the foster parent, revoke the foster parent's annual licensing, or refuse to approve payments for certain expenses, these measures are unlikely, with the shortage of qualified foster parents in some areas.

The difficulties in this dual responsibility of the social worker and the foster parent for the child are now ironed out somewhat more than in the past through foster parents' group sessions. In fact, foster parents in many areas have now organized and made a number of demands on the agencies, such as higher per child payments and more stable relations with the agency. There is a national foster parents' organization.

The difficulties in this triad relationship increase when the social worker is white and the child and foster parent black.

Home Finding

Home finding is another job the agency is involved in; this, of course, is the service of finding suitable foster homes. The agency often advertises for such homes. In many urban areas it has been hard to locate satisfactory foster homes; some agencies have turned to rural areas to locate homes and even other states, but this is frowned upon, since then families cannot visit.

Looking at the ideal, one can say the basic qualifications are that there be a stable family situation with both spouses in the home, that the foster parents have acceptable childrearing practices, that they like children, and that they be mature and responsible.

A major consideration in choosing a foster home up until this past decade was the standard of the home. There were agency regulations about house condition, space requirements (such as the availability of a room for the child), safety requirements, and even the neighborhood environment. Housekeeping standards were scrutinized to see if the home was clean, sanitary, and orderly. Home finding social workers, middle-class themselves, used middle-class standards to evaluate the suitability of the home. A poor family, even a very stable one, was often not considered desirable. Regulations such as the following one dating from 1972 in Alameda County, California, were issued: "The income of the foster family from employment or other resources shall be reasonably steady and sufficient to maintain an adequate standard of living for the family, as far as essential needs are concerned."

A family whose composition did not fit the middle-class norm was often considered undesirable; thus single parents, a major group in the black community, were excluded. The age of the foster parents was also taken into account, with the feeling that older couples, perhaps over 45, should be excluded, as should very young ones.

While these criteria, especially those on room standards and housekeeping, have hardly been abandoned, many of them are now more liberal, and single women, including some never-married women, are considered, as are older couples. The criteria on house condition and socioeconomic level have also been greatly liberalized, especially in areas where it is hard to get foster parents. While middle-class social workers may set up criteria according to their own childhood experiences, if foster homes are hard to find they may have to adjust their criteria to this situation. Today most agencies have some black social workers, who might be better equipped to judge acceptable black foster parents than their white counterparts.

Problems with Foster Care

Many children can never adjust to a substitute home. Also, such a home can seldom be considered a permanent arrangement, because the natural parent at some time may want to take the child back. Thus it is always an unstable situation. It is important to have understanding and mature foster parents who can handle these problems. Many foster parents cannot. Also, many have trouble working with teenagers and understanding and accepting the teenage culture.

Foster parents may have their own children they are giving their main time and energy to; they may, in fact, indicate to foster children that they are not as high in their affection as their own children and are somewhat different in status from them. Some foster parents even take on the fostering job for the money and treat the work in an impersonal way. They may have several foster children from different homes. If one child's behavior is such that the child is difficult to handle, they may ask the agency to remove that child from their home. A social worker might know of a number of children, especially in their teens, who have been moved from home to home. Fanshel (1976) found in a study of 624 children in long-term foster care that 28 percent had had three or more placements and 30 percent had had two placements, leaving less than half (only 42 percent) who had been in only one home among this sample. If children get into trouble with the law, are incorrigible, or act out in violent ways, the foster parents may no longer want them.

We would like to think most foster children stay only a short time in foster care, but a nationwide Child Welfare League of America study in 1968 found agencies reporting that about a fourth of their placements, for all agencies, stay in the foster home for more than thirty-six months. Illegitimate children and minority children are more likely to be in a foster home a long time, study after study shows. If the child is not returned to his or her own home within a year, the stay is usually a long one and the chances of returning home are low. If the natural parent seldom visits the child, it is likely that the stay will be a long one, studies show.

New measures are now being taken to try to improve the situation of the long-term foster child. Cases are being reviewed to see whether the natural mother visits or has any type of contact with the child. In some states, such as New York, the "permanently neglected" child, as defined by lack of contact with the parent, is freed for adoption under new legislative regulations. In other cases, where there is some parental contact, the agency may hold discussions with the parent or parents to see whether the child can be put up for adoption, or on the other hand, whether the parent is now ready and qualified to take the child back. The problem often is that no one wants to adopt these children either because they are too old to be desirable or because they are from minorities.

Another major move is to subsidize the child after adoption and even pay the adoption fees. In a number of cases the foster parents would be willing to adopt the foster child they are caring for if they could continue to receive the monthly maintenance check from the agency. Such adoption would be desirable because it would free the child from the present triangular relationship of agency supervision, natural parent, and foster parent and give him or her a permanent home.

A related possibility is to encourage, in general, the adoption of minority children who are presently put in foster care for the reason that no adoptive parents can be found.

Another possibility is to pay greater attention to the natural parents and their counseling needs. Traditionally, when a child has been removed from the natural home to a foster home, the emphasis has been on the foster home relationship. Little time has been given to correcting the family situation that originally brought the child into foster care; often such work is a very minor aspect of the caseworker's job. However, if the home situation could be improved, in many cases the child could return.

Such an effort is especially needed in the first year, before the parents have withdrawn from feelings of parental responsibility and affection and before the child has settled too deeply into the foster home relationship. Demonstration projects have shown that major supportive efforts to correct family problems can mean the return home of a number of children, a desirable situation not only to improve family life but also to save the taxpayer long-term foster care expenses. It may be that all the parent needs is a chance to adjust to a changed marital situation, or counseling to correct neglect or abuse, or a decent day care service to help with the care of the child. Too often, instead of providing this help, the agency turns its back on the family after the child is removed. With heavy caseloads, families' situations are often not reviewed periodically unless they demand it.

In some areas today this has changed and periodic agency review of each case and even court review is demanded. Costain (1979) points out that "dissatisfaction with the foster care system has increased with awareness of the numbers of children placed away from homes who could have remained at home if supportive social services had been provided their parents" (pp. 277–278).

A last trend to mention is greater use of group homes; this is a type of foster home where a number of teenaged children, often eight to twelve of them, are housed in an agency-rented or -owned house that is staffed by agency-salaried workers, often couples. For the teenaged child who has gone through a number of foster placements, this is the best solution, since he or she usually has trouble trying to establish a new relationship with another foster family. In fact, teenagers, in general, have trouble shifting their affection to a foster family; many are simply hard to handle and are immersed in a teenage culture that foster parents have difficulty working with. For all these reasons a group home, with its more generalized, diffuse emotional relations and its larger group, can be a more suitable setting. Its somewhat better-educated staff, as regular agency employees, can more adequately handle the emotional problems many of these young adults have.

In summary, the direction of policy on foster care is more counseling of natural parents, a greater attempt to put children back into their own homes, more provision of supportive services to the natural family, and the use of group homes for teenagers. Other trends are to make more foster children available for adoption and to subsidize the child after adoption and, in choosing foster parents, to be more flexible on a number of criteria.

ADOPTION SERVICES

Another traditional child welfare service is adoption, in which the child is legally given a permanent new family and legally released by the biological family. Several nonprofit private agencies, such as the Children's Home Society and the Catholic Charities, are prominent in this field, but in recent years public social agencies have expanded their services, especially for hard-to-place children.

Traditionally, in the United States the typical adoption is by a white childless couple legally adopting a 2-month old illegitimate child of a white unwed mother. However, today there is a shortage of such children; the white unwed mother today often keeps her baby; often a pregnant unwed white girl has an abortion. There is a surplus of minority children, even though black unwed mothers often keep their child, as well as a surplus of older children and physically handicapped children. Because of these circumstances adoption procedures have been changing and agencies are trying innovations to "screen in" adoptive parents for these hard-to-place children at the same time they carefully select the best parents for the few white babies.

Historically, the legal adoption of a child has been for the benefit of the adult, often to provide a male heir, and not the child. In the United States, concern for the child rather than the adopting parents was expressed as early as 1851, when Massachusetts passed a law focusing on the child; the law said that the new parents must petition for adoption, that judges must see that the new home is a fit one, that the guardian of the child must consent, and that there must be complete legal severance of the relationship of natural parents and child. Most states have adopted somewhat similar laws, some much later than others.

Today a thorough investigation is done of the suitability of the adopting parents by the social welfare agency in all cases it handles. However, there still are a number of independent adoptions where such an investigation, if done at all (it can be done at court request), is more superficial; these are adoptions where the child is obtained from a source other than a social welfare agency, such as through a doctor or lawyer.

Last, there are adoptions by relatives; these make up about half of all adoptions. Of the *nonrelative* adoptions, agency adoptions make up the bulk of the cases, 65,350 children in 1971; they account for over three-fourths of nonrelative adoptions today.

The Child Welfare League of America sets standards for agency adoptions, as it also does for foster homes. An agency worker looks into the social and health background of the child—the social background so that the adoptive parents are not later surprised to hear the child is illegitimate or the mother had mental problems, and the health background in order to give the adoptive parents information to tell the child later at an appropriate age.

The agency investigation of the adopting parents is an extensive one. What the agency is trying to avoid is the unhappy matches of children and adoptive parents that were sometimes made before such procedures were brought in. The agency wants the couple to have been married for several years, to have marital stability, to be in good health, and to be financially stable.

Because of the present shortage of white babies awaiting adoption, agency selection is now stringent for those wanting white babies; agencies are likely to screen out prospective adoptive parents who do not have proof of infertility because they have decided that the limited number of such babies should go to those most in need. The agency in such cases demands that they be married couples, and preferably not too old or young to carry out childrearing.

The agency gets the information on adopting parents from interviews with the applicants, home visits, application forms, and references. These traditional agency procedures have been criticized as too extensive and involving too much red tape, too many interviews, and too lengthy a process, often taking many months.

Another complaint is that agencies are staffed by middle-class white social workers trained to be selective. In reality today innovative outreach programs are needed to attract new kinds of adoptive parents, including many from minority groups, to meet the need for homes for the majority of the children up for adoption today. Costain (1979), reporting on a 1975 Children's Bureau study, says there are as many as 100,000 children awaiting adoption. Many of them are not white babies, who are so few in number and so quickly adopted, but are older children, especially older minority children, and children with special problems. Many of these are presently in foster homes.

Most applicants want a baby, and therefore the question is how to attract adoptive parents for the many older adoptable children. Agencies have to change their ways to do this: criteria need to be revised, adoption fees lowered, time for adoption speeded up, and the all-white agency image changed. Some agencies, especially public ones, are doing this. For example, Gallagher (1967), reporting on trends in adoption, says that "the Los Angeles County Bureau of Adoptions placed over 4,000 children, . . . an increase of 54 percent over the preceding 2 years; included were children from Mexican-American, American Indian, Oriental, and other minority ethnic groups" (p. 13).

Billingsley and Giovannoni (1971) were among early advocates of innovative techniques to attract black adoptive parents and of reversing agency techniques to screening *in* rather than screening *out* adoptive parents.

Before they could do this, many agencies had to overcome their assumptions that black couples were not interested in adopting children, that black women did not wish to surrender their babies for adoption, and, in some areas, that there were no black children awaiting adoption. An Urban League nationwide project on black adoptions found:

> The agencies' first task was to stimulate interest in adoption among members of the Black community, in order to increase the initial pool of applicants. It was in this area that the [traditional] agencies had perhaps met their worst failures, and where they appeared least successful in manipulating their own behavior. [Billingsley and Giovannoni, 1971, p. 188]

Then when agencies finally did take on the job of advertising for black adoptive parents through the media, Billingsley says, they did not address "the appeals to the large areas of concern, such as the apprehension a Black couple might feel in approaching a white agency."

Today some agencies have tried to remedy this by hiring minority personnel. Also, the agencies have changed the criteria for adoptive parents to include working mothers, older mothers, even singles. Agencies still, however, find there is a reluctance for some black families to apply even when they have an acceptable socioeconomic position, partly because such an income position is not felt secure enough or because there is concern over the background of the children up for adoption or impatience with agency paperwork. A number of black parents wishing to adopt find they can do so privately, sometimes children of relatives.

Many American Indian children and foreign-born, usually Asian, children have also been placed in white homes. These are called *transracial* adoptions. Adoptions of children from other countries have increased, partly because some white applicants see it as a chance to find a child available for adoption. Well over 80 percent of these children are from Asia. A number are illegitimate children of relationships between American soldiers stationed overseas and Asian women; others are refugee children, as from Vietnam in the mid-1970s. Many are abandoned children from orphanages in Asian countries. Some are adopted by American relatives or by those having the humanitarian desire to give such children decent homes, but many are adopted simply by those wanting a child in their family. Screening of potential adoptive parents and of children is done by such social welfare agencies as the International Social Service agency. They handle the legal aspects and paperwork in both countries and meet all requirements for the United States Immigration and Naturalization Service to process the child's immigration. In 1970, Kadushin (1974) reports, 2400 such children were admitted for adoption.

Another source of adoptive children today is foster children, as mentioned earlier. Some agencies are making considerable effort to free foster children for adoption. A major need is to do this at as early a date as possible because the age of the child is important to an adoptive parent. Even today, with all the efforts to increase adoptions of older children and minorities, most adoptive parents want to adopt children under 5. Yet studies show adoptions of older children usually work out.

Subsidized Adoptions

Subsidization can be given to any potential parent, but it is most frequently given to foster parents. It may be simply a subsidy of the adoption fee or it may be for the medical expenses for a handicapped child or the special education costs for a retarded child. It may be temporary or long-term maintenance payments to replace the foster child payments to foster parents who are adopting the child in their care. Many states now allow such payments, with New York and Illinois leading the way, but the number of recipients of this subsidy in most states is often low. Such a subsidy seems desirable, since such an adoption will then give the foster child a feeling of being a permanent part of the foster family.

Gray-Market and Black-Market Adoptions

Over three-fourths of all nonrelative adoptions are agency adoptions (65,350 in 1971). However, there are also what we call "gray-market" and "black-market" adoptions. In these cases an agency is not involved, thus not providing its extensive investigation and screening procedures; the case, if it is legal, comes directly to the court. Of course, the court is likely to demand some sort of social investigation and a hearing and, of course, require consent of the biological parent(s). However, the thorough agency procedure is missing. In the most common, the gray-market adoption, an intermediary who knows the biological mother, such as a doctor or a lawyer, arranges the adoption; such adoptions (about 17,000 in 1971) are legal in most states. The doctor of the unwed mother may know a family wanting to adopt a child and bring the two together. A lawyer may hear of an unwed mother wishing to put her child up for adoption and take care of the legal work. The lawyer and the doctor may work together. In these cases the adoptive parents will usually pay a legal fee, but if this is not excessive it is considered acceptable.

The problem here is that the child's needs are not as carefully served, since no agency has a part in accepting or rejecting the adoptive parents on the basis of the usual criteria. If the adoptive parents' motivations are in terms of ego-satisfaction, the child may be put into an unsuitable home. In fact, adoptive parents rejected by an agency as unacceptable may turn to the gray market for a baby: the family with an alcoholic husband, a mentally unstable wife, or serious marital problems.

In the gray-market situation the adoptive parents have less assurance that the adoption is entirely legal and there will be no interference by the biological parents. In many cases, the unwed mother has not been given adequate time to make her decision to put her child up for adoption; she might make the decision in the hospital and later regret it.

Black-market adoptions present even more serious problems. These are cases of selling babies to adoptive parents. For example, an unwed mother, often one who wanted an abortion but turned to that solution too late, may be contacted by someone who has a buyer and can make secret arrangements. A child may be taken across state lines or smuggled into the country for adoption. No one knows the extent of such adoptions, but with the extreme scarcity of white babies today it is likely that black-market adoptions are on the increase. Such selling of babies is, of course, illegal in all states. It puts the adoptive parents in jeopardy of having their child taken away at some future date by the biological mother or of being blackmailed by the biological mother or others. For the child, it means the possibility of being placed in an unsuitable home.

CONCLUSION

There is a need for better policy measures to ensure against black-market and gray-market adoptions. There is a need for innovative approaches to increase adoption of hard-to-place children. There is a need for the subsidy of adoption fees and in some cases for providing the continual maintenance costs of a child to low-income adoptive families, including foster families. There is a need to stop child abuse. In all these cases the goal is to improve the societal functioning and the quality of life of children.

The type of provision discussed in this chapter is provision of services. In some cases they are of a universal nature, but for some, such as day care, a means test or sliding scale of payment may be used. The services are offered on the basis of need other than income in a number of cases, such as child abuse. Delivery may be by a voluntary agency or a public agency, although public agencies have become more involved in recent years in providing all these services. Staff is usually highly trained to carry out this professional work, although paraprofessionals are used as foster parents and to some extent in the day care field. Values favor assistance for most of the types of services discussed here, including agency adoptions and child protection services. One could say that values against adopting older and handicapped children do affect the adoption and foster home situation.

In both of these areas, as well as in child abuse, we need to take new directions; for adoptions we need to work more with the hard-to-place, and for foster children, more with the natural parent. For child abuse cases we need to treat the parent as well as the child. For day care we need to help the nonlicensed home.

As far as resource scarcity and policy is concerned, there have been more funds for child protection services but not enough funding for services related to placing the hard-to-adopt child or to subsidize foster parents to adopt, except in some locales, even though these would be cost-effective, saving on long-term foster payments. Even the funding of day care centers could be considered cost-effective, since it can lead to keeping young people adequately socialized and directed toward education and nondeviant behavior.

Chapter 10

Policy Alternatives for the Elderly

INTRODUCTION

One major area where social policy decisions must be made is in providing services to the elderly. This group comprises approximately 24 million people in our population. Many elderly require services as they develop physical, economic, psychological, and social limitations. In the last ten years the federal government has greatly stepped up the variety of programs to meet the many different needs of this large group. Types of provision include meals, transportation services, recreational programs, home nursing care, housing assistance, and income maintenance. Social policy alternatives are continually being established.

Any social policy recommendation must take into account the great variations in the health and other circumstances of the huge population of people 65 and over in our society.* One must take into account the fact that there are many subgroups within this 24 million and a variety of

*Some data are in terms of those 62 and over, the OASDHI retirement age, and some, 70 and over, but 65 and over seems the most commonly used grouping.

different types of services are needed to meet a variety of needs. No one course will fit the needs of all the elderly. As one "Gray Panther," an 81-year-old woman, said, "We're just like everyone else but older. We want to be seen as individuals."

At the same time one must realize that increased age does cause special problems for many. The extended longevity of the elderly has meant many now live into their eighties and some into their nineties, and thus there are a number who have some physical frailty and financial problems that limit their ability to function without help. Although most aged are still mobile and alert enough to pursue an independent or semi-independent life, they may have problems in shopping, cooking, or keeping up their home. In coping with the everyday demands of living, their decreased energies, caused by the aging process, may mean that adequate services and even alternative housing are needed to allow these elderly to pursue their normal routine. Such services can be useful in preventing them from moving to an institutional setting, which is a more dependent situation. Besides the provision of services, for some elderly, provision of specially designed individual apartments and congregate living arrangements with common dining room can give them the type of environment that allows independent or semi-independent living.

THE CHARACTERISTICS OF THE AGED

In 1970 the elderly in America made up over 10 percent of the population and one-fifth of the households. Because of an increased life expectancy, the fastest-growing subgroup is the group 75 and over, now over 8 million, a fact that greatly influences the type of services and housing needed. Forty percent of the elderly were 75 and over in 1970.

Marital Status and Sex

In 1970, almost a third of the entire elderly population was composed of widowed women; of those 80 or over most were widowed. A number of widows were financially and psychologically dependent on their husbands before widowhood and so have a need for legal and financial counseling.

Elderly men are usually married, and most 65 to 74 usually live with their wives.

Almost half of all elderly in 1970 were married and living with their husbands or wives.

Ethnicity and Race

The aged population has an overrepresentation of foreign-born and an underrepresentation of blacks; only 8 percent of the aged population is black. The low life expectancy of blacks is responsible for this. This group is in special need of services and housing, because, compared to the white elderly, there are more living in poverty, more are women, and more are in poor housing. Black elderly have less availability of congregate housing or nursing homes, although they are well represented in public housing.

Household Composition

A situation that may cause a need for services is the fact that over one-fourth of the elderly live alone; twice as many elderly women live alone as men, indicating there are a number of isolated widows. Only 4.8 percent of the elderly in 1970 lived in institutions.

Location of Relatives

In evaluating the situation of those living alone, the location of their family indicates how much their needs will be met. Shanas (1969) reports that for one sample of the aged who had children, half lived within one hour's drive of them and only 16 percent lived more than an hour away; over one-fourth of them lived with their children.

This writer in 1973 did a large, nationwide study of the aged in government-subsidized, specially designed apartments and congregate housing developments (with common dining room and hotel-type rooms) in Canada. It was found that a number of the elderly residents of these units did not have children in the area; 44 percent had no children alive or none living in the immediate area. However, of those that did have children in the area, most had daily or weekly contact.

Financial Status

In order to meet increased needs on their own, the elderly must have an income. Almost half of American elderly households in 1970 had incomes of $3000 or less, and many incomes were much lower. While 1980 figures will obviously be higher, with inflation the general cost of living is considerably higher. One out of four elderly persons is poor. Elderly persons living alone in 1970 were even more likely to be poor, about half of them so.

In 1970 annual income of the elderly went down drastically for both men and women as their age increased, with women and blacks 75 and over in very bad straits. Few elderly, only 14 percent in 1970, had incomes of $10,000 and over, thus indicating that only a small number could pay the cost of living in private retirement facilities such as Leisure World. Retirement incomes are often far below what is needed to keep up former life-styles, including living in one's private house. Almost a third of homeowners had incomes near or below the poverty level in 1970. Elderly persons' homes are their only financial asset in many cases, and they are continually confronted with the need to sell to get liquid funds.

Health Status

The aging process means physiological change. Changes, however, need not correspond to changes in chronological age, for the functioning of the physical organism is not the same for every 64-year-old or every 80-year-old. There are a number of physiological processes that generally decline with age, but individual characteristics may cause the decline to be quick for one person and slow for another. Thus one person at 75 may be immobile while another is actively working and exercising. Cottrell (1974) explains this biological process by saying:

> There are only a few of the characteristics of older people that are universal among them. Of the traits that they do share, not all show up at the same age in all older people. Senescence is a catchall word that is often used when no other more specific one, like blindness, arteriosclerosis, aging, or arthritis, will fit. In another sense, it covers all of the adverse conditions that accompany old age. In still another, it means only the results of "normal" aging. In this sense, senescence characterizes everybody who lives long enough. In time, the skin gets wrinkled, mottled, and while easily broken, heals slowly. Appetite fails and weight is often reduced. Muscle tonus declines. Usually one or more of the senses declines in sensitivity. [P. 8]

The body burns up food less efficiently for an older person than for a younger one, and the excess turns to fat. For the aged, exertion is harder, taking more energy. Fat replaces some of the heart muscles, meaning that the heart does not provide the proper amount of oxygenated blood and thus the person is breathless. This can also cause coldness in the feet and hands. The veins and the arteries may be clogged, with fatty deposits doing the clogging.

Changes in nerve cells cause slower response. As one gets older there is also difficulty in recovering from stress, including the death of one's mate. Change can make one emotionally sick. The sensory system deteriorates. One has a decrease in the sense of smell, in ability to see and in ability to hear, all factors affecting housing needs.

The National Health Survey showed that over 40 percent of elderly Americans in 1970 had some "activity limitation" caused by a chronic condition and that 20 percent were limited in physical mobility, housebound, or bedridden. Arthritis-rheumatism and heart condition were the most common activity limitations, with one-fifth naming each.

NEEDS RELATED TO PHYSICAL, FINANCIAL, AND SOCIOPSYCHOLOGICAL CONDITION

The aged, like other human beings, have the basic common needs of shelter, food, health care, and opportunities for interaction with others.

Because of the physiological, psychological, and economic limitations related to the aging process, the elderly find some of these needs intensified and, above all, unmet.

Some needs are related to role change. The elderly person may reluctantly face role changes, some connected with their jobs and some caused by financial circumstances or physical conditions. Today many face institutionalized retirement from employment. The change from the work role to a leisure role is not easy for most in a society that is strongly influenced by the work ethic. The job took time, provided status, and provided friendships. Aspirations were toward occupational achievement. Retirement represents a change in one's role, a discontinuity. The degree to which people adapt varies. It often depends on their previous leisure habits and how much they associate with those going through a similar retirement process. There is definitely a lack of institutional provision for the new role and status. One also has fewer roles in retirement. Bengston (1973) says, "The number and kind of social contacts decreases; roles are literally lost as retirement, widowhood, the death of friends, and decreasing physical mobility leave the individual increasingly to his own resources" (p. 30). The aged have a role ambiguity, because there is no clearly defined role for those moving into old age. The elderly are given a negative status.

Several gerontologists, such as Cummings and Henry (1961), speak of *disengagement* of the elderly, a mutual withdrawal from society as they grow older, a decreased interaction. They call it a double withdrawal—of the society from the individual and of the individual from society. Research shows, however, that there are wide variations in how much the elderly withdraw; some widows are more active than they were when younger.

Some elderly make their retirement a reengagement rather than a disengagement. They feel they are now released from undesirable work and can pursue long-term leisure interests. They retire *to* something, not *away from* something. They may move to a community with a high concentration of elderly and a variety of leisure activities. They may even take college courses. Studies of retirement show attitudes have changed. Many workers now look forward to retirement and have made plans for it. Yet for many aged there may be either a vacuum or an inability to adjust on their own to occupational retirement, death of a spouse, change in status, reduction of income, or movement from a familiar neighborhood. Social service agencies must meet the needs caused by these changes and losses.

Needs will vary for different age groups. Some members of the 75 to 85 age group will have serious disabilities and therefore physical immobility, but others will be healthy and have only minor physical frailties. Yet practically all aged in their seventies and eighties, even if suffering only from minor infirmities, need help from time to time; the realities of the aging process mean that many develop physiological deficiencies as time goes on, ranging from loss of energy and loss of memory to complete immobility. (See Table 10-1.) Reduced energy and other ailments mean inability to bend or to climb stairs. Physical frailties will hinder heavy housekeeping and maintaining a large home.

Being capable of only a low degree of physical exertion means having special needs. In housing for the elderly doors must be easy to open, cupboards easy to reach, and rest places readily available. Their reduced energy means that if the aged are to continue living in their existing housing they need assistance with maintenance and even housework. In some cases, however, it may instead mean that they need to move to alternative, specially designed units.

Health conditions, causing slow movement, result in mobility problems for the elderly. For those who have mobility problems the practical range accessible from home becomes smaller, so that they can get about only in their immediate neighborhood, finding the energy expenditure too great for long-distance trips. For some there may also be a disengagement

Table 10-1   Surveyed Elderly's Health Status, by Development Type

	Development type		
Health status	Mixed**	Self-contained apartments	All
Seriously limited ability*			
Number	13	2	15
Percent	7.0	1.7	5.0
Moderately limited ability†			
Number	41	12	53
Percent	21.9	10.3	17.5
Slightly limited ability‡			
Number	70	38	108
Percent	37.4	32.8	35.6
No incapacity⸹			
Number	63	64	127
Percent	33.7	55.2	41.9
Total			
Number	187	116	303
Percent	100	100	100

*Seriously limited ability in areas of walking or seeing or hearing; unable to accomplish many daily tasks on own.

†Moderately limited physical ability or capacity as noticeable handicap in one activity or faculty; needing limited or continuous aid.

‡Slightly limited physical ability or some minor difficulty either in moving about, communicating, or keeping house.

⸹No incapacity and able to keep house.

**Mixed is congregate and apartments in the same development.

Note: Interviewer asked resident in depth about physical limitations and then checked the best-fitting category.

Source: Canadian user survey, by author, reported in Huttman, Housing and Social Services for the Elderly, Praeger, New York, 1977.

from life and a low degree of social interaction; outreach programs are needed.

When aged persons with little mobility have to stay in their units it means that services must be brought to them or they must be taken to services. When possible, the person should live where services are close. When developments are planned for the elderly, they should be sited close to needed services, such as a grocery store, medical centers, and recreational facilities, unless good transportation to these places is provided.

The mobility problem means more attention must be paid to public transportation. Because of physical limitations, many elderly can no longer drive automobiles or walk long distances to a bus stop or to services. Therefore the availability of special transportation or a nearby bus stop has to be taken into account; the latter often influences the siting of housing developments for the aged.

Other special needs of the elderly may cause them to require medication, a special diet, or walking aids. These problems mean that nursing or homemaker services must be provided in their own homes or apartments, otherwise congregate housing with special nursing services is required if they are to avoid nursing homes.

However, physical limitations may make elderly persons hesitant to move out of their present housing. The exertion both for the search for the new unit or development and for the move to it is too much. An elderly person may not use specially designed housing or the Section 8 leased housing program for these reasons.

Psychological factors also may cause a reluctance to change living units for more suitable ones in better locations. It is psychologically difficult for aged persons in their seventies to make a change in living arrangements; they usually are more established in their ways than younger persons. They frequently have lived in their homes for many years and consider them familiar territory. A move can be stressful. Elderly persons worry more about such changes than younger people, and they suffer actual illness from the stress. They need counseling on moves and help in the actual move. They need help in establishing new friendships after the move. There is not always a willingness to make new friends at 70.

Financial Needs

Retirement from the work force means a lower income; widowhood, too, may alter economic circumstances. Savings decrease as inflation causes higher costs; health conditions mean medical expenses increase. The elderly need income assistance to cover costs.

Even with this help the elderly still need assistance in finding cheap housing. Income deficiencies often mean they will live in inadequate housing, such as transient hotels or mobile homes, to keep housing costs low. Even this housing may take more than a third of their income.

Money problems may also mean the elderly will try to economize on food. In some cases they have even been known to eat dog food. The resulting inadequate nutritional intake may lead to health problems.

The degree to which old people have changed needs depends on past life-style and psychological orientation and, above all, present physical state, much more than chronological age.

To cover these needs a wide variety of services are required, services that will allow the elderly to live independently and assure that their welfare is cared for in an atmosphere free of the debilitating effects of the institutional world of the nursing home. The types of services to cover these needs can range from recreational and social services to minimal nursing care, homemaking, and food preparation. They can range from financial assistance to transportation and improvement of the neighborhood.

SERVICES TO MEET THE NEEDS OF THE ELDERLY

The Need for Social Interaction

Many elderly are lacking social interaction. Many in our Canadian survey said they "needed company" or felt "depressed," "lonely," or "isolated" or "wanted to be close to other people in the development" and enjoyed a place in which it was "easy to make friends."

Senior citizen centers can play an important role in providing social contact. Many centers, besides running their normal recreational program and having special events and tours, now run separate programs for the frail elderly. Some senior citizen centers have area outreach programs to make contact with the more isolated elderly. Some have members who actively run the program (although others take a paternalistic approach to the elderly, even treating them as children).

The senior citizen center today is a source of information and referral services and provides educational programs. It may also provide legal services. (An extreme type of legal service, often requested by the old person's children, is conservatorship and protection of the elderly person's possessions; this service is usually performed in cases where the elderly person has memory loss.) Sometimes this community senior citizen facility is included in the housing complex.

A number of other groups, of course, run recreational programs for the elderly, including many city parks and recreation departments, church groups, and neighborhood groups.

Seniors' housing complexes usually have a number of social interaction programs and facilities. This is especially true for congregate developments, where not only is there a common dining room—which makes them congregate—but there are also many recreational rooms. In either apartment or congregate complexes these may include a lounge, a library, a television room, arts and crafts rooms, an auditorium, and sports rooms or outdoor areas. Activities may include songfests, crafts, movies, bingo, or bowling. There is often a tenant association.

In many cities social contact services include the *telephone contact service*. This is a volunteer program, possibly a daily service, in which a volunteer checks up on the aged person's health and also simply acts as someone to talk to. The *friendly visitor program* is one in which volunteers visit weekly, or on some regular basis, those aged persons who are identified as isolated or somewhat nonambulatory and in need of contact. They often pick up prescription drugs or groceries for the elderly and, above all, check on any medical problems and if necessary alert a physician or get the person to a health clinic or similar facility. In housing complexes for the elderly another social contact service might be a buddy system, whereby persons on the same floor are designated as "buddies" and asked to check on one another. Another health alert system is an alarm in the bathroom and possibly the living room that can be pushed or pulled in the event of special need or an emergency, such as a fall on the floor. The alarm system is very common in Danish, British, and Dutch housing for the elderly.

Information and referral, social work counseling, and legal and financial counseling are other kinds of social contact services. Councils on aging are groups in each area offering the important information and referral service, giving the elderly and also their children advice on where they can go for different kinds of assistance.

There is a real need for an information and referral service; many of the elderly don't know where to go, as the Richmond, Virginia, Redevelopment and Housing Authority reported before Congress in 1975:

> Many old people who are eligible for financial assistance do not receive it. 6,700 elderly citizens in Richmond are eligible for financial assistance but only 2,200 are receiving old-age assistance, aid to the blind, or aid to the permanently or totally disabled. 5,600 elderly citizens are believed to be eligible for food stamps but are not receiving them. . . . the range of programs supported by public and private funds is not known to the potential recipients. [*Adequacy Hearings,* p. 1019]

Social workers, whether in a council on aging or another agency serving the elderly, may also be a source of counseling to the elderly in financial and health decision making. Social workers may have to contact their elderly clients rather than wait for them to seek help, and then the social workers must follow through to see that the elderly persons actually make their appointments or go for the services. In the case of the physically immobile, the social worker may have to see that an escort is provided, and in the case of a somewhat confused person he or she may have to go along, or see that an aide does, to fill out forms, answer questions, and provide documents. Relocation workers in city redevelopment agencies often take on this job.

Social work counseling may include efforts at increasing socialization for those somewhat disengaged from society. Deterioration of health may include loss of memory, delusions, and confusion. Elderly people may develop a deep depression that turns them from happy, sociable people to people who want to die, who are pessimistic. Massive loss of memory, usually due to brain damage, may mean that a person needs help remembering meal hours if in a congregate development; if that person lives in an apartment, there may be problems remembering to turn off the stove and to take medication. Confusion and disorientation can inhibit meaningful social relationships, nondisruptive participation in group recreational activities, or the ability to dress and bathe. A confused person may wander out of a housing development or nursing home into traffic and forget the way back.

Another kind of disengagement, one that may be related to confusion, depression, physical incapacity, or even alcoholism, is deterioration in both personal care and care of the apartment or room. Social workers can point out these problems to old people who have them. If the problems are in an early stage, the social workers may be able, through casework, to talk them out and try to introduce corrective measures. If the counseling is done in a housing development for the elderly, then the social worker may also help the development staff, especially in a congregate development, to compensate for the problem. For example, the worker may see that the staff reminds the person of mealtimes, has a housekeeper clean the person's room, or has a personal aide or staff member help the person dress or even take care of occasional incontinence.

In some advanced cases of confusion, for example, the social worker, after trying first to work directly with the elderly person, may want to deal with the family as well. Sometimes a family member refuses to face the fact that the father or mother has such a problem and may even resent being told. In other cases the family has known of the problem and has made its decision on this basis to put the person in a housing complex or nursing home (even though it might not have told the development staff about it). The job for the social worker is to get the family to speak frankly about the problem with the community service workers or housing development staff or nursing home staff. In many developments and nursing homes the policy is not to tell the family of a problem until it is so serious that they can no longer handle it and, if a housing development, try to evict the relative.

Another job of the social worker in some agencies and housing developments is to arrange hospital stays for elderly persons, see that their rooms or apartments are held while they are in the hospital (most housing developments will hold a paid room for a certain number of weeks), and visit them in the hospital if time allows. Social workers may also be responsible for trying to fit them back into their own homes or housing complexes and seeing that they get temporary homemaker or housekeeping assistance.

Services to Meet Physical Needs

The important physical needs of the elderly center around difficulty with housing, cooking, and shopping. One type of provision is a meals-on-wheels service run by a volunteer group in the community. In this program, a noon meal is cooked in an institutional setting, such as a hospital or church, and volunteer drivers deliver it to those in need in the area. The volunteers, during their brief contact with housebound elderly, can also learn about other needs these persons have.

A more popular way of supplying meals to the elderly today is through the lunchtime meals programs run at many centers. These are often run under Title VII of the Older Americans Act and are held in churches, senior citizen centers, ethnic-group centers, public housing projects, and many other locations. The program pays for a good part of the meal cost; there is a low charge to recipients but no means test, and no one can be turned away, except when the designated number of places is filled, as it often is. The program is designed "to meet the nutritional and socialization needs of elderly who are felt to not eat adequately because they cannot afford to do so or lack knowledge and/or skills to select and prepare nourishing and well-balanced meals or they have limited mobility which may impair their capacity to shop and cook for themselves or they have feelings of rejection and loneliness which obliterate the incentive to prepare and eat a meal alone." Since up to a fifth of the Title VII nutrition and meals program funds can be used for the supportive services that must be included, this program is a real help in any community. Often transportation to the meal program is provided. Social activities are arranged before or after the meal.

The advantages of providing the elderly with meals services are numerous. For one thing, they get nutritious food. In a number of cases elderly persons do not fix nutritionally sound meals because they live alone or because they are not educated in preparing them. They do not want to bother cooking full meals, or cannot afford to do so, or have difficulty preparing meals.

For many elderly an advantage of the center meal service is that the meal period is beneficial as a time for socializing. An elderly Niagara Falls, New York, project tenant said before Congressional hearings in 1975:

> In our building, I see many people who show the subtle but constant evidence of physical decline. Perhaps often a form of malnutrition. Quick evaluation might conclude that proper food and diet regulation is all that is needed to correct the situation. I disagree.
>
> The depressing and sickening circumstances of day in and day out eating alone is the true deterioration factor. In my humble opinion a glass of milk and a biscuit consumed in the happy and loving companionship of others, could be a more healthful benefit than meals-on-wheels, where one must still eat alone. . . . [Arthur Patterson, *Adequacy Hearings,* p. 920]

Once a day aged persons who otherwise might be isolated have a chance to get together in a dining room. It is a time when staff can watch their daily health condition, when the elderly can be encouraged to take part in other activities, and when referral to needed services can be made. These meal periods can provide a routine and a sense that the day has a purpose for retired persons. Dining in a social group can be a great morale boost for the person to whom the day is otherwise meaningless. Aged persons on the Title VII meals program have made such statements as "I had nobody to talk to until I came to this nutrition project" and "Now I have friends, where before I didn't, since all my friends had died off."

The eligibility for this program is based on need. There is no means test. The method of delivery is through existing centers serving the elderly. The staffing is by the professional staff from various backgrounds that run such centers; paraprofessionals, including elderly persons hired to work there; and, in the cases of churches and many senior centers, volunteers.

Homemaker Service   A person who has just returned from the hospital or has permanent trouble doing housework (making beds, cooking) may benefit from daily or weekly homemaker service. The charges may be on a sliding scale. As with all services for the elderly, the number of available homemakers is small compared to the degree of need.

If more homemakers were available we might be able to keep many of the elderly in their own homes instead of moving them to nursing homes. In Denmark, the author found there was a great emphasis placed on supplying homemakers to the elderly, often on a twice-weekly morning basis, in order to encourage them to stay in their own homes. The small country of Denmark has over 40,000 homemakers to serve the elderly and families in need.

In the United States many needing homemaker service are in their own homes, but those in specially designed apartments for the elderly sometimes require this assistance too.

The health condition of a resident will determine the degree of help necessary. Help may be needed just in heavy work, such as vacuuming, washing floors, and cleaning windows. Some, if they need more complete housekeeping help, may need it only on a weekly basis or for a period after returning from the hospital, while others are so incompetent or in such poor health that they need it on a daily basis.

Eligibility here is based on need, with priority given to the low-income elderly. Delivery is often through an established nonprofit agency. The staffing is by trained homemakers, often with a professional administrator—possibly a social worker—heading the program.

Transportation Services   Limited mobility is a problem many aged have. In our Canadian study, in congregate housing a third, and in apartments a fourth, had difficulty getting places, and another tenth in congregate housing said they did not go out. Some of these aged used walkers, canes, and even wheelchairs. (See Table 10-2.)

Table 10-2   Local Travel Ease, by Development Type

	Development Type		
Travel base	Self-contained apartments	Congregate with some self-contained apartments	All
Difficulty getting places			
Number	28	62	90
Percent	24.1	33.1	29.7
No difficulty			
Number	86	104	190
Percent	74.1	55.5	62.7
Does not go out			
Number	2	19	21
Percent	1.8	10.1	6.9
No answer			
Number	0	2	2
Percent	0.0	1.3	0.7
Total			
Number	116	187	303
Percent	100	100	100

Source: Canadian user study, Huttman, *Housing and Social Services for the Elderly*, Praeger, New York, 1977.

Many elderly need transportation assistance if they are to keep living an independent life and participate in the community. Means must be used to see that socialization with relatives and friends and in community organizations continues, for otherwise old people will become isolated in their own homes or segregated in housing complexes for the elderly.

Many elderly live in areas from which such major needs as medical offices and grocery stores are inaccessible. This may occur if they are in specially designed housing as well as when they are in their own homes. It is especially true if they live in rural or suburban areas.

Since many over 75 or even over 65 do not drive, good bus or subway services, if they exist, can increase their mobility and make needed services more accessible. The aged in our Canadian survey considered good transportation a high-priority need. Many aged consider the most important feature of any neighborhood its nearness to good transportation facilities, as well as to grocery stores.

The surveyed Canadian elderly complained there were limited or too distant bus stops, infrequent service, or poor routing. In some cases those in housing complexes used a taxi as a group or had relatives and friends drive them to needed services. In the several cases where outer-area developments or a related agency supplied transportation, as with one Montreal development, the rate at which persons got out one hour or more a day was higher than for other outer-area developments.

In many cities special transportation services are available to take the elderly to community services, to shopping facilities, and to church. In some cases these are minibuses run on a regular basis or on a phone-in basis. In some places, taxi costs for such trips by the elderly are covered by the city, as in Hayward, California.

Eligibility is again based on need. Delivery is usually from an agency providing other services to the elderly, such as an area office on aging, that both coordinates many programs and subsidizes some itself. The staff, of course, includes drivers, who, one hopes, are social work–oriented.

Services to Meet Health Needs

The elderly, who continually fear that their mobility will be sharply decreased by a sickness or that medical aid will not be readily available in an emergency, worry about services to meet health needs. The aged also worry about the costs of hospitalization, even though they are covered by Medicare. In 1969 the American elderly had medical bills amounting to $14 billion, and only 70 percent of that was covered by Medicare, Medicaid, or any private health plan; if just Medicare coverage is counted it covered only about one-half of all medical costs. The elderly rightfully consider coverage of all medical costs a major need.

The need for medical assistance, in our Canadian study, was expressed as a desire to have someone available in times of health emergencies and, in a number of cases, to have a nurse visit once a week. The Canadian aged in the study feared they might become sick with no one knowing of their illness. They gave examples of persons who had become ill and had to go for hours without help, as in this case in a Toronto development:

> An older lady fell in her apartment on Sunday morning and had broken her arm. She became unconscious. There was no staff on Sunday and none of us visited her. It wasn't till afternoon that she was conscious enough to call out and for us to finally hear her. Since there was no staff on Sunday, we didn't know where to call. We finally got a doctor through the hospital.

The aged have also expressed a need for community health clinics that will cater to their needs, partly because doctors in private practice often give them little attention and are even unwilling to serve them, especially if they are under Medicaid.

Future medical problems are of as much concern as present ones. Elderly people worry that when their health deteriorates, even if they are only slightly impaired, there will be no alternative to the dreaded nursing home. A number of aged, in our studies and others, have expressed the need for more alternatives, including a residence with some nursing staff that isn't a full-scale nursing home. In our survey the majority of those interviewed wanted a complex with different levels of care, from apartment and congregate housing wings to a nursing wing, so that they could feel secure in knowing they would be cared for.

One group in need of more services, including medical services, is those in public housing for the elderly. Thompson (1975) reports:

> Many tenants now in public housing have "aged" in their present quarters as have those in private housing in the community. An increasing number of public housing authorities are faced with the fact that either they must evict the more frail or impaired who cannot sustain the shopping, cooking, or heavy housekeeping chores designed for the hale and hearty, or they must develop on a crash, and perhaps, ill-founded basis—some semblance of the services these aging occupants need to maintain at least semi-independence in a residential setting. [P. 1]

Questioning why the federal government wasn't acting, Williams (1975) asked, "Why should we wait for large scale transfers from public housing to nursing homes or hospitals? Why should we fail once again to take preventive measures rather than give illness and helplessness a head start?" (p. 5). Some recent congressional funding for supportive services for public housing has been one answer.

Some Types of Provision   Some of the major types of provision for those elderly in their own homes are visiting public health nurses and such special services as regular checkups, flu shots, and cardiac facilities in a regular hospital or clinic.

The public health nurse, or a nurse supplied by some other agency, may on a temporary or permanent basis visit those elderly who have some health problem but are able with this care to stay in their own home. This visiting nurse can give shots and medication, take blood pressure, give the person a bath, take care of podiatry needs, or provide other needed services.

In inner-city areas with a concentration of elderly, medical clinics especially catering to their needs have been established. Elderly in the area of a hospital might get preferential treatment there.

Another medical service is the day care programs now provided in many cities. These programs are directed at the frail and impaired who have physical problems or have only a marginal degree of competence. The day care program in a number of cases serves elderly persons who live in their children's homes, although over half utilizing the program live in their own homes, sometimes with a spouse or a son or daughter who takes care of their needs. Those day care programs of a medical type substitute for the nursing home; those closer to the social model meet the social contact needs of the frail or confused elderly. Where there is a relative who normally cares for the elderly person, the day care program relieves this relative for a good part of the day, yet it allows the aged person to get the enjoyment of being with the family evenings and weekends, which may not be possible in the nursing home.

The kinds of needs these day care programs serve, and the type of aged utilizing them, may differ from program to program. If the center is the medical model with nurses and physical therapist it can serve stroke victims and others in need of physical rehabilitation. Some are run by hospitals or nursing homes, as is the Levindale Hebrew Geriatric Center and Hospital in Baltimore. In our nationwide survey we found some are also housed in multiservice senior centers, rehabilitation centers, homes for the aged, and even social service departments. Monk (1975) found that most centers serve at the most fifteen to twenty elderly.

Day care programs are, of course, much less costly than nursing homes, but many states have not given them the funding they need. In some places, where they are of the medical model, Medicaid can pay for the poor client's costs.

Medical services include medication, modified exercise, and treatments. In many hospital-affiliated centers, services are available from the inpatient resources of the hospital; they include podiatry and occupational, physical, and speech therapy. Bathing and dietary services are also provided, plus an extensive range of recreational programs.

Many centers, especially the social model, lack the medical services. Recreation is a common denominator in all centers; almost all provide counseling, social services, and meals. As funding improves and the day care center's potential as an alternative to the nursing home is recognized, the number of services offered may grow.

In these centers the usual routine is for a driver to pick up many aged participants and even wheel their wheelchairs to a van. The program usually runs from 9 or 10 A.M. to 2:30 or 4 P.M. After the people get to the center there is a coffee and socialization time; organized activity, such as arts and crafts, discussion groups, films, games, or music; individualized activities aimed at rehabilitation, such as exercise, physical therapy, and counseling; a hot lunch at noon followed by a rest period; and then more rehabilitative and recreational activities.

Medical services are also provided to varying degrees in congregate housing and, in rare cases, apartment complexes or retirement communities. While congregate housing is not a 24-hour nursing care or health facility, it is for semi-independent or slightly impaired elderly who are still ambulatory. Many residents are fairly old, and after a stay of a year or so they may acquire a number of health problems.

The 1972 HUD congregate housing guidelines say:

> In-house medical services are desirable, with regular service hours, preferably 24-hour coverage through the use of para-medical personnel and health aides, with telephone access to a physician on call, and a backup hospital relationship for medical crises or serious illness. The clinic should include a variety of activities such as eye, hearing examination, cancer detection and podiatry care. [P. 14]

Many elderly in congregate housing have health conditions that mean these services are needed. In our surveyed Canadian congregate housing, interviewers assessed 42 percent as "obviously ill" or "somewhat infirm." One finds the elderly themselves saying that a major priority for them is nursing services; availability of health care is a major reason why they were or were not satisfied with the development.

Some housing developments for the elderly, because they also have a nursing home or nursing wing, can better fill the need for medical services in the development. Such multilevel care existed in a number of complexes the author visited in Holland and Denmark. In the many residential homes for the aged (similar to our congregate housing) in Holland, there is a nursing bay for temporary nursing care; some have a nursing home wing.

In Denmark a number of the newer nursing homes have a *service flats* wing where elderly live in their own apartments; these people are served by a nursing staff and also, in emergencies, by the nursing home personnel.

Most agree that such provision of nursing assistance, as well as meals and housekeeping help, can keep a number of elderly out of nursing homes.

Nursing Homes   Another major type of living arrangement for the elderly that provides medical services is the nursing home, where 24-hour nursing service exists. This type of facility has been an expanding one in the last ten years, partly because of the flow of federal dollars through Medicaid, Medicare, the Hill-Burton program, Kerr-Mills, and even the 1959 Housing Act. As Brody (1975) points out, "resources" are created by various streams of reimbursement for which the individual is eligible, so that the nursing home and its residents have become the main recipients of government aid. In contrast, mental hospitals have been closed down and congregate housing has received limited support. But nursing homes have increased greatly in number, doubling their capacity since 1966 to over a million elderly in 1976. Between $5 billion and $7 billion was spent on nursing homes in 1976, with the federal government paying half the bill and state and local government another large share. Nursing homes employed over three-fourths of a million workers to care for these million elderly.

A number of studies have shown that a proportion of these elderly could be serviced in facilities with less than full-time care if they existed. As Morris (1971) pointed out, "Between 250,000 and 300,000 people are annually assigned to costly institutions for reasons other than medical needs." He added, "The paradox is that our programs are designed to pay too little to keep such persons at home . . . but will readily pay an average of perhaps $400–$500 a month to keep the same person in an institution." Tobin (1974) quotes a Buffalo nursing home study where 27 percent of the institutional population did not need this type of care; he gives lack of alternatives and significant responsible relatives as a main reason for institutionalization. In fact Elaine Brody has found that older people in institutions differ from the general population of older people in that they have far fewer family members and often come to the nursing home after the death or illness of a close relative. Some chronically ill come when their families reach the saturation point of stress or the endurance limit of caretaking. Sometimes the sons and daughters are themselves already elderly persons in or near retirement.

The basic reason most elderly come to the nursing home—failing health—cannot be ignored. It must be realized that many of these elderly are in such a deteriorated health state that alternative housing such as congregate housing will not work, even though, as stated above, it will work for some. Brody (1975) found that institutionalized elderly generally were of advanced old age (82 on the average, compared to 72 for all elderly) and had a much higher incidence of chronic physical and mental impairment resulting in functional disability (an average of almost four disabilities per person), and that between 50 and 80 percent were mentally impaired. Thus there is a group that really needs this level of care. The problem is to sort them out, possibly by the functional assessment tests being developed by Jones, Lawton, and others, tests which cover behavioral social assessment as well as physical health status. At present decisions on placement of a sick elderly person are often made hastily after a hospital stay and are determined by the availability of living arrangements and the availability of financial aid for certain types of living arrangements.

Nursing homes range from those with few professionals available, a low proportion of nurses to total staff and residents, little equipment, and little individual treatment, warmth, tolerance of deviance, and physical attractiveness, to the other extreme. According to Curry (1973), the larger the home, the more likely a more impersonal atmosphere, institutional routine, and nonresidential, "homelike" look.

In general this long-term care may cause, as Reichert (1975) stresses, "premature functional death." He says:

> It may be assumed that all candidates for long term care, i.e., all those whose functional capacity is severely restricted as a result of physical or social trauma, chronic disease or aging, constitute the population at risk of premature functional death, substantially *caused by the total impact of the long term care processes themselves*. [P. 6; italics added—E. H.]

The atomized, fragmented, machine approach to the patient dehumanizes what should be an intensely personal and human experience in both the hospital and the nursing home. In the latter, Reichert says, all aspects of functioning are depleted. He adds that these patients in many cases rarely see a doctor, with a fourth in one study reported not having had a visit from the doctor in the previous thirty days.

A chilling fact is that while "only" 5 percent of America's elderly are in nursing homes or other group quarters, 1 out of 5 seniors will spend some time in a nursing home during his or her life. The job of planning a better housing policy for the elderly is centered on the need to develop alternatives that keep them out of nursing homes as long as possible. If these alternative facilities also provide services and activities that keep them alert and in an independent or semi-independent state, the "last-resort" nursing home may never be needed for many. The result is a more rewarding life for a portion of our aged population and a lower tax bill for our younger population.

Financial Assistance for Medical Expenses   The elderly in the United States have a large part of their medical expenses met by the universal-type health program called "Medicare." This insurance program for men and women 65 and over was brought in as a 1965 amendment to the Social Security Act. It has two parts, the first a compulsory hospital program that covers most hospitalization costs, and the second, Part B, a supplementary voluntary medical insurance program to cover doctor bills and certain other services. The person pays a monthly premium to get this second part, which includes physicians' services in a hospital, a clinic, a doctor's office, or the patient's home; home health visits by a nurse or homemaker; x-ray, radium, and other therapy; diagnostic tests, and related equipment. The patient is required to pay a deductible for such service and a small copayment.

In Part A of Medicare, ninety days' hospital costs in one spell of illness are covered, although the patient pays the first $180 and after the first sixty days of hospitalization he or she pays an amount per day toward the next thirty days of coverage. (In contrast, most national health plans in northern Europe allow indefinite use.)

The program also partially covers the costs of a stay of up to 100 days in a nursing or convalescent home if it follows a hospital stay of three or more days. The program pays in full the first twenty days of a stay in such a home and then for the remainder of the stay covers a part of the cost.

The program is not means-tested but is for all persons 65 and over. The problem as of 1979 is that retirement can start at 62 but Medicare coverage does not start until 65.

Medicaid   Because Medicare does not completely cover all expenses some elderly poor must turn to the medical program for the poor in the United States, Medicaid (or, in California, MediCal), to pay these additional expenses. If they are long-term patients in a hospital or a nursing home, they will especially need to turn to this financial source. In California it has been estimated that two-thirds of those in nursing homes have their bills paid by MediCal. The proportion would be higher if more nursing homes were willing to take MediCal cases; many will not do so.

Medicaid (or MediCal in California) is, of course, a means-tested program. If one is already on SSI (Supplemental Security Income) one automatically qualifies. The federal government shares the cost with the state government. It is not just for the elderly. The largest group of users is actually the poor families covered under the AFDC program.

General Financial Assistance to the Elderly

A main problem many elderly have is that they are poor. The most important financial assistance to the elderly is the Social Security Retire-

ment Insurance program and the related survivors program (OASDHI).
This is an insurance program, established in 1935 under the Social Security
Act, whereby retired contributors age 62 and over and their dependents
receive monthly pension checks from the federal government; on their
death their survivors continue to receive such checks. If they are disabled
they may qualify at an earlier age.

A retired worker who has contributed to the federal fund for a
sufficient period of time through payroll deductions qualifies for this
pension; during the working years the employers also contribute to the
fund.

Over 90 percent of all elderly, rich and poor alike, are eligible for
OASDHI. This is a universal benefit, not based on financial need. The type
of provision in this case is a monthly check. The delivery system is a special
federal agency, the Social Security Administration.

In 1977, 17 million persons and 3.5 million of their dependents
received checks. In addition, 7.5 million survivors, from widows to young
children, received checks. Costs totaled about $80 billion for these parts of
the program.

Most retirees' main source of income is the monthly OASDHI check.
There is an automatic cost-of-living adjustment. Persons over 72 receive
full benefits even if they do not retire and have earned more than the
allowable amount per year.

SSI (Supplemental Security Income) is another financial assistance
program whereby an elderly person can get a monthly check from the
federal government. This one is means-tested and is for elderly poor whose
total income from OASDHI and other sources does not exceed the poverty
level. Blind and disabled persons also qualify for this program; in 1977
about half the 4.4 million recipients were elderly.

As with other means-tested programs one must fill out an application
stating income and assets from various sources and then be judged for
eligibility. However, regulations on assets are fairly liberal, so that a home,
a car, personal effects, and household goods of reasonable value need not
be included as assets. SSI is administered by the Social Security Administration, along with the retirement and survivors insurance program
(OASDHI). This situation has existed since 1974. Before then SSI was
administered by the local welfare office along with the AFDC program.
This change, plus an easier application procedure, has taken considerable
stigma out of the program and made more needy elderly willing to apply.
Also, because the home is no longer considered in assets calculations,
homeowners can now apply. While SSI is a federal program, many states
supplement the low monthly payment the federal government allocates for
recipients.

Housing Services

Comfortable, reasonable housing designed and located to compensate for some of the limitations of old people is a major need. This housing needs to be safe, to give a sense of a place of one's own, and to help the aged person recover some mastery over the environment. It must take care of physical limitations by providing elevators, ramps, easy-maintenance units, and adequate heating systems. It must meet such social concerns as landlord relations, homogeneous grouping, tenant contacts and privacy, and safety from strangers.

A basic need the elderly have is for a choice of housing alternatives. Some will want to stay in their own home and need financial help, such as a housing allowance, and support, such as homemaker services, to allow them to do this. Others need a more sheltered environment, as described above, but one still allowing them a high degree of independence. Specially designed apartments may fit this need. Other elderly, due to certain physical and mental impairments, need an environment with more supportive services, such as congregate housing with a group dining room.

Housing Conditions of the Elderly   Today only a few elderly, perhaps one-half to two-thirds of a million out of 24 million elderly, live in specially designed units. Seventy percent own their own home. Regardless of whether they own or rent, many live in units with housing deficiencies.

Many inner-city elderly, especially the elderly poor, live in inadequate housing. In an HEW study of aged on OAA (now SSI) (HEW, 1973), about 40 percent of the 2 million surveyed were living in apartments or homes with substantial physical or structural deficiencies. Most OAA recipients in Boston were estimated in one study to be living in substandard housing. Some elderly, especially men, live in run-down transient hotels in inner-city areas or in private homes taking a few elderly boarders. Some of these inner-city residents are like Mr. M., who lives in a transient hotel in a skid row area of Los Angeles.

A "Home" on Skid Row

Mr. M. resides in a four-story hotel that was built in 1910. There are thirty-one rooms; the rooms do not have private baths. The renters are mainly older single men on small pensions. A few are winos. The hotel's rooms need painting. In one hall there are still signs of the fire they had last year when an aged man, smoking in bed, set his mattress on fire.

> The hotel is not safe; nonresidents wander into the small, poorly decorated lobby. Checks are stolen from the mailboxes. This transient hotel is on a skid row street with dark, unpleasant bars and pawnshops. Mr. M. does not like to walk outside at night. However, since his social security check cannot cover a much higher rent, he will keep this cheap room and hope for the best.

In 1970 more of the elderly (8 percent) in the United States lived in housing without plumbing than the proportion of the general population that lived this way. The rural elderly had bad housing, with almost three times the proportion of rural units (16 percent) as that of central-city units for the elderly lacking one or more plumbing facilities. Among elderly black people, almost one-fourth had inadequate plumbing.

Elderly people live mainly in older units. In 1970, over half, 58 percent of elderly-owned houses were built before 1939. Renters are very likely to live in old structures. Almost half of elderly-headed, owner-occupied households have resided in their homes for twenty years or more.

Overcrowding is not generally a problem for the elderly. In fact, many elderly overutilize space. In 1962, one study showed that over half the elderly surveyed had three or more rooms per person.

Heating is a serious problem in many old people's quarters. In the study by HEW (1973), almost half said that not every room in their dwelling unit was heated in winter. In one study the author did of a sample of elderly poor in eight cities in 1974, many said they had inadequate heating. In this particular study other housing problems mentioned were leaking roofs, rats, inadequate electric fuses, and incomplete plumbing.

Problems of Homeowners   Of the 70 percent of the aged living in an owner-occupied home, many suffer from several types of housing deprivation. Rural homeowners (and more rural than urban elderly are homeowners) and elderly black homeowners (although fewer black than white elderly are homeowners) are especially likely to live in poor housing. A number of the owners (316,000) own mobile homes; many mobile units, with age, develop a variety of structural defects.

For all these elderly people maintenance is a major problem. The elderly often reside in older structures that are likely to need repairs, whether for a sagging porch, a leaking roof, or an unpainted wall. Many aged lack either the physical strength or the funds to make these repairs. This is especially true of older women.

A number of elderly are hesitant to take out a bank loan on their home in order to make improvements, both because they want to pass the home on to their children debt-free and because they do not want the loan burden when they are on a fixed income. A few aged have received government rehabilitation grants or loans, but this is a very small proportion of the elderly with maintenance problems.

Another problem for aged homeowners is increased property taxes and insurance, as well as costs for electricity, heating, and water. Property taxes have escalated. In 1970 property taxes amounted to 8 percent of income for all elderly owners. While many municipalities and many states have property tax exemptions for the aged, this by no means relieves them of the entire tax burden. Housing expenses, when taxes, insurance, heating, electricity, water, sewerage, and garbage bills are added together, were likely (in 1977) to be $150 to $200 a month or more; this is the probable total if the mortgage is paid off. Because most aged owners have low incomes, these expenditures for housing, which do not include repairs and maintenance, represent a considerable chunk of their monthly budget. It is estimated that, on the average, elderly owners spent at least one-fifth of their income for essential housing expenditures; for many it is closer to a fourth or a third, especially if they are 75 and over.

For aged renters housing costs make up a higher proportion of total costs than for the general population. Almost half the aged renter households in 1970 paid a third or more of their income for rent. Of aged female renters, almost two-thirds aged 75 and over living alone paid over a third of their income for rent. The one-person aged household in general suffered from a high rent-income ratio.

Aged renters, even more than owners, are on the losing side of inflation, with no equity in a house and no chance of selling it at a higher price but only the expectation of higher rents each year. Their only hope is inclusion in the Section 8 program, which would give them a type of housing allowance while they stay in their present residence or when they move to a qualifying unit.

Financial Assistance   For renters, financial assistance can consist of some sort of rent subsidy. A very large proportion of the elderly pay over one-third of their income for rent; this can be brought down to one-quarter by government assistance through the Section 8 program. This leased housing program, while it usually requires the elderly person to move to a standard private unit under contract with the public housing authority, allows some elderly to receive such aid in their present unit *if it is standard* and has a rent within specified limits.

In some cases the housing authority leases all the landlord's units in a building and those already living there who are eligible come under the program. However, under Section 8 the authority usually asks the applicant to search for a unit. The person is judged eligible according to income and then is given a certificate. Then he or she must go out and find housing. The applicant, not the authority, will negotiate with the landlord.

The public housing authority also counsels the applicant about what constitutes a safe, decent, and sanitary standard unit that will be eligible under the program. It also prescribes allowable unit sizes as well as allowable maximum rent levels by unit size. There has been a problem in setting allowable size for the single elderly person. HUD would like to limit the single person to an efficiency unit, but many housing authorities want to allow one bedroom.

The Section 8 program is mainly for existing private housing, but more and more it also includes new units, especially for the elderly. The housing authority may work out an arrangement with a developer whereby a project is built, usually with the subsidy under Section 202 for a below-market interest rate for housing for the elderly, and then units are leased to the elderly participants under Section 8.

Section 8 leased public housing has the advantage of allowing the aged to live in housing dispersed throughout the city and in units not set apart; they may live in their former residences. However, in these early days of the program, it has meant that in many cases they have been housed neither in new units nor in specially designed complexes that have facilities and design features useful to the elderly. The elderly under this Section 8 program are not concentrated in a large complex that can be easily serviced by such community organizations as visiting public health nurses, meal preparation services, or transportation services. Of course, some experts feel that the elderly suffer from being segregated in large, separate complexes.

In most cities the low vacancy rate at the present time makes it hard to find units at acceptable Section 8 fair market rents. In one large study it was found that in cities where there was a low vacancy rate the eligible elderly were much less likely to use the program.

Various types of housing assistance can be given to the elderly in their own homes. Rehabilitation grants are one type of assistance to a homeowner. Because many aged own homes in deteriorating inner-city areas that are designated as conservation areas or, in former days, as code enforcement areas, some of them benefit from Section 312 rehabilitation loans at below-market interest rates or, if they have low income, from grants or from other rehabilitation programs mentioned in Chapter 12.

Elderly owners can also get financial assistance toward their housing costs through property tax relief programs. At the close of 1974, forty-eight states and the District of Columbia had authorized eighty-three different programs; the elderly received preferential treatment in all but three of the programs, according to Abt Associates, who did a study of these programs. In many states the programs are aimed basically at the elderly.

Specially Designed Housing Developments   One-half million to two-thirds of a million elderly live in specially designed developments. Some are subsidized housing units, such as public housing, or nonprofit Section 236 housing, which gives a rent supplement so that poor or moderate-income elderly have to pay no more than 25 percent of their income for rent. In some subsidized housing, rents are also lower because a subsidy for a below-market interest rate is given, such as that under Section 202 or Section 236. Other elderly are in the more expensive Section 231, or in private rental or congregate housing, in life care developments, or in a residential community.

While in some of these kinds of developments low rent is one type of assistance given, even here there are other important types of assistance; for the nonsubsidized developments these other types are the main attractions. The types of assistance include specially designed units, development complexes with a variety of facilities, and an assorted variety of services provided by an in-house staff as well as a community-based one. All these features meet the needs of certain aged.

Specially designed developments are especially useful to those who start to develop special needs, often in their late seventies, but still want to live as independent a life as possible; for some they are useful as a cheaper unit. In both cases, these elderly would like a small, modern unit that is easy to clean and on which exterior maintenance is done by the management. They want a development that has design features that mean less exertion in their old age. They may desire housing with special facilities that cater to their social and physical needs, such as a recreation room and even an infirmary. Many want the friendship of other elderly people and the social activities often afforded in such a setting. The elderly and also their children want to know there is staff that can be called upon if there are emergency health needs. Today many elderly also want another type of security: a well-lighted, protected building safe from intruders.

Most of these elderly want an apartment where they can still cook and live a fully independent life, but some who are physically limited though not ill need a more sheltered environment, congregate housing, with meals served in a common dining room, possibly some housekeeping assistance, and even some nursing staff. Such a supportive environment will allow them to get about on their own; at the same time it provides backup services to cover their deficiencies. These particular elderly moving into congregate housing are at the point in their physical and possibly mental deterioration where staying in their own home is not an advantage but more likely a case of serious lack of needed help in getting adequate meals or keeping a house clean or possibly receiving needed medical and nursing care. Wilma Donahue took this view when she said before the 1975 Senate Special Committee on Aging that:

> Specially-designed housing with a variety of associated services [is needed by many] older people who must now live under growing apprehension of having too soon to seek refuge in long-term medical care facilities as they progress through the later years of their lives . . . and who must struggle against rising odds to maintain themselves in the community. . . . Assisted residential living, especially congregate housing, would extend significantly the period of time impaired though not ill older people are able to remain in the community enjoying the independence, autonomy, privacy, and social relationships that constitute the very essence of meaningful life. . . . Family members, vitally concerned with the well-being of older relatives, would be relieved of most of the burden of trying to provide continuing assistance to them and of the extreme sense of guilt usually associated with consigning aged parents to a nursing home from which few return. [*Adequacy Hearings*, p. 894]

Specially Designed Apartments   All apartments designed specially for the elderly, whether public housing, nonprofit, or luxury private housing, usually are designed to meet the physical needs of this group. The units in the complex have complete kitchens; and the developments, even public housing and nonprofit Section 236 rentals, have special facilities such as a communal room, a reception area–lounge, a self-service laundry room, and possibly one or two offices for visiting or development personnel; some have a dining area where outside groups serve a noon meal.

Housing developments for the elderly generally have services available, to varying degrees, but most are provided by the community and not the development. Many American public housing authorities have community services divisions that work with all the elderly public housing developments in their jurisdiction and try to get activities going; they also contract with community agencies for services. The most common management-initiated services are in the realm of encouraging telephone contact service, friendly visiting, voluntary transportation assistance, and, now, hot lunches under Title VII of the Older American Act.

Congregate Housing   Congregate housing developments have a common dining room and housekeeping services and so meet a number of needs. In many congregate complexes there are hotel-type bedrooms rather than fully equipped apartments. There are usually numerous facilities. Congregate housing is considered housing for ambulatory elderly who can walk to their meals and do not need major nursing care. However, it is assumed these elderly have enough physical and mental impairments that they need some help, in the form of personal services and some limited nursing assistance.

Donahue (*Adequacy Hearings,* 1975) estimated that over 3 million could use congregate housing as a substitute for nursing homes. Congregate housing is a semi-independent environment. It is a far cheaper housing arrangement than a nursing home. The director of the Maryland State Office on Aging (*Adequacy Hearings,* 1975) recommended HUD support of experimental sheltered housing, adding, "This sum is peanuts compared to the billions of dollars being invested in unnecessary institutionalization."

Nursing homes will still continue to be used for the impaired elderly who do not need them, because the alternative of congregate housing does not exist in many cases. Lawton (1975) says the number of congregate housing units is "minuscule," and one source counted fewer than 400 congregate housing developments in 1974.

CONCLUSION

Housing assistance can be given in a number of ways. It can be financial assistance to the elderly in their own private units, or it can be provision of specially designed housing that offers services, facilities, special features, and staffing, as well as cheap rent in government-subsidized specially designed units. Provision of services is a chief attribute of these apartment and congregate housing developments, for the provision of standard, architecturally pleasing shelter is not enough for the elderly. This is only the shell in which a community of people in need resides. To make this housing a satisfactory environment in which the elderly can enjoy an independent or semi-independent life style, one must think beyond shelter. As the National Center for Housing Management, in its 1974 manual on housing for the elderly, says in discussing the role of management in providing social services:

> To provide shelter, well-maintained and financially sound, has been the traditional goal of management and consequently the basic role of housing managers. However, it has become increasingly clear with social change that managers have to assume responsibility to see that the social needs of their residents (the elderly are a special instance) are met. [Chap. 9, p. 1]

The Center warns in this manual that "the housing manager must attempt to provide guidelines in meeting these needs, if for no other reason than the fact that the economic and physical well-being of his housing development may be endangered by ignoring the social needs of the residents."

This is the type of role social workers in the housing field must keep in mind. For housing for the elderly is far more than just shelter.

Summary

This call for services in housing for the elderly can be generalized to a call for all services to the elderly. This chapter has described the real needs and also has given details on the types of services that can be provided for the aged. In thinking of social policy for the aged one must keep this variety of services in mind. The main goal is to help compensate for their physical, financial, and social limitations.

Most needs of the elderly are universal needs, not just needs of the elderly poor. Most services are offered to a variety of income groups, although specially designed housing is more available for the poor through the public housing program. Many nonprofit organizations are involved in delivering services. Many are staffed by paraprofessional workers, even the elderly themselves. Some, such as senior citizen centers, are multiservice centers often with workers from agencies on hand once a week, such as a public health nurse. Many have an information and referral function or a general coordinating function.

The value assumption embodied in any legislation to help the aged is that they are a deserving group. Also, because of their number and voting power, they have a strong power base, and considerable funding is given to help them today. They receive priority in the allocation of limited social service resources, including Title XX monies. Cost-effectiveness here can be measured in terms of success in keeping the elderly out of expensive nursing homes or out of the hospital, both of which are often paid for by the government.

Chapter 11

The Juvenile Justice System

by Dr. Terry Jones

INTRODUCTION

The social unrest and the rediscovery of poverty during the 1960s further highlighted the condition of the juvenile justice system in the United States. To some extent the present unrest in the juvenile justice system serves as a reminder of the history of the development of separate treatment for youthful offenders.

Just a little over a hundred years ago children were treated for their crimes in the same manner as adults. While the age of juvenile offenders was considered important in determining whether they should be held responsible for their acts, in most respects the treatment was similar to that of adults. The juvenile was likely to be held in the same jail as an adult criminal, go before the same judge, and even be sent to the same correctional facility. We have made great movement in the last century in changing the way we treat juveniles, and with that movement has come both agreement and disagreement about the role and function of the juvenile justice system and its relationship to the youth of America. The pages that follow examine the development of the juvenile court, probation services, and diversion programs in an effort to give the reader an understanding of how we have attempted to meet the needs of those in danger of leading criminal lives.

HISTORICAL BACKGROUND OF THE JUVENILE COURT

While most authorities have come to regard the Illinois Juvenile Court Act of 1899 as the first such legislation establishing a juvenile court in America, it is important to recognize that the separation of children from adult offenders in the justice system is an evolutionary process that dates back at least to Napoleonic France. In fact, in the United States, the Juvenile Court Act of 1899 culminated nearly 100 years of reform efforts by child-saving organizations all over the country. After Illinois' pioneering efforts, other states soon followed: Wisconsin (1901); New York (1901); Ohio (1902); Maryland (1902); and Colorado (1928).

Haskell and Yablonsky (1978) note that before the establishment of juvenile courts and

> . . . as recently as the latter part of the nineteenth century, children were tried for their crimes exclusively in criminal courts in both England and the United States. The age of the child was considered a factor in determining whether or not he should be held responsible for his acts, but in most other respects his treatment resembled that accorded an adult charged with a crime. [P. 25]

By 1869, Massachusetts had recognized a need for change. It was the first state to pass a law altering the court procedure in cases involving children. The legislation did not call for a juvenile court, but it made provisions for the investigation of cases involving children coming to court. By 1872, Massachusetts had enacted legislation which called for separate trials for children who violated the law, and by 1880 legislation was enacted establishing the first separate detention facilities for children.

To properly understand the development of the juvenile court, it is instructive to examine the context of American society in the latter part of the nineteenth century. People (many of them foreigners) were moving to cities in record numbers, crowded conditions prevailed everywhere, there was an increased focus on protecting property rights, and crime was a constant threat everywhere. In addressing this issue, David Bakan observes:

> Drinking, sexual immorality, vagrancy, and crime were not only intrinsically threatening to orderliness, but were also particularly distressing influences on the young. The rapid breeding, the continuing threat of "street Arabs,"

evoked a strong cry that the state intercede in restraining and training the young. [P. 981]

It is Bakan's belief that these conditions acted as a catalyst for the child-centered social movement legislation and special legal procedures for "juveniles," and therefore the invention of adolescence.

In theory, the Juvenile Court Act passed by the Illinois legislature in 1899 was to separate out cases involving children, whether they be dependency, neglect, or delinquency, and to bring them under the jurisdiction of a separate court for the purpose of rehabilitation. The sad fact of the matter is that this ideal was never fully realized. In actuality, the juvenile court appears to be nearly as punitive as adult courts. For example, an Ohio Youth Commission Study (1974) reveals that:

> **1** The younger the offender, the longer the period of institutionalization.
> **2** Classification for rehabilitation lengthens the period of institutionalization and does not reduce the rate of recidivism.
> **3** Children with the longest institutional sentences have the highest rate of parole revocation. [P. 7]

The juvenile court was also designed to prevent juveniles from being incarcerated with adults. In researching this matter for *The Child Savers*, Platt (1977) notes:

> A survey by the National Council on Crime and Delinquency found that close to 90,000 juveniles spent some time in adult jails in 1965. A more systematic survey conducted by the Department of Justice reported that there were 78,000 juveniles in jail on a given day in March 1970. [P. 190]

Further noting the gap between rhetoric and actual practice, Wilensky and Lebeaux (1965) observe that:

> What is dominant philosophy, however, is not dominant practice. A large proportion of youthful offenders find themselves in the hands of criminal courts with punitive ideology. The quality of juvenile courts is often no better than the criminal courts. An estimated 50,000 to 100,000 children are confined each year in jails—often illegally. [P. 22]

In summary, the Illinois Juvenile Court Act of 1899 sought to offer humane treatment of the juvenile offender separate from adults and on an individualized basis. The idea of *parens patriae,* or the court's obligation to use great latitude in resolving the problems of troubled youth, came to be the order of the day. Hearings were to be informal, the judge to be seen as a kindly parental figure. Offenses were not to be judged criminal acts, and punishment was to be set aside for rehabilitation. In effect, the legal rights of children were frequently overlooked for the principle of service and rehabilitation. Now, after almost eighty years of experience with juvenile courts, there seems to be some question whether the principle of service and rehabilitation has been too high a price to pay for the lack of respect for legal rights.

THE JUVENILE COURT TODAY

The operation of the juvenile court, in theory, is centered around saving the child from being a criminal or from continuing a life of crime. Through the old English Common Law term of *parens patriae,* the court and the judge, acting as a counselor, play a substitute parent's role in cases involving youth under the age of 18 who have been abandoned or neglected or are dependent or delinquent. In concerning itself with the overall behavior of the juvenile, the juvenile court has traditionally held jurisdiction over matters that are only considered law violations because of the age of the participants. For example, curfew violations, refusing to attend school, and runaways are cases that are unheard of in adult criminal court. In the juvenile court, they are referred to as "status offenses" and in many states are being transferred to the jurisdiction of social service agencies.

The procedure of the juvenile court is quite different from that of adult courts. To begin with, under the juvenile court's jurisdiction, the child is not to be considered a criminal or to have committed any criminal offenses but to be a person in need of help. The common phrase heard throughout the juvenile courts and the juvenile justice system is, "We treat the child and not the offense." A great deal of attention is focused on individualized justice and child-centered treatment. To arrive at such noble goals, the juvenile court has had to establish a whole different set of operating procedures from those found in adult criminal courts.

In juvenile court, the procedure is characterized by an air of informality. The hearings are frequently held in the judge's (many states use juvenile court referees) chambers, where the legalities of the adult courts are kept to a minimum. Instead of being arrested in the strict sense of the term, children are given a summons. They may be detained, not in a jail but in a juvenile facility, or at least segregated from adult offenders. In juvenile court proceedings, children do not plead guilty or innocent to a crime but admit or deny the allegations of petitions filed against them. Children are not convicted but are adjudged wards of the court. There are a range of possibilities open to the court, from probation in the home of their parents to placement in private, city, county, or state facilities for juveniles. A very important aspect of the juvenile court process is that being adjudged a ward of the court does not necessarily cut the juvenile off from adult privileges such as voting, entering the military, or future civil service appointments. In fact, in most states there are provisions for having juvenile records sealed after a specified period of good behavior. It is worth noting, however, that even with the safeguards listed above, contact with the police or other involvement with the juvenile justice system puts the juvenile in a stigmatized position in regard to being considered for military service or employment.

Out of the child-saving movement of the progressive era came a juvenile court system that almost totally disregarded the legal rights of the child in favor of "a fatherly judge who would see to individualized treatment and, if necessary, rehabilitation." Over the years there have been a great number of changes in the juvenile court. Chief among these changes has been the move toward a more legalistic approach to the juvenile court proceedings prompted by the *Miranda** and *Gault*† decisions. This movement toward a more legalistic approach is due, in great part, to the criticism and reported failure of juvenile court practices over the past eighty years.

Criticism of the Juvenile Court

Criticism of the juvenile court ranges from overcrowded court calendars to the abuse of the rights of the children and their families who come before it. Over the past fifty years, the most consistent criticism of the juvenile court system has come from groups expressing two different perspectives. Outlining these opposing perspectives is instructive in understanding the conflict in the juvenile court system. Platt (1977) identifies the essence of this conflict as one between "legal moralists" and "constitutionalists" when he states:

> To the "legal moralists," the juvenile court is a politically ineffective and morally improper means of controlling juvenile crime. To the "constitutionalists," the juvenile court is arbitrary, unconstitutional, and violates the principles of fair trial. The former view concerns the protection of society, the latter addresses the safeguarding of individual rights. [P. 190]

In essence, the legal moralists take the position that "a crime is a

---

*Essentially, in the *Miranda* decision the Supreme Court ruled that warnings must be given, that the suspects have the right to counsel, that they have the right to remain silent, and that any statement they make may later be used against them.

†See the section under "Criticism of the Juvenile Court" for a discussion of the *Gault* decision.

crime" and that persons who break the law, whether juveniles or adults, should be punished appropriately. They see the juvenile court system as one that pampers juveniles and therefore encourages criminal activity. California appears to be moving in this direction with its recent legal requirement that 16-year-olds involved in violent crimes be treated as adults.

On the other hand, those who advocate the constitutionalists' view take the position that the juvenile court's lofty humanitarian goals have not been achieved. Specifically, they have charged that:

> The child lost many of the constitutional protections that are commonly associated with adult criminal procedures. For example, in many juvenile courts, the child was not given a written notice of the charges to be considered at his hearing. The child was not allowed to have a lawyer represent him at the hearing and was not extended the privilege against self-incrimination. The opportunity to cross-examine witnesses was absent in many proceedings involving juveniles. [Platt, 1977, p. 190]

By 1960, however, the United States Supreme Court began to challenge the authority of the juvenile court and to question the use of *parens patriae* as the justification for denying children their rights under the Constitution. Several states, New York, California, and Illinois, to name a few, moved to a more legalistic juvenile court system even before the now famous *Gault* decision. In 1967 the Supreme Court ruled in favor of Gerald Gault, a 16-year-old Arizona juvenile. The *Gault* case guaranteed juveniles:

1 Timely notice of the specific charges
2 Notification of the right to be represented by counsel in proceedings that might result in commitment to an institution in which the juveniles' freedom is curtailed
3 The right to confront and cross-examine complainants and other witnesses
4 Adequate warning of the privilege against self-incrimination and the right to maintain silence

When the *Gault* decision was announced in 1967, many states had already anticipated it and were administering a more legalistic juvenile court. According to Judge Purchio, in the Alameda County Juvenile Court in California:

> The same legal safeguards are present in juvenile court as there are for adults. This has been a fact in Alameda County for many years, nationally only

recently. Attorneys are appointed for the minors if they do not have them. [Douthit, 1976, p. 3]

The *Gault* decision was supported by research findings that juveniles appearing before the court represented by counsel fared better than those who had no representation.

The issue of legal representation of juveniles in court raises another concern related to the function of the juvenile court. In 1972, 1.7 million juveniles were taken into custody. With this number on the increase and the juvenile court continually feeling the pinch of crowded court calendars, there has been added speculation about the quality of the representation juveniles receive in juvenile court. In juvenile court, there is a good deal of concern about time and efficiency of operation, and since frequently the juvenile is represented by the public defender, there is concern that a collegial relationship develops between judges, prosecutors, and public defenders. In short, many of the criticisms leveled at the adult court are beginning to be directed at juvenile court.

In summary, there are a number of distinctly relevant criticisms of the juvenile court, but the most serious have to do with the denial of rights. For example, juveniles do not have the right to:

1   Be released on bail pending disposition of their cases
2   A trial by jury
3   A public trial at which reporters and other interested persons may be present
4   The same amount of proof of guilt as in an adult court. (In juvenile court, decisions are made on "a preponderance of guilt")

On this last point, the California Supreme Court recently ruled that a juvenile may be declared a ward of the court on the testimony of an accomplice even if it is uncorroborated. Under the California Penal Code an adult may not be convicted of a crime on the testimony of an accomplice unless there is other evidence connecting the suspect with the offense. Such a ruling keeps in place the tradition that juveniles have fewer rights in court than adults.

Guiding Principles of the Juvenile Court

Despite the criticisms leveled against the juvenile court over the years, the stated goals of protecting and rehabilitating the child remain constant. In fact, there is a good deal of belief that the move toward a more legalistic juvenile court makes it a more conducive instrument for reaching these goals.

While the juvenile court has become more legalistic over the years, the concept of individualized justice and *parens patriae* remains the guiding principle. The state, through the judge or referee and its other officials, seeks to direct delinquent children away from crime and toward a more meaningful life. In order to accomplish this each child brought before the court should be judged as a unique individual with a unique set of circumstances to be taken into consideration before a decision is rendered.

The administrative arm of the court responsible for carrying out this individualized approach to juvenile justice is the probation department. In most states, probation officers working with delinquent children have education and field training in social work, sociology, or related fields. Generally probation workers are civil service appointees, and always there is an attempt to attract people with integrity and a concern for children.

PROBATION

The National Commission on Law Observance and Law Enforcement defines probation as:

> A process of treatment, prescribed by the court for persons convicted of offenses against the law, during which the individual on probation lives in the community and regulates his own life under conditions imposed by the court and is subject to supervision by a probation officer. [Friedlander and Apte, 1974, p. 489]

However, when we think in terms of probation for juveniles, there are some distinct differences in procedure. For example, in the case of juvenile probation there is no conviction, in the technical usage of the term, but an adjudication. As in adult probation, the juvenile probation order allows the child liberty under some form of supervision in the community. Generally, he or she is placed in the custody of parents, friends, relatives, or foster parents.

The guiding principle of probation is the suspension of sentences to allow children an opportunity to conduct themselves in a law-abiding way with guidance from probation officers, parents, relatives, and friends. The juvenile court judge, or referee, sets the terms of probation and reserves the right to revoke it if the terms of the agreement are violated or if another offense is committed.

Not everyone who commits an offense is granted probation. Factors considered in granting probation include:

    1 The child's previous record of delinquency as well as any previous delinquent tendencies

    2 The child's family history including information concerning the composition of the family: the occupation of the parents, their earnings, and other conditions which may affect the child's conduct

3 The neighborhood in which the child lives

4 The child's conduct in school and his general educational background, including his progress in school

5 The child's work record (if he has been employed)

6 The child's interests and activities outside of school

7 The child's general health and personality [National Probation and Parole Association, 1957, p. 53]

More and more juvenile court judges are letting it be known that they are also quite concerned about the *nature of the offense.* In fact, as previously mentioned, some states have moved to have 16-year-olds who commit violent crimes tried as adults.

While most authorities do not want to admit it, race also appears to be a factor in determining who is granted probation. The black child is more likely to be arrested, brought before the court, and denied probation than the white child.

Probation as we know it today was first introduced in the United States by John Augustus, a Boston shoemaker, who provided bail for a poor drunkard who was on the verge of being sentenced to the house of corrections. Seeing the success of this case, he took on others, offering them supervision or "probation" for a prescribed period of time.

The provisions of probation vary somewhat from state to state. In most states, the probation service is attached to the court with the chief probation officer being appointed by the judge. A few states have centralized probation systems, but most of the 3068 counties in the United States have autonomous probation operations within the limits established by state legislation.

An important rationale for probation is that it is far less costly to the taxpayers to maintain persons in the community than to institutionalize them. In addition, it is less stigmatizing to the individuals and allows them maximum opportunity to change their behavior in a far less threatening environment. However, the other side of the picture is that the law is to protect society and not necessarily to release law violators back into the community to continue their lawless ways. Probation's attempt at minimizing the danger to the public in granting probation begins with a social investigation of each juvenile case. This is where a skilled probation staff trained in understanding human dynamics is a must. Probation is to be recommended *only* if the probation officer is convinced that the juvenile will be able to use the opportunity to constructively adjust his or her behavior. If, for some reason, the probation officer feels the juvenile is a poor candidate for probation, he recommends to the court commitment to an institution.

A juvenile who has been placed on probation and declared a ward of the court may be placed at home with his or her own parents or with relatives, a guardian, or in some instances friends of the family. At this point, the court has legal guardianship of the child. In probation supervision, generally a worker, using social work skills or some variation thereof, engages the juvenile and his or her parents in an attempt to develop a more positive behavior pattern. In some areas, male probation officers supervise only male juveniles while female probation officers supervise female probationers. In recent years there has been a tendency to integrate caseloads, with male and female workers supervising both male and female probationers.

One of the most serious difficulties with probation supervision is that probation officers generally lack the time or the expertise to properly supervise juveniles with serious emotional problems. Even if they had the expertise, the size of the caseloads (100 to 200 in some states) works against most effective counseling techniques. Nearly all probation officers are dissatisfied with the size of their caseloads and point to the lack of time for rehabilitation or therapy of any kind. Despite all the criticisms of probation, it appears to be a more humane way of dealing with selected offenders than institutionalizing them.

CORRECTIONAL INSTITUTIONS FOR JUVENILES

Juveniles who are found to be so delinquent that they cannot benefit from probation in their homes or with foster families are committed to juvenile institutions. In the past, such institutions have been called "reform schools" or "training schools." These institutions grew out of the disenchantment with placing dependent and delinquent children in almshouses and prisons with adults during the eighteenth and nineteenth centuries.

The first reform school, or training school, in the United States was the New York City House of Refuge, founded in 1825 by the Society for the Reformation of Juvenile Delinquents. The intent of this institution was "to save neglected and vagrant children from the destructive influence of adult prisons."

As these institutions are currently run, there is heavy emphasis on education, guidance, and rehabilitation, but this has not always been the case. Early juvenile institutions were characterized by their sunup-to-sundown policies that stressed manual labor, codes of silence, and corporal punishment. Now there is an attempt to offer juveniles a controlled environment in which they can begin to work on a positive plan for their return to the community. In some of the better institutions in the country, a number of services, such as medical, mental health, academic, vocational, and recreational services, are woven together into a rehabilitative program geared to place juveniles back in their communities in the shortest possible time. In most all juvenile institutions, there is an emphasis on control under which the juvenile must learn to accept limits and conform to the rules of the institution. The idea is that juveniles who are successful in meeting obligations, controlling behavior, and following rules in the institution should be able to transfer this behavior to the outside community.

Once the court decides to commit a juvenile to an institution, it generally has a wide range of options. In most states a juvenile can be committed to a public or private institution. In the case of the public institution, it may be city-, county-, or state-operated. In the case of private commitments, the placement may be to a sectarian or a nonsectarian institution.

Traditionally, difficulties with juvenile institutions have centered around overcrowding, the mixing of severely disturbed children with those with lesser degrees of disturbance, and the confinement of minor offenders with serious offenders. Couple this with the fact that juvenile institutions have traditionally been built in geographically isolated areas where it is difficult to attract high-quality staff, especially of minority background, and you can begin to uncover the traditional sore spots in juvenile institutional care. The crowding together of juveniles in hostile surroundings with staff that has a difficult time relating to them, their culture, or their way of life frequently compounds the problem of institutionalized juveniles instead of ameliorating their difficulties.

With California taking the lead in 1940, many states enacted youth authority acts. In addition to establishing juvenile institutions, these acts generally called for the youth authority to offer consultative services to local communities, conduct research on the causes of delinquency, and develop preventive services and diagnostic treatment facilities. The California Youth Authority places an emphasis on diagnosis, prevention, and rehabilitation. It has established two reception centers (one in the north and the other in the south) for diagnosis and evaluation of youths committed to the Authority. In addition, the various counties may commit juveniles to the Youth Authority for diagnostic evaluation. These diagnostic evaluations include examination and studies by social workers, physicians, psychiatrists, psychologists, and teachers. If the child is being returned to his or her county of origin for treatment, a diagnostic study and a set of recommendations are sent to the court. On the other hand, a child who is to be placed in a California Youth Authority institution is classified according to age, sex, mental capacity, and similar criteria, and an institution is selected. After a period of adjustment, generally from six months to two years, the juvenile goes before the Youth Authority Board, which has the final say on his or her release. Before the release, a plan is developed for the juvenile's return to the community. The parents are contacted, and decisions are made whether the juvenile will work, attend school, or join the military. Parole service is established for the juvenile with the ostensible purpose of offering guidance and supervision on entering the community.

It should be noted that the Youth Authority is for the most serious juvenile offenders and it is a rarity that a first-time offender is committed. In many instances these institutions are juvenile prisons that breed delinquent activity, gang association, and even homosexual activity. These places frequently have the reputation of being "junior state prisons," and the juveniles who are paroled are stigmatized accordingly.

While California has one of the more sophisticated youth authorities, most states have similar arrangements for the treatment and prevention of delinquency. There has come a recognition that the state, with all its resources, has the ability to wage the most concentrated attack on delinquency. Some argue, however, that such treatment is too centralized and far away from the people and tends to alienate the youth even further. They contend that it would be far better to turn to massive community treatment programs and to deemphasize the role of the state as a service provider. As the situation currently exists, the quality and quantity of service varies from county to county and state to state primarily because of resource inequities. In summary, juvenile institutions have many of the same problems as adult prisons, but their emphasis is shaded more toward rehabilitation and guidance than custody.

DELINQUENCY PREVENTION

Attempts at delinquency prevention are nothing new. Programs to keep people from breaking the law can be traced back as far as the beginnings of the law itself. In the United States, however, its formal history dates back only to 1899 and the establishment of the first juvenile court in Chicago.

While we still do not know all there is to know about the causes of juvenile delinquency, we have not been timid in trying to formulate programs for delinquency prevention. For the most part these programs have been based more on faith than on a scientific approach to the prevention of delinquency. Gould (1971) refers to our efforts at delinquency prevention as "prescientific." He contends that our efforts are in the prescience phase because of:

> . . . confusion over the concept of delinquency, and just what it is that must be controlled; ignorance of the causes of delinquency, the conditions that, if

changed, would effect a reduction; and ambivalence about the goals of treatment, whether to be committed to preventing further delinquency by some effective and humane means or whether (or instead) to wreak revenge and impose retributions for past behavior regardless of future implications. [P. 173]

No matter how prescientific we have been, rising juvenile crime rates and the urban disturbances of the 1960s, participated in by a significant number of minority youth, escalated our efforts in delinquency prevention and control. OEO, Model Cities, the Law Enforcement Assistance Program, and the United Way, to name a few, were all active in putting funds into delinquency prevention efforts.

On a national level, the first effort to formulate strategies for the prevention of delinquency was the establishment of the Juvenile Delinquency and Youth Offenses Act of 1961. This act set the federal government up in a leadership position in delinquency prevention by seeking to coordinate efforts in the field by public and private agencies. The overall objective of the act is to develop techniques for the prevention and elimination of delinquency by encouraging states and local governments to actively engage in demonstration projects which have delinquency prevention and control as their central focus. The emphasis is on getting the community involved in doing the necessary planning and implementation in preventing delinquency.

A wide range of programs focusing on delinquency prevention have come and gone over the years. One of the most publicized was the Mobilization for Youth in New York. It was put together with the help of the School of Social Work at Columbia University in 1962, and had as its objective the reduction of delinquency in a slum area in New York City. The project was based on the theoretical assumption that if juveniles could become employed, they would stand a chance of increasing their social status and begin to perform more like their more successful peers.

Similar projects in Washington, D.C., and Philadelphia were based on the assumption that if "roving leaders," people who could relate to juveniles with problems, were dispersed throughout the city in high-delinquency areas, they would have a positive impact on curbing delinquency. These roving leaders were to counsel youth, assist them with everyday problems, and, above all, keep the lid on possible gang warfare.

In Richmond, California, the Dynamic Youth Group was formed by a juvenile probation officer in the mid-1960s. It operated on the assumption that if you provided wholesome recreational opportunities for youth in a controlled setting the delinquency rates would fall.

In a new project out of New York, Project Joey, the objective was to provide employment in the private sector for up to 1000 New York City teenagers on probation before the project ended in June 1978. According to Sheila Rule of the *New York Times*. The Project hopes to instill in these young people good work habits, a sense of responsibility and optimism about their future" (December 3, 1978).

Effective evaluation of these projects is difficult, if not impossible. In some cases the projects were operated in a fashion that makes evaluation difficult. In others, it's a matter of defining what is meant by preventing delinquency. Is a person delinquent by being in danger of committing an offense or only after being caught and labeled by authorities? Another point to consider is that most of these delinquency prevention programs were operated in low-income areas with the assumption that the lower economic class, especially minority lower classes, were more prone to lives of crime. Now there is a growing recognition that middle- and upper-class juveniles may be just as crime-prone as, if not more than, the lower classes. This further complicates the task of evaluation of delinquency prevention programs, because sizable delinquency-prone groups have been omitted from exposure to the various programs.

The goal of delinquency prevention and control is addressed through a number of strategies. Two of the most prominent strategies focus on social control and reducing provocation. The social control programs are mostly identified with the efforts of the juvenile court and probation services. Programs dealing with reducing provocation are those that offer employment, educational, and recreational opportunities to the target population. The rationale is that meeting the target population's needs will reduce the need to engage in delinquent behavior.

Strategies for delinquency prevention tend to be focused on either individuals, groups, or institutions. Those that focus on the individual or on groups are geared toward providing skills, guidance, or jobs. Those that have an institutional focus attempt either to change agencies that deal with juveniles or to create new ones. It is not uncommon for agencies to focus attention in all three areas. The Mobilization for Youth organization discussed above is an example of this. For individuals it attempted to develop job skills and the confidence that goes with successful job hunting; in dealing with groups, it provided counseling and efforts to reduce gang activity; and in regard to institutions, Mobilization for Youth was active in seeking changes in schools, in the practices of police, and in the juvenile courts.

During the 1960s juvenile authorities slowly began formalizing the concept of juvenile services in police departments. With the aid of federal grants, youth service programs began to appear in police departments across the country. The rationale is the accumulated evidence that the police officer is really one of the first links in delinquency prevention efforts. The officer has the authority to arrest, admonish and release, or refer the juvenile for further services. In many larger cities specially trained juvenile officers process all arrested juveniles and make decisions about the extent to which the juvenile will become further involved in the juvenile justice system.

Youth Service Bureaus

By the late 1960s, there had been enough experience with delinquency prevention (not all of it successful) to recognize a need for a more coordinated effort. The President's Crime Commission Report recommended the creation of youth service bureaus on the local level that would be designed to provide comprehensive counseling and recreational and rehabilitative services for juveniles (HEW, Youth Administration, 1973). These services were to be available to juveniles regardless of their involvement with the juvenile court.

Youth service bureaus operate on the assumption that the juvenile court has not been successful in rehabilitating juveniles who come under its jurisdiction and that juveniles would be far better off being diverted from the justice system. Kenneth McCreedy (1975) interprets the recommendations in the President's Crime Commission Report to mean that the bureaus were to be established as substitutes for juvenile courts. What generally has occurred around the country, however, is that youth service bureaus have been established as supplements to the juvenile court. For example, the Youth Services Bureau in Richmond, California, known as the Youth Outreach Program, is actually funded and operated by the probation department and is a support service to the probation department. It handles youth who are considered to be predelinquent; all others are referred to traditional probation procedures.

The typical youth service bureau is financed by a mixture of federal and local funds and has diversion from the juvenile justice system and delinquency prevention as its primary objectives. The majority of these programs are located in economically depressed inner-city areas and provide counseling, referral, tutoring, and recreational activities as their primary services. Juveniles are most frequently referred to youth service bureaus from schools, law enforcement agencies, and parents. As could be expected, these juveniles are referred for unacceptable behavior, personal difficulties, and some professional service need. In some instances, especially on parental or self-referrals, the juveniles come to youth service bureaus out of a need for companionship and recognition by responsible adults.

In summary, youth service bureaus operate on the assumption that it is better to divert the juvenile from the formalized juvenile justice system. There is a further assumption that the juvenile court system does not work, is arbitrary, and acts to stigmatize youth more than to rehabilitate them.

PROBLEMS AND POLICY ISSUES IN THE JUVENILE JUSTICE SYSTEM

With the rights explosion of the 1960s came an increased recognition that the rights of juveniles were being routinely violated through the practices of the juvenile court system. In addition to the questionable legal practices within the juvenile court system, there has come the additional question of the broad, arbitrary nature of laws regarding juvenile behavior. Empey and Lubeck (1971) note:

> Given the broad mandate of the juvenile court and the catchall character of the statutes which define delinquency, there are virtually no nondelinquents. Juveniles have committed and commit acts daily which, if detected, could result in adjudication. Consequently, from the standpoint of social control, it is necessary to question the utility of legal norms about which there is such ambiguity. [P. 21]

This ambiguity and the catchall nature of juvenile laws make it necessary for the exercise of a great deal of discretion on the part of law enforcement agencies. This discretion creates a filtering process that has resulted in a particular type of juvenile's reaching the formalities of the juvenile court. In 1970, the filtering process had the result that roughly 500,000 juveniles, out of a potential 4 million who had police contacts, actually appeared in juvenile court. Going to a juvenile correctional institution represents the ultimate in the screening process, and it is rather instructive to note who gets filtered into these institutions. According to the National Assessment of Juvenile Corrections report, "Black youth accounted for almost 33 percent and native Americans for 8 percent of the reformatory population in sixteen sample states" (Vintner, 1978). This study goes on to report that a disproportionate number of imprisoned youth come from working-class and minority backgrounds.

CONCLUSION

In effect, the policies of the juvenile justice system are heavily dependent on the exercise of discretion on the part of correctional staff. While this discretion is supposedly exercised for the good of the minor, we find an overrepresentation of low-income and minority groups in juvenile court and juvenile institutions. The time-worn phrase "treat the juvenile and not the offense" gives juvenile authorities the flexibility to be "compassionate and understanding" in the case of middle-class white youth and "strict and no-nonsense" in the case of lower-class and minority youth.

Above all, the policies of the juvenile court lead to the stigmatization and labeling of youth in a way that is unnecessarily detrimental to their future positive development. What is really needed is programs focusing on problem behavior rather than programs that have a tendency to label youth for life.

Critics of the juvenile court suggest that we would be better off scrapping the present system for dealing with juveniles and moving in the direction of establishing viable youth service bureaus. It is their contention that juvenile matters should not be treated in a legal system but more in a service system that focuses on rehabilitation and guidance. They contend that the juvenile court is far too stigmatizing to accomplish this goal.

Juvenile justice policies have traditionally focused on including the youthful offender within a system specifically designed to address their condition. In actuality, the juvenile justice system has been less than successful in this area. It has been more like a revolving-door system that has formally identified a group as juvenile delinquents and set them aside as a stigmatized group in American society.

Once caught within the web of the system, given the right set of circumstances, juveniles could be helped. For the most part, however, it has been a situation of excessive punishment, on the one hand, and on the other, lenience to the extent that violent offenders return to the streets in short order with little or no punishment. These two divergent conditions within the juvenile justice system—and they do exist—precipitated the development of social policies that separated the status offender from the delinquent and treated the youth involved in serious and violent acts in a harsher manner.

The removal of status offenders from the juvenile court process, as previously mentioned, is recognition of the belief that many young people are inappropriately being involved in a formalized process that produces highly questionable results. This, coupled with the rise of legalism within the juvenile court, has generated a narrower view of delinquency.

In addition to a narrower definition of what delinquency is, policies of the 1980s will, no doubt, continue to drift in the direction of harsher treatment of those found to be delinquent. As violent crimes by the youth population increase there is a growing expectation that society has the right to be protected and that the culprits ought to be punished. In effect, the societal need to be protected from its "dangerous classes," i.e., juveniles who commit violent crimes, is influencing the movement of juvenile policies away from treatment to punishment. In addition to becoming more punishment-oriented, future social policies are going to be increasingly concerned with identifying that group most appropriate for this increased punishment.

In short, it appears that we are entering a new era in juvenile justice policy that is more formally recognizing the use of punishment. While we may never formally recognize the need to meet violence with violence and punishment within the justice system, such policies do appear to be a move in that direction.

Social policies in the justice system that propose to increase the level of punishment to delinquents involved in crimes of violence may have some deterrent effect, but they do little to get at the causes that breed such crimes. For many youth, violence is one of the few "resources" they have in this society. Future social policies that focus on increasing the potential contribution to society of our youth population will have to be increasingly considered if we are to make progress in the development of a sound juvenile justice system.

Those planning policy in the area of the juvenile justice system must be increasingly aware of the politics of their efforts. Juveniles can be, and are, used as "political footballs." While there is a need to "listen to the people," there is also a need to have policy that is not just politically expedient. Calling for laws that put juveniles in jail may win votes for politicians, but do they generate solutions to serious problems within the justice system?

Criticism of the juvenile justice system will continue, and change will, no doubt, follow the criticism. There has been great movement since the establishment of the first juvenile court in Chicago in 1899. The move toward "legalizing" the juvenile court, the youth service bureau, and community-based corrections has gathered steam. It appears that the major thrust of the future will be toward diverting potential delinquents from the formalized justice system. Emphasis will be on early detection and prompt, effective treatment, and punishment for those involved in crimes of violence. As part of this thrust, we must be careful not to further impinge on the rights of minors, for no matter how noble the cause, we must question any such effort that tramples on the rights of those least able to protect themselves from the arbitrary use of power and authority.

Policy on Housing and the Physical Environment

Policy on Housing and the Physical Environment

REASONS FOR IMPROVING HOUSING CONDITIONS

A decent home for every American family was a goal put forth in the 1949 Housing Act. Added to this goal in 1978 were President Carter's urban policy goals of saving our central cities and making them more attractive places in which to live and work. Descriptions of many inner-city areas in the 1970s indicated these cities were in desperate need of revitalization, having large areas of abandoned and decaying housing, bankrupt social services, deserted factories, outdated transportation systems, and unkept and unlighted streets; their population was consisting increasingly of the poor, minorities, and the elderly. Much housing in both central cities and rural areas was considered inadequate, according to 1970 census data and local housing surveys.

Social policy strategists have long been concerned with both neighborhood environment and housing conditions. As Friedlander and Apte (1974) point out, "For over a century, the field of social welfare has included in its scope the quality of housing" (p. 21). Many sociologists and social welfare scholars have made housing their special area of research;

these include sociologists Herbert Gans, Sylvia Fava, William Michelson, Suzanne Keller, and Robert Gutman and social welfare researchers Alvin Schorr, David Donnison, and L. K. Northwood.

Poor housing and a poor neighborhood environment are felt to have a number of social effects, although direct correlations between bad housing and various social problems have been hard to fully substantiate. Those ill-housed are felt to be handicapped in chances for upward mobility and equal opportunities by Sternlieb (1973), Huttman and Huttman (1974), and Schorr (1964). Alvin Schorr says:

> First, it would be difficult to find any aspect of housing that does not play a role in the way people live, and, more precisely, in their ability to learn and relax, their specific pattern of functioning with each other, and their view of the world. All these matters have to do with the prevention of poverty. [P. 74]

Sternlieb (1973), in his study of housing for welfare recipients, points out, "At the very least, housing is a necessary and essential, if not sufficient, condition for the material upgrading of life styles, hopes and aspirations of New York City welfare recipients" (p. 218).

Bad housing conditions, such as overcrowding, are also considered to have a negative influence on family life, though there may be cultural differences. Beyer (1969) says, "Almost every person is affected in day-to-day living by the kind of house in which he lives . . ." (p. 3) and adds that families living in the slum do not have social opportunities equal to those in decent housing.

Some researchers have thought that bad housing negatively affects human growth and satisfactory functioning. For example, Friedlander and Apte (1974) state, "It has long been recognized that a milieu with rich resources, warmth and consistency in human relationships, and sufficient stimulation favors physical and emotional growth, just as a deprived conflict-ridden and disruptive situation tends to stunt and warp growth for many" (p. 21).

Sternlieb (1973) talks about the negative effects of residential segregation of the poor. He says that while the hideous conditions of the slums of a generation or two ago, the lack of even the basic amenities, the tremendous overcrowding, no longer exist, we have:

> . . . the increasing residential segregation of welfare recipients. This is a function not only of the sheer growth in their number but . . . of their increasing concentration within what for lack of a better term must be referred to as welfare buildings, welfare blocks and welfare neighborhoods. . . . Their exclusion from the rest of society imposes enormous physical and emotional strains upon them. [P. 218]

Others, such as the early University of Chicago urban sociologists Clifford Shaw and Edwin Sutherland, have related slum housing and neighborhoods to the likelihood of living a criminal life. In 1904 Jacob Riis spoke in quite unscientific terms of the slum atmosphere as poison, saying that "wickedness and vice gravitate towards it [the slum]. Its poverty is hopeless. . . . Recovery is impossible under its blight" (p. 3). This exemplified the environmental determinism view, one taken seriously in the early 1900s. As Sternlieb (1973) says, "The social thinkers of the 1930's, reared on Jacob Riis's vision of the slum as the generator of all social ills, completely accepted this relationship."

Recent research has not been able to prove a direct relationship between bad housing and delinquency or other social problems. In this regard one must heed Titmuss's warning that while "bad housing and blighted cities shape people and diminish their lives . . . what is indeed remarkable is not the minority of people who acquire patterns of so-called pathological behavior but the vast majority who do not" (Schorr, 1964, p. xi).

Titmuss was right in downplaying the determinist view of relating environment to behavior; many sociologists in the 1950s and 1960s did likewise, pointing out the importance of social class, ethnicity, and other factors. However, as Popenoe (1977) says, these critics left a vacuum, and he asks, "Can it be that the residential environment really makes no difference?" (p. 8). The many social science researchers working in this field in the 1970s felt that the environment did make a difference in some way.

The Historical Picture

In the eighteenth and nineteenth centuries the fact that health was affected by living in the unsanitary conditions of the slum tenements in factory towns in Britain or immigrant areas of large American cities seemed easily proved. Epidemics raged through the crowded tenements. Social reformers considered such conditions a reason for demanding improvement in housing and formed such groups as the Boston Committee on the Expediency of Providing Better Tenements to the Poor in the late 1800s. Another group pushing for improved ventilation, lighting, and cleanliness of tenant houses, the New York City Citizens Association, described these diseases in the slums in 1865:

> Typhus fever and consumption are found in the overcrowded tenant-houses, and in dark and noisome quarters excluded from sunlight and fresh air. Cholera infantum, dysentery, diarrhoeal diseases, and various typhoid maladies are found in badly drained and neglected streets and alleys, and in

cellars, or in damp and filthy domiciles surrounded by nuisances and poison effluvia. In such localities . . . the average or constant sickness rate in the families so situated is very high. . . . [Palley and Palley, 1977, p. 162]

These types of health conditions that either were influenced by unsanitary conditions or were easily spread in crowded slum housing are not with us today. Others, such as lead poisoning of children, again considered more likely to occur in the slums, have been highlighted lately. The high infant mortality rate in the slums, twice to three times the national average, has been mainly related to prenatal and postnatal care, but overcrowded and unsanitary housing probably also influence this condition.

The major reason social policymakers today want to provide better housing for the poor is to provide them with an environment equal to that of the rest of the citizens. According to the late Richard Titmuss, decent housing should be provided as a right. He said, "People want better housing as a matter of social justice and as a precondition of more freedom for themselves and their families. They do not want it in terms which seem to imply that they require to be 'saved' from delinquency or some other subcultural infection" (Schorr, 1964, p. xi).

This present goal of providing the poor with a modern unit in an acceptable environment to improve the general quality of life is also pointed out by Sternlieb (1973), a leading housing researcher in the United States. He says, comparing social reformers of the slums in the late 1800s with present researchers, that the early concern was over poor health and vice, while "the battle today, at least in some places, has shifted from improving the absolute quality of housing—the reduction of very severe overcrowding, providing more adequate toilet facilities and the like—to one of comparative quality of housing" (p. 11).

A question here is, How bad is the housing situation of the American poor? What proportion of our population is in housing considered inadequate by today's norms for the middle class?

HOUSING NEEDS

In the United States there are still many households that have an unsatisfactory housing situation. The major statistics on this come from the U.S. Bureau of the Census. Through the 1960 census, housing conditions were rated as "sound," "deteriorated," or "dilapidated," but because of the unreliability of the evaluations these were dropped in the 1970 census and only lack of adequate plumbing facilities was used. In 1960, 26 percent of all units were structurally deteriorating or dilapidated or lacking adequate plumbing. In 1970, with data available only on inadequate plumbing, 7 percent of the total housing stock lacked adequate plumbing; this was 4.7 million units. Most of these units without plumbing were in rural areas. Only a third were found in standard metropolitan statistical areas (SMSA) (these SMSAs, which include the areas' suburbs as well as the central cities or smaller cities, are the main urbanized regions in the United States).

For urban areas, since they have basic housing codes, lack of plumbing is not a good indicator of whether there is poor housing stock. In the 1960 census, when structural deficiencies were included, about a tenth of all the units were substandard in all the SMSAs; the SMSAs had over half the national housing supply.

More localized data come from other sources. The New Jersey State Department of Community Affairs in 1975 estimated that in Newark alone 40,000 units were substandard.

For the entire country Hartman (1975) makes the rough estimate that probably 8 million of the 23 million rented units in 1970 were substandard by local housing code criteria. He also feels that in some cities the number of substandard units has been *increasing*. For example, he reports that in New York City a study in the early 1970s showed that the number of unsound housing units had increased from 420,000 to 525,000 in a 5-year period.

Certain groups fare especially badly in the housing market; one is the low-income elderly. A 1971 HEW study of 2 million OAA (now SSI) households found that 40 percent were in housing with substantial physical or structural deficiencies.

A study of welfare recipients' housing in New York City in 1973 by Sternlieb showed that they were likely to be concentrated in buildings with the lowest maintenance rating and were greatly overrepresented in buildings constructed before 1902.

Another criterion for housing deficiency is overcrowding, that is, 1.01 persons or over to a room, excluding bathrooms. In 1970, 8 percent of all households had a ratio of over 1.01 persons to a room.

Cost of Housing

Another housing deprivation the census considers is the proportion of income used for rent. In 1970 the census showed that 4,512,000 renter households paid 35 percent or more of their income for housing. Since in the United States the government assumes one should pay 25 percent of one's household income for rent, these people are considered to have a high rent-income burden. Actually, to many experts, 25 percent is considered too high for low-income persons.

Many elderly with only one or two persons in the household and collecting only a pension have high rent burdens; half pay more than 35 percent of their income for rent, and with the very low vacancy rate in rental housing in many urban areas they are now likely to pay more.

The situation for the elderly homeowner (and 70 percent of the elderly in 1970 owned) is not much better. While most no longer have a mortgage to pay, their property taxes (even in areas with some property tax relief for the elderly), their insurance, their utilities, and their repairs have meant heavy housing costs. Though in a number of urban areas the market value of their home rose considerably in the 1970s, it benefits them only if they sell or take a second mortgage, which most do not want to do.

Because of the rise in housing costs in the late 1970s, lower middle-class persons who did not own a house, such as young couples, were also beginning to feel housing deprivation. The dream of owning their own single-family dwelling with a lawn and garage was no longer available to many couples as it had been to their parents in the post–World War II days. In an increasing proportion of cases the home buyer now had to have a second wage earner in the family, usually the wife, if the household was to buy a house; in 1977 half the buyers did. In addition, over half of those buying in 1977 had no children.

The 1977 report points out that in many cases, even with two wage earners, over one-third of these new home buyers paid over 35 percent of family income for housing because of high prices. By normal rules, 3 out of 4 Americans have been priced out of the house-buying market.

Housing cost is increasing faster than income; rents are increasing at high rates, especially in areas with low vacancy rates and little new multifamily construction.

HOUSING GOALS

This situation demands an attempt to outline needed priorities or general goals for the field of housing and the physical environment. These goals should be separate from strategies for achieving the goals.

1.   A first obvious goal is to provide housing at an affordable price, taking no more than one-fourth of a household's income. Downs (1976) gives the goal as decreasing the financial disparities between the cost of decent-quality housing and the incomes of poor households.

To correct this, housing costs must be subsidized. The unit must be subsidized to allow a cheaper mortgage payment, or the person must receive aid to pay the high rental cost, for example, through a housing allowance. The person's overall income could also be increased through such measures as a guaranteed annual income.

Subsidies to decrease the price of the unit can take many forms. *Help to the building* can be a government subsidy of the interest rate so that it is *below market interest* for the buyer; thus the group or person paying the mortgage on a building or house pays smaller payments because the interest rate on the money borrowed is lower. For example, the monthly payment can be lowered from $425 per unit if the interest rate is, say, 11 percent to $385 if the rate is about 6 to 7 percent.

Another way to subsidize the housing is to insure the mortgage, that is, to guarantee that the mortgage money will be paid to the lending institution. Banks are more willing to lend to developers to develop a tract of houses if the developer has such insured mortgages; the developer can then build mass tract housing at cheaper prices than otherwise. This is done in the FHA program.

Another way to provide cheaper housing is for a federal agency to build it, or pay for it to be built, and to manage it under government subsidies and charge tenants a rent equivalent to only 25 percent of their income. This is what public housing does.

One form of *help to the person* is to subsidize the rent of those in private standard units whose low income makes them eligible for help: they pay 25 percent of their income toward the rent and the agency pays the rest. This is the Section 8 program. The problem with assistance to the person is that no new units are built and that the person is not in a building managed by personnel who can provide services to disadvantaged persons. Yet if public housing units carry a stigma and the buildings are subject to vandalism and crime, the person may be better off in a private unit with a variety of tenants.

Another type of assistance to the person is to keep rents low by imposing rent control, as has been done for a long time in New York City and is now done in a number of California cities. Subsidy costs are incurred in running the rent control administration and in the loss of tax revenue resulting from low rents. The problem here is that a very stringent rent control program, with only very low rent increases allowed, will discourage landlords from keeping up their buildings or even holding onto them at all. It could lead to abandonment, a serious problem in a number of cities.

Another subsidy to homeowners is to allow them to write off certain housing expenses, such as mortgage interest and property tax, on their federal income tax.

General income assistance is also a way to meet rent expenses. Some would say that instead of giving specific assistance for housing and incurring the special expenses of running such programs, the policy should be to give the poor general income assistance to meet all needs. Downs (1976) recommends as a cure for the disparity between the cost of good-quality housing and the income of poor households either raising direct income supports for the poor households or giving them a housing allowance, an indirect income support. The National Association of Housing and Renewal Officials (NAHRO) in 1977 made raising income a federal housing goal, saying that it is an essential base for improving freedom from the day-to-day struggle for minimum shelter and that without it efforts cannot succeed to conserve, build, and rebuild American cities. At the same time NAHRO also supported housing allowances to low-income and moderate-income households (those with 50 to 80 percent of median household income in the area) and, in periods of high inflation, an interest rate reduction to middle-income families. Specific grants for housing assistance, rather than general income assistance, appeal to housing experts, since they assure that the money will be used for standard units, as the grants stipulate, while general assistance allows recipients to live in substandard slum dwellings.

Housing allowances are the most popular type of housing subsidy today. These are grants to the household to make up the difference between the market rent for their occupied unit and a certain portion of the household's income considered the acceptable housing expenditure (in the United States, 25 percent). To qualify, the low-income household often has to live in certain types of housing, such as standard units or certain subsidized units. For example, in Holland those receiving a housing allowance in the mid 1970s had to live in the more recently built nonprofit housing association units, heavily subsidized and regulated by the government; the purpose was to make these newer, expensive units available to low-income families. In Britain and other European countries, the use of a rent rebate or housing subsidy allowance has also allowed the government to increase the rents for the units. Since in Britain about 30 percent live in local-authority housing and in Holland many live in government-subsidized nonprofit housing, many can afford to have the very low rents increased; yet there are always some families that cannot meet a higher rent, and a housing allowance, based on household income, gives them relief when rents are raised. In Sweden also housing allowances help many families, even though the building itself receives some government subsidy assistance through mortgage money at below-market interest rates and capital development funds. In the new towns around Stockholm the government owns the land and the government or cooperatives own many of the rental buildings.

2. A second goal is to see that all Americans have a decent, comfortable housing unit that is sanitary, clean, and safe. Many poor now live in substandard units. The housing need not be a new unit, but it must be standard, with adequate plumbing, and decent electric wiring, heating, and upkeep; and it should not be overcrowded.

3. Another priority is increasing and stabilizing housing starts, that is, new construction and rehabilitation of units. Increasing the number of housing starts is basic to fulfilling the need for decent, standard, physically adequate units for all. It is also basic to lowering housing cost, because

reduced housing starts mean that vacancies go down and with such scarcity rents go up; the low- and moderate-income households are forced to stay in low-standard units, often at high rents. As Downs (1976) says, "A crucial determinant of conditions in inner-city housing markets is the rate of new housing construction in the suburbs (where most new housing is built)" (p. 13).

A number of policy questions arise here. Should one build new housing for the middle and upper classes with the assumption that the existing standard units will then filter down or "trickle down" to low- and moderate-income groups, that as the middle class moves into the new units their standard units will become available to lower-income families?

Should one build new housing for poor- and moderate-income families? To only subsidize the poor in existing units does nothing to help increase the housing stock; and the filter- or trickle-down policy does not in reality trickle units to many poor, because rents can be lowered only so much and may still be too high for the poor. Also the units that filter down are often not available to minorities because of discrimination.

Should one put the major emphasis on rehabilitation, which can improve inner-city areas and preserve valuable housing stock? The problem is that rehabilitation often costs as much as new housing and does not add to the present housing stock; it can, in fact, reduce the number of units in a building.

4.   Utilization of housing construction as a stimulus to the economy is a general government policy that greatly affects subsidized housing starts. Policymakers trying to improve the state of the economy use housing subsidies to encourage building and to provide construction jobs during economic recessions. The 1937 policy to build public housing had as its aim providing construction jobs as well as providing housing for the poor. Downs (1976) sees as a housing objective in federal housing policies that of overall economic stabilization, causing countercyclical changes in total housing production to help stabilize the overall economy. Subsidized housing is also used in stabilization of housing production itself; in recessions subsidized housing keeps the number of housing starts up.

In 1968 the Kaiser Commission, which was established to look into American housing needs, set a goal of 2.6 million housing starts a year for ten years, based on the number of substandard units, the degree of demolition, shifts in household formation, and the special needs of the elderly and other such groups. This goal was seldom met but was most nearly reached in years that private contractors and builders took up new housing subsidy programs because they did not have enough private construction work. As Nenno (1978) reports, only in 1971–1972, when subsidized starts were high, did total starts come anywhere near 2.6 million.

As Downs (1976) says, the federal government's key housing policies are still determined more by its attempts to influence the general level of prosperity, which is given higher priority, than its attempts to affect housing in particular. And he adds that these countercyclical policies, because they can improve people's income, may be more important in giving people a chance to get decent standard housing than federal attempts at a housing subsidy program. Yet Downs also continually points out the need for a high production of new units if we are to give low-income people decent housing.

5. This would mean a *continual* stable production of subsidized housing rather than the cyclical production we have now, whereby subsidized housing is increased at certain economically advantageous times or when new political interests dictate it. Former HUD Secretary Patricia Harris put stabilization of provision as a goal; certain statistics on housing need show that a priority should be given to this.

6. Another priority is to improve blighted neighborhoods that now have abandoned housing and substandard units as well as inadequate services, few parks, and unappealing surroundings. As Downs (1976) says, there is a need to correct such maladies as undesirable neighborhood conditions caused by the concentration of many very poor households in the least desirable housing, inadequate provision of public services, and exploitative local merchants and other institutions.

Revitalization of central cities and improvement of inner-city neighborhood environments was an overall goal dominating HUD's urban policy group in 1978. The situation in poverty areas of central cities described by the Douglas Commission (1968) is worth noting; it found that inner cities had six times as high a proportion of substandard housing units as other parts of these cities and that, compared to the suburbs, the housing density was forty times as great; the proportion of nonwhites living in the central poverty areas was ten times that in suburbs. By 1978 this situation was much worse.

That these slum conditions were of a magnitude to be of concern to policymakers is indicated by Hunter (1964) in *The Slums: Challenge and Response:* "Slums, representing 20 per cent of the average American city's residential area, cost taxpayers 45 per cent of all city service expenditures and still produced excessive health, welfare, housing, crime, and fire problems" (p. 6).

The deteriorated state of many central-city areas resulted in abandonment of the decaying housing and of the city itself. Places like the South Bronx and Bedford-Stuyvesant, both in New York City, became symbols of this decay and despair, with their many blocks of abandoned apartment houses, burned buildings, and closed stores; their population of welfare recipients, drug addicts, and delinquents; and their notoriety as places of crime and violence.

The focus of the 1978 Carter Administration urban policy was "to save our central cities, to strengthen them and make them more attractive places to live and work." In the recommended 1979–1981 funding for the urban policy initiatives, over two-thirds of the dollar outlay was for the goal of restoring the economic health of the cities. With some inner-city areas having unemployment rates for teenagers at 30 to 40 percent in 1977 and for adults considerably higher than the national average and having a continued loss of industrial activities to the suburbs, there was rightful concern with this problem.

Some specific suggested policies under this goal were locating federal facilities in central cities, procuring a considerable proportion of federal supplies from firms in "labor surplus areas," providing funding to cities suffering fiscal strains, and giving fiscal relief on the cities' portion of welfare payments. A top recommendation was to establish a program to help credit-worthy private firms to locate in distressed areas through the use of various financial assistance programs.

NAHRO in 1978 had a similar objective of neighborhood conservation and rehabilitation. Interestingly, this organization, as chief national spokesperson for professional housing and redevelopment officials, usually a group interested in housing per se, put heavy emphasis on the provision of social services in the neighborhood as a priority. NAHRO said that "systems of transportation, employment centers, public facilities and public services are the essential framework in which housing can be located." The Carter Urban Policy Initiative (1978), however, put only 7 percent or less of the funding in social services.

NAHRO in its report emphasized creating "human-scale environments." It said, "The ultimate success of efforts to conserve, build and rebuild America's physical resources depends on the ability to provide for the individual the identity that advances his or her personal hopes and aspirations." It proposed human-scale neighborhoods and architecture that enhances the larger physical environment and spoke of the need to recognize that the "neighborhood community, whether defined in terms of the inner-core of the metropolitan city, a suburban subdivision, or a rural market place, is the building block around which community improvement should take place" (1977, p. 505).

This sounds closer to what sociologists and social workers would recommend than what housing policymakers, usually economists and professional housing, construction and realty leaders, would recommend.

7. Another major goal is to disperse low- and moderate-income people in housing throughout the whole area rather than concentrating them in undesirable inner-city neighborhoods. By dispersal some progress can be made in the goal of achieving a greater income and racial mix in our communities instead of the extreme segregation existing today and to increase the housing choices available to low-income and minority families,

a 1978 HUD housing strategy. NAHRO in its 1978 goals states that "all individuals must be able to obtain any housing without discrimination," and adds, "Anti-discriminatory policies must be vigorously pursued at all levels of government and all forms of federal assistance should be denied any community that follows exclusionary practices of any kind" (1977, p. 501).

Downs (1976) sees opening up the suburbs and the outlying portions of central cities to new and moderate-income housing as a key urban objective that is desirable not only because present low-income housing includes physically inadequate dwelling units and is in undesirable neighborhoods but also because we cannot build a large number of housing units for such groups within central cities, since there is not enough land and what exists is for nonresidential uses. He adds that creating new housing through relocation and clearance is impractical; and last, most new jobs are being created in the suburbs.

The movement of moderate-income people out of inner-city areas will also facilitate the rehabilitation of inner-city housing, and this may encourage middle-class people to move back to the city and provide a social mix there.

To date such efforts to build housing for low- and moderate-income people in the suburbs have not been very successful. Due to opposition, subsidized housing with below-market interest rates (under Sections 236 and 202) has only in a minor way been sited in suburban areas. Some Section 8 housing, that is, the program of rental of private units by poor who are receiving a type of housing assistance, is found there. Through HUD efforts to get suburban communities to develop local housing assistance plans, whereby the community assesses its housing needs, there has been some push to get suburban communities to realize the need for more low- and moderate-income housing and to act to supply it. HUD has also given various incentives to suburban communities to develop low- and moderate-income housing, including bonuses for mixed-income communities and extra community development funds.

FEDERAL HOUSING POLICIES IN THE LAST FIVE DECADES

Social reformers have long had an interest in the unhealthy conditions of crowded tenement areas of central cities, but the federal government did not play a major role in housing until the late 1930s. However, local governments were early instigators of building codes and public health regulations on ventilation, lighting, and cleanliness because of concern of social reform groups. For example, the Boston Committee on the Expediency of Providing Better Tenements to the Poor, founded in 1846, pushed for local codes because of its concern with a cholera epidemic and its worry about slum conditions in Boston's working-class Irish areas. In these areas many structures lacked drainage and ventilation, factors that led to such epidemics. The Council of Hygiene and Public Health of the Citizens Association of New York in 1865 was reporting similar conditions.

By the early 1900s these health conditions of the slums had been corrected. However, during World War I and in the Depression period there was little housing built and much substandard housing still existed. In 1937 a federal housing law came in to support localities in building low-rent housing for the poor. It followed the earlier (1934) National Housing Act, which gave the federal government a role in promoting private home ownership by insuring mortgages (now known as FHA- and VA-insured mortgages).

Since then federal government policies have taken a number of forms, some subsidizing the building (either a publicly owned or a private building with some costs reduced by subsidy grants) and some subsidizing the person. The early provision of public housing units for the poor was in the late 1960s overshadowed by a new approach, subsidies for mortgages at below-market interest rates for buildings by nonprofit and limited-dividend groups. It was later supplemented and to some degree replaced by greater assistance to the poor person through coverage of rent in private housing, through the Section 8 housing allowance.

The government in reality has given its greatest assistance to the middle class by insuring the mortgages of new housing, and thus encouraging such building, and by the indirect subsidy of allowing deductions on federal taxes for mortgage interest and property taxes. It has also supported rehabilitation and neighborhood conservation.

Housing Starts

Before describing these policy directions in detail we should warn that these various strategies have not increased housing starts to the degree needed to meet established goals.

The number of housing units recommended in the national goals stated in the Housing and Community Development Act of 1968 was 26 million new and rehabilitated housing units (6 million of them low- and moderate-income) to be built in the ten-year period 1969–1978, or 2.6 million units a year, a goal set by the Kaiser Commission of 1968 on American housing needs. In the 1960s annual housing starts were normally 1 to 1.5 million units. This situation was only slightly improved from 1969 to 1978, with average starts per year at 1.76 million if mobile homes were excluded, and only 2.1 million if they were included. In 1969–1973, only subsidized housing starts brought the total anywhere near the goal. In this period, there was increased building by nonprofit and limited-dividend groups using new government subsidy programs for below-market interest rates. Downs says this situation of increased building under these new subsidy programs stimulated the most massive housing production in American history.

The years 1971 and 1972 were record years for total housing production. This all changed from 1973 on because of Nixon's moratorium on most subsidized housing programs; 1974, 1975, and 1976 saw a great drop in the number of assisted housing units. This meant that for the ten years 1968–1978, assisted housing produced for low- and moderate-income families was less than half the projected 6 million housing units. In the post-moratorium period of 1974–1976 all assisted or subsidized new housing starts plus rehabilitation came to far less than 200,000 a year. (See Figure 12-1.) This was a period when demolition and abandonment of units was still high and poverty-area units in inner cities were still becoming inadequate by local housing codes.

It is not surprising then that many people turned to buying mobile homes (over 250,000 units per year); in recent years these have represented over 10 percent of housing starts and in some years far higher.

These data on housing starts show some upsetting characteristics of subsidized housing production in the United States. The number of units produced is low and the importance of different types of subsidy programs

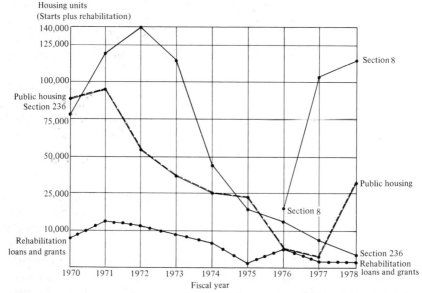

Figure 12-1 Annual subsidized housing production: Fiscal Years 1970 through 1978 (July 1–June 30). (*Source:* "Annual Reports on the National Housing Goals," U.S. Department of Housing and Urban Development.)

changes very much from year to year. Nenno (July 1979) in giving these data says, "The erratic quality of federally assisted housing effort in the decade since 1968 is dramatically demonstrated" (p. 344). Each administration has brought in its own programs, some so poorly subsidized and structured that they were doomed to failure from their inception. This has caused ex-Secretary of HUD Patricia Harris to make as her first of six basic elements of a housing strategy "achieving a stable level of construction for assisted housing."

TYPES OF HOUSING SUBSIDIES

The variety of strategies described above are found in the programs listed in this section. Each has some positive aspects but also a number of limitations. Since a number of alternatives are required to meet the needs of different groups, no one policy alone will work.

FHA- and VA-Insured Mortgages

The Federal Housing Administration (FHA) program insures mortgages so that if borrowers default on their mortgage payments the lenders' losses are covered by the federal government. A similar program of insured mortgages for veterans is under the Veterans Administration (VA).

Our discussion will center first on these large FHA and VA programs. After World War II these programs provided major incentives for building the massive tract developments in the suburbs, since banks and savings and loan groups were more willing to provide mortgages if they knew the FHA and VA guaranteed these loans. This increased the available market of buyers for the houses. Because of this favorable sales climate developers could get front money to go into this mass building enterprise, and they turned acre after acre of suburban farmland into such developments as Levittowns, for the lower-middle-class and skilled-working-class families. Much of the postwar growth of suburbs can be attributed to the FHA and VA assistance through insuring mortgages as well as to the federal government's highway program.

In the 1950s 26 percent of all mortgages for nonfarm housing starts were FHA-insured mortgages, and another 10 percent were VA-insured but by 1965 the prevalence of both dropped sharply, since by then there were some more efficient private mortgage lenders who did not have the limitations of FHA regulations.

The FHA in the postwar years made home ownership financially possible for many American families. FHA's usefulness in the early postwar years, Hartman (1975) points out, was to restore lender confidence in mortgage loans and to radically reshape the mortgage instrument itself, i.e., by replacing a pattern of short-term loans (with a five- to ten-year amortization period) and high down payments with one of long-term loans with low down payments. FHA policies also, he says, served to lower interest rates by virtually eliminating risk to the lender through the insurance features.

The FHA in recent years has taken on more central-city loans to higher-risk borrowers in higher-risk areas. Some are for low-income home ownership (Section 235) and some for rental units (including the Section 236 program). Unlike FHA's basic mortgage program, these have encountered substantial default rates. But this may be the right course; as Aaron (1972) says, "Whatever improvement in the mortgage market FHA and VA could bring to general borrowers has already occurred. The useful role of those institutions now is to underwrite other forms of loans traditionally regarded as unsound, for example, to home buyers who live in run-down areas, rural areas or minority enclaves" (p. 90).

The traditional FHA program for insuring mortgages on single-family, owner-occupied homes has covered many more homes than all other federally assisted housing programs. Through 1970 FHA had given insured mortgages for over 6 million units. In one year, 1970, it insured over 400,000 units. To this must be added VA-insured loans and also the Farmers Home Administration (FmHA) loans through the Department of Agriculture, which are offered in small towns where private credit is often unavailable. This FmHA program was a rising program in much of the late 1970s, giving assistance for over 90,000 units a year.

All these federal assistance programs for the middle class have covered far more units than conventional public housing. Conventional public housing in the ten years up to 1978 added only 440,101 units to the housing stock and in all its lifetime up to 1978 produced only about 1.2 million units.

Income Tax Deductions for Housing

The middle class is also given another housing subsidy, possibly the largest financial one of all. That is the indirect subsidy through the deduction of property tax and mortgage interest payments on the federal income tax return. The Treasury Department estimated for 1971 that the saving to homeowners from deducting property tax and mortgage interest payments from income on their federal income tax was $5.1 billion, according to *Housing Affairs Letter,* July 28, 1972. In other words, the federal government collected $5.1 billion less in 1971 than it would have collected if it did not allow these deductions. Some call this a "tax break," but since it makes owning a home considerably cheaper for a household one can call it an indirect housing subsidy. Twelve percent of the average homeowner's housing costs one could say were paid for by the federal government in 1965 to 1967 simply because the government allowed the taxpayer to make mortgage interest and property tax deductions. This tax saving accrues more to middle-income and higher-income owners than to working-class owners, since the more affluent tend to itemize deductions on their income tax form and also tend to have higher interest payments.

Housing Subsidies for Low-Income Americans

Assistance to lower the rent for low-income Americans can take many forms. One way is to give direct cash assistance for general needs, including housing. However, most experts find benefits-in-kind highly preferable, because direct cash assistance has often been found not to improve the quality of a person's housing.

In-kind assistance can be standard housing units under a public housing program, or it can come through Section 202 or 236 nonprofit housing programs. It can be a housing allowance, as under Section 8, with stipulations about the type of housing so that overcrowded and substandard units are not used.

Housing presents an example where in-kind assistance may be better than cash simply because the household on its own cannot easily get the commodity even when it has cash. At the same time, a frank discussion of housing programs for low-income Americans shows that in-kind assistance also has problems; it sometimes does not meet the objective of providing safe, decent units. But let us start with the deficiencies of the cash side, public welfare.

Public Welfare and Housing   One of the largest housing subsidies for poor households is an indirect one, the part of the welfare check that is designated to meet housing costs. Since there were 3.5 million AFDC households in 1977 and several more million SSI households, one could say that through these programs the government is giving housing assistance to a considerable number of households. One could also include the many elderly, disabled, and blind who use a large part of their OASDHI check to pay for housing; for many elderly this check is almost their sole income. This subsidy differs from a housing allowance (Section 8 is to some degree a housing allowance) in that recipients of welfare and OASDHI receive a lump sum to cover *all* expenses while a housing allowance is given specifically to cover housing costs.

Some say it is better to give an overall lump sum. In this lump payment, however, the amount of the budget designated for housing is very low, and even the welfare administrators acknowledge it has little relevance to realistic housing costs in an area. An HEW report, *The Role of Public Welfare in Housing* (1969), found that the average AFDC housing budget was $400 a year. Most welfare recipients must use the other parts of the budget for housing, therefore skimping on food and clothing. Many pay more than 25 percent of their income for housing, since few recipients (less than 10 percent) are in low-rent public housing. In 1969 HEW estimated that in total approximately $1.1 billion in welfare funds was spent on housing (most likely that figure is over $2 billion today); this does not even cover OASDHI recipients. This large amount is much, much more than all federal annual expenditures on public housing.

The problem is that this housing is often slum housing, because the housing budget per household is so low and because welfare recipients (and especially minority recipients) are discriminated against in the private housing market. Sternlieb (1973) found in his study of New York City welfare recipients that they were the ones most likely to live in the poorest-maintained and the oldest housing; second, he found, over a period of time welfare recipients became more and more concentrated in certain buildings. They were most likely to be in buildings with code violations. Roach infestation was a problem, and safety in the area was bad.

Other studies verify the fact many welfare recipients live in bad housing. A 1971 study of elderly persons under OAA (now SSI) showed that about 40 percent of 2 million recipients reporting lived in homes and apartments with substantial physical or structural deficiencies. A Washington, D.C., study showed that 50 percent of all AFDC families lived in poor housing, and the above-mentioned 1969 HEW report concluded that "on the basis of available data it is estimated that at least one-half of all assistance recipients live in housing which is deteriorated or dilapidated, unsafe, unsanitary or overcrowded" (Hartman, 1975, p. 111).

Welfare departments have inadequate staff or resources to help their recipients find decent housing, although some give out apartment lists and all try to direct those in need to emergency housing. Welfare departments have no power to make recipients move into standard units, and with the low cash budget they give recipients they can hardly insist on it. Mogulof, an early researcher on welfare housing, concluded that in many communities "we shall continue to use public funds to sustain the residence of poor people in housing that all of our standards point to as indecent or unfit" (1967, pp. 562–563).

Public Housing   The traditional federal housing subsidy program for the poor in the United States has been the public housing program, which was started under the 1937 Housing Act. This, unlike a housing allowance, is assistance to the building, not to the person. Traditionally the federal government provided capital to build or, under turnkey programs, to buy the public housing units. In a number of cases several buildings have been constructed on a site to constitute a project, with populations up to 13,000 or more.

The 1937 Act structured the program so that local communities had considerable control. First, they had to decide whether or not to develop a public housing program at all; many suburban and most rural towns did not. In addition, the number of units to be built had to be decided by a voter referendum.

Those cities that did take up the public housing program established a local housing authority (LHA) to build the housing, select the tenants, and administer the program, and, through rent revenue from tenants, to cover operating costs. In recent years voters in some cities who had formerly rejected public housing for families approved housing authorities' building housing for the elderly.

The local political power structure has considerable policymaking power over the LHA, because City Hall appoints the public housing commissioners, who, as a commission, oversee the local program. The local community makes a contribution to the program, because property taxes are not collected on public housing; however, it does receive a payment from the housing authority "in lieu of taxes," an amount that varies according to the housing authority's financial state and its relationship to City Hall. This exemption from property taxes has always bothered many local government officials and caused them to demand, in many cases, that public housing be put on sites least likely to be desirable for private commercial or residential development.

Over time, the federal financing of the local housing authority has changed. Many authorities have been in serious financial troubles because tenant rents have not covered operating costs and because modernization of projects has been seriously needed. The Brooke amendments in the early 1970s requiring that LHAs take no more than 25 percent of a household's income for rent seriously cut the LHAs' revenue from many low-income tenants; and the fact that they were asked to have a certain proportion of tenants from the very-low-income group meant lower rent revenues. Hartman (1975) reported that a number of housing authorities had cut services and lowered their maintenance level to reduce costs and were on the verge of bankruptcy.

Problems of Public Housing   The problems of the conventional public housing program are not new but started in the early postwar period. Before World War II the public housing program, brought in only under the landmark 1937 Housing Act, was small. At that time it served mainly white families in poverty due to the Depression and other unfavorable economic conditions. During the war the housing program was expanded to house war workers. Many of these tenants stayed on after the war. Veterans moved in, but by the 1950s many from both groups either were evicted because they had become too affluent for the public housing income limits or had moved to take FHA or VA housing in the suburbs or other more suitable housing.

In 1949 a housing act came in that promised all American families a decent home; public housing is considered a major way of achieving this. However, in reality the program has grown slowly. By the 1950s its clientele were often those priority cases displaced by urban renewal projects; many of these were very poor black persons living in cities' worst slum housing areas. As Freedman (1972) says:

> It would have been a travesty of the purpose of the housing programs if public housing did not include a high proportion of the most hostile and alienated members of the poverty culture. This could not help but mean life in many of the big city projects would be ridden with tension and difficulties. . . . with the systematic removal of the more successful families, the element making for cohesion and stability was gone. [P. 110]

Without stringent maximum income limits there would have been more income mix. In Britain council (local authority) housing has, until the mid-1970s, gotten a wide mix of working-class families, as has nonprofit association housing in Holland, again nationally subsidized by government.

The families in American public housing are the very needy, as are the increasingly large numbers of elderly in separate projects. (Otherwise these elderly, now over a third of all residents, differ from families in their characteristics and problems.) Over three-fifths of the non–old-age units in public housing are occupied by female-headed households, many on AFDC. Over a third in this type of household have four or more minors. Almost half of all the nonelderly families are on welfare.

The fact that public housing projects in the 1950s and 1960s were *large* only intensified a bad situation, concentrating the poor in high-rise projects. The continual complaints against the large size of the projects and their bad location led in the late 1960s and in the 1970s to scattered projects with smaller populations; it was hoped that these could be placed in somewhat more desirable areas, but this goal was only partially realized.

Architecture and design also contributed to an unfavorable situation, giving the public a negative image of public housing. Policies led to an institutional look that identified projects as housing for the poor. The buildings had a stripped-down, mean, and skimpy look, with little trim or landscaping. The fact that many were high-rise buildings—considered unsuitable for families with children—marring the skyline with their ugliness did not help matters.

The poor who are the users in general do not consider public housing a decent home, although many want the low rent that living in it allows. Nonuser poor see it as a place where only "riffraff" live. Some users feel like second-class citizens, treated not as consumers or clients but as charity cases, disrespected and abused by the housing authority staff. Many housing authorities have been run in an authoritarian manner with many rules.

Even though public housing authorities, such as New York City's, have tried to be more selective and to keep the number of welfare recipients in the projects down, the result has been the reincarnation of slums, as Moore (1969) says about one Chicago high-rise public housing project:

> From the very beginning the project was the embodiment of urban poverty. Tenants from the former slum dwellings that . . . Blackmoor replaced, as well as other urban renewal refugees, secured a lease in this cluster of high-rise homes but could not discard their poverty. All the tangled problems rooted in generations of destitution found in big-city slums everywhere abound in Blackmoor. . . . Relief is an assumption; crime, unemployment, and delinquency are routines; broken windows, broken bottles, and broken spirits are commonplace. [P. 38]

The problem is that simply to provide a clean unit at cheap rent is not enough when the inhabitants are low-income families with many problems. As Clark (1965) warns, "Merely to move the residents of a ghetto into low-income housing projects without altering the pattern of their lives . . . menial jobs, low income, inadequate education for their children . . . does not break the cycle of poverty" (p. 253). The projects were usually segregated, although at one time elderly whites were sometimes mixed with minority families. By 1970 over 70 percent of all public housing tenants were nonwhite, a change from the early postwar days. More nonwhites are in family projects than in old-age projects. In 1970 the proportion of nonwhites varied by state: Atlanta, Georgia's non–old-age public housing and Chicago's were over 90 percent nonwhite, while in Minneapolis the proportion was much lower.

Housing projects other than those for the elderly have also been condemned for inadequate facilities and services, such as playgrounds and day care facilities for children. Moore (1969) quotes one tenant who says, "The people who built this place certainly didn't know nothing about human beings, especially children. . . . it's 7,000 of them here, and one playground and two tot lots." This female tenant complains, "The playground is three buildings away, and I live on the eighth floor. . . . look at that tot lot over there with all of those broken bottles or other junk scattered about" (pp. 11–12).

This lack of places for children to play means they use hall corridors as streets, stairwells for gang meetings and poker games, and elevators as playthings. Vandalism has become common. Because in many projects over half the residents are children, they dominate the scene, even causing some adults, such as the elderly, to be fearful. As Rainwater (1970) states, "The elevators are dangerous . . . the laundry areas aren't safe . . . the children run wild and cause all kinds of damage . . ." (p. 11). The lack of upkeep has added to this negative look, a factor partly related to the type of occupant and the large child population. The situation became so bad in the Pruitt-Igoe project, St. Louis, that few families were willing to move in, and in the early 1970s these high-rise buildings were actually torn down.

Turnover in public housing projects has been fairly high, with about one-fifth leaving in a given year.

All these factors have caused experts to condemn public housing as a program that has not met the criteria of providing a decent home but has "merely institutionalized our slums." Although the projects do provide cheap and relatively clean housing for a number of poor, one does ask if building such projects is the best way to help house the poor: at a cost of $30,000 to $50,000 a unit, are we getting value for money? Many experts have said no, and in 1973 there was a moratorium on this program as well as on other low- to moderate-income housing subsidy programs. Before that time 30,000 to 50,000 units, on the average, had been built each year, and even about 90,000 in 1969 to 1971; in 1978, when the program was active again, only 29,847 units were built, and many were in projects for the elderly. A type of housing allowance, the Section 8 program, has taken over as the main housing program for the poor.

Recent Attempts to Improve Public Housing   In recent years a number of programs have been initiated to improve both existing projects and any future ones. Future family projects are not likely to be high-rise or large, and they will be on scattered sites. The architecture is likely to be better, and more rooms for needed facilities will be found. Under the modernization program older public housing projects are getting a face-lifting with new paint and needed repairs and the like. Under the Target Project Program (TPP) the worst projects are getting money for modernization and service facilities. General federal community funds are being used for many services under Title XX and other programs.

The 1961 housing act permitted the inclusion in housing projects of neighborhood facilities. Community services are enticed into the project. These could be day care centers, a visiting nurse service, recreational programs and classes, a welfare worker once a week, or a Title VII meals program for the elderly. Attracting such services is the job of the housing authority's community service division, which also may provide some services of its own. The staff produces a newsletter. The community service division may arrange special bus tours and events for elderly tenants or teenagers. The staff may try to find summer work for project youth.

The community service division can also help organize and maintain tenant organizations. It may work with the tenants to establish different committees; however, the recent trend has been for tenant involvement to go far beyond this. Tenants have moved into project jobs and even project management, have been appointed to the public housing commission, and have even run rent strikes to achieve their demands on rents, regulations, and increased security maintenance. There is now a National Tenants Organization (NTO). Today tenants are usually given preference in job openings in the project. Sometimes they are running the whole project, making all types of decisions and hiring staff.

Decentralization of housing authority management is now occurring. Some authorities, such as the San Francisco Public Housing Authority, are getting Urban Initiatives Program money to decentralize management and maintenance, among other things. A few housing authorities are now setting up an office for community service staff in their major projects and are also moving to provide resident managers (sometimes residents themselves) who may have some social service work as part of their job. In the past many projects did not have managers on site; this often meant that gangs of youth took over at night; in projects for the elderly it meant that no emergency help was available.

The tradition in American public housing authorities in the past has been not to accept the social service approach, long ago pioneered by Octavia Hill in Britain, an approach in which the poor are recognized as having a number of problems and in which other assistance besides housing is needed if these people are to be rehabilitated. American public housing authorities are now changing to move closer to this point of view. HUD now allows public housing authorities, to a limited degree, to provide supportive services themselves, instead of always acting, often unsuccessfully, as coordinators of reluctant community service organizations. It is now understood that to try to revitalize "distressed" projects such services must be provided.

TPP (Target Projects Program), brought in in the mid-1970s, is an example of the new trend of HUD; the new Urban Initiative Program follows somewhat the same direction. Under TPP a total of over 142 projects, those considered distressed projects, or problem projects with high vacancy rates and bad reputations, were given massive funding to "turn the projects around" into projects with a better image and a satisfactory environment. While this included modernization of the buildings, the projects also got extensive security and social services.

One example of this TPP program was reported in "Omaha's South Side Terrace Homes" (1977, p. 508). The residents of this 36-year-old, 522-unit development helped plan ways to turn around the troubled project; their critical concerns were security, exterior and interior maintenance, resident job opportunities, recreation, and traffic safety. A commitment to community services meant for Omaha city agencies providing a multiplicity of programs to the project residents. Recreational facilities were improved. To meet a tenant priority of creating more of a community atmosphere, the South Side Terrace project was divided into seven minineighborhoods with distinct exterior colors and features. With the assistance of the city of Omaha, a neighborhood center was developed just across the street from the project. This center offered a variety of services that range from medical care to job placement services, and a long-planned complex for day care and recreational activities was started.

This illustrates what NAHRO researchers summarize as a main lesson to be learned from the TPP program: "A public housing project does not and cannot exist as an island in the midst of a surrounding neighborhood or environment". . . . but [only] as part of that environment" (Schneider, 1978). "The problem of distressed projects must deal with the influences of the surrounding neighborhood, in such matters as security . . ." (Nenno, 1978, p. 592). This last point these researchers made was that the continued availability of funding for protective services is crucial to improving bad projects. In general, crime has become a serious problem in public housing projects in the last decade. Many projects have had to hire security guards to satisfy tenant demands.

Neighborhood Conservation and Rehabilitation   Rehabilitation of private residential and commercial areas was also a major housing focus of the late 1970s. The HUD Urban Initiative Program stresses rehabilitation of inner-city areas. Under most rehabilitation plans, the total neighborhood environment is tackled, not just the house, with improvement of street lighting, sidewalks, landscaping, and park facilities. Less emphasis has been put on provision of services, although during the Model Cities program days in the 1960s provision of services was the program's main focus and it and rehabilitation went hand in hand. Some programs are limited more to patch-up and minor repairs and others to gutting buildings and starting anew; this may depend both on funding and on the condition of the neighborhood housing stock.

Under such programs as FACE there were strong powers to get every owner on the block to come up to code enforcement, either by taking out a rehabilitation loan or, if low-income, getting a grant. In many programs today there is less compulsion. In the 1960s and 1970s city redevelopment or urban renewal agencies, usually separate from the housing authority, bought up buildings and rehabilitated them. An example was Oak Center in Oakland, California. In 1977–1978 a considerable portion of community development funding went for rehabilitation, but cities also were getting Section 312 rehabilitation funds, a subsidy enlarged in 1978. Some cities also had monies raised from bonds for such work, with the city building department running the program.

While the effort to rehabilitate old areas of the city rather than tear them down has merit and fits in with the present interests of preserving the old, there are a number of the same problems there were with the earlier approach. In the 1950s and 1960s the emphasis had been on *demolishing* buildings; as late as the period 1971–1973, 700,000 units per year were torn down by urban renewal and redevelopment agencies or by highway departments, while others were abandoned (Downs, 1976). The problems with this approach became so massive that citizens, especially the poor, demanded a halt to such programs. The units torn down had usually housed the poor and minorities, who lost their low-rent housing and had no alternative but to crowd into other slightly deteriorating areas and turn them into slums. The problem was that not enough subsidized moderate- and low-rent housing was put on the urban renewal sites, especially in the 1950s. Instead, luxury and middle-income high-rise buildings were built. Second, there often were fewer units on the site after renewal than before, or even no housing units if the site was used for commercial development. Last, the land was often left vacant for five years or more, again cutting down on the available housing stock.

In the early days those dislocated were given little assistance in relocating, but by the late 1960s there were substantial moving and relocation grants. A whole division of relocation officers helped displaced households to find new housing and satisfactorily adjust to a new environment. They helped arrange moving and paid the expense and then paid a relocation grant settlement to cover the higher rents paid during the next year. The division included social workers, who worked with the harder cases, such as the confused, senile elderly, alcoholics, and the mentally ill, and often arranged with other agencies for counseling. Today these relocation officers carry on a similar job for those in housing slated for rehabilitation. In some programs residents are only temporarily relocated because the program is geared to having them move back in, but usually the move is permanent because of the long repair time, the higher rent of the renovated units, and the decrease in the number of units under the rehabilitation plan.

Rehabilitation is not a cheap solution. First, a thorough job will often cost as much as building new housing. Second, it is hard to get contractors and carpenters and other builders who are capable of doing a good job of rehabilitating. Last, the work may not be lasting, so that the unit in a few years returns to its former state; this is especially true for patch-up jobs, where paint is thrown on, leaks corrected, wiring improved, windows leaded, but little substantial structural work done. The question comes up when to tear down and when to rehabilitate. The state of the buildings in the area must be taken into consideration. If rehabilitation work is chosen mainly because it preserves the social network of the neighborhood, then one must see that the same people can come back into the units and are only temporarily rehoused. This will likely mean a subsidy to the person, such as a Section 8 subsidy, for the new, higher rent after rehabilitation. It also means the residents must help plan the rehabilitation of their area, as they sometimes do today.

The Section 8 Housing Assistance Program   Section 8 is like a housing allowance but has more restrictions and administrative work than most. It is for low-income people, and, in fact, since 1974, it has been required that 30 percent of the recipients be very-low-income. It is assistance to the person; it is not assistance to the building, which conventional public housing, rehabilitation assistance, and FHA- and VA-insured mortgages are. It is not a program to produce new units and thus does not meet one of the important housing needs Downs (1976) stresses in his objectives (a goal rehabilitation also does not meet). Provision of Section 8 assistance, however, can be used to encourage developers to build units, for example, under the Section 202 program for the elderly, since they know they will get renters if these renters in turn can get Section 8 assistance. It also encourages rehabilitation; certain Section 8 allocations are set aside for rehabilitated units.

Section 8, like its predecessor Section 23, is a type of rent supplement or housing allowance whereby the public housing authority or a similar agency pays that part of the rent of a private existing or new unit that is the difference between the actual rent of the unit and 25 percent of the household's income. This is the main program the public housing authorities have had for new applicants in the late 1970s, since little conventional public housing has been built; the authorities' other jobs have been to manage and modernize present housing projects and fill their vacancies and collect rent. Some housing authorities, such as county authorities, have only Section 8 programs. By 1978 there were almost 600,000 units under the program, mostly existing units but also 166,000 *new* units and 22,000 rehabilitated units with Section 8 tenants.

Section 8 clients are counseled by the housing authority on how to look for units. (Section 8 differs from Section 23 in that clients must find their own units.) They are given lists of likely available apartments; they are told how to check whether the unit is standard and how to negotiate a lease. Armed with a housing authority eligibility certificate based on an income check and given an allowable maximum *fair market rent* for an apartment with a certain number of bedrooms, the applicants look for an apartment and when they find one they inspect the unit for standardness and they negotiate the lease. They then return to the housing authority, which inspects the unit; if it is all right, the applicant moves in under the program.

Some applicants can stay in their present units if their rent is not above the fair market rent and if the unit is standard.

In view of the problems of traditional public housing, is a housing allowance program a better means of assisting the poor with their housing needs?

The first advantage of a housing allowance program is that the users are scattered over a wide area and mixed in with nonsubsidized tenants instead of being housed only with other program recipients. They live in housing that does not carry a stigma as housing for the poor, as public housing does.

Landlords in some localities like the Section 8 program because it assures them that they are likely to get the rent each month and can turn to the housing authority for help in evictions or cases of property destruction or other tenant-landlord matters, although to a lesser degree under Section 8 than under the former Section 23. They get a security deposit. They can also more easily qualify for rehabilitation grants, such as those under Section 312, because they are involved in the Section 8 program.

There are several other advantages of the program. It puts the poor in existing rather than new housing, in most cases, so that the public and the apartment owners' lobby are not as opposed as they are to conventional public housing. It also utilizes housing units that are covered by property taxes, unlike public housing. For users, it gives them a freedom of choice of units and even allows them to stay in their present unit. It gives them more privacy than the more highly regulated public housing. It allows them to be fairly anonymous recipients of Section 8 assistance, unlike public housing tenants. Many, especially the elderly, will not apply for public housing; elderly make up about one-third of those in existing units under Section 8 and three-fourths of those in new units. The program has had a high HUD-approved allocation, with subsidies for 300,000 units in 1978; in most areas these were quickly filled and there were long waiting lists. The estimated total subsidy per household for leased public housing (Sections 23 and 8) is one-third less than the conventional public housing operating cost subsidy, Downs's group (1976) reports.

There are also disadvantages to the program. Minorities and those considered somewhat deviant from the normal tenant will have trouble being accepted by private landlords. A developer of new units, such as those subsidized under Section 202, may select the tenants and may again exclude deviants.

Many poor may also be too fearful and inarticulate to explain the program to the landlord and negotiate a lease or to fight discrimination. Some housing authorities, such as the Worcester, Massachusetts, one, try to reduce this fear and give help. Some applicants, including elderly ones, have transportation problems in looking at potential apartments. All these factors can make it hard for some disadvantaged to utilize the program; for these many housing authorities feel it would be better for their staff to handle tenant-landlord relations.

Another problem is that the maximum allowable fair market rent must be high enough for the area. With a low vacancy rate in many cities, rents have risen, and there is a scarcity of low-rent units.

In this program the unit needs to be standard. If area rents are high, public housing inspectors may accept units for inclusion under Section 8 that are not standard or barely so. If this happens, the program is not meeting the aim of providing a decent home for the poor.

Below-Market Interest Rates   Another type of subsidy has been given to moderate-income applicants, those having a maximum income considerably higher than the public housing income limit. Here the interest rate on the mortgage for building the units is kept considerably below the current interest rate and the loan is insured. This subsidy to encourage building rental units goes to the nonprofit and limited-dividend groups that develop and manage the units. Thus it is a move away from public provision of housing for low-income people to the use of nonprofit groups for moderate-income people.

The initial program came in in 1959 as Section 202 housing for the elderly, that is, nonprofit housing developments receiving government assistance in the form of reduced interest rates as well as tax benefits and insurance of the mortgage. In 1961 a program came in for families as Section 221(d)(3) housing, originally planned for those displaced by urban renewal but later broadened as Section 236 rental housing. Some of those in Section 236 housing (less than 15 percent) were under the rent supplement program, whereby renters paid only 25 percent of their income for rent. The number of users of the Section 236 program shot upward in 1969. Downs (1976) says:

> Because of the 1970 recession, builders had trouble getting adequate mortgage credit in 1970 for conventionally financed units. But Section 235 [home ownership for low-income persons] and Section 236 financing were available, so thousands of builders shifted to the new direct subsidy programs. Non-directly subsidized housing starts fell in 1970 to the lowest total since 1950. But subsidized starts shot upward from 163,360 in 1968 . . . to over 430,000 in both 1970 and 1971. [P. 99]

This was thus a program pleasing builders and pushed by their lobbies. The increased 1972 nonsubsidized housing starts and the problems of Section 236 and 235 brought on the 1973 moratorium on these programs.

Section 236, when going strong in 1971 and 1972, produced many more units than public housing had. In 1978 the program was somewhat revised. Section 202 never shot up the way 236 had, but in the late 1970s it was pushed as a major program for the elderly, to be used with the Section 8 program.

A major problem that Section 236 sponsors had was their lack of management experience; they were often church and service club groups and often failed in the job. They let rents go in arrears, let in tenants who caused problems, and in general mismanaged the housing program. These sponsors often did not have the front money to cover unforeseen maintenance and repair expenses. In addition there was shoddy construction of the developments, causing considerable repair problems. Site selection was also poor. In late 1971 one in every fifteen Section 236 projects was in default. Things got worse by 1973–1974. HUD tried to use some of the Section 236 projects in default for Section 8 tenants and tried to turn some into Section 202 projects.

Section 235   Section 235 home ownership for the poor was another idea utilizing private units that had promise but failed because the provisions were poorly thought out and the administration of the program had many serious defects.

This program was to make the poor feel more a part of the community by giving them home ownership and thus giving them a reason to keep up their homes. However, the HUD-FHA program saddled many poor (400,000 units were covered from 1968 to 1974) with heavier housing payments than they could afford and housing that quickly became slum units. The housing cost was high, because while the subsidy to keep costs at about 20 percent of income covered mortgage payments, insurance, and taxes, it did not cover maintenance, utilities, and heat, which could bring the total up to 30 percent or more of income. Also, as a household's income went up, the amount it had to pay in the mortgage went up, often to the recipient's surprise. In the 1974 recession period, often the opposite happened, and the owner, possibly unemployed, could not meet the mortgage payments.

One-third of the units in the program were existing housing. What often happened was that the Section 235 owner was paying suburban housing prices for slum housing. The owners, often minority families, were pressured into signing mortgages for deteriorated housing that had been given a quick cosmetic uplift and some patching up; these houses often had structural problems and defective heating or plumbing. The program, the House Banking and Currency Committee stated in a 1970 report, was "a bonanza to fast-buck real estate speculators" (Hartman, 1975, p. 138).

Again the federal government found itself in possession of units as low-income owners, unable to afford the repairs or meet the mortgage payments, walked away from the units. In Detroit alone the government took title to 5000 single-family homes and tried to resell them on the open market. FHA has now allowed some units to be put under urban homesteading programs, whereby an owner agreeing to do needed repairs or have them done pays a low amount for the unit; the whole process is supervised in detail. In 1978 HUD was reviving the program somewhat, using stricter regulations and supervision and tighter selection of participants.

New Communities

The final type of subsidy to mention is the subsidy coming under the 1971 New Communities Act. This was for various types of front money (money to build roads, sewerage systems, police and fire stations, and the like) for the development of new communities. About 15 such American new towns got some degree of federal funding in the early 1970s. These new towns were all privately developed by large development corporations, and HUD funds were only a minor assistance in the whole development process. These developments were to be 20 percent low- and moderate-income housing, mainly Section 236 and Section 235 housing. While some—such as Jonathan, Minnesota; Columbia, Maryland; Reston, Virginia, and possibly Park Forest South, Illinois—came close to this, most did not.

The new-town idea came from Britain, where after World War II the British, instead of building all their new housing on the fringes of their already sprawled large cities, such as London, chose to build some housing in entirely new towns, usually 30 to 40 miles from a large urban center and surrounded by a greenbelt, that is, a large open space. The cost was borne almost entirely by the national government. In these planned communities people would both work and live, making life more logical and efficient and building a more cohesive society. The Mark I new towns built around 1947, such as Stevenage, were to be around 60,000 in population. At first some of the new towns looked barren and dull, but gradually they built up a community life and recreational activities and new-town blues were no longer so evident; relatives from London resettled together in the new towns and a second generation grew up there. The employment situation was good until the 1974–1975 recession, when Britain's economy took a downturn and new-town jobs fell off. The larger Mark II new towns of the 1960s have fared fairly well, but again growth has been impeded by recent national economic problems.

The Swedish government, like the Dutch and French governments, among others, has also developed a number of new towns, most noticeably around Stockholm on land the city owns. Here the idea is that by fast transportation residents can commute back to Stockholm for work. There are high-density housing, shopping centers, and recreational centers in nodules with a subway stop in the middle; at the fringe around the center or nodule there is extensive parkland. As in the British new towns, the housing design and general planning and landscaping are very good.

This type of planning appeals to the architect and the utopian dreamer. Instead of patching up decaying inner-city units and instead of putting housing in an unplanned sprawl of a suburb, one can start anew. One can plan landscaping, desirable densities, well-located public facilities, a mix of housing of different costs, and planned parks and motorways.

Unlike European new towns, which have proved quite successful (and in the case of the Mark I British ones have paid for themselves and even given their developer, the British government, a profit, because of increased land values), the American ones have run into financial troubles and often gone bankrupt. American new towns compete with many private suburban developments. In the 1974–1975 recession period, at the height of their development, they were unable to find buyers for their units. These new towns never got the money they had hoped for from the federal government (through HUD), and, in fact, opposition built up to giving large federal grants to what was mainly a white middle-class enclave when the inner cities needed the money so badly. Around HUD in 1975 the word was that new towns don't work. Yet a number, such as Jonathan, which the author studied, were providing a very satisfactory environment for the residents and a type of community where different income levels did interact together. As one writer said, by 2000 we'll be back to praising new towns, for we will need to house people somewhere and they are a better solution than the present unplanned urban-sprawl development. One could add that the next time we build them we need to provide more extensive government financing and government supervision of the planning, as is done in northern Europe.

A REVIEW OF CURRENT POLICIES

The foregoing sections show that as of 1978 government housing subsidies are mainly Section 8 housing assistance and rehabilitation of inner-city units and areas. Even FHA- and VA-insured mortgages have dropped as a percentage of all mortgages. Thus for new housing we must depend almost entirely on the private market, except for some nonprofit housing under Section 202 and to a very minor degree Section 236. This private market produced a high number of units in 1977 and 1978, about 1.8 million and 2.0 million, respectively, but at a high cost. Will middle-class people, paying high interest for such units, be enticed into them, so that the trickle-down or filtering process can work and the poor will get the housing they vacate?

In the past some have argued that this process will not work well enough to help many of the poor, especially the minority poor. Rental or sales prices will never be low enough to allow the poor to rent the units vacated by the middle class as they move into new housing; the income of many poor is just too low.

Downs outlines the complexities in the trickle-down or filtering theory for the different levels at which housing assistance subsidies can be inserted. He says that "new units inserted at relatively high levels in the income distribution start longer 'chains of movement' generated by every new housing unit created" (an average of as many as 3.8 households upgrade their housing in such a chain), but, he adds, only about 10 percent of those households have low incomes. Direct housing subsidies that cause low- and moderate-income–level insertions start shorter chains—probably averaging about 2.0 households—but nearly all households involved have low and moderate income. He adds that while the insertion of housing at the high-income level seems to cost less, the indirect subsidy of income tax deductions might make it as expensive as the insertion of low- and moderate-income housing, and in the latter case the lower-income families get new housing units.

Should we return to building units for the poor? For the elderly, we are saying yes. For others?

Housing assistance to the poor, such as that under Section 8, has many advantages in giving the poor funds to pay for available rentals. But one must always guard against substandard units and the selectivity of landlords. Minorities may not fare well under the programs if no effort is made to combat housing discrimination.

The neighborhood must be improved and services provided if the whole milieu of the poor is to be uplifted. Will we consider this important enough to put major funding behind this effort of neighborhood conservation and housing rehabilitation?

Most would agree that a satisfactory housing policy must include a number of different programs in order to meet the different goals mentioned in the beginning of this chapter. However, these programs must be carefully constructed so that they do not lack components that are needed if they are to succeed. Some say of HUD's past efforts that they were constructed in such a way that they were doomed to fail. One could include Section 236, Section 235, public housing, and new-community subsidies in this group.

CONCLUSION

Analyzing policies in the housing area in terms of the framework for policy analysis given in Chapter 1, one can say that there are a number of unmet needs in relation to housing and the neighborhood, the most imperative a lack of low-rent units. Some causes of this are the low rate of construction in some years, the high cost of building, and the shortage of subsidized units. In this chapter a number of housing goals have been listed, including more units of affordable housing and better, safer neighborhoods. These goals above all are aimed at improving the quality of life as well as providing resource redistribution and the improvement of intrasocial relations.

Implementation strategies take a number of forms. As far as eligibility is concerned there are some programs for the very poor, such as conventional public housing and Section 8; some for the moderate-income, such as Section 202; and some for the middle class, such as tax deductions and FHA- and VA-insured loans. One could say that different income groups get different types of help. Benefits can be either assistance to the building or assistance to the person. Section 8 is assistance not in cash but of the voucher type. The organizations involved are usually housing agencies that have professional staff and many rules and regulations.

Several values play a part in the choice of a type of program. The value of owning one's home lends support to some programs, such as FHA-insured loans. A negative attitude exists toward using government (public) housing and housing deviants.

Power groups with different values and financial interests, from home builders and realtor groups, which oppose public housing but support some other programs, to tenant groups, are very much in conflict here.

Chapter 13

Policy to Decrease Discrimination against Minorities

INTRODUCTION

The most discussed and debated social policy issues in the last two decades have concerned strategies to decrease discrimination against minorities and women in our society. From the time of the 1954 *Brown* desegregation case through the civil rights movement and the period of urban riots (all described in Chapter 3), the attention of the American public has been centered on strategies for providing equal opportunities and a greater share of total societal resources to minority groups. Policies to decrease discrimination in the 1960s at first seemed simple but in operation became more complex and evolved into such controversial strategies as busing or quota systems in employment and college admissions. This evolution in strategies has brought on fierce debates, cries of reverse discrimination, and a barrage of inconclusive court decisions. Wilkinson (1978) was right when in his book, *Brown to Bakke,* he said of the 1954 *Brown* school desegregation decision:

Brown may be the most important political, social, and legal event in America's twentieth century history. Its greatness lay in the enormity of injustice it condemned, in the entrenched sentiment it challenged, in the immensity of law it created and overthrew. It is rich in national insight, a beginning point of American introspection. It was a crossroads, not just for an outcast race, but for an outcast region, a testing ground for liberal values and theory, a challenge for the rule of law and the authority of the Court. [P. 6]

One could add that the Civil Rights Act of 1964 was likewise the "advent of an uncertain perceptibly better, though unmistakably imperfect new order," as Wilkinson said of the *Brown* case. The means of pursuing the goal of racial justice, the uncertain and imperfect strategies, are what have confronted social scientists and activists from the *Brown* period to the 1978 *Bakke* period and on to today. The goal is agreed on by most Americans, a goal, as the American Civil Liberties Union says, of seeing that in a free society every individual enjoys equal access to employment opportunity and the means of self-advancement without invidious discrimination. Most Americans also agree that certain groups in our society have in the past suffered from long and widely practiced invidious racism and that today many of their members are still in disadvantaged positions in our society due to this.

Evidence shows that the quality of life for many members of America's various minority groups is far below that of the average American. The access to opportunities for education, employment, and housing are just opening up. Past and present discrimination practices against such groups as American Indians, Hispanics, Chinese-Americans, and, above all, members of the black community, have led to a variety of consequences. Discrimination in employment has meant that their incomes are far below those of white families and their unemployment rate is high. They are greatly underrepresented at the higher levels of the corporate hierarchy. Discrimination in housing has meant that the affected groups are crowded into substandard housing in ghetto areas, where city services are inadequate and police protection minimal.

Health conditions, another indicator of quality of life, are poor in these urban minority residential areas. The sanitation conditions in the ghetto, the unavailability of doctors, and the lack of funds for medical expenses, as well as ignorance of such preventive health measures as proper prenatal care, cause a variety of health problems, high illness and infant mortality rates, and a lower life expectancy than that of the general American population.

While minority status and low income often coincide, they need not. Discrimination is a situation affecting the quality of life of middle-class as well as poor minority members. Middle-class blacks or Hispanics also suffer from housing segregation, from lack of police protection, from health problems associated with ghetto living, and from attendance at inferior schools. In this chapter minority status and low income status are treated as two distinct categories.

In this chapter the term "minorities" refers mainly to racial and ethnic minorities that have suffered long and widely practiced discrimination, although it is realized that many of the policy measures discussed also apply to religious minorities, such as those of the Jewish, the Mormon, or any number of other religions, and to women, who, while an actual majority of the American population, because of past and present discrimination against them are considered to have minority status. "Ethnicity" here refers to national origin, while "racial" refers to physical traits, such as color.

The degree to which a group is identified as a minority group is related to the degree the members of society view the group *in terms of* their ethnic and racial identity and furthermore treat them in terms of this group identity, both discriminating against them in housing, employment, and education and indicating prejudice against them on attitudinal scales measuring this.

An indicator of whether minority status is a dominant aspect of life for a particular group is the degree of prejudice or negative attitudes other groups in the society have toward them, as exhibited in surveys asking such questions as "Would you want a member of this group as a neighbor, as a supervisor in your job, as a dinner guest, as a student in your child's school?" By these various measures of social distance, one finds that the ethnic-racial groups most likely to be given minority status and treated in a discriminatory way in our society are black citizens, Hispanics (including Mexican-Americans and Puerto Ricans), American Indians, and various Asian-American groups.

WHY DISCRIMINATION IS A SEPARATE SOCIAL POLICY ISSUE

The NASW recently brought out a book (Cafferty and Chestang, 1976) directed at making social workers recognize the importance of ethnicity in formulating social policy. Here we go further and point out that policies to combat discrimination are an important part of the whole social policy field today.

This chapter is needed because a noticeable degree of discrimination still exists for many minorities and thus is still a social problem. For many minority groups barriers cause loss of opportunity to be in the mainstream; for black teenagers, with their high unemployment rate, this may mean genocide. As the Kerner Commission (1968) pointed out, "white racism" has caused America to consist of two separate societies, white and black, and this presents a problem of great magnitude that can lead to disruption and deterioration of American society in general. If a hundred of our central cities erupt again in riots, as Newark, Detroit, Watts, and other cities did in the mid-1960s, we may again have billions of dollars of damage, many thousands of people arrested, hundreds killed, and thousands injured. The potential for rioting still exists. In 1977 this warning came from Secretary of Housing and Urban Development Patricia Harris after the looting during New York City's electric power failure: "The potential for social disruption is immense" (1977, p. 19). The looters, mainly black youth, were characterized by Urban League director Vernon Jordan (1977) as:

> . . . the victims of a society that willfully destroys its own cities. The destruction they wrought [during the power failure] was a more violent mirror image of the destruction of lives and neighborhoods caused by impersonal forces in our society—discrimination, unemployment, poverty. Lawlessness cannot be condoned, but our society must draw the right conclusions from such terrible incidents—people have to be assured of a stake in the society; they must have jobs and decent housing if we want them to act in conformity with society's rules. The resources that will be spent to repair the damages could have been better spent in preventive programs that might have avoided the disaster. [P. 4]

OBJECTIVES OF POLICY

If policies could be implemented to integrate the 12 percent of our population that is black into the whole society in terms of employment and disperse them throughout city and suburban areas instead of concentrating them in ghettos and rural shanty areas, the chances of poor health, poor education, and poor neighborhood environment would decrease and income would likely increase. If ghetto areas were made livable places and their residents prosperous the quality of life would be better.

One could hope that social policies could be devised to do the same for the other minorities. These policies must be devised to decrease discrimination against these groups and to give them the chance to freely develop their maximum potential and to enjoy a quality of life equal to that of white Americans. Minorities themselves are vocal in expressing these goals of equal treatment. American politicians and policymakers in response are presently wrestling with the various legislative and administrative approaches to reducing segregation and discrimination, expanding on the antidiscrimination legislation, court decisions, and administrative orders brought in during the turmoil of the civil rights movement and then the riots of the 1960s, as described in Chapter 3.

In some instances policies to meet the needs of certain minority groups must be tailored to suit their different historical circumstances and different world views or cultural orientations. For example, for the Mexican-American or the Chinese-American minority there may be bilingual education needs. For the American Indian policy may center around improving life on the reservation for those who wish to follow the traditional way of life and observe tribal rites. However, for most minority groups the following policy goals are basic objectives:

1 A major goal is greater participation in the work force at all occupational levels and reduction of the unemployment rate.

2 Another is equal treatment of minorities and whites when on the job, in regard to promotion, fringe benefits, tenure status, and layoffs.

3 Another related goal is improvement of the income position of minority workers, not only as individuals but as households.

4 An important goal in achieving the above is provision of programs to increase hirability of minorities, such as better formal education, manpower training programs on or off the job, or public work experience.

5 Major policy measures are also necessary to strengthen the minority family and keep the male head in the household.

6 Another aim is to decrease discrimination against minorities in house purchases and rentals outside ghetto areas and to improve ghetto-area services.

7 Another goal is increasing the integration of schools and providing the means for greater accessibility of college and professional school. This is a goal controversial in the minds of many whites, and hard to implement, as we shall document.

8 A last important goal is improvement of the health conditions of minority members through the use of preventive programs, increased access to health facilities, and more attention by health personnel.

ASSESSING NEED

The present social, economic, and health position of various minorities gives us an indication of what policy measures are needed. The situation of the black population will be covered in detail, and then conditions for other select minorities will be given in brief. This focus on the black group is justified on the basis that they are the largest of the American minorities; the analysis of their conditions can be applied to other groups.

The Socioeconomic Situation of the Black Population

The economic position of the black population in America can be measured by median family income, individual income, occupational level, unemployment rate, and the proportion in poverty and can be followed over a period of time.

Occupation   Black males who were in jobs during the period 1964–1974 substantially improved their occupational position. In 1964 only 16 percent of males of black and other minority races were in white-collar work, while by 1974 one-fourth were. The improved position was not only in the lower-status sales and clerical jobs but also in professional and managerial work. White males, however, still had a much greater proportion than blacks—43 percent—in professional, managerial, and higher-level sales positions in 1974. Indeed, well over half of black males were in blue-collar work. They were overrepresented in low-paying service activities, with 15 percent in them compared to 7 percent of white males in 1974.

Yet the demand had increased for college-trained blacks with the introduction of affirmative action plans; this occurred at the same time more blacks were getting some college education. Because of this situation Welch (1973) and others found that the occupational distribution of these *well-educated* black males was by 1970 more similar to the distribution of whites than to that of the rest of the black male employed population. Farley (1977) found that in managerial and sales work nonwhite gains continued in the 1970s, a good sign, but in general nonwhites were still far below whites.

As far as improvement of the occupational position of black women is concerned, many of them moved out of private household services in this period. The proportion in these services decreased from 56 percent in 1964 to 37 percent a decade later. The proportion in white-collar work almost doubled, from 22 to 42 percent, in the decade; but white employed women in 1974 were even more likely (64 percent) to be in white-collar work. For black women the great increase was in clerical jobs.

Job Authority   A related pessimistic note is that several studies have found black males much less likely to be in positions of job authority than whites. Lyon and Abell (1979) found from analysis of a large sample of young male workers that racial discrimination was relatively low when these workers first entered the job market but as they continued their careers occupational advancement and pay increases became more dependent on race. In a longitudinal study they found that young black workers, after being hired, in early stages of advancement were rewarded less than whites, even if they had the same years of education. They state that "white workers are rewarded at a much higher level for equal amounts of two of the most important contributors to occupational rewards—schooling and work experience" (pp. 214–215). However, they say that because many black males lack this educational achievement, so important for advancement, they are even worse off and thus one policy for decreasing the racial gap in occupational prestige is to encourage blacks to stay in school longer, even though they will not get the same return on their investment as whites.

Kluegel (1978) has equally pessimistic findings on young blacks' job authority compared to whites'. He says that blacks' upward occupational mobility has been mostly in moving into higher-level occupational positions and not into higher job-authority positions. For all in his sample, job authority (holding such supervisory jobs as manager or foreman) of black men averaged roughly half that of white men; for young black males it was only slightly better. He suggests that since higher wages go with higher job authority this is part of the reason for the black-white disparity of male incomes.

Income   Two measures of income are family income and individual income. Because college-educated blacks and those with good work experience by the early 1970s had moved into better positions, their individual income went up to 70 percent of that of their white counterparts by 1974. This was helped by the fact that besides the increase in college-educated blacks there was a steady exit of a number of older, low-earning black workers through retirement and death.

The earnings of individual black women in full-time employment had almost gained parity with those of white females by 1974, while they were only three-fourths of white women's income in 1964.

Family income differences between blacks and whites remained much higher, because here the fact of unemployment entered in. While black male employment picked up in the 1960s, it fell with the recession of the mid-1970s. In addition, while many households had had at least two wage earners, a traditional situation for many black families, in the mid-1970s there was often only a male worker or in other cases only a low-earning female worker. This was at a time when there was a great increase in the number of white wives in the labor market. White families by 1975 were slightly more likely than black families to have a second worker. In addition, more white families stayed intact, while the rate of black family separation became alarmingly high, to the point where by 1974 over a third of all black households had single female heads. This meant that household income was very low, as was the median family income figure for the whole black group. Thus we have a situation where black median family income was 54 percent of that of white families in 1964, rose to 61 percent in 1970, and fell back to 58 percent in 1974; in 1974 it was $7808, compared to $13,356 for white families. (See Figure 13-1.)

Within the black community there were great differences in family income, depending not only on whether they were in professional rather than service or other low-level occupations, but also on whether the family was a two-worker or one-worker household, a female-headed household or

Income (in current dollars)

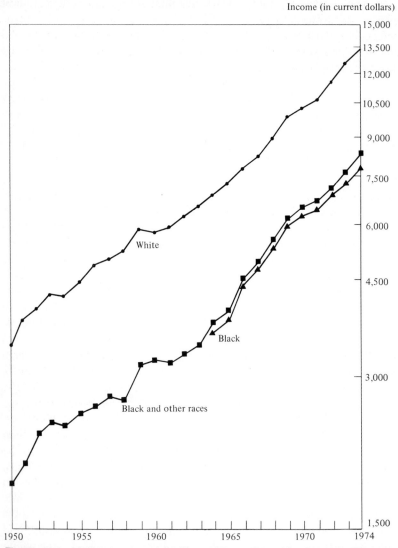

Figure 13-1 Median income of families: 1950 to 1974. (*Source:* U.S. Department of Commerce, Social and Economic Statistics Administration, Bureau of the Census.)

one with an unemployed male head. The income of black female-headed households in 1975 was only $4898; these made up a third of black households.

There was a growing group of black families by 1974 with incomes over $15,000; the proportion had doubled in the decade. Yet only 19 percent had such incomes, compared to 42 percent of white families in 1974.

At the other end there were still many very-low-income black families. A third had incomes below $5000 in 1974, compared to 11 percent of whites. In the South, where half of all blacks still lived, in 1964 half the families lived below the poverty level, so that the fact that only a third did a decade later (1974) was an improvement.

Unemployment   The key to the whole picture lies in the degree of unemployment among the black population. In the late 1960s the economic expansion and the force of affirmative action measures helped the racially segregated twin labor markets to combine somewhat. Prime-aged black males with work experience and education were hired into high-wage industries. Munnell (1978) said that "creaming," or taking the most qualified black males, was done in this period, while little effort was directed toward increasing overall black employment.

With the slowdown of the economy in the 1970s even some of these experienced black males lost their jobs on account of institutional factors, mainly the seniority criterion in the layoff policy of their firms. The last hired became the first fired.

The most alarming situation in the 1970s, however, was the high unemployment rate among black teenagers; without work experience, education, or technical skills these youth suffered a dramatic drop in employment in the 1970s. This affected the overall black unemployment rate. In 1964, 27 percent of black youth aged 16 to 19 were unemployed; by 1978 it was 39 percent. At the same time white teenagers had an actual decrease in unemployment to 14 percent. Because many black youth withdrew from the labor market, the full extent of unemployment was considered even higher than this 39 percent. The increase in the minimum wage seemed one cause, affecting black youth much more than whites. Black males aged 20 to 24 also had considerable unemployment.

Goodlett (1979) says black underclass youth were considered the "untouchables." He quotes Ward's article "Black Youth: The Endangered Species," which warns that an entire generation of black youth have become a useless, expendable, nonfunctional, nonproductive human waste material. Because the system refused to educate them, he says, or even to educate their parents, these young expendables have become the nation's number one social liability.

For all black males 20 and over in the work force unemployment was about 7 percent in 1974, unfortunately double that of white males and higher than in 1970. (See Table 13-1.) For black females 20 and over the 1974 rate was also high, at 8.4 percent; for such white females it was 5 percent.

Family Composition   Black families increasingly were female-headed, with over a third headed by a woman in 1975, compared to a fourth in 1965. In 1975 only a tenth of white families were headed by a

**Table 13-1   Unemployment Rates, by Sex, Race, and Age:
1964, 1970, and 1974**

(Annual averages, %)

Sex, age, and race	1964	1970	1974
Black and other races			
Total	9.6	8.2	9.9
Men, 20 years and over	7.7	5.6	6.8
Women, 20 years and over.	9.0	6.9	8.4
Both sexes, 16 to 19 years	27.2	29.1	32.9
White			
Total	4.6	4.5	5.0
Men, 20 years and over	3.4	3.2	3.5
Women, 20 years and over.	4.6	4.4	5.0
Both sexes, 16 to 19 years	14.8	13.5	14.0
Ratio: black and other races			
to white			
Total	2.1	1.8	2.0
Men, 20 years and over	2.3	1.8	1.9
Women, 20 years and over.	2.0	1.6	1.7
Both sexes, 16 to 19 years	1.8	2.2	2.4

Source: U.S. Department of Labor, Bureau of Labor Statistics.

female. Put another way, half of black children under 18 in 1977 did not live with both parents. This breakup of the family can be largely attributed to economic conditions; data show that unemployment rates and separation rates for the black community run parallel.

Education   Part of the problem that many blacks and other minority members have in seeking and keeping jobs is that they lack the educational training needed for the job. Black high school dropout rates have traditionally been high. Yet they were lowered considerably between 1967 and 1977, from 35 percent to 25 percent. This means, however, that one-fourth of the blacks going into the job market lack the basic credential for any job, a high school diploma.

As far as years behind their proper grade in school is concerned, blacks again made great improvements by 1977, with only 10 percent aged 16 to 17 behind their normal grade, compared to 18 percent in 1967.

The increase in college attendance was very high, although many blacks were attending local two-year colleges. By 1975 a fourth of all blacks aged 18 to 19 were in college; in 1960 it had been 6 percent. Blacks made up 11 percent of the college population, about their proportion in the general population.

Health Status   The life expectancy at birth for the black population continued to be below that of whites, 67.0 years, compared to 72.1 for whites in 1974, meaning that whites stayed alive 5 years longer than blacks on the average.

The infant mortality rate (death of the child in the first year per 1000 live births) was very bad for blacks. In 1974 it was 24.9 for blacks, much higher than the white rate of 14.8. In some inner-city areas, such as East Oakland, California, it was so high that federal authorities were funding a large program to reduce it.

Housing   Blacks have been more likely than whites to be in inadequate housing. While the proportion of black households in units lacking all plumbing facilities dramatically decreased from 1950 to 1974, to a low of 9.6 percent in 1974, blacks were nevertheless likely to live in overcrowded conditions (1.01 persons or more per room); 12.6 percent had such conditions in 1974, compared to 4.5 percent of white households.

Many blacks still lived in older units in inner cities, and a much smaller percentage of them owned their own homes: only 38 percent in 1970, compared to 64 percent of white households.

Few blacks lived in the suburbs in the 1970s; at the same time, in many central cities half or more of the population was made up of black residents. There had been a heavy black migration out of the South during and after World War II, with well over 2 million migrating north and west in the years 1950 to 1966 alone and mostly to cities; this migration slowed down in the 1970s, and some reverse migration, back to the South, occurred. The increased black population in the cities was crowded into segregated, expanding ghetto areas; by Taeber's Measurement Index of Segregation (1964) 86.2 out of 100 Negroes in the twenty largest cities in the United States would have had to change the block on which they lived in order to create an unsegregated population distribution, according to the 1960 census data; in the 1970s the situation was about the same. Hermalin and Farley (1973) report that the proportion of blacks in the suburban rings of the twenty-nine major urban areas remained 4 percent in 1950, 1960, and 1970 and that most of these black suburbanites lived in segregated areas, such as inner-core areas of old suburbs. In the 1970s there was a slight improvement: the proportion rose to 6 percent of the suburban population in 1977. At that point 55 percent of the country's 24.5 million blacks lived in central cities, with another large group in Southern rural areas. Considering that the suburbs in the mid-1970s had half the country's population, this severe underrepresentation of blacks presented a serious problem, since employment openings were increasingly in the suburbs.

It wasn't that all blacks could not afford the suburbs; as income figures showed, the number with middle-class incomes far exceeded the number in the suburbs. This was the conclusion of Hermalin and Farley (1973), who compared the proportion of whites of a certain income who lived in the suburban rings with that of blacks of that income that lived in the suburbs. They stated, "Substantial changes in the racial distribution in urbanized areas would occur if the representation rates of blacks at every value of housing level equaled that of whites." If the suburbs were opened up to black households with sufficient income to buy a house, they found, then "overall in 1970, the proportion of Black households in the suburban ring would increase from 16 to 43 percent" in the twenty-nine metropolitan areas studied (p. 602).

Some say the reason why blacks are underrepresented in the suburbs is that black families prefer not to live in suburban areas. However, a Harris poll in 1967 found that two-thirds of those blacks surveyed said they were willing to live in integrated neighborhoods and preferred them to segregated neighborhoods.

Most researchers attribute the underrepresentation of blacks in the suburbs directly to discrimination. Kain and Quigley (1975), in a massive recent study of housing markets and racial discrimination, bluntly report that the intensity of black residential segregation is greater than that documented for any other identifiable subgroup in American history.

Hermalin and Farley (1973) from their research consider real estate practices and public attitudes as the cause of the absence of blacks from the suburbs. They state, "We believe then that the current level of residential segregation must be attributed largely to actions and attitudes, past and present, which have restricted the entry of Blacks into predominantly white neighborhoods" (p. 608). Then they quote Judge Roth in the Detroit school busing case:

> Government action and inaction at all levels, federal, state and local, have combined with those of private organizations, such as loaning institutions, real estate associations and brokerage firms to establish and maintain the patterns of residential segregation through the Detroit metropolitan area. [P. 609]

And they quote Amos Hawley (1973), who describes a web of discrimination—"real estate practices, the mortgage lending arrangements, the climate of opinion and the like . . . which deter Blacks from obtaining the housing for which they are economically qualified" (Hawley, p. 19).

The U.S. Commission on Civil Rights in its 1974 study also verifies that there must be extreme discrimination at work, saying:

> Racial segregation in residential patterns persists both because of past and present discrimination in the sale and rental of housing and because of income disadvantage. Since at every income level, whites are more likely than Blacks to live in the suburbs, racial discrimination in housing may be more deeply entrenched than economic or income discrimination. [Wallace, 1977, p. 350]

Pascal (1967), in his large RAND study of residential segregation, Harvard's John Kain and his group of economists (1975), in their Urban Stimulation Model work, and real estate researcher Anthony Downs (1976) all agree with these findings that discrimination is a major cause of black families' underrepresentation in the suburbs. Wallace (1977) summarizes these views, stating, "The major explanation for residential segregation is the Blacks are discouraged from entering high quality housing markets because of prohibitive search costs, discriminatory treatment by sellers, agents and market institutions and high non-economic costs from personal and community harassment" (p. 356). As far as mortgage loans are concerned, a 1974 U.S. Controller of Currency study (Charlton, 1975) shows that minority-group applicants were rejected almost twice as often as white applicants in the same financial bracket.

Several myths need to be dispelled. One is that housing prices go down when black families buy on a block. Study after study, including the Laurenti study (1960) in three cities, shows that when an area becomes integrated, property values are more likely to stay the same or go up; in such studies an integrated area is compared with an all-white area with similar-quality housing. Data on the market values of houses are usually collected over a number of years. The Laurenti study found that in 41 percent of the comparisons of 5417 properties, the prices of properties in integrated areas stayed within 5 percent of the prices in control or all-white areas; in 44 percent of the cases, prices in the integrated area were relatively higher than prices in the control area by 5 to 26 percent at the end of the 12-year study period; only in 15 percent of the cases did prices in the integrated area end lower.

Another myth is that white sellers will sell only to white buyers. Studies such as Werthman's of suburban Foster City (1965) show that white owners would prefer minority middle-class neighbors in their area to lower-class neighbors of any racial or ethnic group. In a 1972 National Opinion Research Center (NORC) poll, 84 percent of the whites sampled said, "It would make no difference if Negroes with the same income and education moved into the block," and 55 percent "disagreed slightly or strongly that whites have a right to keep Negroes out of their neighborhood."

Many real estate brokers like to perpetuate both myths, because then they can seize on the opportunity, after integration of an area has begun, to "block-bust," that is, to encourage white owners on the block to sell. Because the real estate agent can usually get a higher selling price out of a black family eager for decent housing, in such situations the agent can make a sizable profit. Such practices are now outlawed, although they are known still to exist; also, many white owners now band together when a black family moves onto the block and agree not to sell and instead welcome the black family into the neighborhood; fair housing groups have helped create this type of response.

Residential segregation caused by housing discrimination has several negative effects. First, it adversely affects job opportunities for minorities, since many new labor market openings are in industrial parks and office complexes in the suburbs and if minorities do not live in the area their chances for such jobs are more limited, especially since the jobs are at sites generally inaccessible by public transportation. Suburban public transit, at its basic level, is organized to get suburban commuters into the city rather than central-core residents out to suburban jobs. Second, minorities' exclusion from the suburbs perpetuates school segregation; dispersal of minorities in suburban as well as city housing would in fact mean school busing efforts and other desegregation plans would not be needed.

Other Ethnic and Racial Minorities

The life conditions of a number of other minorities are likewise below that of the white population, and there are indications that a certain degree of discrimination still exists for these groups. In the 1970 census 6.3 million people were recorded as Chicano, that is, people of Mexican-Indian descent. This group includes very recent immigrants as well as those who have lived here for generations; many still live in rural areas. In 1970 the median family income of this whole group was $4908. About a fourth were estimated to live below the poverty level. The unemployment rate was over 12 percent in 1976. The education level was low, with less than a third finishing high school in 1970; however, this has improved in recent years.

For another growing minority, Chinese-Americans, the education level is high, with 37 percent in 1976 going beyond high school. The median income was, however, very low in 1970, only $5223, according to Goodman and Marx (1978). Since there are many new immigrants, including some from the Chinese mainland, the median income for the whole group is likely to remain low; however, for many second- and third-generation Chinese-Americans who have received a college education it is fairly good. The present increased immigration will bring their number to over 500,000 shortly.

American Indians (792,730 in 1970) are in the poorest position, in both income and education. Their income is far below that of blacks, especially if they are in the half of the group still living on the reservation. Their unemployment rate for males is very high, 29 percent in 1975. Only a third have finished high school, according to 1973 data. The rates for such health ailments as tuberculosis are very high. Infant mortality rates are high; alcoholism is a problem for many. For this group it is hard to find a change for the better, yet more are finishing high school each year, health measures have been introduced, and some attempt is being made in urban areas to give them counseling, manpower training, and day care assistance.

SOCIAL POLICY TO IMPROVE THE POSITION
OF MINORITIES

The data in the foregoing section indicate that minorities in the United States, especially the black minority, still fall far below the white population in socioeconomic position and have unsatisfactory conditions in such quality-of-life indicators as housing and neighborhood, health, and education.

The civil rights movement of the 1960s and then the riots indicated that the black population, like other minorities, has for many years not been satisfied with its subordinate position. American Indian, Mexican-American, and Chinese-American groups have likewise demanded (through demonstrations and other means) more equal treatment in American society.

The federal government has embarked on a number of policies to improve the situation. Legislation has been passed, such as the monumental Civil Rights Act of 1964 and then the 1968 Act with its fair housing provisions. The courts have produced major decisions on minority rights, such as the *Brown* school desegregation decision. Federal and state bureaucracies, such as the Equal Employment Opportunity Commission, have been set up. Federal, state, and local governments have started a number of programs to help disadvantaged groups.

Some policies (and laws) are aimed at changing the organizational and structural characteristics of firms, altering employers' attitudes, and making the cost of discrimination more expensive, so that these firms will both hire minorities and, when minorities are on the job, see that they get equal treatment in promotion and fringe benefits and the like. Other policies are aimed at increasing the *number of available jobs* for minorities by providing incentives to firms to expand their work force or by providing public service jobs for disadvantaged persons.

Another set of policies is focused on improving the job qualifications of minorities through more manpower training, public work experience, and college education.

Major antidiscrimination policies deal with desegregating schools, both for the purpose of stopping the development of two separate Americas and instead promoting a unified society by integrating all young people into one school system, and for the purpose of creating a better learning situation for minority children, that is, in integrated schools where there are a variety of role models and high aspiration and achievement levels. Some policies deal with the problem of bilingual school populations, such as in the case of Chinese-Americans or Mexican-Americans, where the lack of ability in the English language is a barrier to learning and to integration into American life.

Another area of policy is fair housing legislation to allow minorities to have a free choice of where to live and to end discrimination in selling and renting outside the ghetto areas. Efforts here may also include subsidizing the building of housing for low- and moderate-income families in non-ghetto, preferably suburban, areas. Policies may also be devised to improve the ghetto housing and the neighborhood.

Another area of policy has been opening up public accommodations, such as hotels, restaurants, and community facilities, to all regardless of race or ethnic or religious background.

STRATEGIES FOR ENDING DISCRIMINATION

The policy means or strategies used against Jim Crow laws on accommodations, the overt type of discrimination, have been the easiest to implement. In fact, in general *de jure* discrimination, that is, discrimination prescribed by law, has been easier to end, whether in the case of laws on public accommodations or laws on school segregation in the South. *De facto* discrimination, which is due to informal practices rather than law, is much harder to deal with and still evading enforcement.

This is true in regard to education and employment. The basis for action against discrimination in these areas is the 1964 Civil Rights Act and the 1968 one, which includes fair-housing measures, and the 1972 amendments including educational institutions under the act. Another basis for enforcement is the Fourteenth Amendment, as well as some executive orders.

The Civil Rights Act of 1964, enacted after massive civil rights demonstrations (described in Chapter 3), has been the cornerstone of a variety of affirmative action programs and the center of controversy in a number of Supreme Court cases. It was based on the Fourteenth Amendment to the Constitution, which stated that "all persons born or naturalized in the United States, and subject to the jurisdiction thereof," shall not be denied the equal protection of the laws. The Civil Rights Act of 1964 prohibited denial of voter registration, and it prohibited discrimination in and segregation of public accommodations from hotels and restaurants to places of entertainment. The act ordered the Attorney General to undertake civil actions on behalf of persons attempting orderly desegregation of public schools. The act empowered the Commission on Civil Rights, first established under the Civil Rights Act of 1957, to investigate deprivations of the right to vote and to collect information on discrimination in America.

An important demand of this major 1964 act was that each federal department and agency "take actions to end discrimination in all programs or activities receiving federal financial assistance in any form." And last, the act said "that it shall be unlawful for any employer or labor union with twenty-five or more persons after 1965 to discriminate against any individual in any fashion in employment because of race, color, religion, sex, or national origin," and that "an Equal Employment Opportunity Commission shall be established to enforce this provision by investigation, conference, conciliation, persuasion, and, if need be, civil action in federal court."

Issues in Ending Employment Discrimination

Title VII of the Civil Rights Act of 1964 has been the basis for affirmative action in relation to job discrimination. It has been directed at changing personnel practices and policies and even employer beliefs, by demanding the end of discrimination in hiring, promotion, transfer, training, discharge, and compensation. It therefore affects the very structure and organization of firms. While it first applied to private employers and labor unions, the 1972 amendment extended it to educational institutions and to state and local government, thus correcting a situation whereby civil service tests often put minorities at the bottom of the eligibility roster and kept them out of state and local government employment.

Even with the enactment of such a strong act, in the field of employment simply prohibiting discrimination against applicants because of race and ethnic background and sex, it was soon found, did not solve the problem. Attempts to get vague equal opportunity measures voluntarily carried out by firms, with few clear guidelines for improving the racial balance of the work force, did not seem to produce major results. To tell employers to be color-blind or neutral (instead of negative) to minorities in their hiring brought only minimal progress in the situation, a number felt. As Ravitch (1979) says, black civil rights leaders began to fear that color-blindness meant a willful refusal to recognize exclusionary practices that operated under the guise of racial neutrality. As Ravitch herself said, "Strict neutrality in admissions and hiring with no efforts to remedy the effects of past discrimination, will leave many Blacks right where they are, at the bottom" (p. 18), though she herself in 1979 was for a middle ground between total color-blindness and group-consciousness (a policy of preferential treatment for minorities).

Institutional Racism Black leaders found neutrality ineffective because of what they called "institutional racism." Institutional racism does not intentionally bar minorities; it instead can be defined as the existence of bureaucratic procedures and a structural organization that, while seeming neutral, in reality disqualify minorities from employment positions or educational places. The very normal and seemingly neutral regulations and procedures of any institution, such as seniority, aptitude and personnel tests, high school diploma requirements, and college admission tests, could, it was discovered, in a subtle and complex way perpetuate the effects of past discrimination, as the *Congressional Quarterly* points out, adding that this knowledge led to the development of the affirmative action concept.

As Ray Marshall points out, there are different types of discrimination, specific overt acts and what he calls "institutionalized systemic forms that perpetuate exclusion and discrimination in the larger society" (Wallace, 1977, p. 364).

While the courts in the first five or six years after the 1964 Act grappled elusively with these problems when discrimination cases came before them, by 1970 the courts began to define discrimination as it occurred in relation to hiring, testing, promotions, and seniority. They also began to focus on the results of policies rather than intent to discriminate. In the 1971 *Griggs v. Duke Power* case the Supreme Court said that even if the employer did not *intend* to discriminate, if employment practices including *past* practices had a discriminatory *effect* it was considered discrimination. If the employer demanded certain job requirements, such as a high school diploma or a minimum height for police, say 5 feet 10 inches, it could be discriminatory, in this case against Asian-Americans. In *Griggs* the Court said that the 1964 Civil Rights Act put on the employer the burden of showing that a job requirement had a manifest relationship to the employment in question. The law was not addressed to motivation but to consequences.

Equal Opportunity　Neutrality and institutional racism meant keeping the status quo. Therefore executive orders and court decisions were made with the idea that one could not simply offer equal opportunity at the starting line. Probably President Lyndon Johnson stated the need as well as anyone, saying in 1965:

> Freedom is not enough. You do not wipe out scars of centuries by saying "now you're free to go where you want and do as you desire." You do not take a person who for years has been hobbled by chains and liberate him, bringing him up to the starting line of a race and then say "you're free to compete" and justly believe that you have been completely fair. ["Rights Revolution," 1978, p. 159]

From 1965 on and especially since 1970, federal contractors had to go farther than simply offering equal opportunity; they had to take "affirmative actions," and by 1970 they had to work under guidelines and establish *goals* for each job classification by race and sex and *timetables* specifying dates when the situation would be corrected. As Dye (1972) said, "Civil rights was gradually redefined from merely legally prohibiting discrimination and segregation to a broader interest in the actual possibility of developing human capacities and sharing in the goods a society has produced and the way of life it has produced" (p. 56), which, he added, means not merely restrictions on government but a positive obligation of government to act forcefully to end discrimination in public accommodation, employment, and housing.

Affirmative action is best defined by the courts. In the challenge to an early affirmative action plan supported by the Department of Labor, the Philadelphia Plan, the federal district court defined it, saying:

> The heartbeat of affirmative action is the policy of developing programs which shall provide in detail for specific steps to guarantee equal opportunity keyed to the problems and needs of minority groups, including when there are deficiencies, the development of specific goals and timetables for the prompt achievement of full and equal employment opportunity. [Wallace, 1977, p. 335]

Affirmative action above all was a strategy establishing timetables and goals in order to bring the characteristics of the internal labor force of the employer into conformity with the characteristics of the external labor market.

As one critic (Glazer) said, "By the early 1970s affirmative action came to mean much more than advertising opportunities, actively seeking out those who didn't know about them and preparing those not qualified. It came to mean setting statistical requirements based on race, color and national origin" ("Rights Revolution," 1978, p. 6).

By 1975, as Wallace (1977) reported, the law, the courts, and voluntary action by firms had established the general guidelines of affirmative action plans that affected practices in hiring and promoting all employees. Wallace concludes that:

> By 1975, the standards of performance on equal employment opportunity issues had been established in both the judicial rulings and through administrative procedures of the compliance agencies. The impact of these measures extended throughout American industry. The evolution of the concept of *institutional* discrimination produced extensive revisions in traditional practices in personnel selection, assessment, and upgrading. Recently negotiated settlements in the steel, trucking, and telephone industries may have upgraded the occupational position of some minorities, thereby reducing the earned income differential between Blacks and whites. However, it is likely such gains were made by those Blacks who were not the most disadvantaged in the labor market. [P. 337]

A number of issues arose around the new concept of affirmative action. The move from equal opportunity at the starting line to a degree of equity per se, that is, provision of employment positions and educational places, was questioned. Critics said that help at the starting line was enough; these critics, as Billingsley (1977) laments, considered unfair those measures to ensure that the disadvantaged keep pace with the advantaged. They were against *special efforts* to bring minorities up to the level of equality shared by the majority, to set up timetables for the equal inclusion of blacks and other minorities in the work force. They said it was not the American way while establishing equal opportunity was. Billingsley (1977) chides these critics for not answering the question of what government and society should do if the opportunity prescription does not result in any substantial degree of equality.

Past Discrimination   Affirmative action was justified on the basis of past discrimination. "The Rights Revolution" (1978) gives this as the main reason for affirmative action measures, saying that they are to make up for past discriminatory hiring practices. Or, as stated in the *Griggs* decision, the 1964 Act's Title VII was to remove barriers that had operated in the past to favor an identifiable group of white employees over other employees. The Court said you can't have practices that freeze the status quo of prior discriminatory employment practices.

In the educational field past discrimination or "benign" discrimination has again been used as a justification for positive admission considerations, as it was by four of the justices in the *Bakke* case concerning the medical school preferential admissions plan at the University of California, Davis. The four justices in their minority opinion on the quota decision said that these should be allowed "if there is reason to believe that the disparate impact [on minorities] is itself the product of past discrimination."

The very words "compensatory justice" are used as the justification for preferential treatment. Critics say that compensation for the past is a dangerous principle raising the questions of what groups should be given special treatment and how much and for how long (Glazer, 1975).

Degree of Disparity   A high degree of disparity is also given as a justification for affirmative action; when the degree of disparity greatly decreases, affirmative action will not be necessary. The vice president of the Ford Foundation, Howard Howe II, answering Nathan Glazer, the critic of affirmative action, said:

> In making his case, I think he [Glazer] ignores the issue of the degree of disparity in comparing minorities with the main body of the population. When statistics show that a racially identified group of 25 million people is as far behind whites as America's Blacks apparently are, they become a powerful argument for special efforts to enhance both the opportunities and success of Blacks. . . . [Billingsley, 1977, p. 539]

And in its 1979 affirmative action statement, the American Civil Liberties Union said, "When discrimination has been *long and widely practiced* against a particular group, it cannot be satisfactorily eliminated merely by the prospective adoption of neutral, 'color-blind,' or 'sex-blind' standards" [for selection, promotion or retention of an applicant]. The group applies this policy to such groups as Chicanos and American Indians, who "because of discrimination have been isolated from the American mainstream and been relegated to second class status and have not been permitted full and equal participation in American society" (Strum, 1979, p. 27).

Preferential Treatment   Another issue is whether policies should move from color-blindness to color-consciousness, that is, preferential treatment, a policy supporters say is needed because there is institutional racism. Preferential treatment plans have especially been attacked when they are in the form of a numerical remedy or quota. In the 1970s both the federal department guidelines and court decisions talked of goal setting, time schedules, targets, and the like.

By 1971 the Office of Federal Contract Compliance was demanding that firms send in affirmative action plans with data on employees' race, sex, and ethnicity and their organizational position and pay level, as well as the background of job applicants and the reason for rejection. Some researchers felt that this continual accounting system in itself helped employers move toward employment and promotion of minorities, just as litigation for noncompliance or the cutoff of federal contracts meant that the cost discouraged discrimination in employment.

Court agreements on litigation over discrimination used quotas; the *Bank of America* (1974) case said that the company not only was to compensate with back pay for past discrimination but was also to increase the overall proportion of women officers to 40 percent by 1978, up from 18 percent.

School districts were likewise asked to have a certain proportion, or to come within a certain range of that proportion, of each race in their student body. Higher education employers under the 1972 Equal Employment Act were included in the demand to increase minority and female employment.

This color-consciousness was seen as *reverse discrimination,* that is, giving preferential treatment to minorities. The attack increased when policy moved from prescribing general racial balance to giving very specific quotas. This word "quotas" was especially held in disrepute, even though in reality the courts when imposing numerical remedies often used the words "quotas" and "goals" interchangeably. As Justice Powell said in *Bakke,* a case involving numerical remedies, any "semantic distinction is beside the point. . . . whether [the numerical remedy] is described as a quota or a goal it is a line drawn on the basis of race and ethnic status." Sindler (1978) gave a somewhat different interpretation of the issue, saying:

> The question was not whether goals or quotas were theoretically the same thing; clearly they were different. Nor was it whether affirmative action mandated quotas, because [through 1977] plainly the procedures called for setting goals. The core of the dispute was, rather, whether the procedures in their *actual* operation often resulted in the *conversion* of goals into quotas because they encouraged or tolerated the employer's use of minority preference devices to achieve his hiring goals. [P. 154]

One could say that some were opposed to narrow "quotas" versus broad "goals," and that others were critical of *any type* of preferential treatment, whether goals or quotas. In the 1978 *Bakke* case the Supreme Court, by a 5 to 4 vote, opposed narrow quotas. Bakke, an older white engineer, had been trying for two years for admission to the Medical School of the University of California, Davis. Davis had a quota system for minority admissions, with 16 places of 100 saved for minorities. Both years Bakke was denied admission while minorities with lower grade point averages were admitted. Bakke charged that he was denied admission because of his race, which meant he was denied equal protection under the Fourteenth Amendment and Title VI of the 1964 Civil Rights Act. In other words, there was reverse discrimination. The Supreme Court ruled 5 to 4 that Davis's quotas were too rigid and not acceptable; one justice, Powell, pointed to Harvard's more flexible plan as acceptable. The majority, with Powell now in support, ruled that race could be considered as an admissions criterion if the university was seeking a diverse student body, as at Harvard, since the university could do this under the academic freedom guarantee of the First Amendment. Powell, by using Harvard as an example, even provided a broad policy framework for university affirmative action programs.

In the 1979 *Weber* case on quotas in a firm's job training programs the Supreme Court ruled that quotas were acceptable. Weber, a white, was denied admission to a voluntary job training program of the company and the union related to promotion to skilled jobs at a Kaiser steel plant; Weber had more seniority than some of the black workers admitted to the program under a plan where half the trainees were to be black. Weber's lawyers claimed this was reverse discrimination forbidden by Title VII of the 1964 Act. Racial preference had occurred. Second, there had been no showing of prior discrimination at Kaiser.

The Supreme Court 5 to 2 majority reversed the lower court decisions and said that in this narrow case of *voluntary* affirmative action between private parties, not involving the state, such a plan was acceptable. This decision thus upheld quotas, saying voluntary affirmative action plans, even those containing numerical quotas, did not automatically violate Title VII, which barred discrimination. The *Weber* decision had the important consequence of assuring employers who enacted voluntary affirmative action programs that they would not be sued by whites on the grounds of reverse discrimination. Thus it gave them the green light to go ahead with programs. This decision also assured these firms that they would not be in the dilemma of having to admit past discrimination or guilt if sued on their affirmative action program (the Kaiser firm had not had evidence of past discrimination). The decision said such proof was not necessary in a voluntary affirmative action program between private parties. Secretary of Labor Ray Marshall said that the *Weber* decision was a vindication of affirmative action as a major tool for achieving equity in the work place. Yet one doubts if the issue of reverse discrimination is fully closed, although it was dealt a clear blow in the *Weber* case. In 1976 several federal district court decisions had ruled against reverse discrimination, including a Virginia Commonwealth University case.

Arguments Pro and Con   The proponents of preferential treatment, including Supreme Court justices, support it for a variety of reasons. Many have argued, as in the *Bakke* case, that preferential treatment is the only way to make up for past discrimination, especially when institutional racism exists. For example, the New York State court ruled in the Brooklyn Downstate Medical School case, which gave certain admission preferences to minority applicants, that reverse discrimination was constitutional "in proper circumstances in cases where this preferential treatment satisfied state interest. . . . It need be found, that, on balance, the gain to be derived from the preferential policy outweighs its possible detrimental effects" ("Rights Revolution," 1978, p. 154).

In the *Bakke* case, the four justices who voted for quotas said it was all right to penalize some whites, if necessary, to overcome past mistreatment of blacks (benign discrimination). Or, as Edwards and Zaretsky (1975) say:

> While there may be an element of unfairness in preferential treatment, some price must be paid to overcome the longstanding pervasive patterns of race and sex bias in this nation. The minor injustice that may result . . . is, on balance, outweighed by the fact that temporary preferential remedies appear to be the only way to effectively break the cycle of employment discrimination and open all levels of the job market to all qualified applicants. [P. 7]

Proponents argue that preferential treatment is supported in the Constitution and in the 1964 Civil Rights Act. They say that the 1964 Act did not forbid discrimination on the basis of race but included an affirmative action statement, as in fact Title VII does. It says, "The court may . . . order such affirmative action as may be appropriate which may include, but is not limited to, reinstatement or hiring of employees . . . or any other equitable relief as the court deems appropriate."

In the 1979 *Weber* case, Supreme Court Justice Brennan again asserts that the act was not a color-blind or nondiscrimination principle. He said that the intent of Congress in the 1964 Act was hardly to bar this kind of voluntary action (voluntary job training programs with quotas) when it outlawed discrimination in employment on the basis of race. Nor was the purpose of the statute to forbid all race-conscious affirmative action, since forbidding this would be at variance with the end the act was trying to achieve. This decision thus upheld quotas, saying that voluntary affirmative action plans, even those containing numerical quotas, did not automatically violate Title VII.

Brennan goes on to say, in the majority opinion,

It would be ironic indeed if a law triggered by a nation's concern over centuries of racial injustice and intended to improve the lot of those who had been excluded from the American dream for so long constituted the first legislative prohibition of all voluntary, private race conscious efforts to abolish traditional patterns of racial segregation and hierarchy.

The Fourteenth Amendment was also used to justify preferential treatment, especially in the case of government employment. In finding racial discrimination in government agencies, federal courts, using this amendment as justification, did such things as demanding the establishment of "priority pools" from which to draw minority and nonminority applicants for such civil service jobs as police and fire fighters in Philadelphia and Boston; and demanding preferential hiring, such as hiring one minority applicant for every two white applicants on an alternating basis, as was ordered in the Minneapolis Fire Department case (*Carter v. Gallagher,* 1972).

Opponents argue that both the Fourteenth Amendment and the 1964 Civil Rights Act were nondiscriminatory, that is, color-blind. Ravitch (1979) considers the 1964 Act to embody the fundamental principle that everyone should be considered as an individual without regard to social origin. She says the alliance of Catholics, Jews, organized labor, liberals, and others that supported desegregation has now been splintered because of the shift of focus from antidiscrimination to group preference. White male, including Jewish male, positions in the academic world and elsewhere became threatened. As Billingsley (1977) says, some members of the Eastern intellectual liberal establishment (including those associated with *Commentary* and *Public Interest*) who had supported efforts to desegregate the South now "provided the intellectual rationale for contemporary efforts to slow down, withdraw and rethink affirmative action programs designed to assist Blacks, disadvantaged minorities, and women to reach equality and equity with the more privileged white American males in all aspects of society." These opponents of affirmative action argue that special treatment is not legal; that equal opportunity but not preferential treatment is the American way; and that preferential treatment is not necessary, since the conditions of minorities have greatly improved and discrimination no longer exists, and where it does, voluntary action, not government enforcement, should be used to correct the situation. Billingsley (1977) argues that "this leaves those already privileged as the gatekeepers of liberty," and he adds, "there is a necessity for social policy and measures of enforcement which stand outside the domination of the privileged majority in embracing the whole of the nation and society."

Opponents argue with the use of statistical counts, percentages, and timetables. They say these could cause a backlash against minorities by whites who have become resentful over these quotas. (Yet Taylor [1978] shows that attitudinal studies in recent years show that white attitudes to having blacks work with them or supervise them have stayed about the same since 1963 and that for certain groups, such as Irish, Slavics, and Italians, attitudes have considerably improved.)

Critics also feel that affirmative action measures violate the normal pattern of employment in the United States, which now, they say, by deemphasizing ethnic and racial categories has produced progress toward equality and parity.

Critics say enforcement measures are too high a price to pay for a change toward greater equality. As Moore (1977) says of the critic Glazer, he sees great power, wielded unremittingly, by the proponents of affirmative action; the EEOC (Equal Employment Opportunity Commission) is portrayed as a veritable octopus, strangling employers' efforts at maintaining standards. Moore adds that no list of actual penalties is provided (most are small), and that about half the work force is not affected by federal compliance issues.

Actually, although the EEOC was established under the 1964 Act, there was little enforcement of this legislation until 1971, when a government contract was revoked. Only in 1972 was the EEOC granted major enforcement powers to bring civil action against employers and unions in federal courts. Before that it had to work by helping individual parties who had filed complaints, which the EEOC then investigated and tried to settle by voluntary conciliation. Conciliation is still the EEOC's main way of working. It had a limited staff to fully investigate and carry forward cases. For example, by 1977 the national EEOC had a backlog of 130,000 cases, and many of these cases weren't considered for three years.

Most states had EEOC programs, some with stronger powers than others.

The equal employment enforcement agencies work under a complex and uncertain process. As Harvard Law Professor Derrick Bell (in Burstein, 1979) pointed out on equal employment laws:

> If the country were really committed to eradicating the social and economic burdens borne by the victims of employment discrimination, it would have fashioned a far more efficacious means of accomplishing this result. At present, the law channels charges of employment discrimination into a burdensome, conciliation-oriented administrative structure that functions, in the mean, on a case-by-case basis, depending on effectively prosecuted litigation and a sympathetic judiciary for even the hard-won progress thus far achieved. [P. 368]

Burstein in his major study of the effects of the EEOC says, "The EEOC enforcement effort was slow to begin and seems modest in intensity, but the demands placed upon the system keep increasing" (p. 379). He adds it is very inadequately funded compared to its task.

The EEOC often has used class action suits or sample cases to get court decisions. Wallace (1977) reports, "The number of cases that can be tried by the federal court is small and additional administrative mechanisms must be developed." She quotes the chairman of the Senate Subcommittee on Equal Opportunities in 1974 as noting that "successful implementation of the act depends upon the effectiveness of the nonlitigation methods of enforcement since the litigation process itself cannot be expected to handle the large volume of charges referred to the Commission" (p. 337). By 1975 industrywide consent cases, such as the AT&T consent decree, began to replace individual cases, Wallace reports.

Seniority   Another issue related to antidiscrimination measures in employment concerns seniority rights. To a large degree this stands out as an obstacle to the fulfillment of affirmative action measures. Seniority rules are a collective bargaining measure. In times of economic recession they affect the retention of members of minorities who are new employees. The seniority system means the last hired is the first fired. To change the procedure, one runs into union rules and basic collective bargaining mandates. In cases in 1968, 1969, and 1971 the lower federal courts ruled that seniority systems organized along racially segregated bases that prevented blacks from advancing on merit to better jobs, systems that had existed before Title VII of the 1964 Civil Rights Act, had the discriminatory effect of perpetuating past discrimination and were unjustified by business necessity. However, in a 1974 Supreme Court case, *Alexander v. Gardner,* the court said that the policy should be to look at *both* the grievance and arbitration clause in the collective bargaining agreement *and* the cause of action under Title VII and that the federal court considered the employee's claim de novo. And in the 1975 *Jersey Central Power* case the 3d Circuit Court reversed a lower court's ruling that layoff procedures must keep the proportion of minorities at prelayoff levels and instead said that seniority took priority.

The Supreme Court in 1976 in *Frank v. Bowman Transportation* approved the use of "retroactive" seniority to increase job opportunities for black truck drivers at the expense of whites in a case where discrimination had been established. "Retroactive" seniority was a new concept; it applied where persons could prove they would have been hired earlier had they not suffered from illegal race or sexual discrimination. Thus, if a minority person had applied and been rejected for a job in 1973 and then had been hired in 1976, seniority rights would have started in 1973, not 1976. Justice Brennan, giving the majority opinion, asserted that if the person was merely awarded a job he should have had earlier, he "will never obtain his rightful place in the hierarchy of seniority. . . . He will perpetually remain subordinate to persons who, but for the illegal discrimination, would have been his inferiors."

Yet in the *Jersey Power* case the courts, at the appeals court level, said in 1975 that antidiscrimination goals could not take precedence over workers' seniority rights. This leaves the whole situation in relation to the seniority system indefinite as of 1977. In general, as Munnell (1978) says, seniority systems have been a major barrier to greater minority employment.

All these issues make one pessimistic about future progress on affirmative action. Yet to say that affirmative action is in the doldrums is wrong. Not only has there been the *Weber* decision, but also the Carter administration in the period 1977–1978 was dedicated to seeing that discrimination complaints were processed faster. By 1978 the national EEOC had cut the backlog of 130,000 complaints sharply. The federal contract compliance programs were also still active: the Department of Labor's program in 1979 announced to Uniroyal that this large government supplier was being debarred from federal contracts because after three years of investigation and litigation Uniroyal was found to have allegedly discriminated against female and minority employees in its Mishawaka, Indiana, plant.

Effectiveness of Affirmative Action Plans on Minority Jobs

Affirmative action plans have attempted to open job opportunities for minorities and to upgrade their wage earnings and occupational status, but in a period of economic recession, the seniority system and contractual wage rigidity, Munnell (1978) concludes, make it hard for affirmative action measures to have much effect. She says that policies under Title VII of the 1964 Act to improve the economic status of minorities should by now have raised the employment and wages of minorities at the expense of white workers. However, she says that, although prime-aged black males have enjoyed some immediate gains, other blacks, such as teenagers, have suffered a steady decline in their labor market position and that even for prime-aged males the recession of the mid-1970s reversed earlier gains. The problem she sees is that while affirmative action has raised wages and promoted the best of the skilled black workers it has not *expanded* employment because of institutional restraints. Employers weren't required to take the part of the black labor force made up of "old-timers" or unskilled, inexperienced teenagers. This situation has put constraints on improving the occupational position of blacks.

Studies on the effects of affirmative action, using EEOC data on firms' hiring and promotions, have given somewhat more positive results. In the massive Burstein study (1979) of EEOC's impact, EEOC was found to have had an independent impact on nonwhite income, although EEOC enforcement and changes in laws, attitudes, and nonwhite education since the mid-1960s all formed a historical package to improve income. These data take into account improved EEOC enforcement since 1972 and show an impact from this. They don't cover the unemployed, a group that increased in 1973 and 1974. Brimmer and others in a large study looking at EEOC data from 1966 to 1973 found that black employment increased at a faster rate in affirmative action firms (21 percent) than for total nonfarm employment (15 percent). Of course, this was before the 1974 recession.

Herbert Hill, the foremost expert on labor laws as they affect black employment, although first pessimistic, by 1977 felt that the years of litigation had begun to turn the tide, so that "by the mid-1970's the impact of the law was evident as court orders began to make the elimination of racial discrimination an economic necessity" (Burstein, 1979, p. 368).

Marshall (1974), again using EEOC data through 1969, found only minor expansion of employment in the South for black females and little for males. Marshall concluded that antidiscrimination laws are a *necessary but not sufficient* factor in improving the black job situation, that for sufficient change to take place programs of job development and training are essential. In another study (Welch 1973) the conclusion was that affirmative action measures stimulated both job training and educational programs because the two together are the key to openings for blacks; the measures helped increase the demand for college-trained blacks.

Job Training Programs

The provision of training can fit the minority worker into the labor market. Since the early 1960s, a variety of off-site and on-site manpower training programs have been introduced. Some are aimed at disadvantaged youth and some at the adult unemployed worker. A few upgrade the worker on the job who already has basic skills. Many are directed at unskilled, inexperienced youth; some combine work opportunities with high school education.

Some, such as the National Youth Conservation Corps or similar state programs or the Job Corps, are run at centers or camps where the trainee works and lives. Most, however, operate in inner-city areas where the enrollees reside, as do the old Youth Opportunity Centers, which give off-the-job training to youths while they live in their own homes. Others are on-the-job training, such as JOBS (in private industry), Neighborhood Youth Corps, and CETA (in public service work), with the latter two putting little emphasis on group training sessions. In some programs using private employers, a monetary incentive is given for taking on the workers. The problem in these cases is that the trainee is not certain of having a job after training is over.

In one program, WIN, participation has been somewhat compulsory for those AFDC recipients deemed employable, unless they have young children or other liabilities.

Training programs often only train youth for low-level jobs, where there may already be a surplus of labor. Also, for many youth even this type of training must be preceded by remedial work to improve basic reading, writing, and math skills. In addition, the trainees often lack the ability to successfully take job tests, to make positive presentations in oral interviews, or to develop basic acceptable job habits.

Emphasis in the 1970s has been more on work experience than training, especially in public-sector jobs. The largest work experience program in the late 1970s was CETA (the Comprehensive Employment and Training Act), whose purpose was to put low-income unemployed persons of all ages into either public service or private jobs; in 1978 about three-fourths of a million persons were in such jobs. As with other such programs, including the large National Youth Conservation Corps, there was a question about how much the workers actually learned skills on the job. They did often at least learn job habits and procedures. And of course, the programs did decrease the number of unemployed persons in the population, as President Carter often testified. The CETA program, however, was often accused of not giving these jobs to the hard-core low-income unemployed but to the "cream" of the unemployed group, including college graduates.

EDUCATIONAL POLICY

School Desegregation

Creating racial balance in the schools has been the major antidiscrimination issue in education. As already shown, this has implied using statistical counts and goals concerning the proportional range of minority students in schools. To achieve this balance, other policy measures, such as busing children, have been implemented. Woodward (1979) says that busing became in the early 1970s the hottest issue of national politics, for suddenly the entire nation, not merely the backward South, "was summoned to sacrifice for integration. . . . The question then arose whether integration was really a worthwhile goal . . . whether it really did anybody any good. . . ." (p. 28).

Some of the earliest desegregation activities and certainly the most controversial and conflict-laden have been school desegregation decisions. In 1954 in *Brown v. the Board of Education* the Supreme Court ruled that separate but equal schools were not in reality equal, since, as the Court said:

> Segregation of white and colored children in public schools has a detrimental effect upon colored children. The impact is greater when it has the sanction of law, for the policy of separating the races is usually interpreted as denoting the inferiority of the Negro group. A form of inferiority affects the motivation of a child to learn. Segregation with the sanction of law, therefore, has a tendency to retard the educational and mental development of Negro children and to deprive them of some of the benefits they would receive in a racially integrated school system.

Before 1954 the *Plessy v. Ferguson* decision of 1896, which said that separate but equal schools and other facilities were in accord with the Fourteenth Amendment to the Constitution, was the guiding policy statement, and seventeen Southern states even required the segregation of the races in public schools.

After the 1954 *Brown* decision changes were slow in coming, partly because this Supreme Court decision was far ahead of public opinion. States and federal district courts acted slowly on litigation; states produced obstructions to desegregation and caused long delays. Only a small proportion of the total black school population was attending integrated schools in the South a decade later. But the 1964 Civil Rights Act (and then the Office of Education guidelines) changed this with its recommended termination of financial assistance if communities and states receiving federal funds refused to comply with desegregation orders.

Mississippi lost a fight in the Supreme Court to delay desegregation; the Court demanded that states move ahead to desegregate with "all deliberate speed." Progress still was slow, but in 1971 the courts directed the schools of Charlotte-Mecklenburg, North Carolina, to do whatever was necessary—including busing children away from their neighborhood school or gerrymandering districts—in order to bring about truly nondiscriminatory assignments (Ravitch, 1979).

Even though many tense situations and temporary conflicts developed, each fall more schools opened as token desegregation facilities; by 1972 the point was reached where well over half the black students in the South were attending schools with some whites. De jure segregation was gone. In fact the situation was better in the South than in the North, where only about one-third of the schools were desegregated (Wilkinson, 1978).

By 1975 some northern schools were actually more segregated (due to residential segregation) than earlier, because many white families with children had fled to the suburbs for a variety of reasons; this was true in such cities as Chicago, Detroit, Baltimore, St. Louis, Washington, D.C., Cleveland, and Philadelphia, to mention only a few. Integration was difficult to accomplish in these cities, since there were so few white children left to take part in integration efforts.

Yet in the late 1960s and the 1970s most big cities had established elaborate desegregation plans to comply with federal demands, a necessity if federal funds for education were to be forthcoming. Most of these plans involved extensive busing of children from one residential area to another to improve the racial and ethnic ratios in the various city schools. In some cases the school district boundaries were changed to make the schools more racially and ethnically balanced; in the past boards of education had often done just the opposite, that is, had drawn school district lines in a way to keep the attending child population homogeneous. Other desegregation plans included turning an entire city school into a school for two or so grades for children from all over the city; thus there might be one ninth-grade or ninth- and tenth-grade school with children coming from all over the city.

Busing caused a great uproar from parents, especially whites. In the South many parents sent their children to private white academies, and in the North and South parents turned to religious schools.

While the opposition was mainly from white parents, there were some minority members who protested, such as the Chinese in San Francisco, who feared the loss of the cultural aspect of the educational system if their children were integrated into schools of other areas; or black parents who disliked having their children bused far away to suffer as isolated, token integrators in white schools. In the same period, in 1967, Pettigrew's reanalysis of the Coleman study of 4000 schools and 600,000 children was showing that black students attending predominantly white schools, when compared with black students with comparable family backgrounds who attended predominantly black schools, had a higher average achievement amounting to more than two grade levels. On the other hand, achievement levels of white students in classes nearly half black in composition were not any lower than those of white students in all-white schools. Because of these findings Coleman and also Pettigrew (1967) supported integration and the use of transportation to achieve it.

While this finding buttressed the United States Commission on Civil Rights' demand for racially balanced schools it did little to change white parents' opposition. Many whites called for the return of neighborhood schools; many moved to the suburbs.

Coleman in 1975, as well as other scholars, turned against busing, saying it caused white flight to the suburbs. However, they also agreed that other factors also caused white flight. Coleman, although reversing his approval of busing following his 1975 findings on desegregation and white flight, pointed out that the loss of white students after desegregation is a one-shot affair, not followed by a continuing, accelerated loss in subsequent years. He says that white flight is occurring anyway but that substantial desegregation does, on the average, hasten the shift of the city to being predominantly black. He adds that the impact is not enormous, simply because it is a one-time acceleration.

Coleman also points out that desegregation effects are much greater when the central city has a high proportion of blacks. As Ravitch (1975) says, studies show that in small cities the effect usually does not seem great, and Giles (1978) shows that when black enrollment after desegregation is under 30 percent, white student withdrawal is low; withdrawal increases exponentially with Black enrollment over 30 percent.

The courts, however, did not abandon their efforts to abide by the 1954 *Brown* decision and end the dual school system that existed in America. In fact the Supreme Court in several cases reiterated that the 1954 decision imposed on school boards a "continuing duty" to eradicate the effects of all official segregation.

In a landmark 1973 Court ruling, the *Keyes* case on Denver schools, the Supreme Court said evidence of *intentional* segregation by the school district need not be proven for all schools but for only a substantial number in the district. If it was found, a presumption was created that other cases of segregation by the district did not occur by chance. This interpretation made it easier for civil rights advocates, who formerly had to prove before winning a case that school segregation was caused by the official actions of some state agency and was not just the result of accident or people's private decisions on where to live.

This 1973 ruling was reaffirmed in the 1979 Supreme Court decisions on the Dayton and Columbus, Ohio, schools. Here the Court said, "Proof of purposeful and effective maintenance of separate Black schools in a *substantial* part of the school system is proof that a *system-wide* remedy is warranted, *unless* the school board can show that other factors were responsible for the dual Black and white system." Evidence of intention in the Columbus case was the school board's conduct. In another 1979 action the Court let stand a lower court decision that Mexican-Americans were intentionally discriminated against by the Austin, Texas, school board.

These 1979 Court rulings, which gave federal judges broad powers to order desegregation, followed a period (1973 to 1978) when most of the conservative Supreme Court's decisions had been to limit the power of the judges to order desegregation. In fact, in this 1979 Columbus decision, Justice Powell, in dissenting, said that "the opinions . . . seem remarkably insensitive to the now widely accepted view that a quarter of a century after Brown v. the Board of Education, the federal judiciary should be limiting rather than expanding the extent to which courts are operating the public school systems of our country." With a basically conservative Supreme Court one cannot predict whether the next decision will be closer to the opinions of those wishing to limit affirmative action, as in the Bakke case, or those pushing for its extension.

Decisions supporting some degree of limitation have occurred in relation to desegregation plans across city boundaries. Areawide city-suburban school integration plans came before the Court in two cases, in relation to Detroit, Michigan, and Richmond, Virginia, where two-thirds of the public school pupils were Negro, so that the plaintiffs argued that "local, state and federal policies resulted in out-migration of whites from the central cities, a piling up of Blacks in the city and the general exclusion of Blacks from the suburbs." Busing of students within these cities was seen as ineffective in eliminating racially segregated schools.

(In fact, advocates of busing, such as Pettigrew in the mid-1970s, only now saw hope in metropolitan or multidistrict busing.)

This litigation argument led federal Judge Merhige in Richmond and Judge Roth in Detroit to order cross-district busing to effect integration, according to Hermalin and Farley (1973). In 1974 the Supreme Court reversed the ruling on the Detroit plan in which fifty-four school districts in the Detroit metropolitan area would have been consolidated in an effort to remedy discrimination in the city of Detroit with the busing of children between districts. The Supreme Court in Milliken v. Bradley ruled that a federal judge could not impose a multidistrict, areawide plan to remedy desegregation in a single district where there was no proof that the other districts had discriminated. Justice Thurgood Marshall called this a giant step backward, a second Reconstruction period. Many felt this ruling meant that the Supreme Court might bar judges from imposing interdistrict remedies in discrimination cases. However, in a Court case in regard to low-cost housing, in 1976, the Court said that because a federal agency had caused the discrimination it could be ordered to place such housing in the suburbs to relieve racial segregation. On school desegregation through busing across city lines in 1979 the ruling is still negative.

At this writing opponents of busing are achieving success on other fronts. In California a proposal to ban state court-ordered busing was voted on in the November 1979 elections and won. In Congress a constitutional ban on court-ordered busing was working its way through committees in 1979. At the same time, school districts in serious financial trouble across the nation were bothered that court-ordered busing was a major budget item. The Chicago School Board in 1979, in fact, used the cost of busing as a defense against carrying out the desegregation plan the government demanded.

While all this indicates a negative attitude by many whites in 1979, it should not indicate government abandonment of desegregation efforts. Besides the Supreme Court's positive 1979 decisions, the Justice Department was investigating ten cities in the North and West as possible targets of school desegregation suits.

Another federal agency, the Department of Health, Education, and Welfare, was using another technique, denying funds to school boards that refused to develop desegregation plans or redistribute teachers to achieve racial balance in faculties. For example, in the school year 1976–1977, HEW ordered twelve of the country's largest school systems, including New York, Los Angeles, and Chicago, to transfer large numbers of white teachers to predominantly black schools and a fair number of black teachers to white schools.

In 1979 the Chicago school system was still slow in taking the needed steps to end segregation, and HEW threatened to take away $100 million in federal funds and turn the case over to the Justice Department if it did not come up with an acceptable, comprehensive desegregation plan. HEW, backed up by evidence in a 102-page document, said that school board action fostered segregation by a number of strategies, including location of schools, establishment of school boundaries to follow racial residential patterns, and assignment of teachers. HEW also said that the board put mobile units in black schools to alleviate overcrowding instead of putting black students in nearby white schools where there were empty classrooms. The rebuttal of the Chicago school superintendent was that segregation was due to housing patterns. HEW also complained that Chicago's voluntary school transfer system had so many restrictions that in some cases it served to promote segregated schools rather than eliminate them and added that whites were sometimes allowed to use the plan to escape integrated schools. The Chicago board was ordered by HEW to come up with a better plan, but interestingly, it was not told it must use citywide busing or racial quotas to accomplish integration. It will not be an easy job for Chicago to find a workable solution, since the white school-aged population is low and any desegregation move will likely mean more white flight to the suburbs (although white flight is shown, by studies, to be due also to other reasons).

In the long run a more workable solution will likely have to be desegregation of the suburbs. If residential housing segregation can be decreased, as Hermalin and Farley (1973) propose, a more permanent school desegregation may occur. However, even less progress has been made in opening up the suburbs than in school desegregation.

One cannot help but be pessimistic. On the twenty-fifth anniversary of the historic 1954 Supreme Court *Brown* decision, in 1979, Linda Brown-Smith, who, as Linda Brown, had been the key student plaintiff, was planning to file an antidiscrimination suit on behalf of her two children because, as her lawyer said, "things in the schools in Topeka, Kansas, are as bad now as they were in 1954. Many schools don't have Black teachers, and others have nearly all Black student bodies." This lawyer, Joseph Johnson, added, "The Topeka school officials just haven't lived up to the law" ("U.S. Marks Anniversary," May 19, 1979).

Affirmative Action in the Universities

Preferential admission policies have been the main issue in the universities. Before *Bakke,* much had occurred. Racial integration at the university level was an issue in the late 1960s and early 1970s. Most Southern states had few Negroes in their prestigious public universities; there were separate institutions of higher learning for Negroes. Major integration fights were carried on at such universities as the University of Mississippi and the University of Alabama. Minority recruitment was demanded by students in Northern and Western universities in order to increase the token representation then found in such schools.

Title VI of the 1964 Civil Rights Act demanded that there be affirmative action programs if institutions of higher learning were to continue receiving federal funds.

Many universities made special efforts to recruit minority students, setting up goals and quotas for numbers of minority students as well as timetables to meet such goals. Under special programs minority students with lower test scores and grades than the average entrant were often conditionally admitted. Some universities held special summer sessions for minority freshman entrants. The universities provided financial help and work-study opportunities to those from low-income minority families. Some universities did heavy recruiting in minority schools to try to attract high achievers to their institutions.

Of course, much more intensive recruiting had long been practiced to attract minority athletes to Ivy League universities. Harvard's search for a *diverse* student population was a policy supported in the *Bakke* admissions case; the condemned specific quotas were not involved. Brown University's recruitment technique was to send a letter to everyone with fairly high College Board scores in certain urban ghetto areas. In selecting a diverse student body, Brown included in its admitted group a number of these minority applicants, even some who were risks in their potential for high college grades. These changes in Ivy League admissions policies mean a remarkable change in minorities' representation at colleges.

However, in the future, minorities' student numbers at Ivy League schools may decrease, for with their financial problems private colleges may no longer be able to take lower-income students but only those who can pay the high tuitions. In fact in 1979 black students at such universities were demonstrating about such matters as the lowering of urban ghetto recruitment efforts, the decrease in financial assistance, and the lack of interest in funding black studies and in minority faculty recruitment. These universities, with their financial crisis, were accused of abandoning a decade-old commitment to black students. While the *Bakke* decision did not forbid recruitment and upheld racial preferences, the general climate for affirmative action was a cooled one.

Everywhere there was indication of a lessening of interest and even a white backlash. Few white students were old enough in the 1960s to understand the civil rights movement or to be knowledgeable about the degree to which minorities had been denied equal education up to that point in history. Therefore compensatory affirmative action for past discrimination, through special minority admission policies, had little meaning to this young white student group and was often resented.

Fair Housing

Fair housing policies can open up the suburbs and all-white areas of the city. This will increase the integration of suburban schools and decrease the worry about the lack of employment opportunities for some minority members.

Policy measures have included trying to reduce housing discrimination in rental and sale of homes, discouraging realtors both from excluding minorities from certain housing markets and from blockbusting, or turning certain housing markets to nonintegrated minority areas. Policy has also been directed at lenders, both in prohibiting discrimination in lending and in pressuring for positive actions by them. HUD also has tried to educate and pressure realtors.

There are also HUD policies to encourage communities to take subsidized housing by offering them additional community block grants and other subsidies.

Another policy of HUD is increasing its vigilance to see that subsidized housing is both integrated and placed outside segregated areas and to see that federally insured housing is open to minority groups.

Another policy direction is to provide federal funds in inner-city areas for improving the quality of life in the ghetto. These funds include grants for rehabilitation programs, urban initiatives programs to bring industry into the inner city, and various area improvement grants.

The most important government directives on integration of housing were the 1964 Civil Rights Act and, even more, the 1968 Civil Rights Act, as well as Executive orders. They were needed because segregation in housing is still very high in the United States. Ghettos still exist, and the suburbs are still over 90 percent white. The blame cannot be put on the supposed inability of minorities to afford suburban house prices, since many black households as well as a number of other minority households do have sufficient income to afford suburban housing, as Hermalin and Farley (1973) proved. The situation is blamed to a fair degree on the discriminatory practices of the real estate industry and the lending institutions that bar blacks and other minority groups from entry into the suburbs and white city areas.

The major policy statements encouraging nondiscrimination include, first, President John Kennedy's 1962 Executive Order No. 11063, which mandated that the federal government "take all action necessary and appropriate to prevent discrimination because of race, color, creed or national origin in the sale, leasing, rental of federally subsidized or insured housing." The Civil Rights Act of 1964 reiterated this, but the Civil Rights Act of 1968 went far beyond coverage of subsidized housing, and it was strengthened again by the amendments in the Housing and Community Development Act of 1974. Title VIII, the Fair Housing provision of the 1968 Civil Rights Act, gave protection against the following acts, if they were based on race, color, religion, sex, or national origin:

1 Refusing to sell or rent to, deal or negotiate with any person
2 Discriminating in the terms or conditions for buying or renting housing
3 Practicing discrimination by advertising that stated housing is available only to certain groups
4 Denying that housing is available for inspection, sale, or rent when it really is available
5 Blockbusting for profit, that is, persuading owners to sell or rent housing by telling them that minority groups are moving into the neighborhood

The 1968 Act also prohibits commercial lenders, such as banks and savings and loan associations, from making different terms or conditions for home loans. It prohibits denying the use of or participation in any real estate service, such as broker organizations, multiple listing services, or other facilities. The law does not apply to the owner who sells the single-family dwelling he or she lives in. State legislation, where it exists, is often similar, with regional variations.

State agencies, rather than HUD, often handle claims of discrimination in private housing. For example, the California Fair Employment Practice Commission (FEPC) is one; the state agency has a number of legal powers, such as demanding rental and related records and interviewing residents in the building to compare the rental arrangements of different tenants. If the FEPC finds that discrimination has taken place in renting, it can demand that the landlord rent to a particular applicant or pay a fine or whatever "compromise" amount the complainant is willing to accept.

The California FEPC also can take the more formal route of conducting hearings, with subpoenaed witnesses. It can send cases to the Superior Court because of inaction. However, all these formal actions are seldom taken. Nor does the FEPC do "testing," that is, sending potential black renters and then whites to a building in which discrimination is alleged to have occurred. Nonprofit agencies are more likely to do both this and a general annual audit to see what degree of discrimination there is in an area and by what type of landlord; the Palo Alto, California, Fair Housing agency, for example, does this with the cooperation of many community groups, including realtors' and apartment owners' associations.

These nonprofit groups as well as public bodies try to educate the public in providing fair housing. HUD and state FEPCs publicize the antidiscriminatory provisions of the laws and advertise the method for making complaints.

As with complaints against discrimination in employment, the government agencies acting under the law to process fair housing complaints have somewhat of a backlog.

Another area where antidiscriminatory policies can be applied is in the area of sales and mortgages under FHA- and VA-insured mortgage programs. Actually in the past the government did just the opposite: it encouraged discriminatory practices.

Federal urban policies in the postwar period actually accelerated segregation. Many early postwar tract developments had housing with FHA- and VA-insured mortgages (see Chapter 12). Such federal insurance of mortgages encouraged lending institutions to give out mortgages to working-class families and to back developers of large suburban tracts. However, in the early postwar days FHA guidelines recommended that such tracts should be "homogeneous" communities; a mixture of racial groups in neighborhoods was considered a greater financial risk. Such guidelines meant most Negro households did not get FHA-insured mortgages. This was admitted in a 1974 U.S. Civil Rights Commission report, which, in reviewing early postwar FHA actions, stated:

> Residential segregation of racial minorities was and is another characteristic of the social environment which has been influenced by federal housing policy. Until 1949 FHA officially sanctioned and perpetuated community patterns of residential segregation based on race by refusing to insure mortgages in neighborhoods not racially homogeneous. [P. 36]

Besides discouraging black participation in the FHA program, at least through the 1950s, and thus forgoing a chance to integrate the early suburban tracts, this type of housing policy, insuring new tract housing units, actually greatly encouraged white families to leave the city. If instead the government had subsidized central-city apartment construction or rents, as was done in Great Britain, the white exodus to the suburbs and the "blackening" of the central cities would have been much slower.

The federal government's postwar transportation program also encouraged the white exodus to the suburbs.

Today FHA makes much more of an effort to be an open-housing advocate, advertising FHA-insured mortgages as open-housing assistance. FHA is now less involved in suburban single-family dwellings, insuring a much smaller proportion of all suburban purchases than in 1960, and more involved in inner-city housing, including multiple-family units. In 1971 FHA was forced to use HUD fair housing marketing guidelines and to have developers working with FHA submit affirmative advertising plans to reach minorities.

HUD in Washington in 1977, under a black Cabinet-level Secretary, Patricia Harris, and a black Assistant Secretary for Fair Housing, Chester McQuire, Jr., was proceeding to monitor subsidy programs more to see that the fair housing law was enforced. HUD was putting more pressure on lending institutions. HUD, according to Secretary Harris, was also telling cities that would not accept their fair share of low- and moderate-income housing that these cities would no longer receive Community Development Block Grant funds. HUD was also offering cities and suburbs that did work together to provide housing for low- and moderate-income people the bonus of Block Grant discretionary funds, 701 Planning funds, and Section 8 subsidized housing assistance, Harris (1977) reports.

Public opinion has in general been against siting either public housing or moderate-income Section 236 nonprofit rental housing in middle-class areas, and especially suburban areas. Local voter referendums are necessary to enable a public housing authority to build a specific number of public housing units in an area; in suburban communities the vote has often been against such building of public housing except when it is housing for the elderly. Such a vote is not necessary on the Section 8 leased public housing program because recipients themselves are leasing privately owned units and then receiving a rent subsidy from the housing authority.

This program has had somewhat more success in placing recipients, including a few minority families and elderly, in suburban and middle-class areas. However, one study showed that minorities under the Section 8 program usually stayed in segregated areas, although often on the fringe.

One major program directed at minority households, the HUD conventional public housing program, has helped to perpetuate the segregation of minorities in inner-city areas. Most public housing projects, until the last decade, have had segregated populations of either white or minority groups (sometimes several minorities) rather than integrated populations of whites and minorities. The siting of many projects was in racially segregated areas.

Protests against such public housing segregation finally culminated in court actions, such as *Shannon et al. v. HUD* in 1970. The court demanded priority be accorded to siting subsidized projects *outside* racially segregated areas. A later court decision in 1973 even allowed HUD to put public housing in white areas beyond the city limits, in this case Chicago *(Gautreaux v. Chicago Housing Authority).* In 1976 the Supreme Court supported this decision of decreasing racial segregation and said that where a federal agency (in this case a housing authority) had been found guilty of segregative practices in violation of the Constitution, the federal government could be ordered to provide such low-cost public housing in the suburbs. The Supreme Court added that to limit relief to Chicago proper would be a shield for an agency found guilty of segregation.

The Section 8 leased housing program does counsel clients on how to deal with discrimination when hunting for housing and explains the clients' rights in such cases. It also helps to work with landlords around discriminatory practices in some areas or cooperate with fair housing groups in the area over the issue. Such groups, as well as housing authorities, compile lists of landlords who will rent to minorities under the Section 8 program.

Rehabilitation, neighborhood conservation, and industrial revitalization in central cities has now become another major policy to serve minority citizens, to improve the ghettos in which they live.

Early federally financed urban renewal projects in the 1950s were often called "Negro removal" programs, because the areas demolished were mainly ghetto areas of cheap, substandard rental housing. Land was often left vacant several years and then developed for high-income nondiscriminatory rentals or commercial use. This left low-income black families with fewer rental units in the city; however, it did allow some middle-income blacks to move into the newer units.

Because of severe criticism, by the mid-1960s the urban renewal program changed to include some moderate-income housing and some public housing; more minorities then found housing in these urban renewal units. The change in the program from demolition to rehabilitation has had varied effects on minority members. Since rents often have gone up after rehabilitation of units, low-income minority families have been forced to look elsewhere for housing rather than return to rehabilitated units, unless the tenants got in under the Section 8 program.

HUD also embarked in 1977 on educational efforts to fulfill the goal of Secretary Harris of developing "strategies to increase the housing choices available to low income and minority families." One 1977 educational effort was the National Conference on Voluntary Concepts in Support of Fair Housing, with 700 fair housing advocates and government and industry personnel present.

In 1977 HUD also negotiated a national fair housing program and a lawsuit settlement with the American Institute of Real Estate Appraisers. Negotiations for a fair housing program were also under way in 1977 with the National Association of Real Estate License Law Officials, according to Harris (1977).

Yet, with all this HUD activity, one must keep in mind the fact that past efforts have had little success. As reported earlier, very few blacks live in the suburbs and those who do are usually in segregated areas of the suburbs. In the cities blacks as well as other minorities still live in ghetto areas, and as more white families migrate to the suburbs the concentration becomes greater. Thus, while the Kerner Commission (1968) talks of the need to end the situation of two separate Americas, black and white, and such experts as Anthony Downs point out that it is imperative to open up the suburbs, one is pessimistic about the prospects for the future. As Wallace (1977) sums it up, "While these recent policies may retard residential segregation in the future, they leave unaffected the consequences of past housing discrimination" (p. 353). And a 1973 federal report on national housing policy states, "The significance of the contribution of subsidized housing is small in comparison to the amount of racial imbalance that exists."

Some optimists say that as the incomes of minority families increase they will be able to move to the suburbs and live in integrated areas, but after analysis of the findings of the mammoth Urban Stimulation Model study, Straszheim (1973) reports, "In short, increases in Black family income in the context of a continued segregated market . . . will not solve the housing problems of blacks" (p. 2–3). Major changes are needed in the real estate industry's and lending institutions' practices. Policies must be devised that get at the roots of these massive problems.

References

Aaron, Henry. *Shelter and Subsidies: Who Benefits from Federal Housing Policies.* Washington, D.C.: Brookings, 1972.

Abbott, Grace. *The Child and the State.* Chicago: University of Chicago Press, 1938.

Abel-Smith, Brian. *Labour's Social Plans.* London: Fabian Society, 1966.

Abrams, Charles. "The Housing Problem and the Negro," *Daedalus,* Winter 1965, pp. 64–76.

Adams, Paul. "Social Control or Social Wage?" *Journal of Sociology and Social Welfare,* Vol. 5, No. 1, January 1978, pp. 46–54.

Addams, Jane. *Twenty Years at Hull House.* New York: New American Library, 1961.

Adequacy of Federal Response to Housing Needs of Older Americans, Hearings before the Senate Special Committee on Aging, 94th Congress, 1st Session, October 1975, pts. 13 and 14.

"Affirmative Action Ruling: Supreme Court Upholds Racial Quotas in Hiring." *San Francisco Chronicle,* June 28, 1979.

"Americans Change: How Drastic Shifts in Demographics Affect the Economy." *Business Week,* Feb. 20, 1978, p. 66.

Ashenfelter, Orley, and James Heckman. *Measuring the Effect of an Antidiscrimination Program.* Princeton, N.J.: Industrial Relations, Working Paper No. 52, Princeton University, 1968.

Atherton, Charles. "Growing Up Obscene: The By-product of Life on AFDC." *Public Welfare,* October 1969, pp. 371–374.

Audain, Michael, and Elizabeth Huttman. *Beyond Shelter: A Study of NHA-Financed Housing for the Elderly.* Ottawa, Canada: Canadian Council on Social Development, 1973, pp. 304–306, 334–335.

Austin, Michael, Alexis H. Skelding, and Philip L. Smith. *Delivering Human Services.* New York: Harper & Row, 1977.

Axinn, J., and H. Levin. *Social Welfare: A History of the American Response.* New York: Dodd, Mead, 1975.

Bakan, David. "Adolescence in America: From Idea to Social Fact." *Daedalus,* Fall 1971, p. 981.

Barth, Michael C., George J. Carcagno, and John L. Palmer. *Toward an Effective Income Support System: Problems, Prospects, and Choices.* Madison: University of Wisconsin Institute for Research on Poverty, 1974.

Beck, Bertram M. "The Voluntary Social Welfare Agency: A Reassessment." *Social Service Review,* Vol. 44, No. 2, June 1970, pp. 147–154.

Bengtson, Vern L. *The Social Psychology of Aging.* Indianapolis: Bobbs-Merrill, 1973.

Bennis, Warren G., Kenneth D. Benne, and Robert Chin (eds.). *The Planning of Change.* New York: Holt, Rinehart and Winston, 1961, 2d ed. 1969.

Bentrup, W. C. "What's Wrong with the Means Test?" *Public Welfare,* Vol. 23, October 1965, pp. 235–242.

Berger, Raymond, and Irving Pillavin. "The Effect of Casework: A Research Note." *Social Work,* May 1976, pp. 205–208.

Beveridge, William H. *Social Insurance and Allied Services.* New York: Macmillan, 1942.

Beyer, Glenn H. *Housing and Society.* New York: Macmillan, 1965.

Billingsley, Andrew. "Review of *Affirmative Discrimination* by Nathan Glazer." *Contemporary Sociology,* Vol. 6, No. 5, September 1977, pp. 537–539.

——— and Jeanne Giovanonni. *Children of the Storm.* New York: Random House, 1971.

Birch, M. Bruce. *The Coming of the Welfare State.* London: Batsford, 1961.

Blaug, M., H. D. Hughes, and Bleddyn Davies. *Social Services for All?* Part Two. London: Fabian Society, 1968.

"Bleak Job Outlook for Young Blacks." *San Francisco Chronicle,* Nov. 11, 1977.

Boulding, Kenneth. "The Boundaries of Social Policy." *Social Work,* Vol. 12, No. 1, January 1971, p. 7.

Bradshaw, J. "The Concept of Social Need." In Neil Gilbert and Harry Specht (eds.), *Planning for Social Welfare.* Englewood Cliffs, N.J.: Prentice-Hall, 1977.

Branch, Taylor. "Who's in Charge Now?" *Harper's Weekly,* May 16, 1975, p. 13.

Briar, Scott. "Why Children's Allowances?" *Social Work,* Vol. 14, No. 1, January 1969, pp. 5–12.

Brimmer, Andrew. *Widening Horizons: Prospect for Black Employment.* May 5, 1974.

Brody, Elaine. "Long-Term Care: The Decision Making Process and Individual

Assessment." In *Human Factors in Long-Term Care.* Report to institute, National Conference on Social Welfare, San Francisco, May 1975.

Brody, Jane. "Doctors Study Treatment of Ills Brought On by Stress." *New York Times,* June 10, 1973.

Bruce, M. *The Coming of the Welfare State.* London: Batsford, 1961.

Buckley, Walter. *Sociology and the Modern Systems Theory.* Englewood Cliffs, N.J.: Prentice-Hall, 1971.

Burgess, M. Elaine, and Daniel O. Price. *An American Dependency Challenge.* Chicago: American Public Welfare Association, 1963.

Burns, Eveline M. *Social Security and Public Policy.* New York: McGraw-Hill, 1956.

Burstein, Paul. "EEO Legislation and the Income of Women and Non-Whites." *American Sociological Review,* Vol. 44, No. 3, June 1979, pp. 367–391.

Cafferty, Pastora San Juan, and Leon Chestang (eds.). *The Diverse Society: Implications for Social Policy.* Washington, D.C.: National Association of Social Workers, 1976.

Charlton, Linda. "2 to 1 Turndown of Minorities for Mortgage Loans." *New York Times,* July 26, 1975.

Chiswick, Barry R., and June A. O'Neill (eds.). *Human Resources and Income Distribution: Issues and Policies.* New York: Norton, 1977.

"Civil Rights Victory on School Integration." *San Francisco Chronicle,* July 3, 1979.

Clark, Kenneth. *Dark Ghetto: Dilemmas of Social Power.* New York: Harper & Row, 1965.

Cloward, Richard, and Irwin Epstein. "Private Social Welfare's Disengagement from the Poor: The Case of Family Adjustment Agencies." In Mayer Zald (ed.), *Social Welfare Institutions.* New York: Wiley, 1965, pp. 628–629.

——— and Lloyd E. Ohlin. *Delinquency and Opportunity: A Theory of Delinquent Gangs.* New York: Free Press, 1960.

Cohen, Wilbur. "Social Insurance." *Encyclopedia of Social Work, 1977.* New York: National Association of Social Workers, 1977, pp. 1363–1364.

Coleman, James. *Equality of Educational Opportunity.* Washington, D.C.: Government Printing Office, 1966.

———, Sara D. Kelly, and John Moore. *Trends in School Segregation 1968–1973.* Washington, D.C.: Urban Institute, 1975.

Commager, Henry Steele. *The American Mind.* New Haven: Yale, 1950.

Compton, Beulah, and Burt Galaway. *Social Work Processes.* Homewood, Ill.: Dorsey, 1979.

Conant, James. *Slums and Suburbs.* New York: McGraw-Hill, 1961.

Costain, Lela. *Child Welfare,* 2d ed. New York: McGraw-Hill, 1979.

Cottrell, Fred. *Aging and the Aged.* Dubuque, Iowa: Wm. C. Brown Co., 1974, p. 8.

Coven, Irving. "Section 8 Existing Housing Program." *Journal of Housing,* Vol. 34, No. 2, February 1977, pp. 84–85.

Cummings, Elaine, and William Henry. *Growing Old.* New York: Basic Books, 1961.

Curry, Timothy, and Bascom Ratliff. "The Effects of Nursing Home Size on Resident Isolation and Life Satisfaction." *The Gerontologist,* Vol. 13, No. 3, August 1973, pp. 295–298.

Cutright, Phillips. "AFDC, Family Allowance and Illegitimacy." *Family Planning Perspectives,* Vol. 2, No. 4, October 1970, pp. 4–9.

Davis, Kingsley, and Wilbert E. Moore. "Some Principles of Stratification." *American Sociological Review,* Vol. 10, April 1945.

Derthick, Martha. *Policy Making for Social Security.* Washington, D.C.: Brookings, 1979.

"Dilemma for Working Mothers: Not Enough Day-Care Centers." *U.S. News and World Report,* Apr. 12, 1976, pp. 49–50.

Donnison, David. *An Approach to Social Policy.* Dublin, Ireland: National Economic and Social Council, The Stationery Office, Dublin, 1975.

Douglas Commission. See National Commission on Urban Problems 1968.

Douthit, Jim. "Juvenile Courts Have Adult Safeguards." *Oakland Tribune,* Oct. 11, 1976.

Downs, Anthony. *Urban Problems and Prospects,* 2d ed. Chicago, Rand McNally, 1976.

Duhl, Leonard (ed.). *The Urban Condition.* New York: Basic Books, 1963.

Dye, Thomas. *Understanding Public Policy.* Englewood Cliffs, N.J.: Prentice-Hall, 1972.

Edwards, Harry, and Barry Zaretsky. "Preferential Remedies for Employment Discrimination." *Michigan Law Review,* November 1975.

Elling, Ray H., and Sandor Halebsky. "Support for Public and Private Services." In Mayer Zald (ed.), *Social Welfare Institutions.* New York: Wiley, 1965, p. 329.

Empey, LeMar, and Lubeck, with Ronald LaPorte. *Explaining Delinquency.* Lexington, Mass.: Heath, Lexington, 1971.

Fanshel, David. "Status Changes of Children in Foster Care: Final Results of the Columbia University Longitudinal Study." *Child Welfare,* Vol. 55, No. 3, March 1976, p. 165.

——— and Eugene Shinn. *Children in Foster Care.* New York: Columbia, 1977.

Farley, Reynolds. "Trends in Racial Inequalities: Have the Gains of the 1960's Disappeared in the 1970's?" *American Sociological Journal,* Vol. 42, 1977, pp. 189–208.

———. "White Flight to Suburbs Not Caused by Busing." *Information: Quarterly Journal of National Institute of Education,* Fall 1975, p. 1.

Fischer, Joel. "Is Casework Effective? A Review." *Social Work,* Vol. 18, January 1973, pp. 5–20.

Fodor, Anthony. "Social Work and Systems Theory." In Beulah Compton and Burt Galaway (eds.), *Social Work Processes,* rev. ed. Homewood, Ill.: Dorsey, 1979.

Freedman, Leonard. *Public Housing: The Politics of Poverty.* New York: Holt, Rinehart and Winston, 1972.

Freeman, Howard, and Clarence Sherwood. *Social Research and Social Policy.* Englewood Cliffs, N.J.: Prentice-Hall, 1970.

Friedlander, Walter, and Robert Z. Apte. *Introduction to Social Welfare,* 4th ed. Englewood Cliffs, N.J.: Prentice-Hall, 1974.

Friedman, B., and Leonard Hausman. *Work and Welfare Patterns in Low Income Families.* Waltham, Mass.: Brandeis University, June 1975.

Fuchs, Victor R. "Redefining Poverty and Redistributing Income." *The Public Interest,* No. 8, Summer 1967, pp. 88–95.

Galbraith, John Kenneth. *The Affluent Society.* Boston: Houghton Mifflin, 1958.

———. *The New Industrial State.* Boston: Houghton Mifflin, 1967.

Gale, Dennis. "Dislocation of Residents." *Journal of Housing,* Vol. 35, No. 5, May 1978, pp. 232–235.

Gallagher, Ursula. "Adoptions: Current Trends." *Welfare in Review,* Vol. 5, No. 2, February 1967, p. 13.

Galper, Jeffrey. *The Politics of Social Services.* Englewood Cliffs, N.J.: Prentice-Hall, 1975.

Gemignani, Robert. "Youth Services Systems." In U.S. Department of Health, Education, and Welfare, Youth Development and Delinquency Prevention Administration, *Delinquency Prevention Reporter,* July–August 1970.

Gil, David. "Incidence of Child Abuse and Demographic Characteristics of Persons Involved." In Ray E. Helfer and C. Henry Kempe (eds.), *The Battered Child.* Chicago: University of Chicago Press.

——— *Unraveling Social Policy.* Cambridge, Mass.: Schenkman, 1973.

Gilbert, Bentley B. *The Evolution of National Insurance in Great Britain: The Origins of the Welfare State.* London: Michael Joseph, 1966.

Gilbert, Neil, and Harry Specht. *Dimensions of Social Welfare Policy.* Englewood Cliffs, N.J.: Prentice-Hall, 1974.

——— and ———. *The Emergence of Social Welfare and Social Work.* Itasca, Ill.: Peacock, 1976.

Giles, Michael. "White Enrollment Stability." *American Sociological Review,* Vol. 43, No. 6, December 1978, pp. 848–864.

Glazer, Nathan. *Affirmative Discrimination.* Cambridge, Mass.: Harvard, 1975.

Goodhue, Carol. "Once Abused, Can Children Ever Return Home?" *Fremont Argus,* June 6, 1976, p. 6.

Goodlett, Carlton. "The Crisis of Youth and Adult Responsibility." *Black Scholar,* Vol. 10, No. 5, January–February 1979, pp. 19–30.

Goodman, Norman, and Gary Marx. *Society Today,* 3d ed. New York: Random House, 1978.

Gould, Martin. "Crime and Delinquency: Control and Prevention." In *Encyclopedia of Social Work.* New York: National Association of Social Workers, 1971, p. 173.

Gouldner, Alvin. "Theoretical Requirements of the Applied Social Sciences." In Milton Barron (ed.), *Contemporary Sociology.* New York: Dodd, Mead, 1964, pp. 640–653.

Greenleigh Associates. *Public Welfare: Poverty, Prevention, or Perpetuation.* New York, 1969.

Griswold, Barbara, Kermit T. Wiltse, and Robert W. Roberts. "Illegitimacy Recidivism Among AFDC Clients." In *Unmarried Parenthood: Clues to*

Agency and Community Action. New York: National Council on Illegitimacy, 1967.

Haggstrom, Warren C. "The Power of the Poor." In Frank Riessman, Jerome Cohen, and Arthur Pearl (eds.), *Mental Health of the Poor.* New York: Free Press, 1964, pp. 205–226.

Hall, M. P. *The Social Services of Modern England.* London: Routledge, 1955.

Hamilton, Gordon. "The Role of Social Casework in Social Policy." *Social Casework,* Vol. 33, No. 8, October 1952.

Handler, J. F., and E. J. Hollingsworth. *The Deserving Poor: A Study of Welfare Administration.* New York: Academic Press, 1971.

Handlin, Oscar. *The Americans: A New History of the People of the United States.* Boston: Little, Brown, 1963.

Harris, Patricia Roberts. "HUD's 'Urban Initiatives' Announced at NHC Meeting." *Journal of Housing,* Vol. 35, No. 5, May 1978, pp. 214–215.

———. "A New Look at HUD." *Black Scholar,* October 1977, pp. 15–21.

Hartley, Shirley. "American Women as a 'Minority.' " Paper presented at World Congress of Sociology, Toronto, 1974.

Hartman, Chester. *Housing and Social Policy.* Englewood Cliffs, N.J.: Prentice-Hall, 1975.

Haskell, Martin R., and Lewis Yablonsky. *Juvenile Delinquency,* 2d ed. Chicago: Rand McNally, 1978.

Hausman, Leonard. "The Impact of Welfare on the Work Effort of AFDC Mothers." *Technical Studies,* Washington, D.C.: Government Printing Office, 1970, pp. 83–100.

Haveman, Robert (ed.). *A Decade of Federal Antipoverty Programs.* New York: Academic Press, 1977.

Hawley, Amos H., and Vincent P. Rock (eds.). *Segregation in Residential Areas.* Washington, D.C.: National Academy of Sciences, 1973.

Hayes, Edward. *Power Structure and Urban Policy: Who Rules Oakland?* New York: McGraw-Hill, 1972.

Hayward, California, City of, Needs Assessment Committee. *Social Needs Assessment, Summary, 1978.*

Heckman, James, and Kenneth Wolpin. "Does the Contract Compliance Program Work?" *Industrial and Labor Relations Review,* Vol. 29, 1976, pp. 544–564.

Heilbroner, Robert. "Benign Neglect in the United States." In John Tropman et al. (eds.), *Strategic Perspectives on Social Policy.* New York: Pergamon, 1976.

———. *The Limits of American Capitalism.* New York: Harper & Row, 1965.

Hermalin, Albert, and Reynolds Farley. "The Potential for Residential Integration in Cities and Suburbs: Implications for the Busing Controversy." *American Sociological Review,* Vol. 38, No. 5, October 1973, pp. 595–610.

"High Court Backs a Preference Plan for Blacks." *New York Times,* June 28, 1979.

Hill, Herbert. "Black Labor and the American Legal System." *Race, Work and the Law,* Vol. 1, Washington, D.C.: BNA, 1977.

Hill, Octavia. *Homes of the London Poor.* London: Macmillan, 1883.

Hoffman, Saul. "Bleak Job Outlook for Young Blacks." *San Francisco Chronicle,* Nov. 11, 1977.

Hohaus, Richard. "Equity, Adequacy and Related Factors in Old Age Security." In William Haber and Wilbur Cohen (eds.), *Social Security: Programs, Problems and Policies*. Homewood, Ill.: Irwin, 1960, p. 61.

Hoshino, George. "Britain's Debate on Universal or Selective Social Services: Lessons for America." *Social Service Review*, Vol. 43, No. 3, September 1969, p. 249.

Howard, Donald G. *Social Welfare: Values, Means, Ends*. New York: Random House, 1969.

"HUD-Funded Tenant Management Corporations Projects Progress in Six Cities." *Journal of Housing*, Vol. 33, No. 10, November 1976, pp. 510–511.

Hunger, USA. Report of a Citizens' Board of Inquiry, Washington, D.C.: New Community Press, 1968.

Hunter, David R. *The Slums: Challenge and Response*. New York: Free Press, 1964.

Huttman, Elizabeth. *Housing and Social Services for the Elderly*. New York: Praeger, 1977. ´

Investigation and Hearings of Abuses in Federal Low and Moderate Income Housing Programs. House Committee on Banking and Currency, 91st Congress, 2d session, December 1970.

Johnson, Haynes. "One Man Who's Going to Vote This Time." San Francisco *Sunday Examiner & Chronicle*, Oct. 24, 1978.

Jones, Terry. "The Police in America: A Black Viewpoint." *Black Scholar*, October 1977, pp. 22–38.

Jordan, Vernon. "A Question of Commitment: The Black Urban Crisis and the Carter Administration." *Black Scholar*, October 1977, pp. 1–9.

Kadushin, Albert. *Child Welfare Service*, 2d ed. New York: Macmillan, 1974.

Kahn, Alfred. *Planning Community Services for Children in Trouble*. New York: Columbia, 1963.

———. *Social Policy and Social Services*. New York: Random House, 1973.

——— and Sheila Kamerman. *Not for the Poor Alone: European Social Services*. Philadelphia: Temple University Press, 1975.

Kain, John, and John M. Quigley. *Housing Markets and Racial Discrimination: A Microeconomic Analysis*. New York: Columbia, 1975.

Katz, Arnold J. "Problems Inherent to Multi-Service Delivery Units." *Journal of Sociology and Social Welfare*, Vol. 5, No. 5, September 1978, p. 649.

Keeley, M. C., P. K. Robins, R. G. Spiegelman, and R. W. West. *The Labor Supply Effects and Costs of Alternative Negative Income Tax Programs: Evidence from the Seattle and Denver Income Maintenance Experiments Part I and Part II*. Menlo Park, Calif.: Center for the Study of Welfare Policy, Stanford Research Institute, May 1977.

Keller, Suzanne. "Does the Family Have a Future?" *Journal of Comparative Family Studies*, Spring 1971.

Kerner Commission. See U.S. Commission on Civil Disorders.

Klein, Joann. "Hoping for a Little More." *California Living* Magazine, Aug. 1, 1976, pp. 19–21.

Kluegel, James. "The Causes and Cost of Racial Exclusion from Job Authority." *American Sociological Review*, Vol. 43, No. 3, June 1978, pp. 285–301.

Knowles, Louis, and Kenneth Prewitt. *Institutional Racism in the Americas.* Englewood Cliffs, N.J.: Prentice-Hall, 1979.

Komisar, Lucy K. *Down and Out in the U.S.A.,* rev. ed. New York: New Viewpoint Books, 1977.

Kramer, Ralph. *Participation of the Poor.* Englewood Cliffs, N.J.: Prentice-Hall, 1969.

―――― and Harry Specht. *Readings in Community Organization Practice,* 2d ed. Englewood Cliffs, N.J.: Prentice-Hall, 1975.

Kriesberg, Louis. *Mothers in Poverty: A Study of Fatherless Families.* Chicago: Aldine Co., 1970.

Kuhnle, Stein. "Development of the Social Policy Strategies in Scandinavia." In *Social Policies in Comparative Perspective, Proceedings of the Social Policies Session, IX World Congress of Sociology, Uppsala, 1978.* Copenhagen: Danish National Institute of Social Research, 1978.

Lampman, Robert. *Ends and Means of Reducing Income Poverty.* Chicago: Markham, 1971.

Laurenti, Luigi. *Property Values and Race.* Berkeley: University of California Press, 1960.

Lawton, M. Powell. *Planning and Managing Housing for the Elderly.* New York: Wiley, 1975.

Lemont, Edwin A. "Legislating Change in the Juvenile Court." *Wisconsin Law Review,* No. 2, 1967, pp. 421–428.

Leonard, Elizabeth. "A History of the Riverdale Children's Association." In Andrew Billingsley and Jeanne Giovannoni, *Children of the Storm.* New York: Random House, 1971, pp. 27–28.

Lerner, Max. *America as a Civilization.* New York: Simon and Schuster, 1957.

Levi, Edith, "Mr. Nixon's 'Speenhamland.'" *Social Work,* January 1970, pp. 7–8.

Levin, Herman. "Voluntary Organizations in Social Welfare." In Robert Morris (ed.), *Encyclopedia of Social Work,* Vol. II. New York: National Association of Social Workers, 1971, pp. 1518–1524.

Levitan, Sar A., and Robert Taggart III. *Social Experimentation and Manpower Policy: The Rhetoric and the Reality.* Baltimore: Johns Hopkins, 1971.

Lloyd George, David. *The People's Insurance.* London: 1911.

Lourie, Norman, and Stanley Brody. "Implications of Recent U.S. Supreme Court Decisions on Residence Requirements." *Public Welfare,* Vol. 28, No. 1, January 1970, pp. 45–51.

Lubove, Roy. *The Professional Altruist.* Cambridge, Mass.: Harvard, 1965.

Lyon, Larry, and Troy Abell. "Social Mobility among Young Black and White Men: A Longitudinal Study of Occupational Prestige and Income." *Pacific Sociological Review,* Vol. 22, April 1979, pp. 201–222.

Macarov, David. *The Design of Social Welfare.* New York: Holt, Rinehart and Winston, 1978.

Malthus, Thomas. *An Essay on the Principle of Population As It Affects the Future Improvement of Society.* 1798. Reprinted Ann Arbor: University of Michigan Press, 1959.

Manard, Barbara, Cary Kart, and Dick van Gils. *Old-Age Institutions.* Lexington, Mass.: Lexington Books, 1973.

Marris, Peter, and Martin Rein. *Dilemmas of Social Reform.* New York: Atherton Press, 1967.

Marshall, Ray. "The Economics of Racial Discrimination: A Survey." *Journal of Economic Literature,* September 1974, pp. 849–871.

Marshall, T. H. *Class, Citizenship and Social Development.* New York: Doubleday, 1965.

―――. *Social Policy.* London: Hutchinson, 1965.

May, Edgar. *The Wasted Americans.* New York: New American Library, Signet, 1965.

McCreedy, Kenneth. *Juvenile Justice System and Procedures.* Albany, N.Y.: Delmar, 1975.

Merriam, Ida C., Alfred M. Skolnik, and Sophie R. Dales. "Social Welfare Expenditures 1967–68." *Social Security Bulletin,* Vol. 31, December 1968, pp. 14–27.

Merton, Robert. *Social Theory and Social Structure.* New York: Free Press, 1957.

Meyer, Carol H. *Social Work Practice: A Response to Urban Crisis.* New York: Free Press, 1972.

Meyerson, Martin, and Edward Banfield. *Politics, Planning, and the Public Interest.* New York: Free Press, 1955.

Michael, Donald. *Cybernation: The Silent Conquest.* Santa Barbara, Calif.: The Center for the Study of Democratic Institutions, 1962.

Miller, Henry. "Value Dilemmas in Social Casework." *Social Work,* Vol. 13, January 1968, pp. 27–33.

Miller, S. M. "Types of Equality: Sorting, Rewarding, Performing," Paper presented at Plenary Session 4, Eighth World Congress of Sociology, Toronto, Aug. 24, 1974.

―――, and Martin Rein. "Can Income Redistribution Work?" *Social Policy,* May 1976, p. 3.

Mogulof, Melvin. "Subsidizing Substandard Housing through Public Welfare Payments." *Journal of Housing,* No. 10, 1967, pp. 560–563.

Monk, Abraham. "The Emergence of Day Care Centers for the Aged: Trends and Planning Issues." Paper presented at National Conference on Social Welfare, Cincinnati, May 1975.

Moore, Joan. "Review of *Affirmative Discrimination* by Nathan Glazer." *Contemporary Sociology,* Vol. 6, No. 5, September 1977, pp. 542–543.

Moore, William, Jr. *The Vertical Ghetto.* New York: Random House, 1969.

Morris, Robert. "Alternative to Nursing Home Care: A Proposal." Presented to Senate Special Committee on Aging, 92d Congress, 1st Session, October 1971.

―――. "Welfare Reform 1973: The Social Services Dimension." *Science,* Vol. 181, Aug. 10, 1973, pp. 515–522.

Mott, Paul E. *Meeting Human Needs: The Social and Political History of Title XX.* Columbus, Ohio: National Conference on Social Welfare, 1976.

Moynihan, Daniel P. "The Crisis in Welfare." *Public Interest,* No. 10, Winter 1968, pp. 3–29.

―――. *Maximum Feasible Misunderstanding.* New York: Free Press, 1969.

―――. *The Negro Family: The Case for National Action.* Washington, D.C.: U.S. Department of Labor, Office of Policy, 1965.

_____. *The Politics of a Guaranteed Income: The Nixon Administration and the Family Assistance Plan.* New York: Vintage Books, 1973.

Munnell, Alicia. "Economic Experience of Blacks 1964–74." *New England Economic Review,* January–February 1978.

Murray, Janet, "Homeownership and Financial Assets: Findings from the 1968 Survey of the Aged." *Social Security Bulletin,* Vol. 35, No. 8, August 1972, pp. 3–23.

Myrdal, Alva. *Nation and Family.* Cambridge, Mass.: MIT, 1968.

"NAHRO, NTO Completing Tenant Employment Study." *Journal of Housing,* Vol. 31, No. 9, October 1974, p. 429.

"NAHRO TPP Services Program." *Journal of Housing,* Vol. 33, No. 11, November 1976, pp. 551–553.

"NAHRO's Comprehensive Statement of Policy Goals and Implementing Actions for Housing and Community Development 1977, IV. Program for Housing." *Journal of Housing,* Vol. 34, No. 10, November 1977, p. 505.

National Center for Housing Management. *Housing for Elderly: The On-Site Housing Manager's Resources Book.* Washington, D.C., 1974.

National Commission on Urban Problems (Douglas Commission). *Building the American City.* Washington, D.C.: Government Printing Office, 1968.

National Health Survey 1969. See U.S. Bureau of the Census.

National Probation and Parole Association. *Guidelines for Juvenile Court Judges.* New York, 1957.

Nenno, Mary. "President Carter's 1978 Urban Policy Initiatives." *Journal of Housing,* Vol. 35, No. 5, May 1979, pp. 217–221.

_____. "The 10-Year Housing Goals." *Journal of Housing,* Vol. 35, No. 7, July 1979, pp. 343–344.

_____. "TPP Experiences Can Help Provide Support for Housing Management." *Journal of Housing,* Vol. 35, No. 12, December 1978, p. 592.

Nevitt, A. A. (ed.). *The Economic Problems of Housing.* New York: Macmillan, 1967.

"New Haven Tenant Board Takes Over Management." *Journal of Housing,* Vol. 35, No. 1, January 1978, p. 36.

The New Supplementary Security Income Program: Impact on Current Benefits and Unresolved Issues. Studies in Public Welfare, Joint Economic Committee, 93d Congress, 1st Sess., 1973.

Niebanck, Paul. *The Elderly in Older Urban Areas.* Philadelphia: University of Pennsylvania, 1965.

Northwood, Larry K. "Some Critical Questions in the Political Economy of Social Welfare: The Carter 'Welfare Reform' Proposals." *Journal of Sociology and Social Welfare,* Vol. V, No. 4, July 1978, p. 538.

OECD, "What's Left?" *The Economist.* Feb. 3, 1979, p. 65.

Ogburn, William. *Social Change.* New York: Viking, 1922. Rev. ed., 1952.

Ohio Youth Commission. *A Statistical Inquiry into Length of Stay and the Revolving Door.* Columbus, 1974.

"Omaha's South Side Terrace Homes." *Journal of Housing,* Vol. 34, No. 10, October 1977, p. 508.

Opton, Edward M., Jr. *Factors Associated with Employment among Welfare Mothers.* Berkeley: Wright Institute, 1971.

Orshansky, Mollie. "The Shape of Poverty in 1966." *Social Security Bulletin,* March 1968, pp. 18–21.

Ostow, Miriam, and Anna B. Dutka. *Work and Welfare in New York City.* Baltimore: Johns Hopkins, 1975.

Owen, Henry, and Charles L. Schultze (eds.). *Setting National Priorities: The Next Ten Years.* Washington, D.C.: Brookings, 1976.

Palley, Marian, and Howard Palley. *Urban America and Public Policies.* Lexington, Mass.: Heath, 1977, p. 161.

Parry, Carol. "Association Testifies on Welfare Proposals in House Subcommittee." *NASW Newsletter,* January 1978, p. 7.

Pascal, A. H. *The Economics of Housing Desegregation.* Santa Monica, Calif.: The Rand Corp., November 1967.

Pearce, Diane. "The Feminization of Poverty: Women, Work and Welfare." Paper delivered at Society for the Study of Social Problems, San Francisco, Aug. 28, 1978.

Pechman, Joseph, and P. Michael Timpane (eds.). *Work Incentives and Income Guarantees: The New Jersey Negative Income Tax Experiment.* Washington, D.C.: Brookings, 1975.

Perrin, Guy. "Reflections on Fifty Years of Social Security." *International Labor Review,* 1969, pp. 249–292.

Pettigrew, Thomas. "Racial Isolation in the Public Schools." In U.S. Commission on Civil Rights, *Racial Isolation in the Public Schools.* Vols. I, II, 1967.

Pincus, Allen, and Anne Minahan. *Social Work Practice: Model and Method.* Itasca, Ill.: Peacock Publishers, 1973.

"Plan to Save 6 Billion." *San Francisco Chronicle,* Nov. 6, 1976.

Platt, Anthony M. *The Child Savers: The Invention of Delinquency,* 2d ed. Chicago: University of Chicago Press, 1977.

Popenoe, David. *The Suburban Environment: Sweden and the United States.* Chicago: University of Chicago Press, 1977.

President's Commission on Income Maintenance Programs. *Poverty Amid Plenty: The American Paradox.* 1969.

Prigmore, Charles S., and Charles Atherton. *Social Welfare Policy.* Lexington, Mass.: Heath, 1979.

Rainwater, Lee. *Behind Ghetto Walls: Black Family Life in a Federal Slum.* Chicago: Aldine, 1970.

———. "The Services Strategy vs. The Income Strategy." *Trans-action,* Vol. 4, October 1967, pp. 40–41.

———. "Toward a Nation of Average Men: Income Equalization and a Just Society." Presented at UDA Airlie House Conference, October 1966.

———and Martin Rein. "The Future of the Welfare State." *Social Policies in Comparative Perspective, Proceedings of Symposium II, IX World Congress, Uppsala, August 17, 1978.* Copenhagen: Danish National Institute of Social Research, 1978.

Ravitch, Diane "Busing." *New York Times,* Dec. 21, 1975.

————. "Color Blind or Color Conscious." *New Republic,* May 5, 1979.

"Record of Section 8 Housing Assistance as of April 30, 1978," Table 3. *Journal of Housing,* Vol. 35, No. 7, July 1978, p. 345.

Reddin, Michael. "Universality versus Selectivity." *Political Quarterly,* January–March 1969.

Reich, Charles. "Midnight Welfare Searches and the Social Security Act." *Yale Law Journal,* Vol. 72, June 1963, p. 1347.

————. "The New Property." *Yale Law Journal,* Vol. 73, April 1964, p. 779.

Reichert, Kurt. "Social Work Contributions to the Prevention of Premature Functional Death." In *Human Factors in Long-Term Health Care,* report prepared for institute on health given at National Conference in Social Welfare, San Francisco, May 1975.

Rein, Martin. *Social Policy: Issues of Choice and Change.* New York: Random House, 1970.

————. "The Social Service Crisis." *Trans-action,* Vol. 1, May 1964, p. 3.

————. "The Strange Case of Public Dependency." *Trans-action,* Vol. 2, March 1965, pp. 16–23.

Rein, Mildred. "Determinants of the Work-Welfare Choice in AFDC." *Social Service Review,* Vol. 46, No. 4, December 1972, pp. 563–564.

————. "Social Services as a Work Strategy." *Social Service Review,* December 1975, pp. 515–538.

Reissman, Frank, Jerome Cohen, and Arthur Pearl (eds.). *Mental Health of the Poor.* New York: Free Press, 1964.

"Resident Involvement Happens in Omaha Project with Help of TPP and Modernization Grants." *Journal of Housing,* Vol. 34, No. 10, October 1977, pp. 508–510.

"The Rights Revolution." *Congressional Quarterly,* 1978.

Riis, Jacob A. *How the Other Half Lives.* New York: Scribners, 1904.

Rivlin, Alice. *Systematic Thinking for Social Action.* Washington, D.C.: Brookings, 1971.

Rohrlich, George. "Social Policy and Income Distribution." In Robert Morris (ed.), *Encyclopedia of Social Work,* Vol. II. New York: National Association of Social Workers, 1971, pp. 1385–1386.

Romanyshyn, John. *Social Welfare: Charity to Justice.* New York: Random House, 1971.

Roosevelt, Franklin D. "Private Economic Power Is . . . a Public Trust." In Faye Rattner, *Reform in America: Jacksonian Democracy, Progressivism and the New Deal.* Chicago: Scott, Foresman, 1964, pp. 90–91.

Ross, Arthur, and Herbert Hill (eds.). *Employment, Race and Poverty.* New York: Harcourt, Brace & World, 1967.

Rule, Sheila. "Project Joey: New Chance for Youths on Probation." *New York Times,* Dec. 3, 1978.

Ryan, William, *Blaming the Victim.* New York: Pantheon, 1971.

————. "Blaming the Victim: Ideology Serves the Establishment." In Pamela Roby (ed.), *The Poverty Establishment.* Englewood Cliffs, N.J.: Prentice-Hall, 1974, p. 173.

Salisbury, Harrison. *The Shook-Up Generation.* New York: Harper & Row, 1958.

Saltman, Julia. *Open Housing.* New York: Praeger, 1979.

Saunders, Irwin, "Professional Roles in Planned Change." In Ralph Kramer and Harry Specht (eds.), *Readings in Community Organization Practice.* Englewood Cliffs, N.J.: Prentice-Hall, 1975.

Saville, J. "The Welfare State: An Historical Approach." In Eric Butterworth and R. Holman (eds.), *Social Welfare in Modern Britain.* London, 1968, pp. 57–69.

Sawhill, I. "Women with Low Incomes." In M. Blaxall and B. Reagan, *Women and the Workplace.* Chicago: University of Chicago Press, 1976.

Sawhill, I. V., G. E. Peabody, C. A. Jones, and S. B. Caldwell. "Income Transfers and Family Structure." Working paper, Washington, D.C.: Urban Institute, 1975.

Schneider, Eugene. "NAHRO's TPP Services Program: An Analysis of Lessons Learned and of Possible Future Impact." *Journal of Housing,* December 1978, pp. 593–594.

Schorr, Alvin. "Against a Negative Income Tax." *Public Interest,* Vol. 5, Fall 1966, pp. 110–117.

———. *Explorations in Social Policy.* New York: Basic Books, 1968.

———. *Poor Kids.* New York: Basic Books, 1966.

———. *Slums and Social Insecurity.* London: Nelson, 1964.

Schottland, Charles I. *The Social Security Program in the United States.* New York: Appleton-Century-Crofts, 1963.

Schweinitz, Karl de. *England's Road to Social Security.* New York: Barnes, 1961.

Shanas, Ethel. "Living Arrangements and Housing of Old People." In Ewald Busse and Eric Pfeiffer (eds.), *Behavior and Adaptation in Late Life.* Boston: Little, Brown, 1969, pp. 133–135.

"The Shape of Poverty in 1966." *Social Security Bulletin,* Vol. 31, March 1968, pp. 3–31.

Sherlock, Basil, and Ingrid Moeller. "Young Adult Fantasies and Goals at the Newlywed Stage: Some Gender Differences." Paper presented at Pacific Sociological meetings, April 1977.

Shriver, Sargent, in George Dunne (ed.), *Poverty in Plenty.* New York: P. J. Kenedy, 1964, p. 9.

Simon, William E. *A Time for Truth.* New York: McGraw-Hill, 1978.

Sindler, Allan P. *Bakke, Defunis, and Minority Admissions: The Quest for Equal Opportunity.* New York: Longman, 1978.

Skolnik, Alfred, and Sophie Dales. "Social Welfare Expenditures, Fiscal Year 1976." *Social Security Bulletin,* January 1977., Vol. 40, No. 1, p. 1.

Slack, Kathleen. *Social Administration and the Citizen.* London: Michael Joseph, 1966.

Smith, A. D., A. E. Fortune, and W. J. Reid. "Notes on Policy and Practice: WIN, Work and Welfare." *Social Service Review,* Vol. 49, September 1975, pp. 396–400.

Smith, Adam. *The Wealth of Nations.* 1776. Reprinted New York: Modern Library, 1937.

Smith, James D. "The Concentration of Personal Wealth in America, 1969." *Review of Income and Wealth,* Vol. 20, No. 2, June 1, 1974, pp. 143–180.

Smith, Russell, and Dorothy Zietz. *American Social Welfare Institutions.* New York: Wiley, 1970.

Spencer, Herbert. *Social Statics.* New York: Appleton, 1880.

Steiner, Gilbert Y. *Social Insecurity.* Chicago: Rand McNally, 1966.

Stern, Phillip M. *The Rape of the Taxpayer.* New York: Random House, 1972.

Sterne, Richard, James Phillips, and Alvin Rabushka. *The Urban Elderly Poor.* Lexington, Mass.: Lexington Books, 1974.

Sternlieb, George, and Bernard P. Indik. *The Ecology of Welfare: Housing and the Welfare Crisis in New York City.* New Brunswick, N.J.: Transaction Books, 1973.

Stone, Helen. *Reflections on Foster Care: A Report of a National Survey of Attitudes and Practices.* New York: Child Welfare League of America, 1969.

Straszheim, Mahlon. *The Effects of the Housing Market Discrimination on the Urban Labor Market for Blacks.* College Park, Md.: University of Maryland, 1973.

———. "Housing Market Discrimination and Black Housing Consumption." *Quarterly Journal of Economics,* February 1974, pp. 19–43.

Strum, Philippa. *Affirmative Action for Women and Non-Black Racial Minorities.* Paper for a plenary meeting, American Civil Liberties Union, June 1979.

Sumner, William Graham. "Influence of Commercial Crises on Opinions About Economic Doctrine." in A. G. Keller and M. R. Davie (eds.), *Essays of William Graham Sumner.* New Haven: Yale, 1934.

———. *Social Darwinism.* Englewood Cliffs, N.J.: Prentice-Hall, 1963.

Surrey, Stanley. *Pathways to Tax Reform.* Cambridge: Harvard, 1973.

Taeber, Karl. "Negro Residential Segregation: Trends and Measurements." *Social Problems,* Vol. 12, 1964, pp. 42–51.

Tawney, R. H. *The Acquisitive Society.* New York: Harcourt, Brace & World, 1948.

———. *Equality.* London: Unwin Books, 1931.

Taylor, D. Garth, Paul Sheatsley, and Andrew Greenley. "Attitudes toward Racial Integration." *Scientific American,* Vol. 238, No. 12, June 1978, pp. 42–49.

Theobald, Robert (ed.). *The Guaranteed Income.* Garden City, N.Y.: Doubleday, 1966.

——— (ed.). *Social Policies for the Seventies.* New York: Anchor, 1969.

Thompson, Marie McGuire. "Congregate Housing for Older Adults: A Working Paper." Presented to the Senate Special Committee on Aging, 94th Congress, 1st Sess., 1975.

Tillmon, Johnnie. "Welfare Is a Woman's Issue," *Ms.,* January 1972, pp. 111–116.

Titmuss, Richard. *The Blood Relationship.* New York: Pantheon, 1971.

———. *Commitment to Welfare.* London: George Allen and Unwin, 1969.

———. *Essays on the "Welfare State."* London: George Allen and Unwin, 1958.

———. *Income Distribution and Social Change.* London: George Allen and Unwin, 1962.

———. "The Practical Case Against the Means-Test State." *New Statesman,* Vol. 74, 1905, Sept. 15, 1967, pp. 308–310.

——— *Problems of Social Policy.* London: HMSO, 1950.

Tobin, Sheldon. "The Long Term Care Institution." Symposium on Health Networks, American Public Welfare Association, May 22, 1974.

Towle, Charlotte. *Common Human Needs.* Washington, D.C.: National Association of Social Workers, 1965.

Townsend, Peter. "Does Selectivity Mean a Nation Divided?" In *Social Services For All.* London: Fabian Society, 1968, pp. 1–6.

Tropman, John. "Societal Values and Social Policy." In John Tropman, Milan Dluhy, Robert Lind, and Wayne Vasey (eds.), *Strategic Perspectives on Social Policy.* New York: Pergamon Press, 1976, pp. 67–81.

Turner, Jonathan, and Charles Starnes. *Inequality: Privilege and Poverty in America.* Pacific Palisades, Calif.: Goodyear Publishing Co., 1976.

U.S. Bureau of the Census. *Detailed Characteristics, U.S. Summary, 1970.* Tables 189, 245, Washington, D.C., 1972.

———. *General Population Characteristics, U.S. Summary, 1970.* Table 49, 1977, pp. 1–263, Washington, D. C., 1972.

———. *Housing Characteristics by Household Composition, 1970.* Table A-4, 1973.

———. "Money Income in 1975 of Families and Persons in the United States." Table 13, *Current Population Reports,* 1977, p. 57.

———. "Report on the National Health Survey of 1970." Table 125 in *The American Almanac: The Statistical Abstract of the United States.* 1974.

———. *The Social and Economic Status of the Black Population in the United States.* Series P-23, No. 54, 1975.

———. *Social Indicators, 1976.*

———. *Subject Report: Housing of Senior Citizens, 1970.* Tables A-2, A-4, B-2, C-2, D-2, 1976.

U.S. Commission on Civil Disorders. *Kerner Commission Report.* 1968.

U.S. Commission on Civil Rights. *Equal Opportunity in Suburbia.* 1974.

U.S. Department of Health, Education and Welfare. *The Role of Public Welfare in Housing.* 1969.

———, Office of Human Development, Administration on Aging. *New Facts About Older Americans.* June 1973.

———, Youth Development and Delinquency Prevention Administration. *The Challenge of Youth Service Bureaus.* 1973.

U.S. Department of Housing and Urban Development. *Challenge 6.* May 1975, No. 4, p. 33.

———. *Older Americans: Facts About Income and Housing.* 1977.

U.S. Department of Labor. *Children of Working Mothers.* Special Labor Force Report 174, March 1974.

———. "Women in the Workforce." *Monthly Labor Review,* 1975, pp. 65–66.

U.S. Federal Reserve System Board of Governors. "Survey of Financial Characteristics of Consumers, 1962." Reported in Census Bureau *Social Indicators, 1973.*

"U.S. Marks Start of Civil Rights Drive: 25th Anniversary." *International Herald Tribune,* May 19, 1979.

"U.S. Says Chicago Segregates Schools." *International Herald Tribune,* Apr. 14–15, 1979.

U.S. Social Security Administration. "Research and Statistics Notes." In *Social Indicators, 1974.*

University of Wisconsin study. See Barth, Michael et al.

Urban Institute. *Child Support Payments in the United States.* Washington, D.C., 1976.

Vinter, Robert D. (ed.). *Time Out: A National Study of Juvenile Correctional Programs.* Ann Arbor, Mich.: National Assessment of Juvenile Corrections, 1978.

Wallace, Phyllis A. "A Decade of Policy Development in Equal Opportunities in Employment and Housing." In Robert Haveman (ed.), *A Decade of Federal Antipoverty Programs.* New York: Academic Press, 1977.

Warren, Michael. In *Proceedings of the Ontario Regional Workshop on Housing the Elderly.* Ottawa: Canadian Council on Social Development and Ontario Welfare Council, October 1974, p. 9. (Mimeographed.)

Warren, Roland. *Social Change and Human Purpose.* Chicago: Rand McNally, 1977.

Watten, Moody. "The Trouble with No Fault Divorce," *San Francisco City Life,* Sept. 25, 1977, p. 10.

Webb, Beatrice, and Sidney Webb. In *United Kingdom Report of the Royal Commission on the Poor Laws,* Cmd. 4499. London: HMSO, 1909.

Weil, Gordon L. *The Welfare Debate of 1978.* White Plains, N.Y.: Institute for Socioeconomic Studies, 1978.

Weissbourd, Bernard. *Segregation, Subsidies and Megalopolis.* Santa Barbara, Calif.: Center for the Study of Democratic Institutions, 1964.

Welch, Finis. "Black-White Differences in Returns in Schooling." In Orley Ashenfelter and Albert Rees (eds.), *Discrimination in Labor Markets.* Princeton, 1973.

Werthman, Carl, Jerry Mandel, and Ted Dienstfrey. *Planning and the Purchase Decision: Why People Buy in Planned Communities.* Berkeley: Institute for Urban and Regional Development, University of California, 1965.

Wickenden, Elizabeth. *"H.R. 1: Welfare Policy as Instrument of Coercion,"* New York: Center for Social Welfare Policy and Law, 1972.

Wilcox, Claire. *Toward Social Welfare.* Homewood, Ill.: Dorsey, 1969.

Wilensky, Harold. *The Welfare State and Equality.* Berkeley: University of California Press, 1975.

—— and Charles N. Lebeaux. *Industrial Society and Social Welfare,* New York: Free Press, 1965.

Wilkinson, J. Harvie, III. *From Brown to Bakke: The Supreme Court and School Integration, 1954–1978.* New York: Oxford University Press, 1978.

Williams, Harrison. "Critique of Existing Legislation on Congregate Housing." Paper presented at the National Conference on Congregate Housing for Older People, Washington, D.C., Nov. 11–12, 1975, p. 5.

Williams, Robert George. *Public Assistance and Work Effort: The Labor Supply of Low Income Female Heads of Households.* Princeton University, Department of Economics, 1975.

Williams, Robin. *American Society: A Sociological Interpretation.* New York: Knopf, 1970.

Willie, Charles. *The Caste and Class Controversy*. Bayside, N.Y.: General Hall, 1979.

Wilner, Daniel, Rosabelle Walkley, Thomas Pinkerton, and Matthew Tayback. *The Housing Environment and Family Life*. Baltimore: John Hopkins, 1962.

Wiltse, Kermit T. "Orthopsychiatric Programs for Socially Deprived Groups." *American Journal of Orthopsychiatry*, Vol. 33, No. 5, October 1963, pp. 806–813.

Witte, Edwin. *The Development of the Social Security Act*. Madison: University of Wisconsin, 1962.

Wolins, Martin, and Jerry Turem. "The Societal Function of Social Welfare." In Gilbert and Specht (eds.), *The Emergence of Social Welfare and Social Work*. New York: Peacock, 1976.

Woodward, C. Vann. "Review of *From Brown to Bakke* by J. Harvie Wilkinson III." *New Republic*, June 23, 1979, p. 28.

Yancey, William L. *The Moynihan Report: The Politics of Controversy*. Cambridge, Mass.: MIT, 1967.

Youssef, Nadia, and Shirley Hartley. "Demographic Indicators of the Status of Women in Various Societies." In Jean Lipman-Blumen and Jessie Bernard, *Sex Roles and Social Policy*. Beverly Hills, Calif.: Sage Publications, 1977.

Zald, Mayer N. (ed.). *Social Welfare Institutions*. New York: Wiley, 1965.

Name Index

Subject Index

Abortion, 13, 41, 64−65, 173, 216
ABT Associates, 247
Accessibility of services, 110, 133
  through benefits-in-kind, 126
  for elderly, 230−231
  income maintenance, 169
  policies on, 149−150
Administrative costs, 157
  of income maintenance, 176−180,
    186−187, 191
  of means-tested services, 117
  of universal services, 119
Adoption, 147, 216−220
Affirmative action, 124
  for American Indians, 69, 115, 327
  through opportunity provision, 133−134
  and quotas, 75−76, 133, 327−331
  (*See also* Discrimination)
Agency regulations, 148−149
  on AFDC, 168, 174−178
  opposition of social workers to, 2

Agency regulations:
  standardization of, 186, 191−192
Aid to Families with Dependent Children
    (AFDC), 2, 53, 166−194, 242−243
  and abortion, 65
  attitudes toward recipients of, 174−178
  Carter and Nixon proposals on,
    103−104, 188−194
  characteristics of recipients of, 46,
    171−173
  cost of, 179−180, 191−193
  eligibility for, 27, 60, 113−115,
    120−121, 125, 165−169
  fraud in, 178−179
  history of, 63, 91, 167
  and housing, 179−182, 189, 191,
    289−290
  as income redistribution, 88
  political considerations on, 157−158
  provision of services in, 131−133, 170,
    191−192, 208

372